strategy. His first major expenditure is likely to go for hiring a top-flight, high-priced professional media manager. When he goes to New York, he may call on Mayor What's-his-name, but not until he has wangled lunch with the big-time editors and publishers. Give him a choice between a spot on the "Today Show" and a gathering at national party headquarters and he will hardly pause over the choice. His schedule is built around media markets in the primary and caucus states. He goes where he goes and does what he does *mainly* to get his message into the newspapers, magazines, and television programs. By far the biggest burden in his budget is for commercial advertising through the mass media. His aides ponder through the night how to get him covered for free without shoving him over into some eccentricity the press will pick up as a "gaffe." In the early obscurity of his campaign, he seeks out the major reporters like a lonely bachelor in a singles' bar. If his wooing works and fame begins to gather to him, he finds himself trailing a vast horde of writers and picture-takers as he marches through various scripted and scenarioed spontaneous encounters. In short, the primary task a Presidential candidate faces today is not building a coalition of organized interests, or developing alliances with other candidates or politicians in his party, or even winning over the voters whose hands he shakes. If he has his modern priorities straight, he is first and foremost a seeker after favorable notice from the journalists who can make or break his progress.

At the other end of the media pipe, citizens are getting whatever they eventually get of the candidate from print and broadcast journalism. Few get to the rallies. Indeed, there are not many rallies to get to anymore. The thousands who experience some airport or shopping-center event with the candidate are massively outweighed by the millions who know of him only what journalists tell them.

To suppose that either the candidate or the citizen is putty in the hands of conniving communicators is absurd. Candidates are made up by their own histories long before the television make-up artist gets hold of them. The citizen also has a mind of his own. The journalist has to find news in the material available. He is significantly dependent on what he judges his audience wants to know and on what the candidate hands him to depict. But it is just that position as middleman that sets the journalist up as the new power-broker, filling the gap vacated by yesterday's bosses.

There he stands, between people and President. Whether he knows it or not, the impressions he composes and conveys are now the blood of Presidential politics. The journalistic tyros of old—the Hearsts and Luces and Murrows, whose impact on politics was often personal and direct—are gone. The collective, loose-jointed journalistic fraternity of today is all the more powerful because its influence is pervasive and indirect and atmospheric, an element of the cultural air we breathe.

Nothing signals quite so clearly the rise of the journalist to political power as the righteous wrath that now descends upon him. Spiro Agnew had his reasons for spraying journalism with indignant alliterations. His protest was but a visible bubble in a great outpouring of criticism from left, right, and center. "Media critic" is now a recognized occupation. Wounded and slain politicians, once they have really decided to retire, blast the media as obsessed with their warts and blind to their beauties. Academics who deign to notice what is happening chime in with their analytic condemnations. Journalists themselves rail at one another for bias and hype and error. There is scattered evidence that some elements of the public, ahead of their time, are looking askance at the media they associate with recent dips in our political fortunes. Just as it happened years ago, when the new ethnic bosses took over from the old Wasp elites in the big cities, reformers and reactionaries join in castigating the new powerbrokers.

That might do some good, though righteous indignation as a teaching technique can be overrated. I think political journalism is improvable; with many journalists, I think the craft has often missed its promise. In the final chapter I say where I think current practice is taking us and suggest changes of direction that might prove possible and productive—without importing a whole new population of reporters and candidates from outer space. But understanding comes first. The interplay of journalism and politics turns out to be crucial to the most important political choice we make, the choice of a President. How has that connection grown up in the American culture? What casts of mind do the contemporary composers of this drama inherit from their traditions? Why have we come to tell the Presidential story as we do?

A solid starting point is the evident fact that we have transformed a quadrennial event into a saga lasting at least two or three years. In the days of McKinley—not so long ago—candidates for President, however burning with ambition and whatever they might do behind the scenes, were not expected to campaign for their party's nomination. Indeed, even after the national convention named the nominee, he stayed quietly at home until the official committee of notification made its way to his doorstep, an occasion of considerable ceremonial moment. Touring and speechmaking, for a really proper candidate, began in a serious way only in September after Labor Day. The public's time of awareness was relatively brief, the process of deliberation and choice concentrated in a few months. Today, thanks to the invention of new opportunities for early testing—the caucuses, primaries, and public opinion polls, and the chance to qualify early for federal funds—the typical campaign is well under way the fall before election year and it is not unusual to find candidates in hot pursuit of the prize well before that. Thus the quest is stretched out to Odyssean dimensions; stages previously compacted in time are elaborated and elongated; the dash becomes a race, the race a marathon, even a crusade. Along that trail, the fortunes and prospects of the candidates rise and fall in an extended series of connected events. For those who would take a serious part in it, prolonged attention and sustained action are required.

Insofar as the people are concerned, their participation is almost entirely vicarious. Except when a primary vote or a poll or a candidate appearance happens their way, they watch and read. It is natural for them to sense the campaign as a developing, continuing story, unfolding a piece at a time through the seasons.

That sense could not suit the journalist better. For the journalist is, at the heart of his calling, a storyteller. His attention is attuned to notice, in the flux of facts, just those features that lend themselves to interesting, novel narrative. The idea of the reporter as blotter, passively soaking up the inchoate slop his perceptual organs get wet with, is too trivial and naïve to give us pause. Reporters are sentient beings and thus selective perceivers. Whatever their political leanings or unique personal biases, their *professional* interest is strongly focused on extracting stories from events. They look in order to tell. As historians of the present, they look for the significant—that is, news that may affect their readers' future for good or ill. So any strung-out sequence of connected events with fateful implications is grist for the journalistic mill. The story must persuade the reader—from paragraph one—that the events reported *will* make a difference. Thus journalists are impelled to drama, not as mere decoration, but as a skill essential to the craft of communication. Day after day, journalists must approach their work with the juices of their own curiosity and creativity flowing, composing stories their busy readers will *want* to read.

Fortunately for journalists (and thanks in no small part to their doings) today's campaign saga is a profoundly human story—the struggle of persons for power. The concentration on the candidate as star traces to an institutional sea change in the Presidency itself. Back in Lincoln's day, cabinet members felt free to challenge the President in public. Over the years the President himself rose up so far out of the Washington crowd that today we name administrations by naming the Presidential incumbent. The President has become by far the most visible feature in the political landscape, the focus of the nation's political interest and emotion. The star system spread from the Presidency to the Presidential campaigns—the Eisenhower crusade, the McGovern movement, the Carter campaign. The new Presidency thus puts a person at the center of each campaign story, a person whose tragedies and victories grip the human imagination.

All these trends come together to dramatize the quest for the Presidency. The material is real. The form is dramatic. The drama of politics has been there since the first, and journalists have written it. What demands attention to the way they do that today is, first, the conjunction in our era of an enormous mass electorate who must be addressed through the mass media; second, the root and branch democratization of the process—traceable to

mass political disillusionment—which has virtually removed other traditional middlemen from respect and authority; third, the opportunity a much
longer campaign offers for dramatic development; and fourth, the
emergence of the individual candidate—the potential President—as star of
the story. To grasp what is happening in Presidential politics today, one
must move past the analysis of the details of issues, regional voting alignments, and systems of party organization, to an understanding of how the
Presidential story has been shaped and shared in the experience of American
political culture.

The parties, as we inherited them, failed. Their giant ossified structures, like those of the dinosaurs, could no longer adapt to the pace of political change. Journalism *could* adapt. Attuned to change—owing its very existence to its ability to tune in to change—journalism took over where the
parties left off. The vitality of a political system originally designed to roll
with the punches of history found in journalism a flexible, sensitive organism
ready and able to respond to the pulse of politics. That emergence renders
relevant a largely neglected history: the interplay of Presidential campaigners and the journalists who tell their running stories.

2

The Pulse of Politics

SEVEN TIMES between 1900 and 1980 the cycle of elections dominated by themes of conflict, conscience, and conciliation beat through American Presidential politics. Radically condensed, the sequence went like this:

Cycle I: 1900, 1904, 1908

1900 Conflict The century opened with the battle election of 1900. Four years before, William McKinley had been chosen over William Jennings Bryan, in a great national sigh of relief that brought an end to a decade of economic hard times. Bryan the Democrat had offered a cure-all, "free silver," but McKinley, a calm, sweet-tempered fellow, personified the nation's need for harmony and peace. Prosperity followed his election. In time the public, spurred on by the newly burgeoning Yellow Press, began to lust for adventure. They got it in the Spanish-American War, which broke out in 1898 and provided the springboard for the century's most bellicose politician, Theodore Roosevelt. Roosevelt came roaring back from San Juan Hill to win the governorship of New York. In 1900 the Republicans nominated him for Vice-President to stand in for quiet McKinley in an all-out political war against Bryan; the two of them put aside their dignities and treated the nation to a hot partisan fight over foreign and domestic policy, racing around the country blasting each other from every available stump.

1904 Conscience McKinley died the September after his inauguration and Roosevelt took over as President. He rapidly achieved immense popularity, a fascinating, self-dramatizing sparker of interest and attention. Roosevelt easily gained the Presidential nomination in 1904 and the election itself turned into a Roosevelt landslide. Such excitement as emerged centered on moral questions: America's duty, in the name of civilization, to rescue victims of brutal regimes, the question of the legitimacy of giant trusts, the problem of civil rights for blacks in the South. The Democrats, in a chaotic convention, heard Bryan invoke God and high principle, and then turned to an unknown, Judge Alton B. Parker of New York, a farm-born nonpolitician valued for his clean and decent character, whose innocence had been repeatedly demonstrated by his reluctance to run for electoral office. Roosevelt, now standing on his Presidential dignity, resolved to rise above the contest, avoiding the hustings as George Washington had. Only near the end of the campaign, when his conscience was challenged by a charge that he had been bought and blackmailed by rich contributors, did TR issue a harsh defense of his moral rectitude.

1908 Conciliation   Roosevelt, recognizing that reaction would set in after his era of action, announced that he would not run again in 1908. His measures had met increasing opposition; he responded by moderating his demands. Bryan did likewise, focusing his rhetoric more and more on the need for a time of peace, though he did not neglect to criticize the opposition. As the election season approached, the economy went shaky, with several temporary but frightening panics and increasing rates of unemployment. Roosevelt's choice as his successor could hardly have symbolized more clearly the nation's readiness for a time of conciliation: William Howard Taft, three hundred pounds of genial good cheer. Taft, with his slogan, "Smile, Smile, Smile," left his opponent—Bryan again—behind by a comfortable margin and eased into the White House.

Cycle II: 1912, 1916, 1920

1912 Conflict   Within two years, the Taftian consensus fell apart. The combative surge boiled up in both parties. Issues of interest—creditor vs. debtor, bosses vs. insurgents, East vs. West—cracked the temporarily smoothed surface of national politics. Taft broke with the Republican conservatives; Roosevelt came back from a hunting trip in Africa to break with Taft as *too* conservative and to battle against him for delegates. Bryan went down to defeat in his own state's convention. At a riotous Republican national convention in 1912, Roosevelt furiously marched his forces from the hall to form the Progressive (Bull Moose) party and took to the field to flail his old friend Taft. All over the country, political meetings broke up in fistfights and challenged votes. Even the Socialists fell apart, their moderates expelling their radicals. Bryan charged again in the Democratic convention, already split into wildly contending camps. The Democrats fought through forty-six convention ballots before the conservative faction finally won out, nominating a new face on the national scene, ex-professor Woodrow Wilson.

1916 Conscience   Wilson won. To the surprise of his backers and opponents, he turned out to be a progressive reformer, driving through Congress a substantial program of novel measures. He also turned out to be a remarkable rhetorician, and the public got to know him as a fervent moralist, given to justifying his every move on grounds of high principle. War broke out in Europe; the jingoes at home began to beat the drum for militant patriotism.

Wilson stood firm against intervention—on grounds of principles he was absolutely sure were right. In 1916 he was easily renominated. The Republicans chose a clean outsider, Justice Charles Evans Hughes, who dutifully campaigned for "Americanism" while Wilson wrapped himself in the Presidency. Questions of who was more loyal to the country pervaded the campaign. Wilson won narrowly. Had Hughes won, the election would still stand as an example of the moral drama.

1920 Conciliation   There followed the horror of the Great War. Peace brought domestic strife—a wave of violent strikes, race riots, bombings, a Red scare, soaring inflation. An exhausted nation was ready for a rest. In 1920 the Republicans found just the man for that, harmonizing Warren G. Harding, with his call for a return to "normalcy." The Democrats, radically misreading the national mood, went for Ohio Governor James Cox, who lit out after Harding with a hard-fighting partisan campaign. Harding the mellifluous conciliator buried him in the heaviest landslide ever recorded.

Cycle III: 1924, 1928, 1932

1924 Conflict   The Presidency killed Harding. His Vice-President, Calvin Coolidge, took over, an odd President for the Jazz Age. By 1924, Harding and his harmony seemed nearly forgotten. A fighting election ensued—but one more strangely focused than any other. Silent Cal Coolidge said little, but he fought off several challengers by adroit, behind-the-scenes employment of the federal patronage. By convention time, he was securely in the saddle, though Senator Robert La Follette and his Progressives split off to wage a vigorous campaign, championing the interests of labor and the farmer. But the combative hit of the season was the Democratic convention; torn to shreds by factional fights, it took the Democrats three weeks of internecine combat and 103 ballots to light on a dull and ineffective Wall Street lawyer named John W. Davis. The party went into the election hopelessly split and debilitated. Coolidge's Vice-Presidential candidate, "Hell 'n' Maria" Dawes, blasted the Democrats while the President kept his silence—and the White House.

1928 Conscience   Coolidge finally decided not to run again in 1928, destined to be another season of moral concern. The Republicans turned to Herbert Hoover of Iowa, a clean-living Quaker untarnished by the political wars, who persistently shied away from any expression of Presidential ambition until his first-ballot nomination. The Democrats nominated Governor Al Smith of New York in a convention as placid as the Republicans'. Then a storm of righteous indignation fell on Smith—that Catholic product of Tammany Hall who favored relaxing the liquor prohibition. The question of character leapt to the fore; Smith was painted as personifying everything alien to the American Eden. Hoover would not even mention his name. The voters chose the native son of pure principle and high ideals.

1932 Conciliation   Almost before he had settled into office, the bottom began to fall out from under Hoover's hopes for continued prosperity. By 1932 the American people, desperate for relief, were ready for any viable alternative. Hoover himself, with the full force of his wooden rhetoric, kept calling for confidence and optimism as the antidote to terror. The Democrats found their cure in Franklin D. Roosevelt, governor of New York, unknown to most Americans, depicted by those in the know as a mild-mannered gentleman of no particular conviction whose jaunty smile seemed to promise better times ahead—another Harding. Roosevelt's major appeal was that he was not Hoover. He floated in on a tide of votes in an election consumed with the quest for an end to trouble.

Cycle IV: 1936, 1940, 1944

1936 Conflict   The trouble did not go away. Roosevelt took action in a startling array of governmental experiments. By 1936, he had aroused allegiance and opposition unmatched in the twentieth century, polarizing the polity. The Republicans, encouraged by the crude polls of that time, thought they had a chance to whip him with Governor Alfred Landon of Kansas. The election was a battle royal. Roosevelt, the smiler of 1932, came across this time as a fighter, damning the "economic royalists," welcoming their hatred. The Republicans pulled out all the stops; some employers even threatened wage cuts if Roosevelt won. Demagogues of the left and right raved and ranted. Fighting Franklin Roosevelt took every state but Maine and Vermont.

1940 Conscience   In his second term, Roosevelt overreached himself. He tried to pack the Supreme Court, the American polity's church. The charges against him escalated from the partisan to the principled: he threatened the Constitution, they said, and he aimed to set up a dictatorship. The Republicans led off a crusade to preserve democracy, handing that flag to Wendell Willkie, son of the Indiana soil, a businessman like Hoover but even freer of the taint of political experience. Willkie's platform for 1940 was a creed, a faith, a reprise of the sacred American promise. Willkie had to be drafted—and so did Roosevelt, who held back until convention time. FDR campaigned as The President, consumed with the developing war in Europe, interrupting that high work for an occasional correction of Republican errors, calling on God to strengthen the patriotic cause. Despite the shock of his violation of George Washington's rule against a third term, he carried the day.

1944 Conciliation   One could say that Roosevelt won the election of 1944 on December 7, 1941, the day the Japanese attacked Pearl Harbor. For the second time in history, Americans went to the polls in the middle of a war. The universal purpose was to get to the end of it. Roosevelt the confident continuer reappeared with his old jaunty humor and comforting certainty intact, calling the nation together like a family around the dinner table, teasing his opposition for attacking his little dog, waving and smiling to the crowds as he drove through Manhattan in the rain. His challenger, New York Governor Thomas E. Dewey, echoed the conciliatory theme by calling for an end to New Deal bickering, but he seemed a bickerer himself as he flailed at the Commander-in-Chief's administrative imperfections. Once again, Roosevelt won by a safe margin.

Cycle V: 1948, 1952, 1956

1948 Conflict   Five months later, he was dead and Harry S Truman was President. The year after that, the war over, the Republicans captured both houses of Congress, as long-suppressed partisan passions revived. Dewey had a hard fight at the Republican convention of 1948, but won through to the nomination on the third ballot. His troubles were as nothing compared to Truman's. On the left, Roosevelt's former Vice-President, Henry A. Wallace, formed a new Progressive party to fight for the Presidency. On the right, the Dixiecrats split off to contend for Governor J. Strom Thurmond. A funereal convention nominated Truman—who proceeded, to nearly everyone's amazement, to battle the Republicans from one end of the country to the other, at last winning a shocking upset victory by the closest of margins.

1952 Conscience   Truman did his damnedest, but by 1952 it was time for a change. War broke out in Korea in 1950; the President was held responsible for failing to beat back the communists and end it. Charges of corruption in and around the White House gained credence, as did the suspicion that the Reds might have too many friends in the Truman administration. Perhaps as important, in an age of increasingly symbolic politics, Truman's image as a scrappy politician lacking in Presidential dignity, a cusser, and a poker player, took hold. Truman saw the signs; he helped get Illinois Governor Adlai E. Stevenson to run—a man of evident high integrity, superbly literate propounder of the American conscience, who preached his sermons like a Puritan divine. The Republicans beat that move with General Dwight David Eisenhower, hero of World War II, son of Abilene, Kansas, reluctantly taking his first plunge into political controversy. Eisenhower conducted not a campaign, but a "crusade." Morals ruled the day and the Republican diatribe against "Communism, Korea, and Corruption" won it.

1956 Conciliation   Eisenhower went to Korea and the war there was settled. Back home the Red scare got going in earnest, complemented on the foreign front by the secretary of state's dire warnings. In the midst of prosperity came new anxieties: massive social shifts, escalating debt, newly demanding minorities. In 1955, the Soviets exploded a hydrogen bomb. Eisenhower, meanwhile, grinned and presided. Adlai Stevenson, renominated, added to the general anxiety by trying to get a fight going in 1956. Eisenhower, renominated, spoke of peace and harmony. The electorate responded: they liked Ike, their warmhearted friend in the White House.

Cycle VI: 1960, 1964, 1968

1960 Conflict   The appeal of placidity slowly waned in Eisenhower's second term; the appeal of adventure sparked again. Ike stepped aside in favor of his aggressive young Vice-President, Richard M. Nixon, who fought his way to the Republican nomination in 1960 over the challenge of New York Governor Nelson Rockefeller. A young Democratic war hero, John F. Kennedy, muscled aside Senator Hubert Humphrey in the primaries and Senator Lyndon Johnson at the convention. A partisan battle ensued as the candidates lashed each other in a flat-out campaign, culminating in a novel confrontation: a series of "Great Debates" on television. Kennedy won by a whisker. The drama of that season was combat, in a new, cool mode.

1964 Conscience   Kennedy was gunned down in Dallas in 1963. President Lyndon B. Johnson went into the 1964 campaign as "Preacher Lyndon," dedicated to the martyred Kennedy's moral purposes: a peaceful resolution of the war in Vietnam and justice for blacks in America—a high-road campaign for grand principles. That year brought forward a new moral champion for the Republicans, who advertised his conscience as his primary qualification for the Presidency. Senator Barry Goldwater of Arizona was hauled into the race by disgruntled conservatives, who undertook nothing less than a reorientation of American political philosophy. Goldwater railed against corruption, not in the name of clear programmatic alternatives, but in the name of civic virtue deductively defined. In the end he lost, but his moral concerns and the wildly deviant paths of policy they dictated dominated the national agenda.

1968 Conciliation   There followed, under Johnson the "dove" candidate of 1964, a hideous escalation of the war in Vietnam, setting off a period of political discord that made the anxieties of the 1950s look like a tea party. Those same years saw the boiling up of violent racial protest, as, in city after city, black ghetto residents and white police confronted each other in the streets. At last in April 1968, Johnson bowed out of contention for renomination. Martin Luther King, Jr., and Robert F. Kennedy were killed by assassins in the spring, chaotic violence seemed spreading everywhere, the country veering out of control. Candidates from one end of the political spectrum to the other called out for peace and quiet, a revival of national unity. The Democrats, meeting in the midst of a riot in Chicago, nominated their chief apostle of brotherhood, Hubert Humphrey. The Republicans turned to a new Nixon, calm and mellow, his lowered voice promising to bring us together again. Nixon won by an eyelash—the peacemaker, the conciliator, the bringer of harmony.

Cycle VII: 1972, 1976, 1980

1972 Conflict   It did not work out that way. Nixon spread the war—secretly. He got at his political enemies—secretly. By 1972, the first secret was out in the open and the second just beginning to emerge. Opponents to the war turned from demonstrations to hard-fought politics. But President Nixon would not meet in public challenge directly. Instead, in a carefully orchestrated image campaign, he presented himself as The President, negotiating with foreign powers, refusing to discuss the issues his opponents threw at him. Thus the story of politics as war had nowhere to go in 1972 but to the Democrats. There, in a long series of hot fights in the primaries, the contest of 1972 found its drama, as moralist Senator George S. McGovern carried his crusade to the nomination and then, in the summer, worked himself out of the election when he mishandled the resignation of his running mate, Senator Thomas Eagleton.

1976 Conscience   Nixon's secret war against his political enemies at last came to light in a slow process of uncovering, leading to his resignation from office in 1974. His Vice-President, Gerald R. Ford, moved into the White House amidst high hopes for moral restoration—an honest man at last. But then Ford pardoned Nixon, raising the suspicion that he was not above a deal. Ford's demeanor helped allay that doubt; he went into the 1976 election season as a straight-shooting down-home American booster. The Democrats, after a long and wearing contest in the proliferating primaries, turned to an outsider from Plains, Georgia, running against the corruptions of the Capitol. Governor Jimmy Carter emerged, preaching the common American values of decency and compassion and honesty. A nation ready for moral revival voted him in.

1980 Conciliation   There were some highly praised foreign-policy moves but as the 1980 election approached, Carter's preacherly rhetoric began to wear thin with a public increasingly anxious over a deepening recession, galloping inflation, and an energy crisis. In the summer of 1979, the President took note of a "crisis of confidence" and the need to restore union. More than 100,000 citizens wrote in to praise his speech. Millions more turned out to see the visiting Pope, with his ecumenical message of love. The seizure of hostages in Iran and a Soviet invasion of Afghanistan rallied the nation to the President's side, while his critics fumed and fumbled. Whatever the outcome of the election, the emerging dominant theme was clear: worn with quarrels and demands for heroic sacrifice, the Americans seemed ready for a little relief, a little healing, a time of concilation. There would be time enough for another hot policy battle in 1984.

The Power of the Pulse

That history happened. My reading of the extended accounts of these elections convinces me that this summary version does justice to the facts. On the record, the pulse of politics describes the major themes that dominated contest after contest. But description is not explanation. *Why* do these particular dimensions of modern politics keep returning to shape the nation's consciousness as we deliberate the Presidential choice? Where does the force of it come from?

The pulse of politics is a mythic pulse. Political life shares in the national mythology, grows in the wider culture, draws its strength from the human passion for discovering, in our short span of life on this peripheral planet, the drama of human significance. Ours is a story-making civilization; we are a race of incorrigible narrators. The hunger to transform experience into meaning through story spurs the political imagination. We seem bound and determined to find in the mundane business of picking a chief executive a saga of the spirit.

That impulse marks us as human. But why do we concentrate so persistently on three themes: conflict, conscience, conciliation?

Part of the explanation may be that they resonate with the most deeply rooted and primitive human memories. No one knows how tale-telling got its start, long before life was reduced to writing. The conflict theme may trace all the way back to preliterate hunting stories, recounted by survivors returning to the fireside to report the frantic search and kill and escape—the origin of the "Embroidered Exploit," one writer thinks. The conscience theme may echo the primordial "Warning Example": a mother, straining to "persuade her child from the fire," tells how another child, another time, ignored the commandment and suffered for it.* The conciliation theme may draw on the appeal of ancient acts of union: the young woman or man, driven by the incest taboo to seek a mate among foreigners, comes back with a tale of courtship and consummation, giving birth to an endless series of sweet stories of love. Reflections of these old sagas might be discerned in the psychological paradigm that dominates our age's thinking: the ego, instrument for coping with the struggles of the external world; the superego, warning against harmful violations; the id, longing after the thrill and ease of sexual satisfaction. They are reflected again in the never-ending popularity of the war story, the morality play, the romantic comedy.

But there are also specifically American reasons for these emphases.

The American war story, from which the theme of politics as conflict derives its very language, reflects our peculiar experience. Here as elsewhere war has had its powerful appeal—cutting through the ambiguities and complexities and frustrations of life with a simple, exciting, rejuvenating

---

*Arthur Ransome, *A History of Story-Telling: Studies in the Development of Narrative* (New York: Frederick A. Stokes Co., undated, c. 1910), chapter 1.

release of aggression. But war often came to other nations by the shock of invasion. In isolated America, the warmakers repeatedly confronted the special problem of arousing the martial spirit against distant enemies who had not yet attacked us. That arousal required propaganda—the substitution of drama for experience as a stimulus to action. Thus our history vibrates with *talk* about war, advertising its anticipated glories in rip-roaring tales of heroism. The war story echoes through the culture; no wonder political storytellers pick up on its thrilling, threatening theme.

Modern newspapering was born in combat; I will trace how that craft grew up with the political fight game and how it helped translate the fighting story from its primitive, axe-murder style to the gentler—but no less decisive—political combat of our time. There its drumbeat rattles to rouse us from the temptations of lassitude.

The politics of conscience bites deep in the American experience. From the Old Testament on, the tense drama of the making and breaking of the covenant between God and His people has electrified Western civilization. The American civilization was founded by Godly people, determined to build a New Zion in the wilderness, a newly chosen people, set apart by the Almighty Himself from the heathen Europeans to the East and the heathen Indians to the West. The Puritan God was no bemused Observer of human folly, content to sit back and watch what His original act of creation had set in train. God was *in* history, the Calvinist God directing every flight of birds over Plymouth, every blast of lightning, the rise of every crop and plague, and the exact course of human events. America was a mission. The Declaration announces our "firm reliance on the protection of divine Providence." Thus America stepped into the family of nations claiming a kind of ordination. Lincoln confirmed it: we were a nation "under God." From then to now, our conscience has never been satisfied by government as a mere practical arrangement to secure our survival and see to the feeding of our animal appetites. If it was never perfectly clear whom God favored for President, it seemed self-evident that the question must be asked.

Our periodic revivals of the politics of conscience owe much to the preachers in the press. While reporters were covering the fights, editors and columnists ministered to our spiritual needs. That moral mission flourished most strikingly in magazine journalism. Magazine journalism on a national scale got underway in the nineteenth century, but it took off, in terms of mass circulation and political influence, in that era of moralistic reformism that culminated in Wilson's reign, the era of the moralizing "muckrakers." Editors got directly into Presidential politics; one brought Wilson along, another fostered Hoover, behind the scenes as well as in the pages of their journals. The success of *Time* and the rise of the columnists lent force to the combination of reportage and moral commentary, recalling the power of the ancient parables, reinforcing the politics of conscience down to our day. Now as then, American politics focuses on the search for a good President to lead a good country.

The politics of conciliation has its own essential suspense: will Romeo and Juliet succeed in getting together despite the Montagues and Capulets? But again, the specifically American experience underscores the theme. We became a nation of nationalities, of strangers bearing conflicting heritages, scattered across a continent. Had we not found the path to union, there would have been no United States. Holding that vast and varied enterprise together became urgent American work, its necessity never more deeply burnt into the national consciousness than when union failed in the 1860s. Just as we are about to smash up the political saloon, someone has to have the sense to yell, "Don't shoot the piano player!" That calls for laughing off our oh-so-serious differences, for positive thinking, for the continual rediscovery of what we have in common. At least since Ben Franklin, Americans have stood apart from the world's stern aristocracies, dour dictatorships, and aching slumlands as a nation of incorrigible hopers and boosters. If we did not invent Santa Claus, we made him our own. Our politics is something we *play*, a great game, and a President is supposed to play that game with a smile on his face. That superficially light and vulgar story, the butt of ironists, is in fact the rock-bottom myth of our political existence.

The prime medium for illustrating the politics of conciliation in the modern era is broadcasting. The early nineteenth century had its "celebrations" mixing politics and entertainment, continued in the late nineteenth century in popular tent theater. But radio and then television reached out eventually to nearly every home, homogenizing the culture. Television burst into mass popularity just as the nation was discovering we liked Ike— and the peace and harmony he came to symbolize by 1956. Broadcasting aimed to please, wrapping politics in fun and games. Today it is our only truly national medium, conveying with unmatched reach and power its core message of conciliation.

In *every* Presidential election season, these themes are reinforced. We could not possibly sort out from the many who present themselves the few who are serious without setting up a fight. Once the leading contenders emerge, it is necessary to inquire into their qualifications—their characters—as potential replacements for George Washington. And then we need to sense whether this or that self-proclaimed hero can in fact draw together the nation's multifarious interests and energies for a unified march into the future. The slower, longer pulse of politics, by which we move from one dominant theme to the next, picks up momentum when, season after season, we confront the necessities of choice.

No wonder then that these myths grip the American political mind. They trace back to deep and original challenges to the human condition. They grow from the bloody ground of this nation's experience. They give our major storytellers their channels to popularity. They make possible our quadrennial progress from many to one. Together, they compose the lifeforce of the American political culture.

I

THE POLITICS OF
CONFLICT

O N JUNE 26, 1796, Washington wrote Hamilton that he was stepping down for "a variety of reasons (among which is a disinclination to be longer buffeted in the public prints by a set of infamous scribblers)." That decision, announced in his September Farewell Address, was "a signal, like the dropping of a hat, for the party racers to start," wrote his friend Fisher Ames. Ames saw an end to national tranquillity, a time "when adversity, disturbance, and panic, shall prevail." He was right. Washington's departure brought on the nation's first real election—a hot partisan battle between Jefferson's Democratic-Republicans (pro-French, prodebtor) and John Adams's Federalists (pro-British, pro-creditor). The *Gazette of the United States* led the way for the Federalists, the *National Gazette* for the Republicans. Adams was appalled: "I have no very ardent desire to be the butt of party malevolence," he said. "Having tasted that cup, I find it bitter, nauseous, and unwholesome." Jefferson wrote later that he had been "a fair mark for every man's dirt," and, "I did not know myself under the pens either of my friends or foes." The election was nearly a draw. Adams won, with seventy-one electoral votes to Jefferson's sixty-eight.

The fighting spirit of 1796—our first real election—springs to life recurrently in American Presidential politics. The leading contenders change, the system changes, the issues and conditions and electoral results change. What keeps coming back, in ever-new versions, is the myth of the fighting candidate beating his way into the Presidency over the bodies of his adversaries. After a time of concord we are ready for a time of conflict. Politics then appears as the rhetorical equivalent of war, offering the excitement of real war without the actual death and destruction real war brings. Like real war, the revival of the politics of conflict provides an antidote to apathy and surrender, the adrenalin of adventure, rousing tales of heroism. It offers a fresh start, breaking away from a dead past, freeing aggression from the bonds of reason, cutting through the ambiguities of moderation. It is a test of courage. It offers meaning: participation in a drama of risk and surprise, an unpredestined story of the human experience in which the gallantry of action overpowers the calculation of result.

Political combat is, for most of us, a spectator sport, a great game to watch and read about. For all our talk of "campaigns," "strategies," "attack," "battle," "victory," and "defeat," we experience political warfare as a romance, a mythic experience. We play at war. The last act of that drama produces a President, who can make real war.

Each of the Presidential candidates whose names title these chapters was a veteran of real combat in real war. Each was profoundly affected by the experience. Theodore Roosevelt's heroic adventure in Cuba massively confirmed his natural bellicosity, which served his career superbly in its early phases and then, in 1912, shot it and his party into shambles. Harry S Truman discovered within himself a whole new dimension of fighting courage in World War I, when he led his rowdy artillerymen through one desperate crisis after another; later he said, "My whole political career is based on my war service and war associates." John F. Kennedy was nearly killed in the South Pacific after months of navy combat, and he came into politics as "Fighting Jack" the war hero. George McGovern was decorated for valorous leadership as a bomber pilot in World War II; his many missions branded into his mind the determination to fight for peace. He lost the election but the crusade for peace was belatedly won, and the victor over him ousted from the White House in disgrace. These veterans linked their war adventures to the political adventures they starred in. Other candidates whose experience with the threat of death in battle had been momentary or vicarious picked up on the same themes and images, sometimes rattling their sabers more loudly than the heroes did. But the political war story did not have to make do with actors hired to play the parts. Real warriors stepped out of uniform and into candidacy, bearing in their personal mythologies the words and music of war.

Journalists also went to war. There they found and tested their own capacities for grace under pressure, but they also found thrilling copy and they came home with their heads full of combative imagery. The story of politics as war as told by journalists took on its basic modern shape just before the turn of this century. In a remarkable historical conjunction, the sudden surge into mass popularity of the American daily newspaper coincided with the Spanish-American War and Theodore Roosevelt's emergent presence. That war fueled the fight between two inventive geniuses, Joseph Pulitzer and William Randolph Hearst, whose yellow presses sometimes resorted to red headlines as they raged for war and, when it came, made the most of it. Their star reporters became celebrities. Their circulations soared far beyond the old records. They wrote about politics in the militant vocabulary. Their fantastic success set a style, the tradition of the press of battle, forever itching for a fight. That spirit lived on in newspaper journalism and spread out into the other media so that today magazines and broadcasting follow the story of politics as conflict with vigor and verve. But the battle story took hold and worked best in newspapers.

Theodore Roosevelt's story can be taken as the benchmark case: a dramatic, aggressive politician finds in dramatic, aggressive journalism the co-author of his destiny. Harry Truman's amazing victory carries that theme forward, but shows also how the strong appeal of the story of politics as conflict can overcome even the nearly unanimous political bias of the storytellers themselves. The newspapers, like his own party, had written Truman off but the saga of his stubborn campaign took hold in the daily accounts—it was news. John Kennedy's rise to power is conflict again, but it marks a sea change in the battle story, from hot attack to cool intellectual riposte, and from a seasonal event to a drama unfolding over years. George McGovern's losing struggle shows how the press, blocked by President Nixon's refusal to campaign out in public where the public could see him, concentrated its forces on the man they *could* see, while Nixon knifed his "enemies" in secret. In the process, journalism developed a whole new art form: the story of the battle against a scoreboard of expectations the press itself set up for the polls and the primaries, a new game Jimmy Carter and his young strategists mastered to win his crusade.

If the pulse of politics beats on as it has in the past twenty elections, the time will come round again for an election of conflict in 1984, doubtless with its own special style and story.

3

Theodore Roosevelt 1900

THEODORE ROOSEVELT *scared* politicians. Woodrow Wilson thought him "the most dangerous man of the age." Mark Hanna, the great Republican boss, called him a "madman." Even Mark Twain saw him as "clearly insane . . . and insanest upon war and its supreme glories." But there were those who loved him. Chief among them were reporters.

Mad as he sometimes seemed, Roosevelt was no radical. On the issues, he was a reformer, a fixer-up-er, an advocate of change within the system. He sounded radical because he roared and pounded and thrashed about. He started off the Presidential politics of the twentieth century with a bang—the election of 1900—and he dominated American politics for a dozen years, even when he was off in Africa hunting lions. A war hero with enormous energy and a genius for publicity, Roosevelt fit the battle story perfectly. He was also lucky. Continually opposed by his party's chieftains, he could not have climbed to the Presidency without an alternative channel to power. For TR, the channel was the new mass-circulation newspaper, exploding on the scene in New York City just as he was gearing up his career. Newspaper journalism had found a new focus and produced a lasting image, the image of the active, combative, crusading, irreverent, emotive, and endlessly surprising journal of the day.

TR and the newspapers were lucky that history handed them the chance to start a real war, one he could fight in and they could report. And in the larger perspective, Roosevelt was lucky in the election that paved the way for his emergence: 1896, when a frightened nation chose comforting William McKinley and began to ease back into prosperity and, in time, to lust for fresh adventures. Peaceable McKinley was as unsuited for the combat of 1900 as Roosevelt was for the gentleness of 1896. Thus candidates come and go, their characters sometimes fitting, sometimes at odds with the pulse of politics.

1896: A Sigh of Relief

By 1896, fear and violence had been wracking the national nerves for a decade, from the Chicago Haymarket riot in 1896 (four protesters hung), to the Homestead uprising in Pennsylvania in 1892 (ten killed, seventy wounded), to the Panic of 1893 (layoffs, breadlines), to the Pullman strike and Debs's arrest and Coxey's "Army of the Commonwealth of Christ" marching to Washington to demand jobs in 1894. That year alone there were some fourteen hundred strikes; more than 660,000 men were thrown out of work. Farmers by the thousands gave up and sold out. There were rumors of "anarchy"—even "revolution"—especially among the wealthy. The un-wealthy did not want revolution. They wanted money. The campaign was about how to get more of it without losing what you had, how to achieve and maintain an easier, safer, more comfortable existence and bring to a close the too-long and too-wearing years of turmoil and distress.

For all its economic complications, the Democratic panacea, free silver, came on as a magic cure for a real disease. Its prescriber was Bryan, the Democratic nominee, who at age thirty-six (barely old enough to be Presi-dent) had already mastered the grand old American oratorical art of sounding profound while committing nothing. Bryan was nominated because the many other contenders could not sort themselves out and because he wowed the national convention with his high ambiguities sonorously delivered. The delegates amened again and again as he warned of those who would "crucify mankind on a cross of gold."

What Bryan was saying was part of what millions of anxious Americans wanted and needed to hear: compassion for their plight, castigation of a ruling class that had forgotten the meaning of the stewardship of power, a prophetic reminder that the pursuit of happiness is a human right above and before allegiance to any particular economic arrangement. He spoke to their concerns, to great and little crowds of them. "The fountains in the hearts of men were stirred," wrote Jonathan Daniels. Bryan himself set out with the feeling that "this is going to be a campaign of sentiment."

Nearly all the heavy thinkers in the universities and the great corpora-tions stood against free silver. Their man was McKinley, then governor of Ohio. He had no magical solution; he *was* a magical solution. His curative powers were, they thought, in his personality more than in his policy—which was not entirely clear, though he was basically against fooling around with the money. "Good money never made times hard" was his campaign slogan and his campaign song was "The Honest Little Dollar's Here to Stay." In contrast to Bryan, whom Roosevelt called "a mere boy," McKinley ex-uded solid maturity. He looked prematurely embalmed, with that little smile funeral directors learn to put on to assure the bereaved of the depart-ed's heavenly destination. Up close he was a sweet man, kind and patient and sturdily humble; he left the hardball politics largely to his manager, Mark Hanna, though he called the main shots.

McKinley was constitutionally against aggressive campaigning. "I cannot get the consent of my mind to do anything that places me in the position of seeming to seek an office and anything I might say or do would at once be interpreted as an effort in that direction," he wrote a friend. "Everything looks very comfortable and anything like seeking to promote my personal interests is very distasteful to me." He would not make or respond to attacks and he would not give out interviews. Instead he set up a marvelous, continuing media event at his homestead in Canton, Ohio. Personally "averse to anything like an effort to bring crowds here," he cooperated with the drummery of the Republican National Committee. The railroads cooperated by setting excursion rates so low that the trip was "cheaper than staying at home," one newspaper said. Nothing was left to chance. The leader of each visiting delegation came to Canton in advance and submitted his statement in writing; anything embarrassing was edited out and sometimes new sections added. Pilgrim bands of veterans, farmers, merchants, church people, and every other kind of group journeyed to his front porch.

It was wonderfully appealing. For that and other reasons the editorial press was overwhelmingly pro-McKinley. In New York, only William Randolph Hearst's *New York Journal* backed Bryan (Hearst held a fortune in silver) and cartooned McKinley as the puppet of a grotesque Hanna dressed in a suit of dollar signs. The newspapers were full of vituperative exchanges by lesser candidates and campaigners and the editors themselves. True to his character, Roosevelt lit out after the Democrats, such as the delegates to the Illinois convention in June—"murderers, horsethieves, burglars, libertines, crooks of all kinds—men who have been convicted of crimes ranging from pickpocketing to arson." By October he was lumping together "Messrs. Bryan, Altgeld, Tillman, Debs, Coxey and the rest" as "strikingly like the leaders of the Terror in France in mental and moral attitudes." But the two Presidential candidates floated above it all, Bryan scarcely mentioning his opponent or his party, gently reproving such hecklers as the Yale boys who threw eggs at him. McKinley simply smiled.

That fall, as if in benediction, the weather brought in a bumper wheat crop in America and a wheat shortage abroad; prices shot upward before the election. McKinley won by more than a million votes. Late on election night, his brother James discovered the winner kneeling in prayer with his mother's arm around him, she whispering, "Oh, God, keep him humble." The *World* editorialized, "The pall is lifted. The paralysis is removed. Apprehension will give way to confidence." Of the inauguration, another New York newspaper headlined, "Republicans Take the Helm. Under Bright Skies and with Fair Winds, the Ship of State Sails for the Haven of Prosperity." The Republicans would hold that helm for sixteen years. In the fall of 1897, New Yorkers returned safe old Tammany to power by overwhelming majorities, setting off wild celebrations in the streets. "To Hell with Reform," read the banners.

The election of 1896 ended in a sigh of relief and relaxation. In the course of it the American electorate reshuffled their partisan loyalties more fundamentally than would happen again until 1936. At the time, though, 1896 felt more like an end of the miseries than the start of an electoral realignment. Four years later, it could be seen as background music for one of the hardest fought shoot-outs in American political history.

The Battle with Bryan

By 1900, Bryan had been pummeled out of his silver obsession by the Democratic bosses, who at last succeeded in persuading him to resist "the allurements of so-called consistency," as one of them put it. Times had changed, drastically. Prosperity was abroad in the land. Silver moved down the list in a program stressing antiimperialism and antimonopoly—and there was Bryan, buying it all, ardently pressing his blessings on the Tammany bosses. Roosevelt strode into the Republican convention and was whooped into the Vice-Presidential nomination by the exuberant delegates. McKinley would stay home again. Hanna told Roosevelt that virtually the whole burden of the campaign would be his. TR was up for it: he said, "I am as strong as a bull moose and you can use me up to the limit."

The issues that year were exceedingly complex, as both parties, sniffing victory, edged toward the muddled middle of the political spectrum. The Democrats were against imperialism but for landed expansion. The Republicans kept bringing up free silver, which the Democrats now wanted forgotten; Roosevelt's party, like Bryan's, was against trusts but found the Democrats' solutions unworkable. They agreed, however, on one enemy: public indifference. Mark Hanna saw "General Apathy" as McKinley's main enemy, and Bryan's manager worried about that having "failed to awaken the lethargic American conscience." It looked like a close fight. Democratic fortunes had picked up in the state elections of 1899; Bryan had lost in 1896, but he polled more votes than any previous Presidential candidate. Arousal could make the difference and so both candidates hit the trail running hard.

The campaign made up in steam what it lacked in substance. In that railroad age, Bryan roared around the country, 16,000 miles of it in seventeen states, making 600-odd speeches in five and a half weeks, thirteen to sixteen hours a day. Roosevelt surpassed that, traveling 21,000 miles through twenty-four states in eight weeks. Aflame with fight, Roosevelt soon got over his early fear that, as second man on the ticket, he would appear "like a second-class Bryan," and left behind his sense of accepting the nomination as "a man absolutely and entirely in the second place whom it is grossly absurd and unjust to speak of in any other capacity." Bryan became "my opponent"—so strikingly so that when Mrs. Bryan came to write the Bryan memoirs she referred to her husband's defeat "by Mr. Roosevelt." Mr. Dooley, the comic sage of the newspapers, had it right: "Tis Teddy alone that's runnin' and he ain't r'runin', he's gallopin'."

He boomed "my beloved Republicans"—and their gallant leader William McKinley when he thought of it—but mainly he assailed the Democrats. Anticipating another fighting candidate sixty years hence, his main theme was this: "It rests with us now to decide whether . . . we shall march forward to fresh triumphs or whether at the outset we shall cripple ourselves for the contest." His book, *The Strenuous Life*, was republished and given wide circulation.

Out in the field, Roosevelt let loose his vituperative vocabulary:

Our opponents have not any more even the poor excuse of honesty for their folly. They have raved against trusts, they have foamed at the mouth in prating of impossible remedies. . . .

Mr. Bryan himself is sufficiently strident when he talks about those figments of disordered brains, militarism and imperialism; yet he coos as mildly as a sucking dove when he whispers his unchanged devotion to free silver. . . . If they came into power, their mere possession of power would throw this country into convulsions of disaster.

The policy of the free coinage of silver at a ratio of sixteen to one is a policy fraught with destruction to every home in the land. It means untold misery to the head of every household, and, above all, to the women and children of every home.

Mr. Bryan seeks to sow seeds of malice and envy among Americans. Jefferson and Jackson he quotes. His political school has nothing in common with theirs. He is a pupil in that most dangerous political school, the school in which Marat and Robespierre were the teachers.

Militarism! Here in this building a week ago Mr. Bryan repeated what he either knows, or ought to know, to be an absolute slander, when he said that our little army had been created with the purpose of putting it into forts to overawe the working men of our great cities.*

The vituperative mode did not come as naturally to Bryan as it did to TR, but he got his licks in. It was "a contest between democracy on one hand and plutocracy on the other"; it was a fight against a "Republican party . . . dominated by those influences which constantly tend to substitute the worship of mammon for the protection of the rights of man." In one supersentence, Bryan laid out the devious hypocrisy of his enemy:

Republicans who used to advocate bimetallism now try to convince themselves that the gold standard is good; Republicans who were formerly attached to the greenback are now seeking an excuse for giving national banks control of the nation's paper money; Republicans who used to boast that the Republican party was paying off the national debt are now looking for reasons to support a perpetual and increasing debt; Republicans who formerly abhorred a trust now beguile themselves with the delusion that there are good trusts and bad trusts, while, in their minds, the line between the two is becoming more and more obscure; Republicans who, in times past, congratulated the country upon the small expense of our standing army, are now making

*Theodore Roosevelt, *The Works of Theodore Roosevelt*, ed. Hermann Hagedorn (New York: Charles Scribner's Sons, 1926), vol. 14, chap. 12.

light of the objections which are urged against a large increase in the permanent military establishment; Republicans who gloried in our independence when the nation was less powerful now look with favor upon a foreign alliance; Republicans who three years ago condemned "forcible annexation" as immoral and even criminal are now sure that it is both immoral and criminal to oppose forcible annexation.*

Republicans, said Bryan, justified imperialism as the American "destiny"— but "destiny is the subterfuge of the invertebrate, who, lacking the courage to oppose error, seeks some plausible excuse for supporting it."

The *New York World* saw the Manhattan throngs for Bryan as "A Whirlwind of Fire," but Roosevelt gave them newspaper drama: "Elmira Toughs Threw Turnips at Roosevelt," "Governor's Carriage Mobbed in the Street by Crowd Who Called Him 'Scab' and 'Fakir' and Hurled Missiles," "Many Men Hurt in a Political Riot," and the next day, "Roosevelt Declares That Coker Incites to Riot and Mob Violence at the Polls." Roosevelt had responded to a *World* reporter with a conversation-stopper: "I will not give any statement of any kind to the *New York World* of any sort or shape"—which the *World* printed on page one. In a mocking editorial titled "A Lack of Strenuousity," the *World* drew on news of another Rooseveltian riposte:

> . . . Asked an impolite question at one point the terrible Teddy only yelled, "That's a lie!" If it was a lie, the man who asked it was a liar; and yet the idol of the cowboys neither shot his ear off nor jumped down and "cut" him nor offered to lick him after the meeting. . . . It is not difficult to fancy the astonishment and disgust with which One-Eyed Ike, Dead Injun Bill and other really strenuous chums of Roosevelt out West will read of this incident.

To a cry of "Down with the trusts!" from a man in the crowd who had evidently taken seriously the condemnation of these monopolies in the Republican platform, the candidate for Vice-President shouted:

> You look like one of those men who work exclusively with their mouths. You interrupt this meeting because you are a hoodlum and nothing else. Now, then, go back to your fellow-hoboes.

> . . . . And yet, as we have said, there is a disappointing lack of strenuousity in Roosevelt's campaigning. If a soft answer turns away wrath, a hard answer fails to "knock-out" anybody. Until Teddy shall actually shoot, stab or lick some of his interrupters it is inevitable that his reputation will shrivel among his kindred spirits.†

When that same month, Bryan again visited New Haven, souvenir-seeking Yale men "grabbed him from all sides, knocked his hat down over his eyes, pulled his necktie awry." The Great Orator was rescued from this desecration by William Randolph Hearst, who shoved the attackers aside and led Bryan to safety.

McKinley and Roosevelt won, by fewer than a million votes in a low

---

* From Bryan's acceptance speech in Indianapolis, 8 August 1900, in Schlesinger et al., *History of American Presidential Elections: 1789–1968* (New York: Chelsea House, 1971), vol. 3, pp. 1943*ff*. Bryan had a phonograph record made of this speech.
†*New York World*, 22 October 1900.

turnout election. Before another year had gone by, an assassin killed McKinley and Roosevelt was President, the youngest ever at forty-two.

TR Rising Like a Rocket

Roosevelt reached this apex of attention by a most circuitous route. By the time he achieved notice his political character had its basic shape. Had he been merely mad, as Hanna thought, he would not have been nearly so interesting. But behind all his clamorous strenuosity was a remarkable personality, a man who had shaped from his triumphs and tragedies an extraordinary approach to life as adventure that found an outlet in voracious reading and wild-game hunting, in remarkable literary productions and in front-line combat, in righteous indignation and an unmatched talent for friendship. He liked the rough and tumble of politics; bellicose he was, but he was also the first American to win the Nobel Peace Prize. He was terrific copy. Writing in 1950, historian Frank Luther Mott said Theodore Roosevelt was "probably more constantly page-one news than any other President the country has had."

Roosevelt had begun to catch the reportorial eye and ear as a young state legislator in Albany in the 1880s. It was his idiosyncracies reporters noticed, the features and manners that set him off from the other typical dude aristocrats who would occasionally drift in and out of that body without disturbing its equilibrium. He looked and sounded different. "Young Roosevelt of New York"—he was just twenty-four—appeared as "a blond young man with eye-glasses, English side-whiskers and a Dundreary drawl in his speech," said one report. His voice was high and his speech halting, but he could easily be heard calling out shrilly for recognition, "Mr. Speak-ah! Mr. Speak-ah!" He broke into the news by demanding an investigation of a stock-jobbing scandal, drawing heavily on evidence fed him by the city editor of the *New York Times*. This outrageous proposal "was like the bursting of a bombshell," a member remembered, at which "a great silence fell over the whole Assembly for a while. It was a thunderbolt to them." Jay Gould, then owner of the *New York World*, ordered this whippersnapper treated with the contempt he deserved. On the substance, Roosevelt won and lost: there was an investigation, but its result was a finding of no wrongdoing. But as he saw it, "I rose like a rocket." He got a reputation. The following year he was reelected by a wide margin, though his party suffered large losses.

Roosevelt's fireworks were the natural stuff of the newspaper story. His journalist friend Mark Sullivan saw that: "Roosevelt's fighting was so much a part of the life of the period, was so tied up to the newspapers . . . as to constitute almost the whole of the passing show." Even his critics had to watch him; one said, "Roosevelt has the knack of doing things, and doing them noisily, clamorously; while he is in the neighborhood the public can no more look the other way than the small boy can turn his head away from a circus parade followed by a steam calliope." Publisher Joseph Pulitzer, who came to detest him, found him nevertheless "wonderfully interesting." Publisher Hearst eventually saw Roosevelt as an "unspeakable blackguard," but he could not keep his eyes off him. His devotion to "the strenuous life" was contagious in this age of Kipling.

Roosevelt the newsmaking legislator emerged as "the most successful young politician of the day," said the New York Evening Post. He mixed into Presidential politics in the Republican convention of 1884 as a vigorously conniving and orating delegate. After two years of ranching and hunting in the Dakotas (to recover from the tragic death of his mother and his wife on the same day), he came back to run for mayor of New York as a vigorous reformer still only twenty-eight years old. "If I find a public servant who is dishonest," he promised, "I will chop his head off if he is the highest Republican in this municipality!"—but he lost in a three-way race. In 1889, Henry Cabot Lodge got President Harrison to appoint him to the U.S. Civil Service Commission in Washington, where he stomped around demanding reform until 1895, when he came back to New York to take over the police commission. On the morning of May 6, 1895, he gathered up reporters Jacob Riis and Lincoln Steffens and marched into headquarters—"Where are our offices? Where is the Board Room? What do we do first?"

New York was awash with corruption. Payoffs to police from brothels, saloons, and gambling houses surpassed $10,000,000 a year. TR, to the delight of the press, swung into action. The New York World wrote up his trial of errant policemen in a front-page story copiously illustrated with drawings of his gesturing hands, teeth, ears, and "eyes, nose and glasses." The lead set the tone:

Sing, heavenly muse, the sad dejection of our poor policemen.
We have a real Police Commissioner. His name is Theodore Roosevelt. His teeth are big and white, his eyes are small and piercing, his voice is rasping. He makes our policemen feel as the little froggies did when the stork came to rule them. His heart is full of reform, and a policeman in full uniform, with helmet, revolver and night club, is no more to him than a plain everyday human being. He is at work now teaching the force that it is paid to work, not to boss.*

Within two weeks of the policemen's trial, he hit the papers again, as "Haroun-Al-Roosevelt," prowling the midnight streets in search of patrolmen to be accosted and corrected. Riis and Richard Harding Davis went with him; "The World's all night and ever-present reporter" Davis saw through his disguise—"a turned-up coat collar and a soft hat"—and brought back the story. " 'This is devilish police work!' exclaimed Mr. Roosevelt, wiping the night dew from his glasses, while he examined the gutters, dark recesses, and open doorways for the missing policemen."

*New York World, 17 May 1895.

Roosevelt's flair for "publicity, publicity, publicity," as a *World* subhead stressed, owed much to his natural friendship with the men who brought in the news. He knew how to help them with their own job. He lived his adventure in action, not fantasy; he went places and did things—physical things—in a time when most fateful decisions were being made behind desks. And he talked their language, the language of lead and hype and sensation reporters needed to get their stuff onto the front page.

Roosevelt's boyish behavior and aggressive idealism endeared him to reporters as friends, not just as feeders on his exploits. Throughout his career he had terrible fights with newspaper publishers—eventually he sued one for $10,000 for calling him a drunk (the award was six cents). When his son Ted was harassed by newshounds at Harvard, Roosevelt wrote him advice he himself could never take: "The thing to do is to go on just as you have evidently been doing, attract as little attention as possible, do not make a fuss about the newspaper men, camera creatures, and idiots generally, letting it be seen that you do not like them and avoid them, but not letting them betray you into any excessive irritation. I believe they will soon drop you, and it is just an unpleasant thing that you will have to live down." But reporters found TR irresistible. One who traveled with him said, "I don't think any sane man could be with him two weeks without getting to like him." Jacob Riis, who revealed *How the Other Half Lives*, became his constant companion in New York City: "For two years we were together all the day, and quite often most of the night, in the environment in which I had spent twenty years of my life. And these two years were the happiest by far of them all. Then life was really worth living, and I have a pretty robust enjoyment of it at all times." Richard Harding Davis became his lifelong friend; when Davis died, Roosevelt called him "as good an American as ever lived," one whose "heart flamed against cruelty and injustice." The great sports writer turned political reporter, Frank Cobb, caught "the Roosevelt obsession." Roosevelt would yell out his office window to his friend Lincoln Steffens: "Hey, there, come up here. . . . I just want you to see the kind of people that are coming here to intercede for proven crooks. Come on. . . ."

Roosevelt always realized how fragile his popularity was, how much in need of perpetual propping up. Some turned against him when he hired a female secretary ("young, small and comely, with raven black hair, and wore a dark closefitting gown," leered the *World*). The German community turned against him for closing beer halls on Sunday—but he joined their protest parade and when an irate guzzler loudly demanded, "Wo ist der Roosevelt?" the commissioner flashed his teeth in a grin and shouted back, "Hier bin ich!" When he closed down soda-water fountains and delicatessens on Sunday, opposition spread. The *World* fabricated and printed a story of a mother taken to court for buying ice on Sunday for her sick child, coming home too late, finding her child dead. He favored a law allowing liquor on Sunday in hotels, defining "hotel" as ten bedrooms and meals. Imaginative saloon-keepers set out ham sandwiches and knocked together ten tiny rooms for prostitution; a furniture company offered to furnish all ten rooms for $81.20; nine months later there were two thousand such new establishments in New York. The unity of the Police Board collapsed. The *World* hit Roosevelt for hypocritical self-advertisement. The *Journal* concluded: "He has a very poor opinion of the majority. But there is one compensation: The majority has a very poor opinion of Mr. Roosevelt." Perhaps most damaging, the cartoonists turned his distinctive features against him, picturing him as a toothy juvenile in a tantrum. But for every editor who decided Roosevelt had fallen from grace there was a reporter who found him fun and fascinating. And he kept moving. On April 17, 1897, he resigned as police commissioner, leaving behind a solid record of reform, to become assistant secretary of the navy. War, real war, brought together his extraordinary dramatic sense and the newspapers' need for conflict, and set him on course for the Presidency.

The Paper War in Cuba and at Home

All in all, the Spanish-American War was the ideal war. It took longer to start than to win. The victory was sharp and clean and total. In no time at all, it seemed, the memory of that other War—of grinding attrition over weary year after year to a still-wounded peace between Blue and Gray—was wiped away and an easier road cleared toward a Great War, a road to Verdun and the Somme.

For more than a decade, Roosevelt had been itching for a war—with Mexico, Chile, Venezuela, Canada, England, whomever. He glorified in "the rugged fighting qualities" a nation needed to "achieve real greatness." Two days after Christmas in 1895 he said, "This country needs a war," although the "bankers, brokers and anglomaniacs generally" were for "peace at any price," and the likes of Harvard's President Eliot (who saw Roosevelt as one of the "degenerated sons" of that institution) were infecting America with "a flabby, timid type of character, which eats away the great fighting qualities of our race." Over the years his belliphilia deepened. A nation "slothful, timid or unwieldy, is an easy prey for any people which still retain the most valuable of all qualities, the soldierly virtues. . . . Peace is a goddess only when she comes with sword girt on thigh. . . . No triumph of peace is quite so great as the supreme triumphs of war. . . . A war with Spain . . . [would bring] the benefit done to our people by giving them something to think of which isn't material gain, and especially the benefit done our military forces by trying both the Army and Navy in actual practice." "It will be awful if we miss the fun," he worried as the event approached, though he vehemently denied that he himself would "expect to win any military glory" or go to battle "in a mere spirit of recklessness or levity."

Roosevelt's saber rattling could not have suited better the purposes of

his hometown newspapers, then passionately engaged in their own "war"—
the war for circulation between Joseph Pulitzer's *World* and William Randolph Hearst's *Journal*. Absent the newspaper fight, the real war might
never have happened and Roosevelt might well have been shunted aside as a
maverick out of phase with the age of McKinley. Day by day, these two
titans of journalism had been brawling and braying their way to unheard-of
popular appeal in New York; their battle shaped history, in and out of journalism.

Joseph Pulitzer—tall, gaunt, with black hair and a pointed red beard,
looking like a cross between Mephistopheles and Rasputin—got there first,
in 1884. An impoverished Hungarian immigrant, Pulitzer had worked his
way to ownership of the *St. Louis Post-Dispatch*. With fierce energy and a
wild journalistic imagination, he revolutionized the paper. "I want to talk to
a nation," he said, "not a select committee." The prose had to be stark.
Not "Quadruplets Born"—"Four Babies at a Time." Politics was his passion
and battle its metaphor; politicians at conventions charged and fell—
"Grant's Column Dies Heroically in the Last Ditch." Pulitzer the foreigner
knew he could never be President: "But some day I am going to elect a President," he said.

The *World* took Gotham by storm. Within two weeks after first publication circulation leaped up by thirty-five percent. When it reached 100,000,
Pulitzer had a hundred cannons fired off and bought every employee a tall
silk hat. At the height of the Spanish War Crisis, nearly 1,500,000 daily copies were sold. Pulitzer exulted. His paper proclaimed itself "forever unsatisfied with merely printing news" and "forever fighting every form of
wrong." In a celebratory issue in 1895 appeared a large drawing of the *World*
as a draped Brunhild, brandishing a huge quill at her quailing enemies. By
1896, the circulation of the competing *New York Times* ("It Does Not Soil
the Breakfast Cloth") was down to a mere 9,000 copies.

Hearst came to town in 1895 and set out to beat the *World*. He looked
like a chronically dyspeptic version of Franklin D. Roosevelt, particularly
when boredom descended on him. Journalism to Hearst was "an enchanted
playground in which giants and dragons were to be slain simply for the fun of
the thing," said a friend. But his *Journal* was no fairytale. With Napoleonic
vision he warred against Pulitzer with stunts, crusades, fireworks, revelations, and "crime and underwear" stories. As reporter Davis and artist Frederick Remington fed him material from Cuba, he demanded more and more
sensation, eventually sending a muscular reporter undercover to Havana to
rescue from prison the pretty daughter of an insurrectionist, a story that ran
on over the weeks to 230,000 words, and culminated in a tremendous parade
through Manhattan and a rousing national tour. At the top of the war coverage, the *Journal* and the *World* were neck and neck in circulation.

The summer of 1897 was frustratingly quiet, a happy time for peaceable
President McKinley. In Spain the government fell and the new regime of-

fered Cuba self-government within the Empire. The new atmosphere of conciliation prompted McKinley to approve a friendly gesture, a visit to Havana by an American battleship, the *Maine*. When the great gleaming white ship eased into Havana harbor on January 25, 1898, courteous Spaniards welcomed her with a case of Jerez sherry and much polite palaver. The next evening, at his first diplomatic dinner in the White House, the President sat the Spanish minister next to him, though nine other envoys had protocol precedence. Meanwhile, Hearst and Pulitzer competed in wild vituperation. *Journal* headlines, sometimes in red, sometimes printed from carved wood blocks because no metal type was large enough, blazed away at Spanish imperfections. Equally heinous crimes, Hearst seemed to be saying, were "Spaniards Butcher Hundreds of Helpless Starving Cubans" and "Americans Taunted in Havana Streets." What could be wrong with President McKinley, pictured in the *Journal* as an enormous snail, refusing to act? Roosevelt said privately that McKinley "has no more backbone than a chocolate eclair." Hearst thundered publicly, "There are little Cuban babies crawling about in the dirt without a rag on their brown bodies, without a crust in their poor little hollow stomachs, that have more natural courage than McKinley. . . ."

The *World* had begun to imitate the *Journal* in earnest as early as the spring of 1896. A new Spanish general, Valeriano Weyler, had been sent from Madrid to suppress the rebelling peasants and Hearst quickly had him nominated "the prince of all cruel generals this century has seen," a "fiendish despot." The *World* traced "The Hideous History of Old Spain" up to current scenes of women clubbed in the streets, massacres, and garrotings. The *World's* own feature writer, Nellie Bly (who had earned her spurs as a reporter by racing around the world in less than eighty days), volunteered to lead a regiment with all women officers against the tyrant. Somehow a dispatch describing Weyler as a decent and capable man sneaked into the *World*, but soon a new man on the scene got the tone right: "Blood on the roadsides, blood in the fields, blood on the doorsteps, blood, blood, blood! The old, the young, the weak, the crippled, all are butchered without mercy. . . . Not a word from Washington! Not a sign from the President!" But it was hard to beat the *Journal* headline, "Feeding Prisoners to Sharks," and the *Journal* story of Spaniards "roasting twenty-five Catholic priests alive."

On the night of February 15, 1898, the *Maine* blew up in Havana harbor; 260 of her 350 officers and men were killed. The government in Madrid and the Queen Regent sent their regrets and sympathy and official Havana went into mourning. The dead were honored, the wounded cared for.

Returning home from the theater, Hearst got a message to call his office.

"Hello," he said, "What is the important news?"

"The battleship *Maine* has been blown up in Havana Harbor," the editor replied.

"Good heavens, what have you done with the story?"

"We have put it on the first page, of course."

"Have you put anything else on the front page?"

"Only the other big news," said the editor.

"There is not any other big news," Hearst said. "Please spread the story all over the page. This means war."*

The newspaper business went wild. Over at the *World* that week one exhausted managing editor, existing on crackers and milk, broke under the strain, dashing madly about the offices crying "War! War!" until restrained and sent home.

Roosevelt raged. Now in Washington as assistant secretary of the navy, he quickly leaped to the conclusion that "the *Maine* was sunk by an act of dirty treachery on the part of the Spaniards." But McKinley said, "I don't propose to be swept off my feet by the catastrophe." "I have been through one war," he said, "I have seen the dead piled up, and I do not want to see another." He called for an investigation—which dragged on and on. In fact, the *Maine* had been a floating bomb, its forecastle packed with gunpowder and its magazines laced with shortable wires. But Hearst would not wait— the *Journal* printed diagrams of just how a Spanish "Infernal Machine" had hit the hull. Roosevelt took advantage of his superior's momentary absence one afternoon to order the Pacific squadron to sea, put the European and South Atlantic stations on alert, order immense supplies of guns and ammunition, and demand that Congress authorize the unlimited recruitment of seamen. When at last McKinley's investigation reported the cause of the sinking as an "external explosion," the die was cast. Even the *New York Times* saw no alternative to war. McKinley suffered on, offering delay and silence, sleepless, dosing himself with narcotics, breaking into tears at a White House musicale. It was no use; he finally had to come around.

The *Journal*'s front-page slogan asked, "How Do You Like the *Journal*'s War?" The paper printed an interview with Theodore Roosevelt congratulating Hearst and company. Roosevelt promptly demurred: "I never in public or private commended the *New York Journal*"—which the *World* printed on its front page, adding the comment that *Journal* war news was being "written by fools for fools." But not long after, TR told a reporter friend, "I have done all I could to bring on the war, because it is a just war, and the sooner we meet it the better. Now that it has come, I have no business to ask others to do the fighting and stay home myself."

Roosevelt, his dramatic instincts intact, took off for Cuba with his Rough Riders—western cowboys and New York swells. Hearst himself appeared one day on the deck of a steam launch off Cuba. Spotting the enemy on the beach, he pulled off his pants and leapt overboard into the surf, waving his revolver. He rushed up to twenty-nine quivering Spaniards and, with his comrades, took them into custody. A burial party was detailed to dispose of a few washed-up corpses, then Hearst hustled the prisoners onto his ship, put his pants back on, and ordered the signals raised to announce, "We have prisoners for the fleet," as his ship steamed victoriously down the line of American battleships. It was the Fourth of July. Photographic equipment was set up on the deck to picture the hapless Spaniards as, quickly persuaded, they huzzahed three cheers for George Washington and President McKinley. Hearst ordered a full meal for the lot before delivering them, while sailors cheered, to the American warship *St. Louis*. He got a receipt: "Received of W. R. Hearst twenty-nine Spanish prisoners." The news was quickly dispatched to the *Journal*.

Another day, a *Journal* reporter, wounded in battle, suddenly had a familiar comforter:

Some one knelt in the grass beside me and put his hand on my fevered head. Opening my eyes, I saw Mr. Hearst, the proprietor of the New York *Journal*, a straw hat with a bright ribbon on his head, a revolver at his belt, and a pencil and note-book in his hand. The man who had provoked the war had come to see the result with his own eyes and, finding one of his own correspondents prostrate, was doing the work himself. Slowly he took down my story of the fight. Again and again the tinging of Mauser bullets interrupted. But he seemed unmoved. The battle had to be reported somehow.

"I'm sorry you're hurt, but"—and his face was radiant with enthusiasm—"wasn't it a splendid fight? We must beat every paper in the world."*

Richard Harding Davis, handsome model for the famous "Gibson Girl's" escort, arrived in Cuba—with eighty-eight other journalists—dashingly attired with a scarf around his hat, high plastic collar, blue coat, trousers tucked into field boots, and field glasses slung at his side. He tried to talk his way into an early landing because unlike the "ordinary reporters" he was really a "descriptive writer." The general who refused him got short shrift in his stories. Davis wrote home to tell his family how Cuba was treating him:

Dear Family: Santiago, July 1898
        This is just to reassure you that I am all right. I and Marshall were the only correspondents with Roosevelt. We were caught in a clear case of ambush. Every precaution had been taken, but the natives knew the ground and our men did not. It was the hottest, nastiest fight I ever imagined. We never saw the enemy except glimpses. Our men fell all over the place, shouting to the others not to mind them, but to go on. I got excited and took a carbine and charged the sugar house, which is what is called the key to the position. If the men had been regulars I would have sat in the rear as B—— did, but I knew every other one of them, had played football, and all that sort of thing, with them, so I thought as an American I ought to help. The officers were falling all over the shop, and after it was all over Roosevelt made me a long speech

---

* Swanberg, *Citizen Hearst*, pp. 155–56; Hearst is also celebrated, though differently, in a tedious novel by Aldous Huxley, *After Many a Summer Dies the Swan* (New York: Harper and Brothers, 1939), and in the film *Citizen Kane*.

before some of the men, and offered me a captaincy in the regiment any time I
wanted it. He told the Associated Press man that there was no officer in his regiment
who had "been of more help or shown more courage" than your humble servant, so
that's all right. After this I keep quiet. I promise I keep quiet. Love to you all.

Richard*

Davis was with Theodore Roosevelt on what TR called "the great day of my
life," July 1, 1898, when he and his irregular forces charged up a hill adjacent
to the San Juan fortifications, under withering enemy fire. Watching the
battle get underway, Davis thought "someone had made an awful and terrible mistake." But there came the intrepid colonel, upright in his saddle, a
blue polka-dotted scarf fluttering from his sombrero "like a guidon," urging
on the reluctant—"Are you afraid to stand up when I am on horseback?"—
and pushing aside the careful regulars—"Let my men through, sir!"—and
then waving his hat as he whooped his meager band to the crest. Roosevelt
stalked about the trenches, "reveling in victory and gore," a friend reported;
"Look at those damned Spanish dead," he crowed.

The New York press went wild with enthusiasm. Davis would never
forget that on that day he "had the luck to be with Roosevelt." The feeling
was mutual: TR gave Davis his picture, inscribed "To my fellow on the firing
line." Back home, Mr. Dooley had Roosevelt laud "me brave an' fluent body
guard, Richard Harding Davis."

Roosevelt came home to a hero's welcome, featured in the papers coast
to coast. In that November of 1898 his famous exploits got him elected governor of New York. Campaigning in October, Roosevelt would step out onto
the rear platform of his train as a bugler sounded the cavalry charge. Seven
uniformed Rough Riders grouped around him. "You have heard the trumpet
that sounded to bring you here," he began. "I have heard it tear the tropic
dawn when it summoned us to fight at Santiago." After his speech, Sergeant
Buck Taylor came front and center: "I want to talk to you about mah Colonel.
He kept ev'y promise he made to us and he will to you." No one seems to
have taken the sergeant too literally when he concluded: "He told us we
might meet wounds and death and we done it, but he was thar in the midst
of us, and when it came to the great day he led us up San Juan Hill like sheep
to the slaughter and so he will lead you."

The day after the election, a reporter told Roosevelt that "a clear trail"
ran from Albany to Washington. TR blew up at him for suggesting that ambition. But the next spring he went out to New Mexico to a Rough Rider reunion and came back talking about the wild greeting he got—"exactly as if I
had been a Presidential candidate." The New York Times so speculated.
Roosevelt issued a denial. But the worm was working. Henry Cabot Lodge
carefully outlined for Roosevelt a strategy to get him elected President in

---

*Charles Belmont Davis, ed., Adventures and Letters of Richard Harding Davis (New York:
Charles Scribner's Sons, 1917), pp. 254–55.

1904. Assessing each conceivable interim alternative, Lodge concluded he
had to go for the Vice-Presidency in 1900. At first TR balked. "I do not like to
be a figurehead," he wrote Lodge, "I should be in a cold shiver of rage at in-
ability to answer hounds like" some of the senators. Up to that time no Vice-
President had ever been elected President. Roosevelt told New York's boss
Thomas Platt that he "would greatly rather be anything, say a Professor of
History." But Platt and company dearly desired to get Roosevelt out of New
York; they intimated that he might not be renominated for governor.

Roosevelt wavered. At first, McKinley's Washingtonians found it funny
that he kept refusing an invitation that had not been tendered. "He came
down here," Secretary of State John Hay wrote a friend, "with a somber resolution throned in his strenuous brow, to let McKinley and Hanna know,
once for all, that he would not be Vice-President, and found to his stupefac-
tion that nobody in Washington, except Platt, had ever dreamed of such a
thing." Face to face with the agitated Roosevelt, Hay said, "I think you are
unduly alarmed. There is no instance of an election of a Vice President by violence." Secretary of War Elihu Root smiled through Roosevelt's denials and
said, "Of course not, Theodore, you're not fit for it." McKinley himself
chuckled softly "about some of T.R.'s characteristics." He decided to leave
the choice to the convention.

Roosevelt did go to the convention—"I would be looked on as a coward
if I did not go." He stalked in slightly late wearing his big black Rough Rider
hat, to the profound excitement of the assemblage. That night western delegates stormed up and down outside Hanna's hotel suite shouting, "We want
Teddy!" An anxious national party official telephoned Washington to report:
"The Roosevelt boom is let loose and it has swept everything. . . . The thing
is going pellmell like a tidal wave." He sought instruction, referring to a base
law of the politician's power: "We cannot afford to have it said that something was done in spite of ourselves." The word came back: "The President
has no choice. . . . The choice of the convention will be his choice; he has no
advice to give." Hanna was furious: "Don't any of you realize that there's
only one life between that madman and the Presidency?"

The midnight scrambles that typify national convention politics (gen-
erating the nervous exhaustion that has led to many a bizarre choice)
rattled on. Roosevelt was nominated in a rafter-packed session to the music
of tumultuous demonstrations. It was announced that he had received every
vote but one—his own. Then he lit out after Bryan.

The Press's President

The following March, Roosevelt, the newly inaugurated Vice-President, presided over the Senate for only four days before that body ad-
journed until December; TR went off to vacation at Oyster Bay. On September 6, 1901, President McKinley, receiving citizens in Buffalo's Temple

of Music, reached out to shake hands with a man who suddenly shot him twice in the body. As the assassin was wrestled to the ground, McKinley managed to say, "Don't let them hurt him." The President died on September 14th. The new President led the nation into a period of intense and prolonged mourning.

As ever, Roosevelt recovered. Not given to humble hesitation, he behaved as if he had been elected President by an overwhelming landslide. Action after action zipped out of the White House—on conservation, the tariff, trusts, and banking, on the Philippines and Panama. "This country cannot afford to sit supine on the plea that . . . we are helpless in the presence of the new conditions," he said. His cousin Franklin remembered TR roaring around in exasperation—"Oh, if I only could be President and Congress too for just ten minutes." He managed to move against the big corporations without totally alienating them. "The criminal rich and the fool rich," he said, "will do all they can to beat me," and indeed they did carp against him as a "political adventurer." But he moved away from trust-busting to regulation, which the capitalists learned to live with, and even to exploit. And when Mark Hanna threatened to run for the Presidency himself in 1904, Roosevelt went around him, maintaining connections with alternative bosses, exercising his patronage power to good effect.

His words—millions of them—poured forth in equal volume. He got on famously with his friends the reporters, providing office space for them in the White House and an endless stream of exciting news. He took fancy-pants ambassadors hiking through the wilds of Rock Creek Park, and when he went hunting he took the press along, hyping his image all the way. "The first bear must fall to my rifle," he said. "This sounds selfish but you know the kind of talk there will be in the newspapers about such a hunt, and if I go it must be a success, and the success must come to me." Famous and popular, Roosevelt enjoyed the endorsement of such papers as the New York Sun, six weeks before the convention in 1904: "RESOLVED: That we emphatically endorse and affirm Theodore Roosevelt. Whatever Theodore Roosevelt thinks, says, does, or wants is right. Roosevelt and Stir 'Em Up. Now and Forever; One and Inseparable!" With no trouble at all he got the nomination. But, sensing the movement of the pulse of politics into its moral phase, he stood Presidentially above the hustings. The Democrats nominated clean but dull Alton B. Parker, an obscure New York judge, whose major political virtue was his personal virtue. Roosevelt was finally smoked out on a morals charge—that he had accepted large campaign contributions from businessmen, who expected to be repaid in nonprosecutions. Privately Roosevelt fumed. "What infernal liars the independent press does contain," he wrote a friend. The "professionally virtuous creatures like the Times, Evening Post, etc." were "venomously attacking" his upright friends; the "mugwump's scoundrelly yell" was "designed to divert attention" from "eminent purists" in their own camp—underhanded bosses and millionaires. Only near the end of the campaign did TR, demonstrating his rhetorical flexibility, take to the stump with righteous indignation and self-defense. He won in a walk and moved into his first elected term.

After the election of 1904, Democrat Parker announced he would not run again, opening a way for Bryan to cap that year's appeal to what he called "the moral sense" of the nation. But Roosevelt, despite all his love of the Presidency as a "bully pulpit," once elected revealed again his old appetite for a fight. His inaugural address called for "the vigor and effort without which the manlier and hardier virtues wither away," and the term that followed sparkled with fighting action as Roosevelt championed more and more progressive reforms. The ripsnorting battle of 1900 was his kind of politics.

Roosevelt's successful rise to the Presidency, confirmed in his election in 1904, was fueled by his remarkable relationship with the reporters of his day. Had the Yellow Press not found the style to tell his story, Roosevelt's determined political opponents might well have succeeded in muscling him off the national stage. Instead, he brought to popular journalism just the vigor and flash it needed. In the course of that adventure, Roosevelt put the story of politics as war on the front page. There it would *stay*. Its vivid imagery and dramatic form would shape political realities long after Roosevelt was dead.

4

Harry Truman 1948

WELL BEFORE the United States entered the Great War, Theodore Roosevelt, though blind in one eye and burning with Amazon fever, raged to get into the thick of it as combat commander of an infantry division. He stormed at the secretary of war—and got polite appreciation of his patriotism. He crawled to President Wilson, that "abject coward," swearing he would not oppose him in politics if only the President would let him go to France and fight. Wilson was affable, but would have none of it. Bitter at being left out and sixty years old, Roosevelt died in his bed at Oyster Bay on January 6, 1919, as Wilson toured Europe in triumph.

In the crowd cheering Wilson in Paris stood Captain Harry Truman, survivor of more rough combat than he cared to remember. Eventually Truman would carry Teddy Roosevelt's fighting spirit into the battle of 1948, scrambling up a Presidential incline a good deal steeper than San Juan Hill to a victory that left nearly all the informed observers amazed.

That election starkly illustrates the power of the story of politics as war. It was Harry Truman's bad luck to come on the scene after Franklin D. Roosevelt, martyred hero of World War II, star of history's longest-running Presidential act. Through the long, grinding years of the Great Depression, millions had swallowed their doubts about Roosevelt—the aristocrat? the socialist?—in the hope that somehow he would turn their troubled lives around. When the war came in a flash on that "day of infamy" at Pearl Harbor, the whole nation swung into line behind Roosevelt; somehow it seemed unpatriotic to vote against the Commander-in-Chief in 1944. The people had sacrificed, some their sons, all some measure of comfort. Roosevelt died while the battle still raged. And there stood Harry S Truman in the White House, surprised by grace, politically naked as a jaybird. The certainty of victory was fixed in another great flash, at Hiroshima. No sooner had military peace been declared than political war broke out—the predictable breakdown of consensus once the national threat disappeared, releasing long-suppressed furies. No mere momentum of succession would ensure his survival. His canny adviser, Washington lawyer Clark Clifford, told him in the fall of 1947 that "the old 'party organization' control is gone forever," its grass-roots patronage cut down by direct federal programs. Despite the long years of Democratic dominance, *Fortune* reported at the start of 1948 only a modest edge for Truman's party: 39 percent of Americans considered themselves Democrats, 33 percent Republicans. "The campaign of 1948," Clifford foresaw, "will be a tough, bitterly fought struggle."

Truman was overwhelmingly disdained by the editorial lords of the press—predominantly Republican—not only as a poor President but as a sure loser. That word from on high was promulgated early and held firm right on to election night. The polls reinforced that prophecy. But the supposed certainty of the outcome helped not at all the reporter in the field, struggling to get his copy in the paper. Editorial speculations on what President Dewey would do after the election necessarily were written in the subjunctive mood—a sorry substitute for a present-tense political war in the here and now. Reporters' pencils were cocked for a fight. Eventually their professional lust for combat won out; an electorate itching for a scrap began to find in the news columns what it was looking for, what the publishers and pollsters had denied. Harry Truman emerged as one hell of a story—a freeswinging grenade thrower whose explosions were all for quotation, running against the blandest news source since Millard Fillmore.

Harry Truman's famous victory shows how a candidate can sometimes sense the national moodswing more accurately than the media do—and beat them at their own game. Truman himself was cut out for that work. He had a long history as a fighter. As important, Harry Truman's incredible self-confidence gave him the strength to learn from his experience, to listen to advice, to exercise his judgment on the facts as he saw them at any given time. There is a piece of the truth in the contemporary romance of Truman the spontaneous consulting his gut and confounding the experts. At the campaign's start he was nearly alone in believing he had a reasonable crack at winning. But the Lone Ranger image slides by the fact that Truman's basic campaign strategy was designed—brilliantly designed—by one of Washington's cagiest minds. Truman's love for the scrappy side of politics was but the raw material; Clark Clifford showed how a fighting campaign can be plotted like an ambush, especially when the candidate is an incumbent President with certain weapons at his disposal.

The Collapsing Consensus

As 1948 dawned, the Democratic party forces could be seen charging off in every conceivable direction except Truman's. Franklin Roosevelt's coalition, which his long reign had increasingly transformed from a New Deal, program-centered alliance into a personal following, began to fall apart when Roosevelt died in 1945. The very next year, the Republicans won a smashing victory—both houses of Congress—by comfortable margins, for the first time since Hoover. Truman had posed the election as a vote of confidence. Democratic candidates for Congress in 1946 left Truman's name unspoken, using recordings of FDR's voice instead. Senator J. William Fulbright—a Democrat no less—took him at his word and proposed that Truman appoint Republican Senator Arthur Vandenberg as secretary of state and then resign, making Vandenberg President.

On the left flank, a new Progressive party split off in anger over Truman's militant foreign policy. Its leader, Henry Wallace, had been Roosevelt's Vice-President before Truman was, and then secretary of commerce in Truman's own cabinet, a famous man with a substantial following, including some extremely adroit Communists who knew how to work the "popular front" maneuver. Truman had fired him—clumsily, to harsh reaction—when Wallace made speeches directly contradicting the administration line. Now Wallace was an announced candidate to take Truman's place. In California and the big cities, Wallace's strength was picking up.

On the right flank, the "solid South" was coming apart at the seams. Not long after Truman took office he ordered the armed services racially integrated. Responding to pressure from civil-rights groups and black veterans, he fought down the generals and admirals who wanted blacks left in the kitchens. Now in February 1948, the President, without consulting his congressional friends, suddenly called on Congress to pass a ten-point civil-rights law, not only forbidding lynching, but also commanding voting rights, an end to Jim Crow in interstate transportation, a fair crack at good jobs.

Immediately fifty-two southern congressmen promptly deserted his ranks and pledged to fight him. Two weeks later, when Truman's voice came over the loudspeaker at the Jefferson–Jackson dinner in Little Rock, 750 Democrats stalked out of the room. Four days after that, Truman's formerly stalwart ally Governor J. Strom Thurmond gathered southern governors to a confrontation with the Democratic national chairman, railing at Truman's "unconstitutional" assault on state sovereignty, demanding that the legislation be withdrawn. Polls showed a sharp drop-off in the President's support among southern citizens, and their leaders, in angry meetings, plotted their next steps.

If the flanks were crumbling, the center was in not much better shape. Labor, long the backbone of the Democratic attack force, would not back Truman: the president of the CIO, Phil Murray, with Walter Reuther, David Dubinsky, and other union strategists refused to endorse him. Dan Tobin of the Teamsters told reporters Truman was nothing but a "squeaky-voiced tinhorn." And John L. Lewis roared his Shakespearean vituperations like a voice from the mine pits. Jewish leaders who had supported Truman when he supported the partition of Palestine were enraged when the American representative to the United Nations, Warren Austin, not having bothered to check his speech with the President, suddenly announced that the

United States was no longer for partition. Wrath descended on Truman's head. Mrs. Franklin D. Roosevelt wrote to say she was resigning her United Nations post; Truman refused to accept that. Furious Zionists felt he had broken his word.

But after all, who else was there to replace an incumbent President as nominee of his party? None other than General Dwight D. Eisenhower, hero of the Crusade in Europe that had brought Hitler to his knees. A poll showed Eisenhower with more than twice Truman's popularity as a President. The Republicans had been after him and he had turned them down on the eve of the New Hampshire primary. Maybe at heart he was a Democrat. Through the winter of 1947–48, the Eisenhower assault—with no help from him—surged ahead, gathering to it an incredible array of Democratic chieftains. The lead squad was none other than the Americans for Democratic Action, which had stood firm with Truman through his battles for civil rights, European recovery, and economic liberality. Eisenhower left the army and came home to be president of Columbia University on February 7, which made him seem all the more available. Before long, everybody who was anybody in the Democratic camp spoke up for Ike as their choice: the mayors of Chicago and New York City, Boss Frank Hague of Jersey City, Mayor Hubert Humphrey of Minneapolis, Democratic chairman John Bailey of Connecticut, Walter Reuther, Chester Bowles, Paul Douglas, Governor "Happy" Chandler of Kentucky, Senators Richard Russell, Claude Pepper, John Sparkman—the list stretched on from page to page. Worst of all, from Truman's perspective, the emerging leader of this revolution was Franklin Delano Roosevelt, Jr., calling upon his father's party to draft Eisenhower, vigorously assisted in that public effort by two of Roosevelt's other sons, James and Elliott. Almost as bad was the silence from Eleanor Roosevelt, excusing herself as nonpartisan because of her United Nations role. She did not endorse Truman until October 1948, to counter Drew Pearson's charge that she must be for the Republican candidate. She enclosed her supporting letter to the President in one to her friend Frances Perkins. It said, "I haven't actually endorsed Mr. Truman because he has been such a weak and vacillating person and made such poor appointments. . . ."—which perhaps gives a clue to what she was telling friends earlier in the year.

By March, said the Gallup poll, it was clear that Truman would lose to any one of Republicans Dewey, Stassen, Vandenberg, or MacArthur, though he would edge out Taft. By April, half the people disapproved while only about a third approved his performance as President. Press speculation centered on whether or not Truman could be persuaded to be reasonable and step aside.

Meanwhile Republican contenders, buoyed by Truman's decline, popped to the surface in significant numbers. The New Hampshire primary pitted New York's dynamic young Governor Thomas E. Dewey against Harold E. Stassen, dynamic, young ex-governor of Minnesota, making his maiden try for the Presidency. Dewey's loss to Roosevelt in 1944 had not prevented his landslide win in New York in 1946. Despite Alice Roosevelt Longworth's skepticism ("You can't make a soufflé rise twice"), Dewey came on strong, winning six of the eight delegates in New Hampshire, the first primary. In Wisconsin, the primary election-eve betting was five to one in favor of General Douglas MacArthur, American proconsul in Japan. The *New York Times* predicted "M'Arthur Victory Due in Wisconsin." But Stassen's vigorous campaigning won him an astounding victory—and Dewey got no delegates at all. The *New York Herald-Tribune* announced that Stassen, having "emerged from the fringe of interesting possibility," was now "in the first division of contenders." The Democratic national chairman, noting "the fallacy of the political judgment of the principal sources of public information," joked that "to insure the election of the Democratic ticket in November we need only have the commentators united in predicting defeat." Stassen won again in Nebraska and surged to first place in the Gallup poll. In April he took Pennsylvania. In Ohio he went against home-state Senator Robert Taft and won nine delegates to Taft's fourteen, a result variously interpreted as a clear-cut Stassen victory (because it was Taft's state) and a Stassen defeat (because he had been doing so much better).

The grand climax of the primary season came in Oregon on May 21. In April the state's two dominant newspapers had foreseen a Stassen win and the betting odds were five to three for Stassen. Stassen stumped the state, building momentum. The Dewey forces frantically organized an advertising and telephone blitz, and Dewey himself swung into action, crisscrossing Oregon, posing in cowboy hats and Indian headdresses, letting himself be captured by the Coos Bay pirates, whose scroll he signed with his own blood. He lashed out at the "softheaded saps" around Truman and blasted Stassen's proposal to outlaw the Communist party as un-American. This was a "new Dewey," people said, a fighter. The main event happened four days before the voting: a great debate between Dewey and Stassen on outlawing the Communists. Sixty reporters and photographers covered it like a prizefight; nine hundred radio stations brought it live to the nation. Stassen depicted the dark Red menace. "Sincere" as Dewey might be, he said, Dewey was advocating "a soft policy toward communism." Dewey threw away his script. In his old prosecuting-attorney style he lit into Stassen, citing chapter and verse of the law, invoking the principles of liberty. "This outlawing idea is not new," he said. "It is as old as government. For thousands of years despots have shot, imprisoned, and exiled their people and their governments have always fallen into the dust." The way to beat the Communist party was to get it "out in the open so we can defeat it and all it stands for." The press verdict went strongly for Dewey. In the voting, he took a smashing 53 percent, winning all the delegates.

The Republican convention was a maelstrom of strife among the factions committed to Dewey, Stassen, Taft, and a clutch of dark horses. Platoons of journalists dashed among the Philadelphia hotels, tracking the ambiguities and alliances. The "Dewey blitz" at last went over the top on the third ballot. In his acceptance speech, Dewey made clear how he would run—as President, leaving to Harry Truman the role of challenger. The fighting Dewey of the Oregon primary faded away to be replaced by a high-minded Dewey who appealed for American unity. The unity needed was "more than material" and "most of all spiritual." "We have found the means to blow our world, physically, apart," he said. "spiritually, we have yet to find the means to put together the world's broken pieces, to bind up its wounds, to make a good society, a community of men of good will that fits our dreams." The exhausted delegates applauded respectfully, and went home.

The Democrats limped into Philadelphia three weeks later "as though they had accepted an invitation to a funeral," said the AP. The *Washington Post* recommended that the Democrats "surrender to the inevitable" and nominate a "custodian." The *New York Post* thought, "The Party might as well immediately concede the election to Dewey and save the wear and tear of campaigning." Two days before the convention, Eisenhower let the steam out of his backers' hopes: "I would refuse to accept the nomination under any conditions, terms, or premises." That left Truman. A Pennsylvania senator did his best to lift spirits at the national committee dinner: "Nobody is going to lie down and die just to confirm a report in the newspapers, and neither is the Democratic party. Who says we're dead?" Senator Alben Barkley thundered through the keynote address: "What is this cankering, corroding, fungous growth which every Republican orator, save one, denounced with unaccustomed rancor, then in their adopted platform hugged to their political bosom as if it were the child of their own loins?" And so on, for sixty-eight minutes. There was a hot fight over the civil-rights plank; Barkley had trouble restoring order. A stirring speech by Hubert Humphrey helped win the day for the liberal plank, 651½ to 582½, but thirty-five delegates from Mississippi and Alabama walked out. And in the balloting for the nomination, almost all the southern delegates voted for Senator Richard Russell of Georgia rather than for Truman and succeeded in blocking the customary move to make the party's nomination unanimous.

The governor of Missouri had nominated Harry Truman as "a soldier, patriot, and statesman whose splendid courage has never faltered in war or peace." Truman marched out onto the podium, thanked the delegates for their nomination, and lit out after the opposition: "Senator Barkley and I will win this election and make these Republicans like it—don't you forget that!"

Captain Harry, President Truman

When Theodore Roosevelt dashed off to Cuba and the battle that thrust him to national attention, he was already well known in New York as a political fighter. Harry Truman had shipped out to his war—and the experience that set his fighting style—as not much of anything. "My whole political career," he wrote later, "is based on my war service and war associates." When at age sixty-four he stood up and barked at the wavering Democratic delegates he may well have recalled how, at age thirty-four, an old age for combat, he had discovered he could lead men out of what looked like hopeless chaos on the battlefield.

Harry Truman grew up happy and busy on a farm in Missouri that abounded with relatives and adventures. But he had very weak eyes and had to wear thick glasses. In a rough family division of emotional labor, he became more or less his mother's boy while his big brother Vivian partnered with their father in the mule business. Harry helped in the kitchen, took piano lessons, cared for his little sister, read a lot of books. The boys teased him some. Sometimes they let him umpire their baseball games, weak eyes and all. At fifteen he quit piano lessons. "I decided it was sissy," he said later. Harry was no shrinking violet, but neither was he one of the boys in their rough-and-tumble play. The jobs he got were bookkeeper, bank clerk, treasurer of a small oil company—indoor work with papers. For all that he was a gregarious fellow, a Mason, and a talker. When war was declared in April 1917, he reactivated his membership in the National Guard in Kansas City and was set to work recruiting. When it came time to elect officers, he hoped to be a section sergeant, but when the ballots were counted he was first lieutenant—his first electoral win. He put on his uniform and drove around town in a red roadster.

Called to active duty, to the dismay of his mother and his sweetheart Bess Wallace, Truman was assigned to Fort Sill, Oklahoma, as a regimental canteen officer. He and an ex-salesman named Eddie Jacobson made a success of that; Truman got good recommendations. He was sent to France for five weeks of artillery training. There he read in the *New York Times* that he had been promoted to captain, and soon he got his first command: a rowdy flock of Irish pranksters loosely organized as a field artillery battalion. It was a loser's assignment: two previous commanders had failed to control the men. It was Truman's first command of anything. "I was the most thoroughly scared individual in that camp," he recalled. "Never on the front or anywhere else have I been so nervous." That day the troops put on a fake stampede of the horses. After dark a fight broke out, cots were broken, and four men wound up in the infirmary.

Harry Truman, everybody's pal, the nearsighted piano player, stood at one of those crossroads of life where a person either cuts and runs or finds and makes his own a new style of action. Drawing on every resource he could muster, Truman broke into a new identity.

Captain Truman called in his noncoms next morning and told them they had better shape up or, "I'll bust you right back." But a month later, suddenly under merciless night attack by Germany artillery, Truman's battalion broke and ran, abandoning their guns. Captain Harry jumped up from the mud his horse had cast him into and let loose a blistering barrage of invective. "It took the skin off the ears of those boys," the chaplain remembered. "It turned those boys right around." They rallied and stood their ground. That was September 6, 1918; Truman's guns were still firing when the Armistice came on November 11. In between he and his boys fought through the hell of the Argonne. Truman did his own recon work—way out front with his field glasses, spotting targets and directing fire. When a French battery nearly hit him with a bombardment he found their captain and blistered his ears. When his colonel threatened to court-martial him for firing outside the sector, Truman told him to go ahead—he would do the same thing again in the same situation.

Thus Harry the clerk became Captain Harry. Later he said he was sorry to have missed a university education, "But I got it in the Army the hard way—and it stuck." He learned that he had guts, that his angry tirades could turn the tide, that he could make fast decisions in dark circumstances. If not a brand-new man, he had found his voice in the thick of battle.

After the war, Truman rode into politics on the shoulders of his army comrades, with a good deal of help from Kansas City's Pendergast political machine. Election after election—as county judge (i.e., commissioner), presiding judge, and twice as senator of the United States—established Truman's reputation as a hard-fighting campaigner of independent stripe, given to harsh words and energetic, grass-roots canvassing. The *Kansas City Times* said of his first primary race for the Senate nomination that in 1934 "in the whole of Missouri history there have been few such spirited contests within a party"; the *New York Times* called it "a record low in statesmanship"; the *St. Louis Post-Dispatch* said it amounted to "the pot, the kettle and stewpan calling each other black." Truman won and went off to Washington dubbed "the Senator from Pendergast." The *New York Times* greeted "Judge Henry S. Truman," patronized for calling himself "just a farmer boy from Jackson County," determined to "keep his feet on the ground." And, "That," quoth the *Times*, "he said in language highly indecorous for a subfreshman." Opposed for reelection in 1940 by every paper but one in Missouri, Truman spoke himself hoarse and won again. From an obscure and humble newcomer he began to emerge with a reputation for hard work and friendship; he caught the President's eye by conducting a thorough Senate committee investigation of defense production, roaring around the country to see what was happening at firsthand. In 1944, Roosevelt was in the market for a new Vice-President; Henry A. Wallace had managed to alienate the party bosses, from Flynn of the Bronx to Kelly of Chicago, as a theoretical maverick. At the convention, he drafted Truman, nailing the hesitant senator with the message, "If he wants to break up the Democratic Party in the middle of a war, that's his responsibility!" By then Truman was nobody's patsy, having stood up to percentage-pocketing contractors all over the country. He was a veteran scrapper.

Franklin Roosevelt died of a cerebral hemorrhage on April 12, 1945; Truman's first day in office was a Friday the 13th. Stunned as he was by the sudden ascension, he immediately plunged into an international crisis with Stalin over Poland. There followed an unending series of crises and innovations; victory in Europe, the founding of the United Nations, the atomic bombing of Japan, the Truman Doctrine to block the Soviets in Greece and Turkey, the Taft-Hartley Labor Act, the Berlin blockade, the Marshall Plan for European recovery. Whatever they would accuse Harry Truman of in 1948—and they found plenty, from poor taste in clothes to softness on communism—no one could say he had let go of the Presidential tiger he was riding.

Up front at the Democratic convention of 1948, where nearly all the troops wanted to run for the exits, old Captain Harry unleashed his thunderbolts. "Now is the time for us to get together and beat the common enemy. And that is up to you," he said. Republican legislation was "rotten"—"it still helps the rich and sticks a knife in the back of the poor." The enemy made all sorts of promises but, "I wonder if they think they can fool the people of the United States with such poppycock as that!" Truman's peroration flamed with militant imagery:

In 1932 we were attacking the citadel of special privilege and greed. We were fighting to drive the money changers from the temple. Today, in 1948, we are now the defenders of the stronghold of democracy and of equal opportunity, the haven of the ordinary people of this land and not of the favored classes or the powerful few. The battle cry is just the same now as it was in 1932, and I paraphrase the words of Franklin D. Roosevelt as he issued the challenge, in accepting nomination in Chicago: "This is more than a political call to arms. Give me your help, not to win votes alone, but to win in this new crusade to keep America secure and safe for its own people."

Now my friends, with the help of God and the wholehearted push which you can put behind this campaign, we can save this country from a continuation of the 80th Congress, and from misrule from now on.

I must have your help. You must get in and push, and win this election. The country can't afford another Republican Congress.

Thus Truman set the tone for his campaign in this strange election: the President running as challenger, the challenger as President. "I was not brought up to run from a fight," Truman said.

The Secret Strategy

The shape of that fight—the grand battle plan—sprang from the cool imagination of Clark Clifford and his team of heavy thinkers in the Democratic research committee. Clifford came out of Missouri, too, but otherwise he was Truman's complement: a tall, handsome, suavely aristocratic success. Their partnership was that of the elegant with the homespun; they hit it off.

Truman made him his special counsel and his most influential adviser. In November 1947, Clifford gave Truman forty-three legal pages of remarkable advice in a secret memorandum on "The Politics of 1948." Way back then, he foresaw that Dewey would lead the Republicans and that Wallace would run as a third-party candidate. Writing before Truman's sharp popularity slide, and the southern revolt, Clifford thought the Democrats could give Dewey the big eastern states and still win, holding the South, the West, and the labor vote. But the giant overall problem was apathy.

In the farm belt, crops were good—thus bad for the Democrats. Labor, too, was enjoying prosperity; the argument that labor had no place else to go but to the Democrats was dangerous: *"Labor can stay home"* as they had in 1946. "The Negro voter," Clifford wrote in his memorandum, "has become a cynical, hard-boiled trader" fully capable of sitting out a contest between the two white parties. Catholics cared about standing up to communism and might stand down if Truman seemed too soft in that direction. In short, the battalions of the Roosevelt coalition might sleep right through the election and wake up to Republican rule.

Clifford could see as easily as anyone that Truman was not going to be able to wring progressive legislation from the Republican-dominated Congress and thus go to the people for their thanks. He could see with equal clarity that the press was hostile and not about to get into a detailed, objective analysis of Truman vs. Dewey on the issues. Instead, Truman would have to find ways to use both these opponents to his advantage, despite their inclinations.

Since Congress could not be won it must be attacked. Truman's State of the Union Message in January should on purpose "select the issues upon which there will be conflict with the majority in Congress," a message "tailored for the voter, not the Congressman," displaying "a label which reads 'no compromises.' " That would put the Republicans on the defensive and steal Henry Wallace's thunder on the left.

"Prominent liberals and progressives—and no one else," Clifford advised, should denounce the Communists in Wallace's camp.

Truman should invoke the " 'magic' of his office" by inviting labor leaders to the White House and asking their *general* advice—for "it is dangerous to ask a labor leader for advice on a *specific* matter and then ignore that advice."

For the broad public, the substance of Truman's message should damn high prices, a widespread worry. But he should also work on his "portrait" in two only superficially contradictory ways. As Chief of State, Truman should put on White House shows for the newspapers, by inviting such "nonpolitical personages" as Henry Ford and Albert Einstein to lunch, followed by dignified announcements. And as Harry Truman, he should hit the road the way Franklin Roosevelt did in 1940 on his Presidential "inspection tours." "No matter how much the opposition and the press pointed out the political overtones of those trips," Clifford said, "the people paid little attention because what they saw was the Head of State performing his duties."

Finally, Truman should drop his stilted, formal speaking style ("as if attempting a phonetic rendition from a foreign language," his biographer says) and let his "infectious personality" show through.

The Presidential Challenge to the President-To-Be

The President did not buy the bring-an-Einstein-to-lunch routine, but the rest of it rang true to him. The State of the Union message laid out a list of advanced proposals in welfare, medical care, education, civil rights, new TVAs, foreign aid, immigration, and a tax bonus of $40 for every American, to be offset by a tax on corporate profits. Not for another dozen years would his package stand a chance of passage. He followed with a barrage of more than a dozen special messages—a "hit 'em every Monday" series—on everything from governmental reorganization to ethyl alcohol control, including his omnibus civil-rights demands. Whatever the newspaper editors thought, and generally they thought ill, they had to report what the President proposed. Congress struck back with investigations of corruption in his administration. The press got in licks at Truman's plan to put a balcony on the back of the White House—"Back-porch Harry," said the *New York Herald-Tribune*, appeared "impervious to the odium of violating good taste, propriety, and historical feeling." But his name got in the papers, linked to rousing controversies.

On April 17, the President gave a dry inflation talk to the American Society of Newspaper Editors in Washington, reading word for word. Then he went off the record for a freewheeling informal chat—in fact, carefully prepared by his coaches—that charmed and amused them into applause. He worked three more Washington speeches that way, all to good response, playing homely Harry in the style of Benjamin Franklin in Paris and Abe Lincoln in Illinois. He got off what the *New York Times* called a "fighting" speech "in the new Truman manner," rapping the Republicans and declaring, "I want to say to you that for the next four years there will be a Democrat in the White House—and you are looking at him!"

By luck the University of California asked him to make the commencement address in June—the perfect hook to hang the "nonpolitical tour" on. His train took off on June 3, with a record number of fifty-nine reporters and photographers aboard. From the first back-platform talk at Crestline, Ohio, on the way to Chicago, the "new Truman" displayed himself: he smiled and said how glad he was "to get away from the White House and see the people as they are. The President, you know, is virtually in jail. He goes from his study to his office to his study, and he has to have guards all the time." At Gary he scathed Congress for working in "the interests of the men who have all the money." And so it went across the country: "You've got the worst

Congress you've ever had," he said and then gave folksy introductions of his wife and daughter. A woman in a crowd yelled that he sounded as though he had a cold. Harry said, "That's because I ride around in the wind with my mouth open." "Lay it on, Harry! Give 'em hell!" they called, and Truman called back, "I will! I intend to!" At Omaha he happened along as his old outfit, the Thirty-fifth Division, was having a reunion parade. The President jumped over the side of his car and marched along with his old barber, having the time of his life. Somebody presented a basket of eggs to him. Somebody else suggested he throw them at Taft. Truman allowed as how he "wouldn't throw *fresh* eggs at Taft." Taft himself helped out by dourly remarking to the Union League Club that "the President is blackguarding the Congress at every whistlestop in the country." Truman's publicity man wired the mayors of thirty-five towns and cities across America, inquiring whether they thought of their communities as "whistlestops," and mischievously leaked the indignant replies.

It was far from all clear sailing. Gaffes pocked the trip, from Truman's offhand remark, "I like Old Joe" Stalin to his blundering dedication of an airport to a "brave boy who died fighting for his country" instead of to Wilma Coates, who died at home. But he drew crowds, big crowds, some at night to see him speak in his bathrobe and pajamas. At Berkeley some 55,000 turned out to hear him give a serious foreign-policy address at the commencement. "His reception has been uniformly cordial," said the *Christian Science Monitor*. "Most reporters on board feel that this warmth has increased as the journey progressed. Just why is a matter of speculation, but it may be that the word has gone around that a scrappy fighter is making an uphill fight."

If so, the word when he returned to Washington had not reached the big-time press. The *Washington Evening Star* said, "The President in this critical hour is making a spectacle of himself that would reflect discreditably on a ward heeler." Republican congressmen called him "the worst President" ever, a "nasty little gamin," a "Missouri jackass"—and they promptly passed three bills over his veto.

Back in Washington, as Dewey was being nominated in Philadelphia, Truman met the Berlin crisis, promptly decided the United States would not be forced out of that city by the Soviets, and instituted the airlift that eventually broke the Russian blockade. All that got reported. Nevertheless, as he went into his own convention, the knowing press knew how hopeless he was. *Time* magazine had written of the Republican Dewey-Warren combination: "Barring a political miracle, it was the kind of ticket that could not fail to sweep the Republican Party back into power." *Fortune* said, "The prospects of a Republican victory are so overwhelming that an era of what will amount to one party may well impend." Thus Dewey confided his strategy to Stassen: "My job is to prevent anything from rocking the boat."

That was the situation as boat-rocker Truman hailed his Democratic mates to the cause as he addressed the convention. But his strategists had supplied one more Presidential spear for him to throw. Near the end of his speech he let it fly:

> On the twenty-sixth of July, which out in Missouri we call "Turnip Day," I am going to call Congress back and ask them to pass laws to halt rising prices, to meet the housing crisis—which they are saying they are for in their platform."

The delegates jumped up and cheered. Truman went on down the list of actions he would demand from the worst Congress ever. "Now, my friends, if there is any reality behind that Republican platform, we ought to get action from a short session of the Eightieth Congress. They can do this job in fifteen days, if they want to do it."

Predictably, Republicans raged. Senator Vandenberg called it "the last hysterical gasp of an expiring administration." In terms of substance, the Special Session was pure farce. It lasted twelve days—six of which were taken up by a southern filibuster to block anti-poll-tax legislation. Congress passed nothing of consequence. Elizabeth Bentley and then Whittaker Chambers, testifying before a Senate subcommittee, alleged high-level Soviet infiltration in the Executive Branch. Truman called the charges "a red herring as an excuse to keep them from doing what they ought to do." And, "Yes, you can quote me," he added. The *New York Times* asked, "Who has put whom on the spot?"

But Truman was stockpiling ammunition—a simple message people could grasp. The Republicans had said they were for new, liberal laws. He had given them the chance to pass some. They had not done so. Therefore they were liars. When the chips were down, the "no-account do-nothing Republican 80th Congress" sided with the rich reactionaries just as they had in Hoover's day.

Hoover's inheritor had his strategy down pat. Like Truman, Dewey had learned his lesson in bitter experience. In 1944, Dewey had started his campaign against the mighty Roosevelt on the high road. To a fired-up crowd of ninety thousand in Los Angeles he offered a speech on Social Security that "fell like a wet rag on the deck," said one observer. His advisers persuaded him to attack—and so he did, right down to defeat at the polls in an election whose keynote was conciliation. Some newsmen foresaw a reprise in 1948 of the fighting Dewey of 1944, hopefully predicting a "rip-roaring" Dewey campaign, but Dewey's top adviser, Hugh Scott (in what he later called, "the biggest political mistake I ever made"), persuaded Dewey not "to get into the gutter with Truman," maybe not even to mention the President's name. This time he would sail above the furor, leaving the Republican factions undisturbed by issue discussions, leaving himself free, as President, to move forward without prior political commitments. He had been on the attack in an election of conciliation, and now above the battle in a fighting election. Wrong style both times.

As the "Dewey Victory Special" glided efficiently down the railroad tracks, the *New York Times* saw Dewey as "acting like a man who has already been elected and is merely marking time, waiting to take office. In his speeches and in his manner there is an attitude that the election will be a mere formality to confirm a decision already made." He wrapped himself in spirituality: "We have sometimes failed in our faith and often fallen short of it. But in our hearts we believe and know that every man has some of the Divine in him, that every single individual is of priceless importance. . . ." He gave little McGuffey-like lessons, such as his talk on how Americans should "use the water we have wisely and well." "Our streams should abound with fish," he argued. He stuck to the well-worn phrase: "teeming cities," "soft, rolling wooded country," "fertile plains"—all the "sheer majesty" of America that the "prophets of gloom" were blind to. "America's future," he announced in Phoenix, "like yours in Arizona, is still ahead of us." Late in the campaign, pinked by Truman's barbs, Dewey did let fly a few shafts of his own. "But he soon got himself in hand," reported the *Chicago Daily News*, "and is back on a high road of rich baritone homilies." He wound up his campaign in Madison Square Garden, dismissing the opposition's fulminations and calling the people, "not to pride and boasting, but to humility. In this momentous time our country is called to renew its faith so that the world can begin to have hope again. . . ."

Truman opened the campaign on Labor Day to a crowd of 125,000 at Detroit in the pouring rain. "It is a great day for me. It is a great day for you. I am just starting on a campaign that is going to be a record for the President of the United States," he said. But Labor had better watch out for the "reactionary of today," "a shrewd man," "a man with a calculating machine where his heart ought to be." Labor had better get busy: "Labor has always had to fight for its gains. Now you are fighting for the whole future of the labor movement." Again he said, "We are in a hard, tough fight against shrewd and rich opponents." He shook his fist. "They know they can't count on your votes. Their only hope is that you won't vote at all. They have misjudged you. I know we are going to win this crusade for the right!" On September 17, Truman's train swung out of Washington for his first major tour, socking it to the Republicans night and day from the back platform. In Dexter, Iowa, he roused up the nightmare of 1929. The Eightieth Congress "has already stuck a pitchfork in the farmer's back," he said, and "I wonder how many times you have to be hit on the head before you find out who's hitting you?" Reporter Joseph Alsop thought it funny to see Truman "almost comically miscast in the role of William Jennings Bryan." But the farmers listened when Truman charged the Republicans with creating an artificial shortage of grain-storage facilities so as to drive down the price of wheat. "I'm not asking you just to vote for me," he said. "Vote for yourselves! Vote for your farms! Vote for the standard of living that you have won under a Democratic administration!" Dewey, meanwhile, was promising farmers—their fields overflowing with surplus grain—that he would not stand for a return to the dust-bowl poverty of Depression days.

In California, Truman blasted the villainous Congress that "tried to choke you to death in this valley," and at the "terrible Congressman" from Fresno, "one of the worst obstructionists in the Congress," who "has done everything he possibly could to cut the throats of the farmer and the laboring man. If you send him back, it will be your fault if you get your throats cut." The rich Republicans "let a little of it trickle down off the table like the crumbs fell to Lazarus." Kept in power, "they'll tear you apart." In Colorado Springs, he hit citizens who had stayed home in 1946: "You got just exactly what you deserved. If you stay home on November the second and let this same gang get control of the government, I won't have any sympathy with you."

Truman's typical back-of-the-train speech was a flat-out call to arms. "Every time I come out this way, I feel again the tremendous vitality of [wherever he was]. This is straight-from-the-shoulder country and it has produced a great breed of fighting men. I am going to call upon your fighting qualities. For you and I have a fight on our hands, a fight for the future of the country and for the welfare of the people of the United States." When he got around to the villain of the piece, his words spaced out for emphasis: "that no-account, do-nothing, Republican, Eightieth, Congress."

As Truman roared around the country scathing the Republican "blood-suckers," the press grew more and more puzzled. Because Dewey was sure to win, the top reporters had been assigned to Dewey's train, leaving the second-stringers to Truman. They knew what their editors expected them to see but they sent in what they saw. What they saw was steadily building crowds, quiet in the early forays, getting noisier week by week. In St. Paul where Dewey had drawn only 8,000, Truman attracted 21,000. In Republican Indiana they turned out by the tens of thousands in town after town. At the Chicago Stadium, 30,000 people crowded inside while another 10,000 listened to loudspeakers outside. At first the reporters were quick to notice that "his epithets do not stir his audiences," however large, and that, coming to hear him rant, "whether they agree or not, they chuckle and applaud," as a report in the Scripps-Howard papers had it. As Richard Rovere saw, "Nobody stomps, shouts or whistles for Truman. Everybody claps," which "does not necessarily mean that people who come out to hear him intend to vote against him—though my personal feeling is that most of them intend to do exactly that." Street-crowd estimates favorable to Truman were explained away: Truman had arrived at 5:00 P.M. Dewey at 4:00, when fewer were off work. As the crowds picked up and sounded off, a ready explanation was Truman's "growing entertainment value," as *Time* put it. Robert Donovan of the *New York Herald-Tribune* explained: "The American people have a very high regard for the office of President of the United States and a very great curiosity about the man who occupies it. When he comes to town they turn out in droves, tack up the welcome signs, bring out the bands, and drag all the children out of school to see the President and, if possible, to shake hands with him. But does that mean they are going to vote for him?" The voters seemed "willing to give Truman anything he wanted except the Presidency," another reporter wrote. Only a few reporters went as far as the *Washington Post*'s Robert Albright in questioning the going wisdom: "Now and then a particularly large crowd or a noisy ovation starts a mighty surge of hope in the rear staff car. Some of it filters forward to the press car, and hard-bitten reporters ask themselves, 'Could we be wrong?' " Hardly, suggested the *New York Times*. Dewey's crowds might be somewhat smaller and quieter than in 1944, "but they accorded to him the utmost of respect."

A *Times* poll of forty-seven journalists traveling with Dewey found them unanimous in the belief he would win; Truman's reporters, polled in October, were eight-to-one believers in a Dewey victory. They did not believe the evidence of their own eyes and of their own stories. *Editor and Publisher* reported that nationwide, four out of five daily newspapers backed Dewey over Truman. In terms of circulation, Dewey's five-to-one advantage in September had risen to eight to one late in October. In mid-October, *Newsweek* magazine put out a poll of fifty leading political writers. They were *unanimous* in the view that Dewey would win.

But Truman kept hammering away, hitting specific issues in a rhetorical style suited to quotation. The Republicans "have begun to nail the American consumer to the wall with spikes of greed," he declared. "President Likens Dewey to Hitler as Fascists' Tool," headlined the *New York Times*. Covering Dewey was dull stuff by comparison: the same speech, the same high and fluffy rhetoric. One reporter traveling with Dewey put his tongue in his cheek and asked, "How long is Dewey going to tolerate Truman's interference with running the government?" Their frustration showed up in their readiness to report Dewey's gaffe when his train suddenly started backing into a crowd: "What's wrong with that damn fool engineer?"—a comment quickly picked up and tossed to labor by the Truman campaign. About the only thing to write about with any sense of suspense was the future—what Dewey would do once he got in office, speculation rendered difficult by Dewey's refusal to expound. *The Kiplinger Magazine* tried a cover story on "What Dewey Will Do" and just before the election *Life* captioned a picture, "The next President travels by ferry boat over the broad waters of San Francisco Bay." The Alsops gave out with a sober analysis of the problems of the Dewey takeover. The *Detroit Free Press* argued that Truman—"a game little fellow, who never sought the Presidency and was lost in it, but who went down fighting with all he had"—should appoint Dewey's man John Foster Dulles secretary of state so progress would not have to halt until inauguration day. Drew Pearson "surveyed the close-knit group around Tom Dewey, who will take over the White House 86 days from now." And the *Chicago Tribune*; before all the votes had been counted, put out a great big headline for the morning after election, "Dewey Defeats Truman."

When Truman told reporters on election day November 2, that he would sweep the country, they laughed. The next day, he laughed. As early as September 9, famous pollster Elmo Roper had quit preelection polling, because Dewey "is almost as good as elected" and said, "That being so, I can think of nothing duller or more intellectually barren than acting like a sports announcer who feels he must pretend he is witnessing a neck and neck race. . . ." Now Roper, in a morning-after confession, said, "I could not have been more wrong. The thing that bothers me most is that at this moment I don't know why I was wrong." George Gallup confessed, "I just don't know what happened."

Truman had won the election. Those questions would be debated for decades. The election was the closest since 1916, so accounting for the small marginal vote that might have made the difference was specially difficult. But viewed against where Truman had been when he started, where he wound up was remarkable. It strains credibility to suppose Truman would have won anyway, without his blistering campaign against the destiny the press had so confidently assigned him. He bucked the tides—of apathy, prosperity, an apparent Republican trend, and the surging confidence of those knowing people who tell the rest of us what is going on.

One important strand of that story is the way Truman and Dewey, with their markedly contrasting campaign styles, were played in the press. Editorial opinion fixed on a sure Dewey scenario and stuck with it. That line snarled the perceptions of the reporters on the scene, as did the estimates they would hear at the train stops from the local politicians—who had read the odds in the papers. The polls, like the pols, missed the impact of Truman's fall campaign, as more and more Americans, reading what Truman was saying between the lines of journalistic opinion, found that to their liking. The narrative of an uphill fight, of charges and issues and courage against the grain, filtered through and took hold. The politics of war once again found its resonance in the newspaper story, a fight the editors put on the page in spite of themselves. Truman did not, however, succeed in electrifying the nation; 1948 was a low turnout election. But his saga came across—thanks to the press's penchant for a fight—sufficiently to arouse the votes he needed to remain as President.

Harry Truman liked to say he was not one of those fellows who "get kicked in the head by a mule and end up believing everything you read in the papers." Returning to Washington, where 750,000 people turned out to welcome him, he must have chortled at a sign on the *Washington Post* building overlooking Pennsylvania Avenue: "Mr. President, We Are Ready Now to Eat Crow Whenever You Are Ready to Serve It."

5

John Kennedy 1960

THE UNITED STATES declared war on Germany on April 6, 1917. On May 29, a second son was born to the Joseph Kennedys of Brookline, Massachusetts. He would grow up to illustrate, for his day, as TR did for his own and Truman for his, how the battle story got translated, in and through the shock of war, from the raucous rhetoric of the Yellow Press to the cool combat of modern politics.

The Great War was over before Baby Kennedy knew about it; as for most Americans, his feeling for it would be vicarious, indirect, mediated by storytellers. Survivors brought back chilling tales of butchery. In communities all over the United States, little units of neighbors had been formed to go off and fight together, in the manner of Harry Truman's artillery company, the myth of San Juan Hill in mind. That system led too often to a town suddenly learning that all or nearly all their boys had been killed in the same battle. The American appearance was advanced by the British, who marched gaily into the maelstrom with their heads full of the glories of *their* turn-of-the-century war against the Boers, dashingly described by such reporters as Winston Churchill, Rudyard Kipling, A. Conan Doyle, and the ubiquitous Richard Harding Davis. What they ran into this time was something else again. The first day of the "battle" at the river Somme, which began on July 1, 1916 and ground on until November 18, killing 419,654 British soldiers, is a vivid example:

> I see men arising and walking forward; and I go forward with them, in a glassy delirium wherein some seem to pause, with bowed heads, and sink carefully to their knees, and roll slowly over, and lie still. Others roll and roll, and scream and grip my legs in uttermost fear, and I have to struggle to break away, while the dust and earth on my tunic changes from grey to red.
> And I go with aching feet, up and down and across ground like a huge ruined honeycomb, and my wave melts away, and the second wave comes up, and also melts away, and then the third wave merges into the ruins of the first and second, and after a while the fourth blunders into the remnants of the others, and we begin to run forward to catch up with the barrage, gasping and sweating, in bunches, anyhow,

every bit of the months of drill and rehearsal forgotten, for who could have imagined that the "Big Push" was going to be like this?*

War underlines the distinctiveness of generations, tightens the age brackets; war renders the elders irrelevant and turns the young toward one another. A style is set, style-setters emerge. In the backwash of the Great War, such novels as Scott Fitzgerald's *The Great Gatsby* and Ernest Hemingway's *The Sun Also Rises*—and gossip about the "Lost Generation's" actual mode of being—pointed the new direction: "gallantry in heartbreak, grim and nonchalant banter, and heroic dissipation," Edmund Wilson called it. Kennedy eventually read most of Hemingway. When, eventually, he chose to write a book himself he started it this way: "This is a book about that most admirable of human virtues—courage. 'Grace under pressure,' Ernest Hemingway defined it." But the posture of the earlier Hemingway also affected him. He mocked his own high inaugural rhetoric at a Democratic fundraiser—"for we have sworn to pay off the same party debt our forebears ran up nearly a year and three months ago." Courage, he wrote, is not just one among the virtues; it "is the basis of all human morality." But Hemingway's definition, he told a pal, reminded him of a girl he once knew. The new combination was conviction and irony, their tension relieved by humor and resolved in a certain style. Kennedy copied into a notebook this sentence of Churchill's, about how one man died in The Great War:

> The War which found the measure of so many men never got to the bottom of him, and, when the Grenadiers strode into the crash and thunder of the Somme, he went to his fate, cool, poised, resolute, matter-of-fact, debonair.†

For many American millions, World War II came as a relief. On the home front, industry revived; the terror of not being wanted was exchanged for the pleasure of choice among good jobs. The attack on Pearl Harbor sank class conflict in a great surge of patriotic unity and morale. For a nation given to moralizing wars, Hitler and Hirohito were satisfying devils. Life picked up; rates of suicide and mental illness fell off. Overseas, the war was far more a matter of logistics and maneuver than the First World War had been; behind each American combatant stood a team of supporters. By the end of it, twenty-five million humans were killed; nearly three hundred thousand Americans died in battle. But our cities came out of it unbombed, our countryside undevastated. Death never hit close to the average American, at home or overseas. Kennedy's experience was unaverage in that respect. He was one of those who got bombed and shot at a few times. He saw men killed on the deck of his small patrol torpedo boat. More of his crew were killed, and he nearly was, when a Japanese destroyer smashed the boat apart and

* Henry Williamson, *The Wet Flanders Plain* (New York: E. P. Dutton, 1929), pp. 15–16.
† Quoted in Arthur M. Schlesinger, Jr., *A Thousand Days: John F. Kennedy in the White House* (Boston: Houghton Mifflin, 1965), p. 87.

dumped them into a sea covered with burning gasoline; the survivors swam three or four miles to an atoll, where they got by for a week on coconuts before being rescued. After recuperating, Kennedy returned to combat. He came home with a severely injured back, suffering intensely from sciatica. A little over six feet tall, he weighed 127 pounds. From overseas, Lt. Kennedy wrote a girl friend:

> I used to have a feeling that no matter what happened I'd live through. It's a funny thing that as long as you have that feeling you seem to get through. I've lost that feeling lately. As a matter of fact, I don't feel badly about it. If anything happens to me I have this knowledge that if I live to be 100 I could only improve the quantity of my life, not the quality. This sounds gloomy as hell but you are the only person I'd say it to anyway.*

Kennedy's brush with death in war was not his last. Years later, undergoing radical surgery to ease the torment of back pain—"I don't care. I can't go on like this"—he heard a priest intoning last rites. The back never did get well; his brother said that at least half his days were sharply painful. But neither despair nor bitterness was his mode, rather a form of debonair stoicism. What lasted in his mind, as in the minds of the first Great War's survivors, were the names of fallen comrades who had set off to fight the last war ever. When he ran for Congress in 1946, his campaign slogan was "The New Generation Offers a Leader."

The Contrasting Contenders

The election of 1960 would see two young warriors square off against each other in a clear illustration of the politics of conflict. After years of Eisenhowerian torpidity, celebrated in the consensus election of 1956, the nation was ready once again to "get moving again," as Kennedy kept recommending—a call to arms, to adventure, to excellence after a period that had come to feel more and more like a national nap. The resultant battle of 1960 would be chronicled in a new way: not as an event, but as a saga, thanks to the inventive imagination of a journalist-turned-bookwriter, Theodore White. White had good material. The candidates could hardly have been more different in their origin and in their character. John Fitzgerald Kennedy grew up in a political family: politics was the regular topic of dinner-table conversation among the four boys and five girls who populated the lively Kennedy household. His father, son of an Irish saloon keeper and himself a former peanut vendor, had become a mogul of big business, a millionaire in his early thirties, but he took a strong interest in his brood collectively and individually, especially insisting that they learn how to compete and—

* Joan Blair and Clay Blair, Jr., *The Search for JFK* (New York: G. P. Putnam's Sons, 1976), p. 286.

better yet—to win. His mother imposed discipline with a set household routine that began every morning with her attendance at mass. The daughter of the former mayor of Boston, she posted news clippings for the children to read in preparation for dinner time. Her daughter Eunice called her "a very compassionate computer."

Jack and his older brother Joe, the star of the family, formed a pair: roughhouse competitors, but friends, classmates at Harvard. Joe was the boisterous, sociable, charming, and athletic one, taking after his father. Jack was quieter, a little withdrawn, and shy, like Mother. They shared the invigorating family experience: a wide-open, expansive, adventurous mini-community, where achievement was valued and love provided. When in 1944, Joe was killed in the war, Jack emerged as the leader in line of his generation of Kennedys; he began to take more seriously the demand for outstanding performance, but he kept his particular theme. His Harvard thesis later struck James MacGregor Burns and Arthur Schlesinger, Jr., with the "emotional detachment" that makes it "so aloof and clinical." He came into adulthood as a doer but also an observer.

Richard Milhous Nixon had a scarring childhood. His father, Frank, a man with a sixth-grade education and a fierce temper, struggled through failure after failure, fighting to keep enough food on the table. Mother Hannah, a severely repressed Quaker lady, nearly lost Richard when his head was torn open in a fall from a wagon at age three, and did lose two other sons, who died of tubercular meningitis after years of nurturing, in Richard's teenage years. Like Jack Kennedy, however, Richard Nixon was his family's scholar; he got through college and the new Duke law school, from which he emerged with the nickname "Gloomy Gus." At school he carved out an identity as a fighter with words, a debater ready to argue at the drop of a proposition. From his mother, who had to keep some kind of good face on the violent and damaging situation at home, Richard learned the overriding importance of image-management. He grew up sad, with a pervading sense of impending disaster, but also with a combative determination to justify himself through the achievement of independent power. In 1942 he went into the navy; as a supply officer in the South Pacific, he experienced little real danger, but widened his horizons. After the war, at the behest of rich California businessmen, he ran for Congress and won, striking hard at his opponent with sly intimations of disloyalty. In 1950, playing the same kind of hardball politics, he got himself elected to the Senate, establishing a reputation as a tough and thorough rooter-out of Communist subversives. Politically inexperienced Dwight D. Eisenhower took him on as a running mate and hatchet man in the Presidential contest of 1952, and, in 1956, swallowing severe doubts, kept him on when he did not take what seem to have been several hints to pull out. Nixon thus appeared on the stage in the 1960s as an experienced, hard-driving, and hard-driven politician, not very nice perhaps, but effective.

The War Hero Reporter-Politician

Kennedy', like Theodore Roosevelt, found a way to play his fighting story outside himself, in politics. Like Roosevelt, his initial ventures drew heavily on his burgeoning reputation as a "war hero." In January 1944, he arrived in Los Angeles. There was a press conference on the PT-109 adventure. The same girlfriend he had written to so gloomily from overseas—now a syndicated columnist for the North American Newspaper Alliance—quoted him thusly: "None of that hero stuff for me. The real heroes are not the men who return, but those who stay out there, like plenty of them do, two of my men included. . . ." But her nationally syndicated column was headlined, "Lt. Kennedy Saves His Men as Japs Cut PT Boat in Half." Back East, Kennedy met the author John Hersey in a nightclub; they took to one another; Jack and another girlfriend went to the theater with the Herseys. Hersey got the idea for a piece on the Solomon Islands saga. Kennedy insisted Hersey question the crew first; Hersey did, and found "absolutely clear devotion to him by the crew." The navy gave him a medal; the *New York Times* headlined, "Lieut. Kennedy Cited as Hero by the Navy for Saving Men of PT Crew in Solomons," and put his smiling picture under it. Closer to home, the *Boston Globe* announced, "Lt. John Fitzgerald Kennedy Gets Medal Today for Heroism." In June 1944, Hersey's long article appeared in the *New Yorker*, recounting the desperate adventure of PT-109 and Kennedy's heroic role in the rescue. The reaction of at least one fellow crew member, the boxer Barney Ross, illustrates precisely how powerfully story can shape the meaning of memory:

> Our reaction to the 109 thing had always been that we were kind of ashamed of our performance. I guess you always like to see your name in print and that Hersey article made us think maybe we weren't so bad after all. We'd never gone around saying, hey, did you hear about us? But suddenly your name's in print and Hersey made you sound like some kind of hero because you saved your own life. So I suppose my reaction to the article was to be pleased with myself. I had always thought it was a disaster, but he made it sound pretty heroic, like Dunkirk.*

The *Reader's Digest* published a condensed version in August 1944; Kennedy's campaigns in 1946 and 1952 put out hundreds of thousands of reprints, and in 1959, *U.S. News and World Report* printed large excerpts as part of an assessment of Kennedy's Presidential qualities.

Kennedy was in and out of hospitals for months. That August of 1944 death bit right into the family: Jack's older brother Joe was killed when his plane exploded over England. In September, his favorite sister Kathleen lost her husband in France. In January 1945, Jack went out to a resort in Arizona to build up his health, and, perhaps, to recover from the family trauma. There he wrote an article on how to keep the peace through strict arms con-

* Quoted in ibid., pp. 333–34.

trol by the great powers, ending with a ringing endorsement of Franklin Roosevelt's Four Freedoms. His father tried to get it published, to no avail. But literary success was on the way. His Harvard thesis, *Why England Slept*, argued that England was late to wake up to the Hitler threat because her people could not see the threat:

> A boxer cannot work himself into proper psychological and physical condition for a fight that he seriously believes will never come off. It is the same way with England. She so hated the thought of war that she could not believe it was going to happen, and the appeasement policy gave her confidence that this hope had some basis.*

The book got many good reviews, a fair number of which expressed surprise that a mere college student could write so well. It appeared on best-seller lists. Then in 1941 he got a piece titled "Irish Bases Vital to Britain" published in Hearst's New York paper, then called the *Journal American*.

After the war, Jack's father wangled him an assignment with another Hearst paper, the *Chicago Herald-American*, to report on the San Francisco United Nations conference, along with some twelve hundred other correspondents, an average of six for every delegate. "Hero Covers Parley for H-A" blared the Hearstian headline. In a month he put out sixteen stories, each with a picture, the by-line "Lt. John F. Kennedy," and a biographical squib describing him as a "recently retired PT boat hero of the South Pacific." His dispatches combined sportiness and skepticism. The conference looked to Kennedy like "an international football game with Molotov carrying the ball while Stettinius, Eden and the delegates tried to tackle him all over the field." After the conference, he went to England to report for the Hearst papers on the British elections, and was one of the few who saw that "Churchill May Lose Election," because he was "fighting a tide that is surging through Europe, washing away monarchies and conservative governments everywhere." His by-line had become plain "John F. Kennedy," though a war-hero synopsis appeared with it.

Back home Jack began making speeches, first to the Hyannis Rotary Club (one Rotarian said he looked like "a little boy dressed up in his father's clothes"), then to Boston Legionnaires, gravely warning of the perils of the peace. In 1946, urged on and helped out by his father, he set his foot across the line into politics. "A Kennedy Runs for Congress: The Boston-Bred Scion of a Former Ambassador is a Fighting-Irish Conservative," said *Look*. One old Irish pol remembered:

> The first day I met Kennedy he had sneakers on. I said, "For the love of Christ, take the sneakers off, Jack. You think you're going to play golf?" It was tough to sell the guy. We had a hell of a job with him. We took him to taverns, hotel lobbies, club rooms, street corners. Young Kennedy, young Kennedy, we kept saying. But they

---

*John Kennedy, *Why England Slept* (New York: Wilfred Funk, Inc., 1940), pp. xiv–xv.

didn't want him in the district. The Curley mob wouldn't go for him right away. They called him the Miami candidate. . . . We had a helluva fight. . . .*

He campaigned flat out, rising at 6:15 A.M., falling into bed at 1:00 or 2:00 A.M., though he had to take time for a back soak and rub during the day. By the day of the primary election, "Kennedy the war hero" and "PT-109" were household phrases in the Eleventh District. Five campaign offices were going full steam. There were ten candidates but Kennedy got the best coverage; one paper had a reporter check on his campaign every day, and Father Kennedy got a newsreel team to make films to be shown in the movie houses the night before the election. Ninety billboards carried the Kennedy message. And the Kennedy family was all over town, holding tea parties and making little speeches. Younger brother Bobby was assigned to work up touch football games with street boys in a rough section. Just before election day, every voter in the district got a *Reader's Digest* reprint of Hersey's PT-109 story—"a knockout blow," one campaigner called it. Kennedy won by a landslide plurality, 42 percent of the vote. The contest against the Republican in November was a formality.

In 1948 Kennedy was reelected to Congress; in 1952 he won a hard contest against Henry Cabot Lodge for the Senate; in 1956 he lost a try for the Vice-Presidential nomination to Estes Kefauver, a cliffhanger, after a senator named Lyndon Johnson tried to help him out—"Texas proudly casts its vote for the fighting sailor who wears the scars of battle." Then he lit out to be President. Along the way, he was reelected senator in 1958, by a big margin. Back in 1954, Senator Kennedy's assistant Theodore Sorensen collared him on the floor and suggested the senator trim a little on a minor measure that "might look bad in some future national campaign." Kennedy gave him a Kennedy answer: "I can't start basing my life on that or I'd be no good in this job or to myself." But starting in September 1956, Kennedy took to the hustings by air, crisscrossing the country again and again, hitting every state, most of them several times, in support of dozens of Democrats, and of himself. His wife said their relationship was "like being married to a whirlwind."

Running the Field

On January 2, 1960, Kennedy declared his candidacy for President; most of the press did not believe him—many thought he was really after the Vice-Presidential nomination, though he said he would not take that "under any condition." He ran in a crowded field of stars and dark horses. Ten governors scanned the political heavens for lightning but the most serious threats were Adlai Stevenson and the Senate contenders—eight of them, including Humphrey, Johnson, and Symington. Ex-President Truman, ex-candidate Stevenson, Mrs. Franklin D. Roosevelt, the congressional leadership,

---

* Blair and Blair, *Search for JFK*, pp. 439–40.

House Democrats, Senate Democrats, state party chairmen, newspaper editors, "influential intellectuals," Americans for Democratic Action, most labor leaders, most black leaders, most governors, and most urban bosses distributed their preferences among the variety of choices. The party's national chairman was a friend of Kennedy's, "but unfortunately," notes Sorensen, "he had more enemies than delegates."

With no significant early support from the Democratic powers and no influential backing from the established kings of journalism, Kennedy would have to go for the prize on his own. Even after he became President, he complained that he was a stranger to the people who ran the country. He would have to find an opening—to make one—through the barriers of opposition and indifference the system and the situation put up to block his path.

Kennedy's only hope was to run in primaries. State primaries had spread like crabgrass from Wisconsin's reforming soil in 1902 to sixteen states in 1960 (by 1976 there were thirty, by 1980 thirty-six of them). They were mean contests: you had to nick your brothers just deep enough to stagger them while you charged through, then bind their wounds and enlist them to your cause. Primaries ate up money and energy and ideas that would be desperately needed to nourish the general election campaign. Kennedy picked eight to try in, Humphrey chose five. Symington, Johnson, and Stevenson stood aside, watching and waiting for the expected deadlocked convention. As it turned out, only two primary contests were crucial, in Wisconsin and West Virginia against Humphrey, and one obscure convention wrestling match, against Johnson.

Humphrey and Kennedy came to Wisconsin and talked in code. Kennedy showed he knew as much about the Wisconsin rivers and woods as any other senator. Humphrey, referring to no particular other, said, "To elect a President it's more important that he be good of heart, good of spirit, than that he be slick, or clever, or statesmanlike-looking." He edged over a bit toward aggression: "Beware of these orderly campaigns. They are ordered, bought and paid for," and on some issues, Kennedy's "record is like Nixon's." But by 1900 standards it was mild stuff. Kennedy won, but not as big as the press had expected, so Humphrey decided to go on to West Virginia. Somehow he had to hit Kennedy, but that came hard to a man of his sunny and sanguine disposition. Later in the primary season, he would issue harsh attacks to the press, then hang his head and tell the reporters, off the record, "I'll have a lot more to say later, and it'll all be petty and cheap, too."

West Virginia was a key battle. Postelection polls in Wisconsin revealed that Catholic votes had helped Kennedy heavily, and preelection polls in West Virginia, sparsely Catholicized, strengthened underhanded attacks that Humphrey himself would have no part of. Kennedy's television documentary started with a shot of a PT boat plowing the waves of the Pacific night. Franklin D. Roosevelt, Jr., campaigning for Kennedy, said

Humphrey was "a good Democrat, but I don't know where he was in World War II," setting off a press flap. But at the candidate level, it was Kennedy against sloth, Humphrey against greed—hardly the stuff to fire the spring-time voter's blood. The candidates sensed that. Humphrey lashed outward:

I don't think elections should be bought. Let that sink in deeply. . . . I can't af-ford to run through this state with a little black bag and a checkbook. . . . Kennedy is the spoiled candidate and he and that young, emotional, juvenile Bobby are spending with wild abandon. . . . Anyone who gets in the way of . . . papa's pet is going to be destroyed. . . . I don't seem to recall anybody giving the Kennedy family—father, mother, sons or daughters—the privilege of deciding . . . our party's nominee.*

Kennedy said publicly, "I have never been subject to so much personal abuse." He lashed out against the vague whispers, getting louder, that he was a papist agent or at least a swearer of oaths superior to the one quoted in the Constitution. "I refuse to believe that I was denied the right to be Presi-dent on the day I was baptized," he pronounced. On television, he looked the West Virginians in the eye and said, as one reporter remembered,

". . . so when any man stands on the steps of the Capitol and takes the oath of office of President, he is swearing to support the separation of church and state; he puts one hand on the Bible and raises the other hand to God as he takes the oath. And if he breaks his oath, he is not only committing a crime against the Constitution, for which the Congress can impeach him—and should impeach him—but he is commit-ting a sin against God."

Here Kennedy raised his hand from an imaginary Bible, as if lifting it to God, and, repeating softly, said, "A sin against God, for he has sworn on the Bible."†

Later in the campaign, Kennedy made a more detailed attack on bigotry to an audience of worried clergymen in Houston; as Sam Rayburn remembered it, "He ate 'em blood raw." Privately, Kennedy would sigh, "Now I under-stand why Henry VIII set up his own church."

In West Virginia, the big virtue of the "religious issue" for Kennedy was that there was not one blessed thing Humphrey could say about it without seeming a bigot, which he wasn't. Kennedy won, 61 to 39 percent, carrying all but seven of the fifty-five counties. After some healing time, Kennedy and Humphrey got back together. By the fall they were joshing like old pals: Humphrey said, "One thing about Senator Kennedy. If he gives you his word and says he is going to do it, he does it. He told me last year he was going to lick me, and he did it," to which Kennedy replied, "He made it so tough last winter that this fall is very pleasant. . . . It is much easier to play Harvard after you have played Ohio State."

Harry Truman, a powerful figure though not yet elevated to political sainthood, weighed in with a blast against a convention "prearranged" and

---

*Theodore C. Sorensen, *Kennedy* (New York: Harper & Row, 1965), p. 141.
†Theodore H. White, *The Making of the President 1960* (New York: Atheneum, 1961), pp. 128–29.

"controlled" by Kennedy, querying, "Senator, are you certain that you are quite ready for the country, or that the country is ready for you in the role of President? . . . May I urge you to be patient?" On the Fourth of July, Kennedy hit back. "Mr. Truman regards an open convention as one which studies all the candidates, reviews their records and then takes his advice," he said, and noted that requiring more than his own "fourteen years in major elective office" would "rule out all but three of the ten names put forward by Truman, all but a handful of American Presidents, and every President of the twentieth century—including Wilson, Roosevelt and Truman." But by August 1960, when the two of them met the press at the Truman Library, it went like this:

QUESTION: What caused you to decide that Senator Kennedy was ready for the country?

MR. TRUMAN: When the Democratic National Convention decided to nominate him for President. That is all the answer you need. The Democratic National Convention is the law for the Democratic Party. I am a Democrat and I follow the law.

QUESTION: On July 2, I believe you said that you thought the convention was fixed. Have you changed your opinion?

MR. TRUMAN: I did not say that. I said it looked to me as if the convention was already made up the way it was supposed to go, and that is what the trouble was. And it was, and it has been done all right, and they nominated this man, and I am going to support him. What are you going to do about that?*

Eventually it was roughly the same with Stevenson on the left, with Johnson on the right. Kennedy admired Stevenson because "he is not a political whore like most of the others." As the tide turned in his favor he was confident that the Stevensonians would come around when they saw that Kennedy's alternative was to turn to Southern conservatives for support. As for Lyndon Johnson, he recessed the Senate and came to the convention as a candidate, warning that "the forces of evil . . . will have no mercy for innocence, no gallantry for inexperience." His backers fixed up a televised "debate" with "young Jack" before the Texas and Massachusetts delegations. Johnson led off patronizing "some people" who had not been as active as he had in the Senate. Kennedy answered easily that since Johnson had not said who he was talking about, "I assume he was talking about some other candidate, not me." Much to the Kennedyites' surprise, Johnson accepted the Vice-Presidential nomination when it was gingerly tendered, partly persuaded by old Sam Rayburn's argument: "That other fellow"—Richard Nixon—"called me a traitor, and I don't want a man who calls me a traitor to be President of the United States."

The Republican primaries struck no sparks. Like Sam Rayburn, New York's Nelson Rockefeller did not like to think of Richard Nixon as Presi-

*John F. Kennedy, "The Speeches, Remarks, Press Conferences, and Statements of Senator John F. Kennedy, August 1 through November 7, 1960," *Freedom of Communications*, part 1, 87th Cong., 1st sess., Sen. Rep. 994, pp. 24–25.

dent, but that sentiment was not strong enough to lure him into the primaries. Like Kennedy, Vice-President Nixon had been out on the creamed-
peas-and-chicken circuit for years, accumulating many small alliances. President Eisenhower's tolerant noninterference left Nixon free to claim a piece
of Ike's enormous popularity. Rockefeller bowed out in December 1959,
though he would bow back in again, more or less, in June 1960, too late to
make any difference. Nixon entered all the primaries and plodded to victory
at the convention. As the national contest began, he led Kennedy in Mr.
Gallup's poll, 50 to 44 percent.

Generating Conflict

To millions of Americans the contest looked like tweedle-dee vs.
tweedle-dum, six of one and half a dozen of the other. The process had
served up a pair of young veterans who got themselves elected to Congress
at the same time and went on to become party politicians. To Eric Sevareid,
they were a couple of "completely packaged products," two "tidy, buttoned-
down men," whose education had taught "wearing the proper clothes, thinking the proper thoughts, cultivating the proper people." Sevareid missed the
good old days of the 1930s, when young men "sickened at the Republic Steel
massacre of strikers . . . got drunk and wept when the Spanish Republic
went down . . . dreamt beautiful and foolish dreams about the perfectibility
of man, cheered Roosevelt and adored the poor." As for "issues," virtually
nothing of importance came across. One was a Democrat (pro-poor), the
other a Republican (pro-rich). Kennedy's devoted helper Sorensen admits
flatly that "the campaign raised no clearcut, decisive issue, and, except for
the Peace Corps, no new proposals"—though near the end Nixon did come
up with a bizarre plan for sending Eisenhower, Truman, and other great
leaders to Eastern Europe to fix things up. The clarity of their issue differences was symbolized by the grand question of whether or not two little
rocky outcrops in the ocean between China and Formosa, named Quemoy
and Matsu, should be defended. Kennedy said no unless the defense was essential to protect Formosa; Nixon said yes because the defense was essential
to protect Formosa. Neither underestimated the threat of his opponent. As
far back as 1957, Kennedy saw Nixon as a "tough, skillful, shrewd opponent." In 1960 Nixon had Kennedy down as "a tough-minded, capable political operator, and a formidable opponent."

A large problem for Kennedy, from at least 1959 on, had been differen-
tiating himself from opponents. Policy position papers would not do it in
1960; instead, he found a style of fighting that joined his purpose and his personality: he would compete as if he were already President—but not as Tom
Dewey had in 1948. As a proto-President, he would fight high, hard, and
cool, communicating confidence all the way.

Early on he defined a contrast with Humphrey. "Hubert is too intense for the present mood of the people," he said. "He gets people too excited, too worked up." Instead, "what they want today is a more boring, monotonous personality, like me." When told of Humphrey's attacks on him, he expressed "not the slightest trace of anger," Sorensen remembered. He answered Truman with aplomb and analysis, met the "religious issue" with argument, as if the doubts had merit. When students at Dartmouth hissed at his mention of Eisenhower, he told them, "You mustn't hiss the President of the United States." Hecklers got to Nixon—"Don't try anything on me or we'll take care of you." Kennedy tossed it off: "Let me speak first and then you, O.K.?" When an angry woman threw her whisky at him, he handed back the glass—"Here's your glass." Learning that Nixon had gone to the hospital as the campaign got hot around Labor Day, Kennedy refused to comment on him for nearly two weeks, though along the way he could not resist a gentle jab:

QUESTION: Senator, when does the moratorium end on Nixon's hospitalization and your ability to attack him?
SENATOR KENNEDY: Well, I said I would not mention him unless I could praise him until he got out of the hospital, and I have not mentioned him. [Laughter.]*

In the four television debates, which gave the campaign its dramatic climax—the first television debates between Presidential candidates in American history—Nixon debated Kennedy and Kennedy spoke to the nation, over Nixon's head, dismissing the Vice-President's charges: "I really don't need Mr. Nixon to tell me about what my responsibilities are as a citizen."

The hard part included a few low blows. Kennedy had known Nixon somewhat when they were new congressmen together, but never thought much of him. The campaign experience lowered that opinion. Nixon unleashed his vituperative vocabulary—"barefaced lie . . . irresponsible . . . despicable . . . running America down and giving us an inferiority complex . . . whimpering and yammering and wringing of the towel. . . ." Kennedy came to feel that "anyone who can't beat Nixon doesn't deserve to be President." Reading Nixon's account of the campaign in *Six Crises*, he said, "It makes me sick. He's a cheap bastard; that's all there is to it." And the ultimate Kennedy put-down: "He has no taste." He hit Nixon in the acceptance speech—"His speeches are generalities from *Poor Richard's Almanac*." After the conventions he struck him for repudiating, "in the short span of 48 hours since his nomination," key parts of the Eisenhower program. Nixon showed "a lack of basic beliefs," "a political captain leaving the sinking ship," whose vaunted claim to "experience" consisted of "policies of weakness, retreat, and defeat," whose "positions change so fast it is very difficult to know where he stands," a man who "has fallen back on the blackmailer's tactic of distorted threats." He liked to list Nixon's Republican fore-

* Ibid., p. 186.

runners and their slogans: "Stand Pat With McKinley," "Keep Cool with Coolidge," "Return to Normalcy with Harding," "A Chicken in Every Pot with Hoover," "Time for a Change"—this last without attribution to Eisenhower—"the weakest and least constructive slogans in the history of American political thought." That technique could veer him over to a lower form of guilt by association: "There are children in Africa named Thomas Jefferson, George Washington and Abraham Lincoln," he would say. "There are none called Lenin or Trotsky or Stalin—or Nixon." Nixon, he noted, was "the only one who has a Negro traveling with him in the North but not in the South." Standing next to Nixon in one of the debates, he heard the Republican refer to "three Democratic Presidents who led us into war"; Kennedy responded, "I don't think it's possible for Mr. Nixon to state the record in distortion of the facts with more precision than he just did."

The cool part was humor. Kennedy had an ear for it, and his staff kept a bulging notebook of gags and mocks. Nixon was far better known, occupying a high official position under an extraordinarily popular President, and took himself seriously. Kennedy had to deflate him; by the end of the campaign he was condescending to him. When Nixon called him "another Truman," Kennedy said, "I regard that as a great compliment, and I have no hesitation in returning the compliment. I consider him another Dewey." Nixon's own try at appearing Presidential rested substantially on his experience in standing up to Soviet Premier Nikita Khrushchev and on his diplomatic work for peace. Kennedy built this response:

They say he has traveled abroad. He has. In Vietnam he urged the French to continue to fight. On Formosa he implied our support of an invasion of the Mainland of China. In India he questioned Nehru's right to be neutral. In Venezuela his goodwill tour provoked a riot, and in the Soviet Union he argued with Mr. Khrushchev in the kitchen, it is true, pointing out that while we may be behind in space, we were ahead in color television. [Applause and laughter]. But does anyone think for a single moment, do they take the Communists so lightly that they think Mr. Khrushchev was diverted for a single moment from his objectives by an argument in the kitchen? Do they think he changed his plans, pulled back his forces since that argument? He could argue in the kitchen every day and move every night. [Laughter.]*

He would try out new variations, see how they went over: "Mr. Nixon may be very experienced in kitchen debates. So are a great many other married men I know." Here is how he got together his "barefaced lie" number. On November 2, in Los Angeles:

This is a beautiful state. I am confident that Mr. Nixon will enjoy it after the election. [Applause] Mr. Nixon is calling me a liar so much every day, and other choice adjectives, that used to be reserved for the California scenes, which is now being exposed to the Nation, it is rather difficult for me to confirm anything other

*Ibid., p. 43.

than to confirm what Governor Brown said, that there are the most beautiful women in California, and I challenge him to call me a liar. [Applause.]*

The next day in Albuquerque, New Mexico, Kennedy noted that Nixon "in that wonderful choice of words which distinguishes him as a great national leader" had called a Kennedy statement "a barefaced lie." "Having seen him four times close up in this campaign and made up [laughter], I would not accuse Mr. Nixon of being barefaced [laughter and applause]. . . ." The next day in Toledo, Ohio: "In the last 4 days he has called me everything from a barefaced liar to an economic ignoramus. I am calling him a worthy member of his party in 1960. [Applause.] He fits right in with Dewey, Landon, Coolidge, Harding, McKinley and all the rest of them. [Applause.]" The next day in the Bronx, New York: "Nixon, in a high-level or high-road campaign which emphasizes the issues, in the last 7 days has called me an economic ignoramus, a Pied Piper, and all the rest. I just confine myself to calling him a Republican. [Laughter and applause.] But he says that is really getting low. [Laughter.]" A surefire laugher was the elephant image: "The fact of the matter is Mr. Eisenhower carried him in twice. You have seen circus elephants, their heads full of ivory, thick skins, no foresight, complete memory. You know when they go around the ring in a circus they grab the tail of the elephant in front of them. [Laughter and applause.] Well, Mr. Nixon, he grabbed that tail in 1952 and 1956, but it isn't there any more. He has to face the people. [Applause.]"†

Such little twits tweaked the sting from Nixon's barbs. Repeating the Nixon charges made Kennedy seem brave; trivializing them made him seem above it all—confident enough not to worry about such puerile propoundments. Then by daring to mock himself—lightly, to be sure—he gained more stature. "In preparation for this campaign," he said, "I had sisters living in all the key states." Tangling the same phrase three times into one speech-sentence, he stopped and said, "We are going to put this speech to music and make a fortune out of it." The body of the speeches was serious; the humor made him seem confident and at ease—like a President.

The line back to Theodore Roosevelt and 1900 can be traced easily in combativeness, partisanship, the link to war. But in an important sense Kennedy's fighting story was not linear at all. For there was more to his stance than a style, more than a biographical sequence. Kennedy's fight was a space battle, a fight for atmospheric territories. He undertook no less a task than the redefinition of the nation's climate of expectations, he did not chart a path, he advertised a mythic landscape, a New Frontier. The purpose of rocketing a man to the moon was not the act itself or the acquisition of that heavenly wasteland, but the sharing of a meaning. "In a very real sense," he said, referring to a spiritual reality, "it will not be one man going to the moon

* Quotations from ibid., *passim*.
† Quotations from ibid.

. . . it will be an entire nation." Rather than pose a goal for Americans to pursue, Kennedy urged pursuit itself—he would "get the nation moving again." He was trying to raise the public's sights above the material horizon, in a time of peace and prosperity: "I think we can do better"—better, not just more. That would call for sacrifice, though he never made it clear who would have to give up what.

Kennedy's main fight was against an "ism"—Eisenhowerism. Speaking to and for a generation, he stressed his vision's historical timeliness:

> Perhaps we could afford a Coolidge following Harding. And perhaps we could afford a Pierce following Fillmore. But after Buchanan this nation needed a Lincoln—after Taft, we needed a Wilson—after Hoover we needed Franklin Roosevelt—and after eight years of drugged and fitful sleep, this nation needs strong, creative Democratic leadership in the White House.*

That seesaw would rock on after he was gone. The war in Vietnam would rouse again the salience of generations, but Kennedy could not see that in 1960. Back in Boston Garden the night the campaign closed, Fighting Jack spoke to his cheering comrades:

> I thank you for your past support. I ask you to join us tomorrow. And, most of all, I ask you to join us in all the tomorrows yet to come, in building America, moving America, picking this country of ours up and sending it into the sixties.

All of that would have struck Theodore Roosevelt as vague in the extreme. Kennedy's "vigah" would have rung a bell with him and he was thoroughly in favor of courage and progress and all that. But in his day, the fighting story took concreter form, got its language from the book of muscle and steel. By 1960, the essential arena of political combat had shifted over into a spiritual spacescape: politics had become a game for sophisticated preachers.

That year's Presidential election was the closest in history: Kennedy won by a whisker. The dominant mood of conflict in that political season failed to differentiate clearly between the contenders. Both of them were fighters, Nixon of the old gut-level, sock-'em-where-it-hurts manner, Kennedy of the newer mode of surgical riposte. Nixon had gone in overconfidently, leaning on his status as Vice-President of the United States, Eisenhower's choice. When he felt the ground slipping from under him, he turned and fought. Kennedy ran flat-out from the first, assuming nothing, plotting out his progress one battle at a time. The public chose the cool combatant over the alley fighter. Nixon read the lesson: never again would he come on in public Presidential politics in the guise of the Old Nixon, also known as Dick the Ripper. Kennedy passed on a lesson to many a contender yet to come: in the emerging journalistic politics, rising from obscurity made a better story than standing pat at the peak of a reputation.

*Theodore C. Sorensen, "The Election of 1960," in Schlesinger et al., eds., *History of American Presidential Elections*, vol. 4, p. 3544.

Campaigning: From Event to Saga

The reporters who took down what Kennedy said in January 1960, at their National Press Club—that a President should "place himself in the very thick of the fight," that "a real fighting mood" ought to pervade the White House—were also searching for a new style for the times. In journalism as in politics, a new generation groped for a way to tell the story and even live it a little. A book would show them how, transforming the fighting story as never before since Hearst and Pulitzer fought it out in New York. Kennedy sparked the change.

Much as the intellectuals of the 1950s and beyond disdained television, it was stylish among men of the mind at the turn of the century to disdain the daily press. Such attention as the scholarly journals were willing to devote to mere news treated journalism as a social problem, like prostitution or dope taking. An article by Delos F. Williams, Ph.D., introduced a detailed statistical analysis (categorizing newspapers as "yellow," "conservative," and "uncertain") with this cautionary paragraph:

> The newspaper *habit* has many vicious consequences. The children in the public schools are often urged to read the papers and keep track of the world's news. And it cannot be denied that the newspaper serves an important end in bringing men to social consciousness and in giving them data upon which to form social judgments. But we must deplore and, so far as possible, overcome the evils of habitual newspaper reading. These evils are, chiefly, three: first, the waste of much time and mental energy in reading unimportant news and opinions, and premature, untrue, or imperfect accounts of important matters; second, the awakening of prejudices and the enkindling of passions through the partisan bias or commercial greed of newspaper managers; third, the loading of the mind with cheap literature and the development of an aversion for books and sustained thought. Thus the daily newspaper often tends to make the intellectual life of its readers one continuous series of petty excitements, a veritable life of the social "senses," and to shut their minds, by mere fulness of occupation, against any appeal that does not find a voice in the daily news sheet.*

In 1937, Leo Rosten reported in *Journalism Quarterly* (the existence of which registered an advance in reportorial dignity) on his survey of 127 of Washington's premier correspondents. Half had not finished college, eight lacked a high school diploma, and two never made it into high school. Rosten worried that "men without a 'frame of reference' and with an uncontrolled impressionistic (rather than analytic) approach to issues are driven to a surface interpretation of events," full of "normative words of ambiguous content." Thus, "Newspaper men evidence a marked insecurity in the presence of social theories or political conceptualization." Their "caustic reportorial reaction" to the intellectual aspects of the New Deal, Rosten speculated along Freudian lines, "soon suggests the projection of doubts of personal adequacy." After the Second Great War, however, all this began to change.

* Delos F. Williams, "The American Newspaper: A Study in Social Psychology," *Annals of the American Academy of Political and Social Science* (July 1900), p. 57.

Journalists-to-be went to college on the G.I. Bill. Tom Wicker went through the University of North Carolina at Chapel Hill, David Broder finished up at the University of Chicago, and R. W. Apple, Jr., got the benefit of most of a Princeton education. The preceding generation's "interchangeable drones," as Timothy Crouse called them, were retiring right and left. The new breed was hip to ideas, accustomed to poking through facts for patterns. "We all read Riesman and William H. White," says the *Washington Post*'s William Greider, "and we looked around us at our college classmates and we thought, 'My God, that's right—that is the way the world is and I don't want any part of it.' " Thus they shared with the spirit of Richard Harding Davis a maverick mentality, with Jacob Riis a lust for reform, with Hearst himself a sense that there must be more to life than met the actual eye.

"Their dominance of the profession was sealed with the rise and election of John F. Kennedy," Timothy Crouse thought. It took youth or extra-ordinary stamina just to cover Kennedy campaigning. "For weeks and months," one wrote, "they must live like tramps—shaken, rushed, fighting with police at police lines, dirty and unbathed for days on end, herded into buses like schoolboys." Or, like soldier boys. By the last month, "everyone is drinking before lunch." At the first primary in New Hampshire, "everyone" traveling with Kennedy amounted to about twenty reporters. Along the way, transporting the news flock required a separate plane, then a second, then a third. On election night in Hyannis, nearly four hundred reporters were present. In between elections, most news happens in offices. With modern specialization, most reporters groove along their narrow beats, making what they can of various bureaucratic bungles and embranglements. Campaigning meant adventure—unpacking the old trench coat and getting outdoors in the field like foreign correspondents of the past, zipping around from one brief encounter to another, testing and confirming how much was left of youthful vim and manly durance. By 1964, New Hampshire would be a mob scene.

In 1960, Kennedy's press secretary, Pierre Salinger, organized the transitions of bodies and baggage; more important, he helped reporters do their work effectively, for instance by supplying instant transcripts of Kennedy speeches. The story-spawning structure of the situation—a relatively unknown (and thus revealable) challenger trying to bring down famous opponents by going directly to the people—helped enormously. By contrast, the Rockefeller pullout grayed the Nixon effort into abstraction. But the main helper for Kennedy reporters was the candidate. They knew early that he had tried his hand at their own game and that his book had won Mr. Pulitzer's prize. His father had peddled papers as a boy; the son had not only been a newspaperman himself—he had married an elegant woman who was also a reporter. They quickly found out they could get to him—directly, on or off the record—on short notice. He rarely palled around with them, was by no means above conning them when practicable, and he let them know it when he felt they did him wrong, but he shared instinctively the newsman's bedrock professional passion: "He has a limitless curiosity about nearly everything—people, places, the past, the future," Sorensen wrote. "Those who had nothing to say made him impatient. He hated to bore or be bored. But he enjoyed listening at length to anyone with new information or ideas on almost any subject, and he never forgot what he heard." His mind as revealed to Arthur Schlesinger was "objective, practical, ironic, skeptical, unfettered and insatiable"—a list most reporters would pledge allegiance to. One of the things he was most curious about was *their* lives and works, particularly stories of their struggles with mossback editors and publishers (Nixon got 78 percent of the newspaper endorsements, virtually all the big magazines), but also the language, the nailing of a lead, the literary art of telling what you know in a reader-grabbing way. He asked their advice— even got a few to do drafts of speeches for him—and gave them his own: "Tell Ken [Crawford, of *Newsweek*] to bust it off in old Arthur [Krock]. He can't take it, and when you go after him he folds." He knew how stupefying it was to listen to the same speech again and again, so he would occasionally slip a reporter's name into an historical anecdote as he orated. He read their copy and quoted back to them the parts he found "classy." Perhaps "he was also all those things newsmen wish to be but are not . . . always immaculate . . . humorous . . . wry . . . attractive to women . . . precise . . . self-confident . . . realistic and romantic at once. . . ," as one remembered. In any case, they called him "Jack" and composed and chorused raucously, in the privacy of the planes and busses, funny songs about his wonders and Nixon's nerdliness. Tom Wicker writes that there was "a feeling among reporters that he probably liked us more than he liked politicians, and that he may even have been more nearly one of *us* than one of *them*. . . ." Nixon, on the other hand, writes Crouse, "had roughly the same number of friends in the press as he did in Alger Hiss's immediate family."

If Jack's buddying, dash, and irony endeared him to the general run of reporters (as Theodore Roosevelt's did), his way of talking intellectually cultivated the brains among them, restlessly fallow for germinating conversation. To the best of anyone's memory he was the first politician to quote Madame de Staël on "Meet the Press." The reporter he married wrote that the men she would have liked best to know were Baudelaire, Wilde, and Diaghilev. Kennedy was given to complimenting authors on their *second* best-known books. He quoted poetry he himself had found. He and his speechwriters went for Latinate paradox and epigram. Norman Mailer found him satisfyingly "mysterious." Arthur Schlesinger, Jr., wrote, "The historical mind can be analytical, or it can be romantic. The best historians are both, Kennedy among them." All that probably impressed the new reporter-intellectuals. Probably more impressive was their sense that, unlike their impression of Adlai Stevenson, Kennedy was a thinker who could act. He opened up a new dimension of political combat in the sixties—the war of ideas—and he meant to fight that right on down into policy. It was lucky for him that they liked him. For as scribbled in his notes for *Profiles in Courage*, the influence of great leaders had a double root: "character—and the impression they gave."

The Making of Theodore White

Looking back on *The Making of the President 1960*—and *1964* and *1968*—in the summer of 1972, Theodore White shared a dark moment with a fellow reporter:

It's appalling what we've done to these guys. McGovern was like a fish in a gold-fish bowl. There were three different network crews at different times. The still photographers kept coming in in groups of five. And there were at least six writers sitting in the corner—I don't even know their names. We're all sitting there watching him work on his acceptance speech, poor bastard. He tries to go into the bedroom with Fred Dutton to go over the list of Vice Presidents . . . and all of us are observing him, taking notes like mad, getting all the little details. Which I think I invented as a method of reporting and which I now sincerely regret. If you write about this, say that I sincerely regret it.*

But when the book had appeared in 1961, it was a smash hit—"like Columbus telling about America at the Court of Ferdinand and Isabella," White remembered. It won a Pulitzer. The book clubs mailed it around. It stayed on the best-seller list for more than forty weeks. Most important, journalists by the hundreds read it and it bent their minds. The fighting story would never be the same.

White's remarkable career in the news world began with a boyhood job selling newspapers in Boston, ten hours a day, making seventy cents for every hundred sold. At age eight he went to public school until 3:30, then for two more hours to Hebrew school. "Memory was the foundation of learning" and what was to be remembered was the Bible, the Old Testament. The rich color of Hebrew stirred him. The chapters were "essentially stories, which explain to ordinary people their place in the now and the hereafter." Surrounding the smaller stories was a grand epic drama of creation and courage, failure and repentance. He read them—in the original—over and over and over again. The other epic to take hold of Theodore's mind was America. What came home to him was the story of liberty, heroes and all. The Great Depression came when he was fourteen. The day the market crashed Theodore wrote in his diary, "No money all week, Pa brought home $2.00 today, Mama is crying again." The bottom of hope fell out of the American saga. Then came the big break, a scholarship to Harvard. "If there is any one place in all America that mirrors better all American history, I do not know of it." He was a "meatball," a grind; classmates like Joseph P. Kennedy, Jr. ran in different circles. He did make friends with Arthur M. Schlesinger, Jr., and

---

* Quoted in Timothy Crouse, *The Boys on the Bus* (New York: Ballantine Books, 1973), p. 37.

learned from the elder Schlesinger, a distinguished professor of American cultural history, that the American story had a pace and swing to it, action and reaction, in sixteen-year cycles. His freshman history teacher, "Frisky" Merriman, "believed history was story—thus, entertainment"; he taught Western civilization as "a vaudeville sequence of thirty-six acts."

. . . . History as it was taught in my four years at Harvard is, in retrospect, a wonder. Quite simply, history was not yet considered a science but was still thought more noble than a craft. The professors were a colony of storytellers, held together by the belief that in their many stories they might find a truth. They still cared about students and lingered after class for conversations. No better preparation for what was to come to me in life could have been planned than what came to me at Harvard, by accident and timing and osmosis of curiosity.*

White found a good place to study in the library of the Harvard-Yenching Institute at Harvard and a sympathetic young mentor in his tutor, John King Fairbank, who asked him to tea. He learned Chinese and won a fellowship to go to China. Thinking he might be able to write history as a newspaperman, he went down to the *Boston Globe,* where a hardbitten editor told him to send copy and they would see. In Hong Kong, agents of the Chinese Republic's Information Service, learning he was a "newspaperman," hired him on the spot. After various detours he was hired as a stringer for *Time* magazine by their new young writer in China, John Hersey, who edited his prose. Then he went off to the combat zone as a war correspondent, feeling lucky "to be where the action was," to become a distinguished magazine writer and author of books on China and Europe that were not only popular but influential. His mindset had been formed in the saga of war. "I rode with that wave and was swept up by it," he remembered.

White was forty-four when in 1959 he decided "to write a book about how a President is made." He talked it over with his wife, whose view was, "It's probably a good book if Kennedy wins. But if Nixon wins, it's a dog." He would chance it.

The idea was to follow a campaign from beginning to end. It would be written as a novel is written, with anticipated surprises as, one by one, early contenders vanish in the primaries until only two jousters struggle for the prize in November. Moreover, it should be written as a story of a man in trouble, of the leader under the pressures of circumstances.

The leader—and the circumstances. That was where the story lay. . . .

If ever a man was made to illustrate White's thesis of history as the intersection of impersonal forces at personality points, it was John F. Kennedy.†

The Making of the President 1960 reported a fight few Americans had had a glimpse of. It is hard to remember today how dreary most Presidential

---

*Theodore H. White, *In Search of History: A Personal Adventure* (New York: Harper & Row, 1978), p. 47.
†White, *The Making of the President 1960*, pp. 454–55.

campaign reporting had been before his book—stories that reached their apex of excitement in the crowd count. His literary-journalistic achievement was to transform the Presidential battle story from a series of isolated acts into a dramatic whole—to see the grand strategy of war in the battles.

First of all, he cast a new light on the characterization of the contenders. The long fight was for the fulfillment of their life ambitions. White used the novelist's way, not the psychologist's—portraiture in the impressionist mode. He could sound a little like Hemingway when that suited the task, as in this on Kennedy:

> This morning he walked up the stairs slowly, a dark-blue mohair overcoat over his gray suit, bareheaded, slightly stooped. He was very tired. He paused at the top of the stairs and, still stooped, turned away. Then he slowly turned back to the door but made no gesture. Then he disappeared.*

Or he could bring out the Dickens in a character like Humphrey:

> "Now, you ask me that? And why didn't I file in Florida too? Well, I'll tell you— any man who goes into a primary isn't *fit* to be President. You have to be crazy to go into a primary. A primary, now, is worse than the torture of the rack. It's all right to enter a primary by accident, or because you don't know any better, but by forethought. . . ." He shook his head and some thought or some question carried him off to the farm problem.†

To write it that way, one had to be there to make note of the postures and intonations, so White got out where the contenders were, and got himself inside the action centers, a war correspondent in the trenches. Henceforth no one unblooded by participation in the battle would sound quite convincing; armchair analysis was out. White set off a fight within the fight: for access to the candidate—and his staff and children and laundress. After all, he had been bearding the Chiangs and Stillwells when he was a mere whippersnapper of a boy reporter. And he inspired a new way of collecting journalistic minutiae—writing it *all* down, from the mohair coat to Humphrey's italics, just in case.

White's second major mark was to construct for his drama a stage setting of operatic scale. The book had a thirty-seven-page chapter on demographics, "Retrospect on Yesterday's Future," detailing the massive shifts— in generations, in where people lived and how they worked and why they voted as they did—out there in the country. He did that the hard way, with the census and a rather hyperbolic vocabulary of change. The audience for the campaign fight was made part of the struggle, brought into the act, not as mere reflectors but as the tides the candidates were riding so precariously. For that he drew on his capacity for tedious scholarship; he made library work—and later the polls and computers—a required subject for political

*Ibid., p. 5.
†Ibid., p. 103.

journalism. The book ended in another stage setting, the Presidency. Reporters were slower to pick up on that long range perspective. Noting along the way that the Oval Office measures thirty-five feet by twenty-eight feet, four inches, he got into what Presidents do, how they are plugged into various networks, how they relate to the world's other top dogs, how power works at that level. The suggestion was that it was a peculiar job and that its special challenges ought to be the measure of the men who sought it. The contest was not, or should not be, a simpleminded morality play. "May the best man win" said it wrong. It was the best *President* we were after.

In the third place, White brought alive for the contemporary era the campaign as a struggle of organizations. "That which most distinctively sets American politics off from that of other nations," he wrote, is "that so few men can set in motion so vast a mass of freely participating citizens." In between these few and that many he saw a developing, steadily escalating swirl of structures and techniques, of area commanders and media managers and pollsters and fundraisers and any number of other proliferations analogous to the galloping articulations in the military establishment. A straight joust was transformed into a vast battle of logistics and maneuver, like a world war. Reporters would have to get at the story much earlier than before. White showed how the starts shaped the finishes, long before anyone had "declared" his candidacy. The early meetings and assignments—seemingly so casual—put in place a reality subsequent organizers would have to beat apart or deal with. By highlighting how Kennedy and Nixon had been at it for so long, White and his subsequent imitators hyped the early lead, taught not only reporters but candidates themselves that the fighting story was now virtually continuous. This emphasis led to an enormous overconcentration on the New Hampshire primary, the first one of the season, and then, in 1976, even farther back to something called the "Iowa caucuses," and, in 1980, the Florida preference poll of October 1979. For a still small but increasing number of journalists, Presidential election politics meant steady work.

But White's fourth influence overshadowed the rest. As noted, he wrote it like a novel, with "anticipated surprises." It was said of Kennedy that he would be valued, not for what he had done, but for what he was about to do. The air of expectation was a large element in Kennedy's "charisma"—and in White's impact; his story led forward, it had page-turning quality, its fascination derived from what was going to happen next. In the reporting of campaign politics, anticipating next week's surprises would become *the* reason for counting last night's votes. Perception served prediction.

The Kennedy Legacy

Happily *The Making of the President 1960* came out before John F. Kennedy became a hero for the ages, a Presidential martyr, who, like Lincoln, was in deep political trouble when murder made him a myth. Kennedy as President achieved little in the way of practical progress while he lived other than the avoidance of disaster, after the near-disaster of his wild try at the invasion of Cuba. In the White House he finally lost his cool detachment with respect to civil rights for black people and moved strongly and effectively to stop the racist nonsense in Mississippi and Alabama. But he would have to die before that commitment culminated in a great leap forward in social justice at home, the new civil-rights legislation his successor, Lyndon Johnson, would force through the Congress. And he would not live to see his minor mission in far-off Vietnam, sequel to Eisenhower's, transformed, under Lyndon Johnson and Richard Nixon, into a horror of mass butchery unprecedented in American history.

While he lived, Kennedy's influence was inspirational, not practical, fundamental, not immediate. For he was the one who lifted the standard of Presidential politics above the comfortable self-satisfaction of the Eisenhower years, attracting into politics and government new battalions of believers in the possibility of progress, the adventure of making a contribution beyond the self.

After Kennedy died, his story became a romance. He was the young and handsome prince of Camelot, adored by his fair lady, charging out to best the political dragons in a chivalrous adventure, slain as a young hero by a lurking assassin. Like Lincoln, like Franklin Roosevelt, like Harry Truman by the 1970s, and Dwight Eisenhower in the 1980s, President Kennedy's memory took on the aura of glory, his stumbles and lapses papered over by the Presidential mythmakers. But for all that, his legacy was a legacy of hope, of anticipation. That forward-leaning attitude fixed itself in the political culture. The drama of the Presidential election acquired the appeal of the about-to-be. Kennedy did not live long enough to see how that drama would degenerate, distorting the choice of Presidents yet to come.

6

George McGovern 1972

JOHN KENNEDY'S rise to power taught a strong lesson to contenders who would follow him in the race for the Presidency—to Barry Goldwater and Richard Nixon as well as to George McGovern and Jimmy Carter: start early. Nixon and Goldwater spent years dashing around the creamed-peas-and-chicken circuit, building fame and obligations. George McGovern declared his candidacy more than two years before he hoped to be sworn in, and he had been running, in fact, for nearly two years before that. Jimmy Carter announced for the election of 1976 before 1974 was over—by which time Fritz Mondale, eventually Carter's Vice-Presidential candidate, had already dropped out of the Presidential contest formally scheduled to start more than two years hence. Carter's own announcement was but the culmination of at least two years of intensive planning and scrimmaging. Thus what used to come on as a concentrated bout every fourth autumn was transformed into a yearlong series of linked-together contests that threatened to render the election itself an anticlimax.

Theodore White's saga-making gave form to the story. In 1968 at least seventeen other White-like campaign histories were in the works, including one by a British team, and by 1972 every second reporter seemed to have a manuscript going. More important, White's dramatic, insider style swept over into daily journalism. The Associated Press ordered its correspondents to get with it: "When Teddy White's book comes out, there shouldn't be one single story in that book that we haven't reported ourselves." The managing editor of the *New York Times* told his reporters and editors the same thing: "We aren't going to wait until a year after the election to read in Teddy White's book what we should have reported ourselves." Reporters—scores of them—muscled their way into the campaigns of 1972, frantically jotting down what the candidate had for breakfast, how he did his hair, what his children thought of him. But it was the dramatic mode of forward action and anticipated surprise that took hold most firmly in the press, as reporters, charging from event to event, learned to set up the conditions for an endless sequence of amazing developments. By 1972, the battle story no longer covered a *campaign* analogous to Roosevelt's foray into Cuba. Now it reported politics as war, where the outcome of today's battle is the setting for tomorrow's. The press's overwhelming emphasis on the fortunes of that war—the exciting ups and downs of the struggle—nearly blanked out what the war was about, the choice of a President. Instead, the coverage focused on the fleeting surfaces, the images in motion as events tumbled across the calendar. Larger and longer-range considerations of meaning and purpose blurred off the edge of the page; deeper considerations of motive and character were skimmed over. Journalism had discovered a new toy, the wind-it-up running story of politics on the go, the dash through the interconnected maze of polls, primaries, conventions, campaign, and election. In 1972, the consequence was not trivial. Thanks in part to this new obsession, we The People put back into office that November a President who would go down in history as a willful butcher of thousands, a subverter of the Constitution, and the only President ever to resign in the face of certain impeachment and conviction.

Nixon Out Front and Out Back

Part of the problem for the press was that as President the Republican contender, Richard Nixon, was old copy. He had been on the Presidential scene for a score of years. His record had been dissected by the press, discovered and rediscovered ad nauseam: gunfighting smear artist in his first race for Congress in 1946 and then for the Senate in 1950, Eisenhower's Vice-Presidential hit man in 1952 and 1956, loser for the Presidency in 1960 and for governor of California in 1962 ("You won't have Nixon to kick around any more"), winning candidate for President in 1968 in the wake of the Democrats' Vietnam debacle. That last startling victory, a triumph of modern imagemaking, had played on journalism's amnesia and hope for novelty. By 1972, the New Nixon was old hat; it would have taken a persuasive reporter indeed to convince his editor that he had anything fundamentally original on Richard Nixon.

Much of the press, especially the center and left periodicals, disdained Nixon. The feeling was mutual. In one month in 1969, Nixon issued to his staff twenty-one confidential requests for counteraction against the reporting of newsmen and columnists. An enterprising young aide named Jeb Stuart Magruder replied with a comprehensive plan to turn the press around—manipulating the Federal Communications Commission by initiating antitrust investigations, getting the IRS to look into their taxes, and other equally vengeful actions. Nixon went into 1972 determined to beat the press at their own game, turning their traditional role into a weakness, exploiting it to his advantage. To get a fight going, reporters wanted to ask him questions, compare him and his stands on issues to the alternatives. But Nixon had learned how dangerous candor could be for him; he simply shut them out. Presidents from Franklin Roosevelt on had averaged at least two dozen press conferences a year. Nixon in the election year of 1972 offered seven. Reporters could not get to him for interviews, instead ruefully trailed him through innocuous ceremonial occasions. "How does the press justify itself this year," wrote David Broder, "if the man who is likely to remain President is allowed to go through the whole campaign without answering questions on his plans for taxes, for wage-price controls, for future policy in Vietnam and a dozen other topics?" But Nixon's nonresponsiveness was a nonstory. Reporters could write once or twice or three times that he was dodging the direct contest, but then their editors would reasonably inquire what else was new.

Not that he was absent from the front pages and television screens. He came on as The President, not as a contender for the office. The press by long tradition had to cover The President in action, so there was Nixon in China, hobnobbing with the mandarins at the Great Wall and over toasts at the banquet table; just as the primary season started in February, there he was off to the Soviet Union and Iran and Poland in May, the Leader of the Free World receiving the tributes of his fellow rulers, exuding statesmanlike dignity and firmness. Visiting back home, on occasion, he took newsworthy Presidential actions, demanding that Congress stop busing for racial integration, calling off the Vietnam peace talks, bombing Hanoi, mining Haiphong harbor, signing an arms treaty with the Soviets, announcing a $750,000,000 grain deal, dispatching Henry Kissinger to Paris, vetoing the HEW appropriation for $30.5 billion, and accepting his party's nomination for President at a precisely scripted national convention in Miami. Like Zeus, he perched atop his office and hurled the press an occasional thunderbolt. All that *had* to be covered, and every gracious reception and official action presented Nixon as he wanted himself presented, as The President.

Meanwhile, across the street from the White House, the Committee to Re-elect the President (dubbed "CREEP") waged an entirely different campaign, a secret fight with no holds barred. Hundreds of thousands of dollars, in cash and in carefully "laundered" (source-obscured) checks from great corporations, fueled that fight. Ambassadorships were auctioned, quiet promises of protection delivered. A special office in the Internal Revenue Service, operating under "Red Seal Security," was turned loose on the tax returns of "enemy" newsmen, on political activists, and Democratic candidates. Wiretappers listened in on the whole range of "enemies," including journalists, and the *New York Times* would eventually report that the Secret Service agents assigned to Nixon's Democratic opponent regularly slipped the White House inside reports on the other party. Phony polls and petitions were manufactured; fake letters published accusing opposition candidates of everything from race prejudice to homosexuality; hecklers and demonstrators were hired—the whole sorry swamp of fraud, forgery, and disruption the later Watergate investigations would uncover, too late to turn the election tide, demonstrating the depths to which a determined Chief Executive could sink in corrupting political controversy. Nixon had good reason to think he could get away with it: the year before, one of his bands of sneak thieves had broken into the office of a psychiatrist who had treated antiwar activist Daniel Ellsberg, rifled his files, and got away totally undetected. As 1972 opened, a press distracted by campaign whoop-de-doo in the colorful countryside lacked the opportunity and incentive to dig out the complex facts of Nixon's Mafia-style operations. Besides, who would have believed them? Nixon's alley campaign went on in the dark. Privately—but only privately—the President called it a war. Thus Nixon played his hand: stonewall the press, feed them imperial drama, and cut down the opposition with your secret police, blackmailers, and saboteurs.

Nixon had reason to run scared. Elected in 1968 in an election of conciliation by a nation longing for a surcease of anxiety, he had plunged deeper and deeper into war in Vietnam. In the spring of 1970, his war adventure in Cambodia fired protest across the country; students were killed at Kent State and Jackson State colleges; antiwar volunteers poured in to elect peace candidates that fall. In the off-year elections the Democrats gained twelve seats in the House and eleven governorships, though they lost two Senate seats. Out of that season arose a new Democratic star to challenge the President: Senator Edmund Muskie of Maine. Muskie looked like a stand-in for Abraham Lincoln; he came on the national scene in Lincoln's persona when, as Humphrey's running mate in 1968, all three network news programs on the evening of September 25 featured his (Lincolnly) mode of handling hecklers. Trying to speak in Washington, Pennsylvania, Muskie was shown being interrupted by shouts of "Stop the war! Stop the war!" Muskie paused. "I will suggest something right now to you young gentlemen," he said. "You pick one of your number to come right up here now, and I'll give him ten minutes of uninterrupted attention." The young gentlemen did that, sending forward a long-haired college boy in dirty jeans, whose tirade soon degenerated into a confused attack on the system. He ran out of steam and Muskie took the mike again. Quietly and steadily, he told the tale of his father, a poor boy from Poland, a humble tailor, who came to America "to take up life and to find opportunity for himself and for children who were yet unborn. And the year before he died his son became the first Polish-American ever elected governor of an American state. Now that may not justify the American system to you, but it sure did to him." The crowd cheered, even the students. In a bit easily edited for television brevity, a mini-drama with a beginning, a middle, and an end, Muskie fixed his image. Then he disappeared in the wreckage of 1968. He reappeared two years later, Lincoln reborn. On November 2, 1970, Nixon appeared on the screen in a ragged rage, haranguing a partisan crowd for half an hour. Muskie, picked by the Democrats to respond, came on. He was sitting in a rocking chair in a Maine kitchen. Coolly, sadly, he spoke of "those who seek to turn our common distress to partisan advantage . . . with empty threat, and malicious slander." The contrast was striking: Nixon as the desperate challenger, Muskie as the patient, correcting father. By January of 1972, Muskie was way up there in the Gallup Poll, neck and neck with Nixon, 42 to 42.

By 1972, the nation was ready for another partisan conflict, a debate about alternatives against the background of *relative* political stability. The chaos of 1968—civil disorder, demonstrations, the assassinations of Martin Luther King, Jr., and Robert Kennedy—was four years old, fading in memory especially among the newly enfranchised masses of new young voters. In civil rights, the fury of black urban rioting ("Burn, Baby, Burn!") had been transformed into a white political issue: busing, a matter of how to achieve racial integration without harming white education. Ending the war, too, had been translated from a question of "whether" to a question of "how": even as he bombed Vietnamese urban centers, Nixon claimed to be first among the peacemakers, with his own secret plan to end the carnage. Radical population shifts—shuffling where people lived and how they made a living—enlivened the sense of what's-in-it-for-me? politics, as old loyalties to place and calling eroded. Not since 1960 had the time seemed more propitious for a contest of policies, as distinguished from principles and palliatives.

The press's problem as 1972 opened was that the shape of the contest looked so obvious: Nixon vs. Muskie in the fall. What to write about in the winter and spring? The Republican picture offered all the excitement of a Victorian wake. Nixon's challenger in New Hampshire, liberal Representative John M. Ashbrook, was getting nowhere; the polls predicted a massive Nixon win. The Democratic scene was another big ho-hum to the busloads of reporters assigned to New Hampshire: Muskie had it sewed up. A New Englander with plenty of money, an experienced staff, and the endorsements of many big Democratic names, Muskie in January could be expected to garner 65 percent of the New Hampshire vote, according to a *Boston Globe* poll. Yawning before the reporters was a great chasm of emptiness and ennui, the terrifying prospect of Nothing Happening.

Into that vacuum stepped a new character, George Stanley McGovern, who, with a lot of help from the journalistic imagination, would spark to life a contest worth covering. In the beginning he was scarcely noticed, and when he was, the adjective the press assigned him was "mild-mannered." His amazing rise and fall furnished the battle story of 1972. Essentially a moralist, McGovern was drafted by fight-hungry journalism for the role of Teddy Roosevelt. What he meant to say got lost in what he was made to mean.

The Deacon from Dakota

The other favorite adjective for McGovern was "decent." He grew up far from America's corrupting coasts, in Mitchell, South Dakota. His father was a Methodist minister, his mother a lady of legendary gentleness. George's life was an outdoor life, a working life, and from it and his parents he took his character and worldview and style. Father—nearly an old man when George came along—fixed in the son's mind a goal and a defense, the goal in a line of Scripture leading off a list of them he would hang on the wall in his Senate office: "Whosoever shall save his life shall lose it, and whosoever shall lose his life for my sake shall find it." The defense came in fatherly conversation. "There was a phrase he always used," grown-up George would remember, " 'making the best use of your time.' He said you couldn't make the best use of your time if you were going to live by fear. That was his message to me: I couldn't be the kind of person who would let fear get me down." From his mother came the sweetness of disposition idealized in the second of his listed Scriptures, "What doth the Lord require of thee, but to do justly, and to love mercy, and to walk humbly with thy God." George started off as the shy son; his brother Larry contributed the dramatics. But George was getting ready. At the dinner table he listened while the Reverend McGovern lambasted the Democrats (except one, Franklin D. Roosevelt) and lauded the Republicans.

As it did for so many other politicians-to-be, high-school debating freed him to speak out, aggressively, past his inhibitions. "It really changed my life, no question about it," he said much later. "If I had not gone out for debate, there is not a chance in the world, in my opinion, that I would have ever come to the United States Senate. It was the one thing that I could do well. It really became the only instrument of personal and social power that I had." It won him a scholarship to little Dakota Wesleyan University, close enough that he could live at home. He was elected class president. In 1942 he won the South Dakota Peace Oratory Contest with a speech on "My Brother's Keeper." In February 1943, he came home from a five-state tournament, where he was named "best debater," to be welcomed at the bus stop by the college president himself—who handed him his draft notice.

As a student, McGovern had taken flying lessons; from the first to last, flying scared him silly. The army, scanning his record and ignorant of his emotions, shipped him off to flight school in Oklahoma, and in February 1944, Lt. McGovern reported for duty at an airbase in Cerignola, Italy, halfway down the boot. They put him in charge of a crew of eight flying a B-24, dubbed the *Dakota Queen*, a speedy but vulnerable type of aircraft the oldtimers called a "flying coffin." He flew thirty-five missions, never missing one, even the day in December 1944, when word came that his father was dead. Bucking the odds, McGovern began to get a reputation for bringing the *Dakota Queen* home, whether or not in one piece. The worst memory was of a 400-bomber raid on the massive ammunition works at Pilsen, Czechoslovakia. An hour short of the target, one engine gave out; they continued with the other three. Thirty seconds before the drop point, another engine blew a cylinder. They dropped the bombs and McGovern ordered the crew to prepare to bail out. At the last moment, the control worked and he was able to stop the wildly spinning propeller. "Resume your stations," he ordered. "We're going to try to bring her home." They drifted out of formation over Yugoslavia, dodging flak as they lost altitude at the rate of a hundred feet a minute. They came out over the Adriatic at six hundred feet and still falling; quickly they threw out everything grabbable—chart tables, guns, and ammunition. Suddenly a tiny island came into view, its miniature airstrip, littered with burnt-out planes, ending abruptly in a mountain. McGovern took the one chance they had. He set the wheels down on the runway and stood on the brakes, skidding to a stop yards short of the mountain. The crew piled out barely in time to see another B-24 crash and explode. "First Lieutenant George McGovern, 22, Mitchell, S.D.," was awarded the Distinguished Flying Cross for "intrepid spirit, outstanding ability, and rare devotion to duty."

Back home with his wife Eleanor, and their new baby, Ann, McGovern slowly got over nightmares of crashing planes and falling bodies and went back to school. Again he won the Peace Oratory Contest, arguing "The practical men have had inning after inning in which they have constantly piled up a higher and higher score on the side of war and chaos at home and abroad. . . . As long as men continue to scoff at idealism, at spirituality, at such ideas as international corporation through the United World Government, and continue to advance the notion of expediency and material gain, just so long will we continue to reap the tragic harvest of so-called practical men." He went off to theological seminary in Evanston and served for awhile as a student minister, but before long switched to history, wrote a dissertation on the Ludlow massacre of miners and their families in Colorado in 1914, and came back to Dakota Wesleyan to teach history. Along the way, in a fit of idealism, he was a delegate to Henry Wallace's 1948 Progressive party convention—just long enough to see what the "fanatics" were doing to Wallace. He wrote letters to the editor on behalf of Democrats and made a few speeches around town. In 1952, he picked the name for their new baby, Steven, after Adlai Stevenson, Democrat for President. That fall, he lost out to an Ivy Leaguer for a job at Iowa State and Stevenson lost to Eisenhower. The reasonable thing was to make a go of the good solid job he already had; instead, he resigned to be executive secretary of the South Dakota Democratic party, a sparsely populated organization generally considered harmless because irrelevant.

By 1956, McGovern had built an organization sufficiently strong to send him to Congress; in 1958 he was reelected in a race against hapless Governor Joe Foss, whose own dog tried to bite him on television. In 1960 he set out to unseat mossback Senator Karl Mundt; when he lost by 15,000 votes he comforted his sad backers with, "Well, at least we won a moral victory." President Kennedy appointed him director of the new Food for Peace program and in 1962, he ran for the Senate and this time won—by two-tenths of one percent of the vote. Yet almost at once he challenged the administration's Cuba policy, in a speech unnoticed by all of the press except the *Sioux Falls Argus-Leader*. As early as 1963 he spoke on "the failure of our Vietnam policy." But then Kennedy was killed and Johnson took over; McGovern continued to express his criticisms, but he voted for Johnson's blank-check Tonkin Gulf Resolution in 1964. In 1968, very late to the game, McGovern was nominated for President in a speech by Senator Abraham Ribicoff, whose remarks were mainly noted for his attack on Chicago's Mayor Richard Daley, whose police were busily bludgeoning peace demonstrators in the streets outside McGovern's downtown hotel. That night McGovern looked out the window and his anger welled up—"Do you see what those sons of bitches are doing to those kids down there? Those bastards."

His slow burn over Vietnam continued to build. As early as November 1965, McGovern went to Vietnam for three weeks, paying his own way, visiting the wounded, listening to what they said. He came back to Mitchell and told the homefolks, "I will never forget it as long as I live"—the napalmed, the blank-eyed boys with their legs blown off. By April of 1967 he was calling the war "a policy of madness" and "the most tragic diplomatic and moral failure in our nation's history." He came from a conservative state; he knew the risks, but, he told the Senate, "The people of a state can easily secure a new Senator, but a Senator cannot easily secure a new conscience." He visited the President and saw Lyndon Johnson crumble into a rambling, incoherent wreck—so much so that McGovern wanted to comfort him. But in December 1969 he called for an immediate ceasefire and withdrawal—"It is long past time to quit saving face and begin saving lives." Nixon, the new President, kept the heat on. On March 17, 1970, McGovern demanded of the Senate, "In the name of decency and common sense, there must be no more continuation of the present war policy, however disguised in rhetoric or more hollow predictions of victory yet to come." The silence of the Senate reaction was "deafening," he said. But out in the country, especially among the young, protest was building. McGovern was speaking to large crowds of them, joining in their marches, though he spoke against violence at home as well as in Vietnam. His stock in South Dakota plummeted. In March of 1970, McGovern's ace aide John Holum drafted legislation to cut off all funds for Vietnam by June 30, 1971. On May 1, 1970, Nixon revealed that the United States had invaded Cambodia. All over the country, campuses erupted in protest, some of it violent, and thousands of nonstudents joined the marches. The cut-off legislation was introduced; in the summer of 1970 it became the rallying point for petitions and appeals and intensive lobbying efforts as new thousands sought some way, within the system, to mark an end to the carnage. Shortly before the vote in September, McGovern stood in the Senate and said:

This chamber reeks of blood. Every Senator here is partly responsible for that human wreckage at Walter Reed and Bethesda Naval and all across our land—young boys without legs, or arms, or genitals, or faces, or hopes. There aren't very many of these blasted and broken boys who think this was a glorious venture. Don't talk to them about bugging out, or national honor. It doesn't take courage at all for a Congressman, or a Senator or a President to wrap himself in the flag and say we're staying in Vietnam. Because it isn't our blood that is being shed. But we are responsible for those young men and their lives and their hopes. And if we don't end this foolish, damnable war, those young men will someday curse us for our pitiful willingness to let the Executive carry the burden the Constitution puts on us.*

The legislation failed, 55 to 39. McGovern had thought 40 votes in favor would have been enough for a moral victory.

At least a year before that vote in September 1970, McGovern had decided to run for President in 1972; he told that to Haynes Johnson of the *Washington Post* in December 1969—but phoned Johnson the next day to squelch the story already rolling out of his typewriter. The negative basis for his decision when to run was the lack of viable alternatives. Prophetic Senators Wayne Morse and Ernest Gruening had spoken out earlier, lonely, helpless voices against the war tide. Robert Kennedy had been gunned down in 1968 and on July 19, 1969, a young campaign worker was drowned in a car driven by Edward Kennedy, whose behavior sharply damaged his reputation. Hubert Humphrey, beaten by Nixon in 1968 and tarred by his long and fervent support of Johnson's war, seemed unlikely for 1972. Senator Eugene McCarthy had had the leadership of the antiwar forces foisted upon him in 1968, but now seemed old hat, demoralized. McCarthy "lacked a sense of moral outrage," said McGovern. So the old "why not me?" feeling bestirred itself again, urged on by a growing popularity, especially among frustrated youth and appalled adults determined to stop the war. Speaking invitations flooded in; in 1969 alone McGovern made $70,000 in honoraria. His media-wise friends began to spruce up his image, getting him out of those "shiny brown suits from Sears" and the ankle socks that exposed his naked shanks as he sat on platforms, pressing him to get some professional help for his nasal twang. Organizationally, McGovern was both hurt and helped by his reluctant acceptance of the leadership of the Democratic party's Reform Commission, a reaction against the overwhelming domination of the 1968 convention by radically unrepresentative delegations typically composed of white male elders selected by local party bosses in obscure and early machinations. Hearings were held around the country, infuriating politicians North and South, but attracting to McGovern the press's attention and a corps of young, talented enthusiasts. McGovern was adamant: "I do not ever again want to see another convention like the one in 1968," he said. The reformers eventually decided to recommend for 1972 that delegations from primary states be composed to reflect the primary vote rather than giving all the votes to the winning candidate, as was traditional. They required that delegates be picked in the year of the convention and—most

* Quoted in Robert Sam Anson, *McGovern: A Biography* (New York: Holt, Rinehart & Winston, 1972), pp. 177–78.

significantly for 1972—that minorities, women, and youth be represented "in reasonable relationship to the group's presence in the population of the states." McGovern was thus instrumental in opening up the party to Democrats shunted aside by the old process—which brought him their support as it alienated the Old Guard. Then there were the primaries; there would be twenty-three of them in 1972, sprawling through the springtime, eight new ones, so that more than two-thirds of the 1972 delegates would be picked in primary votes. McGovern had sprung up from the grass roots, building a following from nothing along the South Dakota highways. If anyone could catch the chance the primaries offered, argued his advisers, McGovern could.

These pressures from the outside got to him. But pressure from the inside thrust him across the line to candidacy. Not averse to the glories of power, McGovern was nevertheless essentially a moralist. As he saw it then, Vietnam was but a symptom of an appalling moral malaise, which had hardened the hearts of the American leadership against their more decent impulses—to bind up the wounds, to feed the hungry, to join justice and humility and mercy in a new surge of national progress. When he announced his candidacy on January 18, 1971, he said that Americans were not seeking an ideological answer of the left or right, but "a way out of the wilderness." He urged that "we try to evoke the 'better angels' of our nature." The campaign he sought would be a revival, a spiritual experience whereby the people would lift their sights and amend their ways.

"Can a Good Man Win?" asked *Nation* magazine. Not in 1972, history would answer. For decent, mild-mannered George McGovern was a man for a different season. He was headed into a cutting party. 1972 would want a fight, not a sermon. Another four years later, the country would be ready for a moralist in the White House. But not yet. In 1972, the press and McGovern himself would lift him up in such a way as to ensure his downfall.

Parcheesi Politics

McGovern stalked into New Hampshire virtually unnoticed by the press; despite more than a year of active campaigning, his poll standing made him dismissable, confirming Joseph Alsop's view of him a year previous as an "amiable and virtuous shallow-pate." All he had going for him was the war issue and some enthusiastic canvassers. The real story had to be about Muskie, but he held an apparently overwhelming advantage. How could the press craft a story from a foregone conclusion?

Journalism found a way. Speculation turned from *whether* Muskie would win to *by how much*—especially in comparison to how well he could be "expected" to win. The development and elaboration of that expectation turned a nonstory into a running story, a foregone conclusion into a battle— Muskie against the number. Muskie's people saw it happening and tried to head it off. One of them called a 65 percent expectation "absurd"; Muskie himself argued that "it's the guy who gets the most votes who wins." But he hedged: "The significance of the victory may depend on the size of my own vote." On January 9, the *Washington Post*'s David Broder set the benchmark. Muskie and Nixon "must not only win, but win with a large enough percentage of the vote that the press acknowledges it to be a victory." The press? Muskie himself acknowledged as much, Broder reported, saying, "New Hampshire is important to me, in part, because you gentlemen of the press have undertaken to make it important . . . in order to test me." Broder then locked onto a number: "As the acknowledged frontrunner and a resident of the neighboring state, Muskie will have to win the support of at least half the New Hampshire Democrats in order to claim a victory." The word zipped around. ABC called 50 percent Muskie's "magic figure," CBS said anything less than that "is going to be interpreted by the press and politicians as a setback." R. W. Apple of the *New York Times* wrote on February 14 that the numbers game "is being played here with unusual intensity, and it puts the news media in the position of arbiters. It is they who are being asked to decide, in advance, what percentage would constitute a 'real win' for Mr. Muskie." Apple did not report who was asking. Editors, one might suppose, hungry for copy. Apple said the national news correspondents "are uneasy about the game. Yet a consensus seems to be emerging around the magic 50 percent; it is cited in more and more articles and broadcasts."

Meantime, McGovern, his squads of canvassers out pounding on voters' doors, lay back. An early poll had shown him at 6 percent, now the national Gallup poll had him at a measly 3. Bravely his supporters said 20 percent for McGovern would amount to a "moral victory."

An increasingly edgy Muskie campaigned on. Not surprisingly, given the content of the coverage, reporters Broder and Haynes Johnson began to find citizens who were uncertain what Muskie stood for. New Hampshire's own dominant newspaper, the *Manchester Union Leader*, regular daily fare for 40 percent of New Hampshire's voters and clearly one of the oddest right-wing rags in the country, had no such doubts about "Senator 'Flip-Flop' Muskie, the Vietnam War hawk-dove-chicken" whose position "is found to be virtually identical to that of the Viet Cong." On February 24, the *Union Leader*'s editorial was headlined "Sen. Muskie Insults Franco-Americans"—based on a letter, probably forged and sent by Nixon's agents in Florida, quoting Muskie as amused by a reference to "cannocks." Franco-Americans made up about a quarter of the Democratic vote in New Hampshire. Panic hit the Muskie camp. Muskie himself determined to speak to the matter in front of the *Union Leader* building the next day. That morning the *Union Leader* reprinted an old gossip story quoting Mrs. Muskie asking reporters to tell dirty jokes, cussing, chewing gum, smoking, and analyzing her hangovers. A furious Muskie stood on a flatbed truck in the falling snow and laced into "this rotten newspaper." When he got to the part about his wife, he choked up, his voice broke, and he stopped. He appeared to be weeping, Broder's story led, "With tears streaming down his face and his voice choked with emotion. . . ." On the CBS Evening News the next night, there was President Nixon with Chinese Premier Chou En-lai, colorfully feeding goldfish from the moon bridge in Hangchow, and then there was Muskie, falling apart in the gray of New Hampshire.

On February 29, Broder wrote of the "erosion in the presumed front-runner's strength that could leave the Maine senator with an embarrassingly low percentage of the vote in the March 7 Democratic primary he has counted on to send his presidential campaign off on a flying start." The networks quickly picked up "erosion." On primary day, some 86,000 New Hampshire people voted. Muskie was reported as having won 48 percent, McGovern 37 percent. The interpretations were predictable. McGovern happily claimed a "moral victory." The New York Times said he had shown "a strong challenge." The Washington Post called it "surprising strength" in contrast to Muskie's failure to get the 50 percent "that would give momentum to his nomination drive." Meeting the press the next morning, Muskie blew up when reporters kept asking him how the New Hampshire results would affect his chances in the next contest—Florida. "I can't tell you that," he snapped. "You tell me and you'll tell the rest of the country because you interpret this victory. This press conference is my only chance to interpret it, but you'll probably even misinterpret that."

In raw votes, Muskie had licked McGovern by a comfortable margin. But McGovern's leap past his expectation made him news. As Newsweek put it that May: "His past failure to make a splash now lends his candidacy an unusual freshness in view of the fact that he has been in the field for almost sixteen months; McGovern is both the tortoise and the hare of this election year." In the new political Parcheesi game, scoring against the board of expectations laid out by the press, McGovern had now sprung to the lead. And that is the way it went through the springtime. Reporters who sensed how farcical the last primary had been kept hoping the next one would prove something. In Florida, the Wall Street Journal's Allen Otten set up the fight. Florida would be "crucial" to Senator Henry Jackson, Muskie would need "a win or a very strong second showing," McGovern "does need to score high in some of the university areas and in Miami, where he is concentrating his efforts." In the event, the big surprise was Alabama's George Wallace—way out with nearly 42 percent, more than Humphrey, Jackson, and Muskie combined, and therefore, said CBS, "real" and "a national Democratic candidate, to be taken seriously by the politicians and the voters in the primaries ahead."

McGovern got a mere 6.1 percent of the votes in Florida. In Wisconsin, the handicappers were hard at it again. The Gallup poll of Wisconsin Democrats on the eve of the primary had McGovern at 5 percent. The next day he came in with nearly 30 percent of the votes cast, sweeping the field. He was on the way, suddenly a surprise in his own right. No one made much of the fact that the polls, based on questions brought to the citizen's doorstep, had been so wildly out of line with the vote, which requires the citizen to make his way to a polling place—in Wisconsin, with a lot of help from young manager Gene Pokorny's hordes of canvassers. The results were further distorted by Wisconsin's weird system: Republicans could vote in the Democratic primary, and thousands did. There being no contest to speak of in their party, they accounted for nearly a third of McGovern's vote and half of George Wallace's.

In less than a month, readers groggy with predictions and percentages could trace through fourteen more primaries and then, on June 6, California–New Mexico–South Dakota–New Jersey, the season dragging to a halt with New York on June 20. Not until halfway down the list—Nebraska, on May 9—was McGovern labeled the front-runner before the vote. In California his old friend Hubert Humphrey lit into him, but contrary to a wildly mistaken preelection poll, McGovern edged him out. The *New York Times* reported on election day that "Senator McGovern, a very distant dark horse to most political analysts only three months ago, has made his startling rise to frontrunner status the most newsworthy political story of 1972."

But the battle was not over. Beaten in California, Humphrey had at first agreed that McGovern should get all those votes, as California rules provided. But then, leaning on the Reform Commission's guidelines, he demanded his share. So did Mayor Daley for fifty-eight Illinois delegates. In tough struggles, McGovern won both fights. But Humphrey held back his endorsement, as did Muskie, and Mayor Daley went away mad. "The Democrats," wrote Broder, "could not bear to wait for Miami Beach to blow their convention and their party sky-high. . . . The broader consequence, many Democrats agreed last night, was to inflame the deep wounds within their party and reduce the likelihood of anyone leading it to victory over Richard Nixon in the fall." The delegates, picked by the new youth-blacks-and-women guidelines, looked different—"like the cast of *Hair*," according to one disgruntled oldster. Reporters, especially the television types now locked in a battle for ratings as Hearst and Pulitzer had battled for circulation, kept alive the suspense of convention coverage. "We'll beat the ass off them!" said CBS's Bob Wussler—meaning the other networks. "We'll beat the ass off them," echoed NBC's Dick Wald. ABC's Walter Pfister expanded the contest's vocabulary: "We're the wave of the future," he said. Up in their anchor booths and down on the floor, they chased and imagined developments by which McGovern could lose. He won on the first ballot, overwhelmingly.

With all the fights about contested delegations, there had not been time for the careful screening of Vice-Presidential candidates the McGovern campaign had planned, but his choice, Senator Thomas Eagleton, seemed generally acceptable.

Indeed, the timing of the whole convention had been thrown off.

McGovern gave his acceptance speech at 2:48 A.M., to a television audience of only 3,600,000 loyal souls.

Eagleton, Watergate

For many of those, at least, it was worth staying up for.

With a full heart I accept your nomination.

My nomination is all the more precious in that it is the gift of the most open political process in our national history. It is the sweet harvest cultivated by tens of thousands of tireless volunteers—old and young—and funded by literally hundreds of thousands of small contributors. Those who lingered on the edge of despair a brief time ago have been brought into this campaign—heart, hand, head, and soul.

I have been the beneficiary of the most remarkable political organization in American history—an organization that gives dramatic proof to the power of love and to a faith that can move mountains. As Yeats put it: "Count where man's glory most begins and ends, and say my glory was I had such friends."

The sentences rolled on, calling for truth, reconciliation, peace at last, justice, and a decent job—clearly the strongest rhetoric McGovern had ever risen to. And at the end came his highest hope:

So join with me in this campaign. Lend me your strength and support—and together, we will call America home to the ideals that nourished us in the beginning.

From secrecy, and deception in high places, come home, America.

From a conflict in Indochina which maims our ideals as well as our soldiers, come home, America. . . .

Come home to the affirmation that we have a dream.

Come home to the conviction that we can move our country forward.

Come home to the belief that we can seek a newer world. . . .

May God grant us the wisdom to cherish this good land, and to meet the challenge that beckons us home.

This is the time.*

As it turned out, 1972 was *not* the time. McGovern's speech mentioned Richard Nixon only twice, almost in passing.

From the opening of the year, McGovern had been describing, in unusual detail, what he would do as President on taxes, defense, civil rights, Vietnam—to the infinite boredom of a journalistic fraternity consumed with the new Parcheesi game. In his typically somewhat stilted speaking style, he had tried to get a conversation going about alternatives, posed in the light of a moral vision a cut above that of recent Presidents. But that was not a fight, that was a deliberation, and in 1972 the press wanted a fight. McGovern's rise, based primarily on his identification as an antiwar candidate and on the consequent labors of thousands of volunteer canvassers, had provided drama

---

* George McGovern, *An American Journey: The Presidential Campaign Speeches of George McGovern* (New York: Random House, 1974), pp. 17–24.

of sorts, but at the cost of substance. In Nixon's virtual absence, the political war story of 1972, translated into an elaborate game of expectations, rendered the general election campaign itself redundant. For the nomination McGovern had won was won at the cost of a hopelessly wounded party, torn to shreds in the combat preceding it.

Meanwhile, back in the Nixon camp, a minor accident suddenly threw the secret campaign into a panic. At 2:30 A.M. on June 17, 1972, a night watchman at the offices of the Democratic National Committee happened to notice that a door latch had been taped open. He did not think much of it; he took the tape off and continued his rounds. When twenty minutes later he came back and found the tape replaced, he decided to call the police. They came and arrested five cowering burglars, in coats and ties and wearing blue surgical gloves. Alfred E. Lewis, veteran *Washington Post* police reporter, phoned in the story, noting that the footpads had in their hotel room an array of break-in tools, cameras, radio and wiretap equipment, a wig, and more than $5,000 in cash. The next day the *Post* put "5 Held in Plot to Bug Democrat Party Office" on page one. Two young city reporters, Bob Woodward and Carl Bernstein, got onto the story; the following day they reported that a "GOP security aide" was among the arrestees.

Knowing what they knew of the range and extent of their clandestine campaign, the Nixon chiefs broke into a collective sweat and quickly moved to hide the fact that the sneak thieves were CREEPers. The President promptly recommended "counterattack," a "PR offensive" to "hit the opposition" for the sake of "diversion," as he put it to his top aide H. R. Haldeman. His press secretary dismissed the break-in as "a third-rate burglary attempt." In terms of electoral politics in 1972, the cover-up succeeded. The *New York Times* initially ran the Watergate break-in story on page thirty. Nearly a month after the incident, the *Washington Star* reported that the burglars, three of whom were Cubans, had been financed by "a right-wing group of anti-Castro Cubans." The event was straight out of "Mission Impossible": Nixon boss John Mitchell had it right in his first private reaction— "It's incredible!" As late as early October, with the election a month away, only about half the public had even heard of the Watergate break-in and four out of five dismissed it as not a strong reason to vote for McGovern. By October 19th, three-fourths of those polled knew what "Watergate" meant, but 62 percent agreed the matter was "just politics."

The Nixon campaign headquarters, as a source of spontaneous news, clamped shut. A uniformed guard met visitors at the door, got their credentials checked, and escorted them personally to and then from their appointments. Even the telephone list at CREEP was secret; a staffer who leaked a copy pleaded, "I'll lose my job if they find out." Suddenly everything was hierarchical and official—and the official line that nothing was wrong held tight.

No wonder then that reporters vied for assignment to the McGovern campaign, where leaks poured forth in abundance, from the half-dozen rival claimants to chieftainship as well as from the newest phone-jockey and one-finger typist. It was the only show in town, put on by a fervent believer in "open politics." Then, in August, developed a hot story of Democratic folly, which, unlike the hidden Nixon knavery, splashed splendidly across the front pages and television screens.

In the heat of the Democratic convention, no one had had time to think hard about who should be the Vice-Presidential candidate. In hurried consultation, a near-random list was quickly boiled down from ten names (including Walter Cronkite) to one, Senator Thomas Eagleton of Missouri. A phone call brought his happy and immediate consent and his reply to a question he may well have thought jocular: no, there was nothing in his past to worry about. But rumors to the contrary soon sprang up. Jack Anderson published a column hinting that Eagleton had been repeatedly arrested for drunk driving. That was not true, but soon *Time* magazine and the Knight newspapers got onto a lead that led somewhere: Eagleton had been hospitalized three times, most recently in 1966, for nervous exhaustion, during two of which he had received electric-shock therapy. He had not been totally candid with the press back then; the public explanations mentioned stomach trouble. But six years had gone by since the last incident. He now told McGovern he had recovered, had learned to pace himself. McGovern, a forgiving soul, not only absolved Eagleton when the story became public, he said he would have chosen him anyhow and that he backed him "1,000 percent." But this news sunk in: an ex-mental patient might have his finger on the nuclear button. The press, never mind the public, was not ready for that, not yet able to see that the man might really have recovered, perhaps stronger for the ordeal. Eagleton had to go. Inside the campaign organization, a confused battle raged; some leaders felt Eagleton had lied to them. The confusion fed the story as McGovern backed and filled, torn between necessity and loyalty. Through the normally news-dead days of August the story ran on. At last Eagleton left the ticket and speculation centered on his replacement. After Edward Kennedy, Abraham Ribicoff, Lawrence O'Brien, Hubert Humphrey, and Reuben Askew turned him down (which McGovern promptly admitted to the press), McGovern tried Muskie, who also refused, and landed at last on ex-Peace Corps director and Kennedy brother-in-law Sargent Shriver, who accepted. The circus ground to a resting place. That week *Time* put McGovern and Shriver on the cover; *Newsweek*'s cover story was on Chinese acupuncture; at the newsstands, acupuncture won in a walk.

That news-spawning fiasco over, another quickly appeared. McGovern, ever dedicated to peace in Vietnam, got a message that the North Vietnamese wanted to talk with his representative. He sent Pierre Salinger to Paris to do that. Returning to New York, Salinger was preceded by a UPI report that he—a private citizen and aide of the opposition candidate—had entered into negotiations with the enemy at McGovern's direction, an apparent violation of a law that went back to 1799. McGovern first denied it, then admitted he had known Salinger was going, but that he had given him no instructions. The impression of chaos and deception was confirmed.

The chaos and deception rampant inside the Nixon campaign was concealed under heavy wraps. On August 21, 1972, the Republicans met in Miami to play out their carefully scripted convention, a "coronation" the press called it, a political drama Theodore White found "dull, harmonious controlled, listless, pleasant, torpid, jovial—above all prim"—and above all that, another news vacuum. Time's Hugh Sidey saw the delegates as "chips from the national foundation"; Eric Sevareid of CBS found them "middle class, middle aged, middle brow"—some comedown, in terms of drama, from the various and accident-prone Democrats. Nixon was offered to America by Nelson Rockefeller (who knew better) as "this man of action, this man of accomplishment, this man of experience, this man of courage, we need this man of faith in America." Accepting, Nixon advertised a "new majority," ready to make the right choice "between change that works and change that won't work," counterpoising the Democrats' "politics of paternalism" against his "politics of people." A saccaharine film biography followed. A journalist, noting his colleagues' silence, recognized that "Nixon's world wasn't our world—we were out of it."

Los Angeles Times reporter Jules Witcover caught what that estrangement meant in 1972: "Because McGovern was the only Presidential candidate in the field," he wrote, "not only the man but all aspects of his campaign underwent examination beyond that to which most previous candidates had been subjected." The Washington Post's William Greider perceived the season's lesson for the reporters' superiors: "After all, most editors thought Nixon was going to win, so why go out of the way to alienate him." Reporters generally liked McGovern personally, far better than Nixon. But once aboard his campaign, the fight-need took over. All through the year, as McGovern tried again to raise fundamental issues of war and peace, justice and mercy, his larger visons were dissipated into relatively trivial issues upon which Democrats disagreed, such as "amnesty, acid, and abortion"—as if he were running for a Methodist bishopric. While Nixon committed secret crimes, McGovern made public mistakes. The crimes went undiscovered. The mistakes sprawled across the national news.

Right Man, Wrong Time

In October, George McGovern spoke to the students of Wheaton College, a Methodist school in Illinois:

The President can be the great moral leader of the nation. He can ask us to face issues, not merely from a political standpoint but in our conscience and our souls. By his words and deeds the President must witness to the values that should endure among our people. . . .

Power cannot be his only purpose. There is no virtue in simply "being President." A candidate should seek the Presidency to serve the nation and call it to a higher purpose. This is the meaning of true leadership. It is not expressed in power, fame and honor, but in the washing of dusty feet.*

Newsweek, in its preelection issue, headlined "McGovern's Politics of Righteousness," accused McGovern of trying "to preach his way into the Presidency on the once implicit and now open proposition that this election is a contest between good and evil—and that if he loses evil will have won." Joseph Alsop wrote that McGovern seemed to think he was "running against Satan" and that "what seems to McGovern self-evident truth seems to a lot of voters colossal self-righteousness."

On October 26, a dozen days before the election, Nixon's secretary of state informed Americans that peace in Vietnam was "at hand." Newspaper editorial endorsements numbered 753 for Nixon, 56 for McGovern. After the election, Nixon chose Christmastide, 1972, as the time for saturation terror bombing of North Vietnamese urban centers. Not until August 1974 was McGovern's charge that Nixon ruled "the most corrupt and immoral administration in history" confirmed and the President driven in disgrace from the White House.

The press had gone into 1972 looking for a fight. Failing to find one between the parties, they found many within one party. On Halloween night that year, nearly all the national campaign correspondents, punchy with battle fatigue, gathered to party with George McGovern. Now that his defeat seemed certain, they could let their affection for him show. That night they gave him a Tiffany silver bowl they had all chipped in for. The inscription on it read, "Resume your stations. We're bringing her home."

---

* Quoted in Richard Dougherty, *Goodbye Mr. Christian: A Personal Account of McGovern's Rise and Fall* (Garden City: Doubleday, 1973), p. 207.

II

THE POLITICS OF CONSCIENCE

AFTER THE BATTLE OF 1796, the election of 1800 focused on morals—"principles"—and found its focus is the question of character. George Washington was dead; the search for leadership would have to look elsewhere.

"The revolution of 1800," wrote Thomas Jefferson, was "as real a revolution in the principles of our government as that of 1776 was in its form." Jefferson's Republicans asked, *"Is it not high time for a CHANGE?"* Jefferson wanted "a Declaration of the principles of the Constitution, in the nature of a Declaration of Rights." His quarrel with Adams, he later told the President, "is no personal contest between you & me. . . . Its motion is from its principle, not from you or myself." Their differences were profound. Jefferson believed "that man's mind is perfectible to a degree of which we cannot as yet form any conception." Adams thought "the first want of man is his dinner, and the second his girl." But the debate of 1800 was no Socratic dialogue. "There is a shorter mode of deciding between the two classes of candidates," declared a Federalist broadside. "This mode is, to choose the best men. If we cannot confide in good men, it is certain we cannot confide in any."

The issue of Jefferson's religion became the cause célèbre of 1800, outweighing every other issue in the public prints. He was a Deist, whatever that meant; it certainly did not mean Congregationalist or Episcopalian. A Connecticut Federalist wrote, "I do not believe that the Most High will permit a howling atheist to sit at the head of this nation." Hamilton urged action "to prevent an *atheist* in Religion, and a *fanatic* in politics from getting possession of the helm of State." The faithful were urged to hide their Bibles, which a President Jefferson would surely confiscate. To the image of Jefferson the mad French revolutionary was added Jefferson the infidel. But despite the pleas of friends, Jefferson refused to get into the debate about his faith, letting stand his statement, "I have sworn upon the altar of God, eternal hostility against every form of tyranny over the mind of man." After a close and complex decision, resolved in the House of Representatives, Jefferson won the Presidency; he was, he said, gratified that despite "many attempts . . . to obtain terms and promises from me, I have declared to them unequivocally . . . that I would not go into it with my hands tied."

The story of conscience is America's oldest political myth, preceding by more than a century the Revolutionary War, which generated the fighting story, and the Constitution-making period of unity and order. From the Puritan beginning to the present day, American politics draws dramatic tension from the clash of ideal and reality, promise and performance. Ours has always been a *purposive* politics. If the story of conflict gets its excitement from the threat of death, the story of conscience derives its appeal from the fear of death in life: the descent into pride and worldly satisfaction, the loss of moral meaning in the whirl of events.

The fit between our aspirations and the available candidates for President has never been exact. We have had to search out the signs of Presidential grace among the politicians who can be persuaded to present themselves. Given our heritage, it was inevitable that candidates would be assessed not only in what they professed to believe or proposed to perform, but also in who they were—their persons. We developed a drama of discovery: find an honest, decent, capable, undeniably American leader to go to the Capitol and clean up politics. If possible, he should be innocent of "politics" in the pejorative meaning of the word, an innocence ideally indicated by fervent personal preference for a private station, a preference overcome only by the fervor of his sense of duty. If possible, he should be an outsider, sprung from the soil of some American Eden, not some urban Babylon. But the essential thrust of the story of conscience has drawn its force from the tension between the nation's moral commitment and the earthly reality of those persons who claimed to embody it in the Presidency.

Each of the crusaders whose stories are related here was a moralizing outsider. Woodrow Wilson "of Georgia and Virginia" served as governor of New Jersey before he ran for President, but in the popular mind in 1912 he was a professor, not a politician, and, in 1916, a moralist *par excellence*, a champion of principle. Wendell Willkie was no politician, he was a businessman from Elwood, Indiana (and Wall Street), who explicitly distinguished himself from the political regulars, including those in his own party, as he espoused "The Faith That Is America"—he called them "you" and "them" not "we" and "us." Barry Goldwater, senator from far out in Arizona, a maverick defector from Eisenhower orthodoxy, put the dictates of his conscience so high above the muck of politics that he seemed an alien in Washington. Jimmy Carter, of the perfectly named town of Plains, Georgia, kept insisting that he *was* an alien to the failed politics of Washington. Carter found his strongest campaign theme in an appeal for a rebirth of American virtue and Godliness. Other beaters of the moral drum, such as Herbert Hoover the

Great Engineer in 1928 and Dwight David Eisenhower the Great General in 1952, went all out for God and Country and Duty and turned their backs on the "easy" way of ordinary political conniving. These candidates—like some who lost out, Adlai Stevenson primary among them—did not merely stand aside from politics, they stood above politics. Each succeeded in turning the national conversation strongly to questions of virtue and vice. Each sparked a revival of interest in the interplay of personality and policy.

Those revivals owed much to the preachers in the press. That mission flourished most strikingly in magazine journalism, although it emerged from time to time in the newspaper press and even in television, as with Edward R. Murrow in his crusade against Joe McCarthy. Magazining on a national scale got underway in the nineteenth century—preceded by pamphleteering in the eighteenth—but it took off, in terms of mass circulation and political influence, in that twentieth-century era of moralistic reformism that culminated in Wilson's reign. The "muckrakers"—actually positive thinkers out to build America, not destroy reputations—set the moral tone and, as important, found in the factual biography a way to make morals sell like beer in the bleachers. Magazine editors got directly into Presidential politics; one brought Wilson along, another fostered Hoover, behind the scenes as well as in the pages of their journals. After the Great War, magazine moralists experimented with new forms and modes, the most successful of which gave shape to *Time*—the news of the week as homily. *Time* blossomed in the Great Depression; in 1940 its God-haunted editor Henry Luce, son of Presbyterian missionaries, undertook to make Willkie President; failing in that, *Time* turned to Eisenhower in 1952. Barry Goldwater, perhaps the first Presidential candidate brought forward by a real public-relations expert, ran up against another, different collection of modern-day Puritans, led by the columnists and editors of the *New York Times*, who judged him comparatively evil and found in Lyndon Johnson a comparatively virtuous alternative. By 1976, journalists in every sort of medium had elaborated new approaches to testing Presidential character, combining morals and psychology; they subjected Jimmy Carter to the whole battery, with markedly mixed results. What held steady through these years in the preaching press was the periodical resurgence of a vision of politics as more than a game, more than a fight, of politics as an essentially moral quest, the search for a good President to lead a good country. Inventive journalists and candidates evolved new ways of telling that story as each new season of conscience followed a season of conflict.

In the Wilson Crusade the candidate himself set out to instruct the world in its ethical responsibilities, but he came into office first in a fighting year, his principles as yet obscure. George Harvey, the editor who sponsored Wilson, eventually broke with him, in a pattern of disillusionment typical not only of Wilson and Harvey but of other relationships between preachers in the press and their preaching candidates. But on the way up,

Wilson and Harvey found one another invaluable, and their alliance produced this century's model of the translation of moral scripture into Presidential reality. Hoover, Wilson's devotee, played out an essentially analogous story with *his* editor-mentor in the moralizing election of 1928. Willkie's story is a product of Henry Luce's story: how a journalist built a myth around one of history's least likely candidates, by a process of celebrification in narrative news. After the Second World War, Eisenhower's indignant assault on Harry Truman's alleged misbehavior—"time for a change," time "to clean up the mess in Washington"—rearoused the moralists, but by 1964, Eisenhower's uncertain preferences opened the way for Barry Goldwater's "conservative" crusade, our century's prime example of political moralism gone wacky with deductive logic. In grand political irony, the nation's moral cognoscenti preferred the "dove" of that year, Lyndon Johnson in his persona as a sensible and skilled professional. A decade of political tragedy followed. Americans, led by their Presidents, descended into a time of cruelty and corruption unique in the nation's history, until they freed themselves by compelling an unscheduled Presidential retirement and a resignation. By 1976, the hunger for moral rejuvenation was abroad in the land again and both Jimmy Carter and Gerald Ford picked up on that theme. The Carter crusade, and its chronicling in the conscience of the press, illustrates how the story of politics as morals had evolved (with a boost from Sigmund Freud) from the revolution of 1800.

7

Woodrow Wilson 1916

WHY HAS JESUS CHRIST so far not succeeded in inducing the world to follow His teachings in these matters," asked Woodrow Wilson of the startled politicians in Paris, as they struggled to patch together a peace after World War I. And he answered, "It is because He taught the ideal without devising any practical means of attaining it. That is why I am proposing a practical scheme to carry out his aims."* Wilson's scheme failed; his own stubbornness helped kill it. But his purpose was "nothing less than the liberation and the salvation of the world," a cause so high that he "would be glad to die that it might be consummated." Long before Wilson went to Paris, he had become just that sort of true believer—this century's brightest and most tragic moralizer in politics.

As Theodore Roosevelt set the pattern for the twentieth-century fighting election, so Woodrow Wilson put in place the century's model of the politics of conscience. His Presidency left a legacy of principle and practical achievement, and then, in the end, of the tragedy that can result when particulars are invested with ultimate moral meaning.

Wilson the moralist first came to Presidential power in a conflict election, the incredible Donnybrook of 1912, as an accidental President who never would have made it had not the opposition Republicans split their forces wide open. The public, diverted by the struggle between Taft and Roosevelt, knew little about him. What they did know of Wilson was brought to them by a conservative magazine editor obsessed with the possibility of bringing true principle to politics by transforming Professor Wilson into President Wilson. No sooner had he succeeded than Wilson turned on him—and on the principles he thought Wilson held dear. In 1916, after a term of remarkable reform, Wilson the moralizing liberal, by then known to one and all, gathered to his political bosom the fervent enthusiasm of the moralizing liberals in journalism: the muckrakers, those champions of the downtrodden against evil corporate power. That year, conscience reigned in

---

* Quoted in Alexander L. George and Juliette L. George, *Woodrow Wilson and Colonel House: A Personality Study* (New York: John Day, 1956), p. 230.

both parties but Wilson out-righteoused the opposition and confirmed his New Freedom as a moral mission. Thus Wilson managed to corral seriatim the right and the left of political journalism who, for all their ideological distinctiveness, shared the sense of politics as a matter of right and wrong.

He was a queer duck, a mystery to political regulars. Son of an overpowering Presbyterian minister, Tommy Wilson was a delicate, slow-learning child; he got all the way through adolescence without finding an effective way to rebel against the family's atmosphere of repressive, intrusive moral concern. Instead, he made it his own. At nineteen he warned himself in an essay to "overcome evil desires, those powerful and ever present enemies, by constant watchfulness and with the strong weapon of prayer, and by cultivating these heavenly desires which are sure to root out the evil one." It was hard going, for he had a passionate nature. Fantasies of leadership gave some outlet: as "Lord Wilson, Duke of Arlington, Commander-in-chief of H.M. Flying Squadron" and at Princeton, "Thomas Woodrow Wilson, Senator from Virginia." The role of character in leadership fascinated him. In the college newspaper he instructed the baseball team: "*Everything* depends upon the character of the captain and the president. With a good captain and an efficient president success is no longer a matter of doubt. . . . The president must above all things else, be a man of unbiased judgment, energy, determination, intelligence, moral courage, *conscience.*" For his doctoral thesis he chose to write on *Congressional Government*, and, shortly after the book was published, he wrote to a friend of his growing passion for a political role of his own:

> I have a strong instinct of leadership, an unmistakably oratorical temperament, and the keenest possible delight in affairs; and it has required very constant and stringent schooling to content me with the sober methods of the scholar and the man of letters. I have no patience with the tedious toil of what is known as "research"; I have a passion for interpreting great thoughts to the world; I should be complete if I could inspire a great movement of opinion, if I could read the experiences of the past into the practical life of the men of today and so communicate the thought to the minds of the great mass of people so as to impel them to greater political achievements. . . . My feeling has been that such literary talents as I have are *secondary* to my equipment for other things; that my power to write was meant to be a handmaiden to my power to speak and to organize action.*

Wilson's personal quest for power could only be legitimate if his father's God approved. And He did. At last elected to the Presidency, Wilson told a supporter, "I owe you nothing. Remember that God ordained that I should be the next President of the United States."

* Quoted in ibid., p. 7.

Wilson's Magazine Mentor

If God ordained President Wilson, it was George Harvey who saw to his candidacy. Like his protégé, Harvey advertised his conscience—but it commanded him oppositely.

"From the day when the first note of independence was sounded to the very present," Harvey instructed an audience at Yale, "the bane of journalism has been the political ambitions of the journalists themselves." As if preaching to himself, Harvey perorated:

What, then, shall we conclude? That an editor shall bar acceptance of public position under any circumstances? Yes, absolutely; and any thought or hope of such preferment; else his avowed purpose is not his true one; his policy is one of deceit in pursuance of an unannounced end; his guidance is untrustworthy, his calling that of a teacher false to his disciples for personal advantage, his conduct not only a gross betrayal of public confidence but also of the faith of every true journalist jealous of a profession which should be of the noblest and the farthest removed from base uses in the interest of selfish men.*

That was in 1908. Thirteen years later, Harvey would accept appointment as Ambassador to Great Britain from a fellow journalist whose scruples were less inhibiting: President Warren G. Harding. But even as he spoke at Yale, Harvey was deep at work guiding Woodrow Wilson toward the White House.

From the moment of his christening in 1864, Harvey was linked to the Presidency and the Democracy: his farmer father, an ardent Democratic maverick in Republican Vermont, named him George Brinton McClellan Harvey, after the haughty, manic-depressive general whom the Democrats would nominate that summer to run against Lincoln. George put out his first newspaper at age ten, earning money for type by weeding onions, and by age fifteen was sole staff and proprietor of the *St. Johnsbury Republican*, which lasted seventeen issues, and contributor of columns on cattle shows and the like to the local papers. Even in those days, he recalled much later, he suffered the newsman's neurosis:

The most poignant sorrow of a minor nature that I have ever experienced was the scarcity of news. I think I was a reasonably humane lad; but even so, I cannot deny the alleviation of regret I experienced when by chance a cow died or a promising colt broke his leg. What I deprecated most was the paucity of crime in that neighborhood. I used to lie awake nights, not exactly hoping that murder would be done in the peaceful region, but frankly admitting to myself that if the spirit of Cain was to take possession of a human soul, in that vicinity, anyway, that was a very good time and the best of places for it to make its appearance. It never did.†

* Quoted in Willis Fletcher Johnson, *George Harvey: A Passionate Patriot* (Boston: Houghton Mifflin, 1929), p. 97.
† Ibid., p. 14.

But if the flow of news was uncertain, George's moral judgment was sure:

> By that time, I knew it all. There was no subject within the wide horizon of thought, from international problems to the correct method of paring potatoes, that I was not wholly competent not only to discuss but to decide with irresistible conclusiveness. I was particularly strong on politics. . . . I had a large and varying assortment of convictions. In one respect, however, they were alike. They were uncontaminated by tints and shades. Everything was either absolutely right or absolutely wrong. I recognized but two colors, black and white.
>
> With extreme sagacity I formulated a method of educating the masses up to an adequate appreciation of the blessings of free trade. . . . I spurned the suggestion of treating it as an economic issue. It was a moral issue, based upon one of the Ten Commandments—I was never quite sure which. *

In other words, he was a natural-born editor. Still not yet of voting age, Harvey dropped in on Joseph Pulitzer in New York; Pulitzer was taken by him and hired him as a reporter. He covered Ulysses S. Grant's heroic struggle with terminal cancer as the old ex-President, in intense and continuous pain, slowly scrawled the memoirs he hoped would provide for his family when he was gone. When Harvey was only twenty-seven, Pulitzer made him managing editor of the *World*. He got so far into the wheeling and dealing that led to Grover Cleveland's renomination and election in 1892 that Cleveland offered him a place as consul general in Berlin. But Pulitzer advised him "to stick to journalism and never more think of office." Although Harvey heeded his mentor and kept the lesson, he itched for a medium through which to speak his mind independently. The next year he resigned and went into private business handling streetcar investments for Wall Street millionaires; in six years he piled up the capital and connections he needed to buy the *North American Review*, a venerable monthly founded in 1815. Harvey became its nineteenth editor and quickly transformed it into his medium, with articles "By the Editor" up front. That same year—1899— he was named president of a nearly bankrupt publishing house called Harper and Brothers, as the only corporation officer who was not a member of the family. He was thirty-five. By hard economy he pulled the decrepit firm into the black. He became fast friends with Harper's longtime backer J. P. Morgan. In 1901, he took over the editorship of *Harper's Weekly*, an outlet for more frequent instructive pieces.

Under Harvey's leadership, *Harper's Weekly* became an important purveyor of manners and morals among several magazines then rapidly growing in circulation and influence. Much as the newspapers gave clearest definition to the story of politics as conflict, the magazine, free of the need for immediate sensation or for dispassionate objectivity, would furnish the best illustration of politics as a moral enterprise.

The roots of *Harper's Weekly* ran way back. Early American magazines,

---

* Ibid., p. 16.

small and irregular, sought readers among gentlemen and consisted largely of articles pirated from the British. George Washington, continually raked over the coals by the newspapers, wrote a Philadelphia publisher that he hoped magazines would succeed, for, "I consider such easy vehicles of knowledge more happily calculated than any other, to preserve the liberty, stimulate the industry and meliorate the morals of an enlightened and free people." Benjamin Franklin may have started the first one in 1741; if so, he thought it not important enough to mention in his *Autobiography*. Thomas Paine hacked out poetry, essays, and popular science as a magazine editor; after three glasses of brandy, "his ideas appeared to flow faster than he could commit them to paper," said a colleague. His revolutionary pamphleteering followed. Noah Webster published twelve issues of a well-spelled magazine in 1787, then lost interest and started a newspaper. In 1821 the *Saturday Evening Post* got going as a cut-and-paste enterprise in Franklin's old printing plant. The first antislavery magazine, *The Genius of Universal Emancipation*, sprang up in Mount Pleasant, Ohio, and eight years later took on a young assistant editor named William Lloyd Garrison.

It was Boston, font of intellectual enlightenment and disdain, that churned up the idea that was to make magazines a big business: the discovery of the "female market." There in 1828, Sarah Josepha Hale brought forth her *Ladies Magazine*, dedicated to "the progress of female improvement." By the Civil War, its circulation had reached 150,000. Sarah Hale probably did more than any other American to make Victorianism popular—not the repressive, prim version the twentieth century would come to mock, but the hopeful, progressive and humane morality the chaotic and violent nineteenth century longed for. Steady reform was the hope; education was the method. Readers were urged to take a bath once a week, not to eat pie for breakfast, to sleep on a firm mattress, and practice "home exercises." Along with "the latest advanced styles" in dress the magazine urged civic virtues—patriotism, tolerance, unity—as equally à la mode. It was the first significant *national* publication, striving to convey an American perspective North and South, until the War dashed that hope.

Moralism's other visage—righteous indignation—glared forth from the pages of *McClure's*, the famous "muckraker" of the turn of the century. Ida Tarbell, Lincoln Steffens, and Ray Stannard Baker let the American corruptionists have it right between the eyes in their issue of January 1903, which reached 350,000 shocked readers. The centerpiece was Tarbell's "History of the Standard Oil Company," which lifted the lid that concealed moguls of industry who "deliberately, shrewdly, upon legal advice" were operating to cheat the public. This fact-packed, tensely narrative account helped make Miss Tarbell "The Most Famous Woman Journalist in the World," said *McClure's*, and helped set the mode of modern "investigative reporting." Even more popular was her biographical series on Lincoln, written to teach "the solemn duties of citizenship"; it furnished a young student named Carl

Sandburg with the "stirring and picturesque material" that inspired his famous biography. Magazines found the space for life histories, capturing the drama of heroes sprung from the American soil. The parable of the person fixed itself in the journalistic tradition.

By the time Woodrow Wilson came along, the voice of the muckrakers had long been part of the national conversation. They traced shocking evils to evil leaders. The fundamental solution, then, was to get good leaders. Theodore Roosevelt the reformer enjoyed their support, but he turned against them as too negative (and gave them their label—muckrakers—from Bunyan's *Pilgrim's Progress*). To do good, you had to "give somebody the power to render it." In the years before the Great War, they were ready for a hero, if only one could be found who believed with McClure of *McClure's* that "the *problem* of life consists in the relation of man to God and the facts growing out of this relation."

Drafting Professor Wilson

One sunny day in October 1902, Harvey and J. P. Morgan went down on Morgan's special train to break bread with Grover Cleveland, Mark Twain, and a few other rich and famous folk, and to hear Princeton's new president give his inaugural speech. Woodrow Wilson wowed them. What he said was high-minded and conservative: the old languages, Greek and Latin, were best; "the merchant and the financier should have traveled minds"; science was all right except for those parts of it "which lie in controversy" and thus "do not constitute the proper subject matter of general education"; mathematics was meant to inculcate "the lifelong accepted discipline of the race," and so on. The title was "Princeton for the Nation's Service." Wilson's style was striking. He was "faultlessly dressed and gave the impression of immaculate cleanliness," one observer saw, "erect but supple," and "his long, thin face wore a smile of joy and pride free of arrogance or conceit," his voice "as clear as any bell," and "both his enunciation and pronunciation were perfection." Lincoln's son Robert told Harvey it was the best of its kind; Harvey said, "Yes, that man could win the people."

Wilson had winning ways, but what did he believe in politically? Harvey went home and studied Wilson's *History of the American People*. It is probable that Harvey focused on the last of Wilson's five volumes, covering the most recent period. There appeared a Wilson that Harvey and his rich, conservative friends could cotton to. Strikes and labor boycotts threatened law and order and were rightfully put down by force. "Ignorant and hostile Negro voting in the South should be stopped forthwith, though perhaps some of the methods were distasteful." Antagonism to Orientals in the West, with their "yellow skin and strange, debasing habits of life," was understandable, and it was reasonable to fear the new European immigrants, those "multitudes of men of the lowest class from the south of Italy, and men of the meaner sort out of Hungary and Poland, men out of the ranks where there was neither skill nor energy nor any initiative of given intelligence," many of whom "had come to America to speak treasons elsewhere forbidden." Monetary inflation of the Bryan type sprung from "crude and ignorant minds." The imperialism of 1898 made good commercial sense.

The next weekend, Harvey is said to have told a houseguest that he thought Wilson "will make a good President of the United States." The man he had in mind was a good, solid, safe, conservative Democrat like Grover Cleveland. Wilson confirmed his surmise in a speech to the Society of Virginians in New York: it was the "populists and theorists who lost elections; the country "needs and will tolerate no party of discontent or radical experiment; but it does need a party of conservative reform, acting in the spirit of law and of ancient institutions." Wilson could speak; Wilson thought right. But Harvey the conscientious also found in Wilson's very person—his character—the qualities of moral leadership. As he put it later in an editorial:

> Certain personal attributes are essential to successful candidacy. Known fidelity to high ideals. Unquestioned integrity. Veracity. Courage. Caution. Intellectuality. Wisdom. Experience. Achievement. Breadth of mind. Strength of body. Clarity of vision. Simplicity in manner of living. Eloquence. Human sympathy. Alertness. Optimism. Enthusiasm. Finally and practically: Availability!*

On February 3, 1906, Harvey spoke at a posh dinner put on by New York's elegant Lotos Club in Wilson's honor, and stated his case: "Woodrow Wilson of Virginia and New Jersey" should be President. His speech, quickly published in *Harper's Weekly*, put Wilson smack in the middle of the Lincoln category—sprung-from-the-soil, bloodguided Americans:

> For nearly a century before Woodrow Wilson was born the atmosphere of the Old Dominion was surcharged with true statesmanship. The fates directed his steps along other paths, but the effect of growth among the traditions of the fathers remained. That he is preeminent as a lucid interpreter of history we all know. But he is more than that. No one who reads, understandingly, the record of his country that flowed with such apparent ease from his pen can fail to be impressed by the belief that he is by instinct a statesman. The grasp of fundamentals, the seemingly unconscious application of primary truth to changing conditions, the breadth in thought and reason manifested on those pages, are clear evidence of sagacity worthy of the best and noblest of Virginia's traditions. . . .†

Harvey—who did not really know Wilson yet—advertised his hero as just right for the conciliation of 1908:

> . . . that type of man we shall, if, indeed, we do not already, need in our public life. No one would think for a moment of criticizing the general reformation of the human race in all its multifarious phases now going on by executive decree, but it is

* Quoted in Francis Russell, *The President Makers: From Mark Hanna To Joseph P. Kennedy* (Boston: Little, Brown, 1976), p. 150.
† Quoted in William Inglis, "Helping to Make a President," *Collier's*, 7 October 1916.

becoming increasingly evident that that great work will soon be accomplished. When that time shall have been reached, the country will need at least a short breathing spell for what the physicians term perfect rest. That day, not now far distant, will call for a man combining the activities of the present with the sobering influences of the past.*

Harvey said he experienced "a feeling almost of rapture" when he contemplated "even a remote possibility" of voting for Wilson for President. That night Wilson went back to the University Club and wrote a note to Harvey: "It was most delightful to have such thoughts uttered about me, whether they were deserved or not, and I thank you with all my heart."

Harvey's hopeful remarks were received as entertaining speculation, except perhaps by Harvey and Wilson—and Wilson soon wrote a friend that he was not taking "at all seriously the suggestions made by Colonel Harvey." But Harvey was in earnest; he was in it to stay; he would stick with the cause. Wilson had found in him that essential ingredient of electoral success: one other effective influential obsessed with the idea that his man must make it to the White House.

Harvey had already wheeled into action. Early in 1906 he had finagled an appointment for Wilson to New Jersey's Commission on Uniform State Laws, Wilson's first public office. That issue of *Harper's Weekly* with his Lotos Club speech, and a full-page drawing of Wilson on the cover, roused conservative editors to enthusiasm for this man who might lead the nation to "a sobering up after the radical 'crazes.' " Harvey spurred on journalists in Boston and Brooklyn and South Carolina. A reporter asked Wilson if he was a candidate, at which "a smile stole over his features," and he said, "While I appreciate most heartily Colonel Harvey's kindness in bestowing on me such an honor, I must say I think there are other wires taller than mine which will attract the lightning." Harvey got a fellow editor, a friend of Wilson's, to pose the same question; Wilson wrote back at considerable length (unlike, say, Sherman) to the effect that Harvey had meant to espouse someone like Wilson, but not necessarily Wilson himself, and added, "Nothing could be further from my thoughts than the possibility or the desirability of holding high political office."

Harvey the publicist went down to North Carolina and inveigled Josephus Daniels, editor of the *Raleigh News & Observer*, into a long, late-night conversation. Not long after, Daniels sent him a copy of his paper celebrating some anniversary of Daniels' editorship, and a picture. "Take it and make it a full page for the 'Weekly,' " Harvey ordered his staff. "Make it as flattering as you know how. It is impossible to overfeed his vanity, and if you plaster it on thick enough, he may feel that he ought to respond in kind toward Wilson." Daniels took the bait and the *News & Observer*, previously devoted to Bryan, found nice things to say of the Professor. The effort would

* Ibid.

pay off later. In 1912 Daniels delivered the whole North Carolina delegation to Wilson and came aboard, after the victory, as secretary of the navy.

Harvey the politician got together with the aptly named Thomas Fortune Ryan, an immensely wealthy contributor to Wilson's Princeton, and discerned that he was ready to back Wilson for President. Ryan was the muscle in the party's right wing, Bryan in the left. Harvey touched base with Bryan in London, on the Fourth of July 1906. Bryan said Ryan should do as "the young man who went to see the Saviour" was told to do—roughly—get rid of his investments in government-affected enterprises and put the profits in government bonds. Then Bryan would go to work to make a reformed Ryan President—or, said Bryan as reported to Ryan by Harvey, "conditions" might "make someone else more available." Ryan was no more ready to sell out than Bryan was to come out for the gold standard, but Harvey had established a link between them—himself—and opened a chink for "someone else."

That fall, the Republicans won a big majority in the New Jersey legislature and prepared to elect a U.S. senator, as they did it in those days. The Democrats stood no chance of electing one of their own, but Harvey thought Wilson could get some favorable notice by being nominated by the party, and so proposed in a *Harper's Weekly* editorial. Then he visited New Jersey's most powerful Democratic conservative boss, James Smith, who was all for the Wilson proposition as a way to stave off the discontented "progressive" Democrats threatening his power. Harvey took the idea to Wilson, who did not exactly say no: he was flattered, but he could not appear as a candidate— an active, open contender—for the honor, particularly because the candidate of the progressives was none other than a Colonel Stevens, who had been his Princeton classmate and was his friend. In vain Harvey implored Stevens to withdraw.

Wilson was embroiled in Princeton politics, where, as elsewhere in Academia, the intensity of emotion is often inversely proportional to the significance of the stakes. The emerging stories of his sort-of-candidacy began to embarrass him; he sent a friend to tell Harvey to turn it off, but the friend reported back that Harvey was "fascinating and suave and I merely got the impression that he intended to go ahead." Wilson himself talked with Harvey in New York and shortly thereafter wrote him a long letter about his Presidential prospects. There were possibilities to be considered, and probabilities.

The Democratic party was too split and confused to want him, Wilson thought. In any case, he was not the right man to be President. Someone more experienced and charismatic would be right. He was too conservative for most Democrats. Anyway, just who were all the bigwigs Harvey said were in Wilson's corner? Harvey wrote back the next day. He presented a list of famous backers collectively capable of buying Guatemala—the cream of Wall Street and the publishing world, classified neatly into those interested in a general way, those interested in a candidate of Wilson's type (the longest list), and those favorably inclined to the actual Wilson. Wilson was impressed. Perhaps . . .

Then a letter came to Wilson from Colonel Stevens. The prospect of a Wilson Senate nomination candidacy was being put forward "as a sign of your willingness to allow the use of your name as a club by the very men who every good Democrat feels to have been the bane of the party and whose leadership has made the state hopelessly Republican." Wilson wrote back: "Possibly it is because I am such an outsider and so inexperienced in such matters, but the whole difficulty is that I cannot bring myself to see the situation as you seem to see it." Wilson saw it from way off. "When it was a question of actual election to the Senate"—never a live question, in fact—"I felt bound to say I could not accept the office; but a complimentary vote, tendered by a minority, involves no responsibility on the part of the recipient, and therefore it seems to me that it would be quite gratuitous of me to say that if it were tendered me, I would not accept it." Withdrawal now would "be intervening *for the sake of settling factional differences.*" He had said he was not a candidate; "no one, I take it, will venture to doubt my sincerity." Stevens wrote "My dear Tommy" back with some facts of life. Stevens knew: the bosses had told him he could have their votes for money. Wilson promptly wrote to Harvey asking him to tell him the "most courteous and convenient way" out of this mess—but thanking Harvey profusely, hoping, "that I may have many opportunities of showing my appreciation and admiration. . . ." Harvey drafted a withdrawal letter—carefully not casting Wilson's support to Stevens. Wilson sent it off at once, virtually as drafted. "The compliment should be paid to someone of those who were active in the canvas," it said. Thus, for the moment, Wilson stepped aside.

All that happened in December 1906 and January 1907. In microcosm, the story shows what Harvey was up against and how he kept punching, in public and private, to chivy his candidate into position. Neither was about to give up. Harvey got Wilson together with Ryan and a conservative New York publisher in March. Both were impressed. In April Wilson began a series of lectures at Columbia on the need for a strong Presidency—markedly departing from his previous preference for cabinet government. Harvey took on a full-time assistant to work exclusively on the Wilson movement. Wilson wrote to a Kansas railroader, "Would that we could do something at once dignified and effective to knock Mr. Bryan once and for all into a cocked hat!" In August he wrote up a "Credo"—protrusts, antiunions—for the benefit of his new rich backers.

The Conservative Candidate

In January 1908, Joseph Pulitzer was amused when Harvey asked him to have the *World* come out for Wilson for President. All right, said Pulitzer, but only if Harvey would write the editorial. Carefully aping *World* style, Harvey pointed Wilson as "a true Democrat who, though steeped in Jeffersonian doctrines, asks not what Jefferson did a century ago, but what Jefferson would do *now*."

Wilson's time was remoter than Harvey could then see. After years of Rooseveltian moral reformism, the nation in 1908 was indeed ready for "a breathing spell" of "perfect rest." William Randolph Hearst, misreading the mood, formed and financed his own party to make himself President in a fighting campaign—blasting Bryan as a "trickster, a trimmer, and a traitor." Roosevelt, too, urged a battle: "In New York we must win by a savage and aggressive fight against Hearstism and an exposure of its hypocrisy, its insincerity, its corruption, its demagogy, and in general, its utter worthlessness and wickedness." Roosevelt's protégé for the Presidency, William Howard Taft, nevertheless exuded conciliation. The Republican convention, instructed by Roosevelt via a special wire from the White House, dutifully nominated Taft on the first ballot; one of Roosevelt's most effective threats against waverers was that it had to be "Taft or me." TR picked up the going theme and said Taft would be "a President of the plain people," without "the least taint of demagogy," avoiding "appeal to any class hatred of any kind." Bryan, moderating his message, thoroughly controlled the Democratic convention, which nominated him on the first ballot. Despite his trimming, the *New York Times* recalled his radicalism, said his election would amount to "a national calamity," and predicted that after his defeat, with the "election over, people will exclaim 'Thank goodness there is an end of that.' "

The election was a great sigh of relief; smiling Big Bill Taft and his running mate "Sunny Jim" Sherman got almost twice as many electoral votes as Bryan. It was a time for peace, not challenge, for a Taft, not a Wilson.

Harvey, caught up in his own vision of Wilson, might well have paused in his labors had he paid attention to what the professor was saying in the spring of 1908. Wilson's crusade inside Princeton University was aimed at integrating graduate and undergraduate education, an inside story that might have stayed there had not Wilson begun to make reportable speeches to alumni groups at Princeton stressing equality of opportunity, generally sounding suspiciously democratic. Also, he told New York's National Democratic Club that government would have to exert "a firm and comprehensive regulation of business operations in the interest of fair dealing, and of a responsible exercise of power." After a vacation in England, he returned in September to speak to a bankers' convention, warning of a fight "between the power of accumulated capital and the opportunities of the masses of the people." The following January, he stepped to the right again: government was regulating too much. But a month later he was defining the essence of leadership as "a universal sympathy for those who struggle, a universal understanding of the unutterable burdens that were upon their backs." By June 1909, he was damning unions as producers of "unprofitable servants"—another rightward lurch. Harvey apparently felt no qualms at these ideological shifts. He got Wilson to write a long piece advocating tariff reform.

When a donor offered Princeton $500,000 for a separate graduate school Wilson, to the shock and dismay of alumni, turned it down as undemocratic. In a flight of rhetoric that seemed a harbinger of Presidential intentions, he told a stunned Pittsburgh alumni group in April 1910, "What we cry out against is that a handful of conspicuous men have thrust cruel hands among the heartstrings of the masses of men upon whose blood and energy they are subsisting." America's "great voice . . . comes in a murmur from the hills and the woods and the farms and factories and the mills, rolling on and gaining volume until it comes to us from the homes of common men. . . . I wish there were some great orator who could go about and make men drunk with the spirit of self-sacrifice. I wish there were some man whose tongue might every day carry abroad the golden accents of the golden age when we were born as a nation. . . ." Wilson was beginning to sound almost Bryanesque.

"There has been nothing in a political way for Wilson these past two years," Harvey told his assistant, "but the effect of the publicity has been on the whole satisfactory." Wilson the champion of campus democracy might win votes. "The time has come now to proceed on a political line." The strategy was to elect Wilson governor of New Jersey in 1910 and President in 1912. Harvey went at that work like a political Siva, holding the bosses' support with one hand, cozening the moneylenders with another, penning editorials for the masses with a third, and stroking his delicately indecisive candidate with a fourth.

After much palaver, Harvey got a tentative green light from the New Jersey bosses in early 1910. But Wilson himself balked. Harvey went to see him and talked himself blue. Finally he hit on a brilliant little piece of diplomatic formulation. He said to Wilson, "If I can handle the matter so that the nomination for the Governorship shall be tendered to you on a silver platter, without your turning a hand to obtain it, and without any requirement or suggestion of any pledge whatsoever, what do you think would be your attitude?" Wilson paced silently for several minutes. Then he replied, "If the nomination for Governor should come to me in that way, I should regard it as my duty to give the matter very serious consideration." Harvey took that thread of hope back to Boss James Smith, of the New Jersey Senate, who tried to tie up his forces with it, but it would not hold. A more definite commitment was essential. Harvey invited Wilson to dinner at his estate at Deal with his forceful friend Colonel Henry Watterson, editor of the *Louisville Courier-Journal*. Wilson reluctantly accepted, then declined by telegraph the evening before the dinner because there was no train that day from Lyme, Connecticut, where Wilson was vacationing, to Deal. Harvey dispatched his assistant by automobile. "If you don't fetch him, don't come back. Go and commit harikiri; and don't send any word." The assistant got sick en route and the car broke down, but he got through and Wilson, surprisingly, threw clothes in a bag and came at once, explaining to his wife, "But Colonel Harvey has sent for me." Boss Smith joined the dinner party. They talked on into the night, but not until the next day, when Harvey and Wilson went up to New York City, did the professor finally warn he would have to write to some friends in Chicago, who had been supporting him in his Princeton efforts, before he could agree to accept a nomination. Harvey persuaded him to go to Chicago in person and at once. Smith quickly got a Chicago friend of *his* to get to Wilson's friends first with persuasive arguments. Wilson came back ready to take the gubernatorial nomination "if it came to me unsought and unanimously and I could take it without pledges of any kind to anybody." After all, he had been preaching "the duty of educated men to undertake just such service as this," and thus could "not see how I could avoid it."

In the weeks before the state convention, Wilson leaned heavily on Harvey's counsel. When biting, funny cartoons hurt Wilson's feelings—his sense of humor did not extend to jokes on him—Harvey laughed them off. Harvey convinced his candidate that one hundred percent unanimity in the nomination would look like a bossed vote; a big win would be enough. At the convention in the Trenton Opera House, Harvey went doggedly to work on delegates, while the opening prayer so tightly locked God in with the Democrats that the crowd broke into fervent applause at the last amen. Harvey found the backroom machinations nip and tuck. He had his assistant spirit Wilson secretly to his hotel room to wait; if Wilson lost, they would have to deny he was in town. But Wilson won on the first ballot with 747½ votes to his nearest challenger's 373. The bosses backed him as a conservative, remembering his older statements. The progressives heard his liberal Princeton messages. Harvey sold him as both—and as a winner. As usual, it was made "unanimous." The secretary announced that "Mr. Wilson, the candidate for the governorship, *and the next President of the United States*" was on his way. Wilson responded with a ringing address: "As you know, I did not seek this nomination. It has come to me absolutely unsolicited. With the consequence that I shall enter upon the duties of the office of Governor, if elected, with absolutely no pledge of any kind to prevent me from serving the people of the State with singleness of purpose." The delegates stood up and whooped in a body louder with each new stirring phrase. A young fellow named Joe Tumulty, who would become Wilson's Presidential Secretary, was converted on the spot: "Thank God!" he shouted. "At last a leader has come!"

In that acceptance speech, Wilson urged the Democratic party to serve as "the instrument of righteousness for the State and for the Nation." The progressives in New Jersey were not so sure. They dug up his more outrageous pledges of allegiance to corporate complaisancy and threw them at him. He kept quiet until mid-October, shortly before the vote, then all at once he emerged with a raft of liberal proposals: direct election of senators, state control of utilities, workmen's compensation. And he promised not to take dictation from any bosses. He won the election by 49,056 votes. And he kept conservative George Harvey, who wrote in *Harper's Weekly* that the choice was "between this most exceptional man responding to a call of civic duty, and the group of men whose impelling advantage is mere lust for power which they have wielded so long to personal advantage and to the shame of the State."

The Democrats won the legislature, too, which meant they could elect a Democratic U.S. senator. Wilson, depicting his action as "part of the age-long struggle for human liberty," whipped the bosses who had supported him and got his man in. That got national attention, resonating with similar moves across the country. He then proceeded to jam through his progressive legislative program: "I got everything I strove for—and more besides," he wrote a friend.

When the Presidential year 1912 opened, Wilson was being widely touted as a candidate. No one did more to make that happen than Harvey. Once having fastened on Wilson as the savior of the day, he seems to have blanked out Wilson's shifting policies; perhaps he read the signs as Wilson did—that he could not be elected President as the tool of the conservative moneybags, that he would have to reach leftward to Bryan's old constituency. Harvey was hooked on Wilson and on his own role in bringing him to power.

The backing Harvey had so laboriously arranged fell apart as Wilson waxed progressive, but Harvey stayed: week by week he published articles on "The Predestination of Woodrow Wilson," "The Problem, the Solution, and the Man," and a large-type banner headlined across the editorial page of *Harper's Weekly* in every issue, proclaimed "For President, Woodrow Wilson."

If Harvey, his eye on the Presidential star, could shift with the tide, Wilson increasingly found his enthusiasm a liability. "I wish I could rid myself of the support of *Harper's Weekly* and Colonel Harvey," he told a reporter, "I do not know why Harvey insists on supporting me. It does me great injury." Harvey was still seen as a pal of the J. P. Morgans of the world; Wilson had a wider audience to win. Finally, bluntly, rudely, and without explanations, Wilson told Harvey to turn it off. Harvey took down the slogan in *Harper's Weekly* and began to move to the periphery of the Wilson circle. The Wilson-Harvey "break" leaked to the press and became the Wilson gaffe of 1912, making him seem a disloyal ingrate, leading the *New York Times* to note: "The question will at once arise in the minds of men whether Woodrow Wilson, with these infirmities of temperament, does not lack some of the highly essential qualifications always associated with the great office to which he aspires." Wilson wrote Harvey an apologetic—though private— letter, and Harvey reciprocated with a friendly note. He would not be the last devotee to return to Wilson, that enigmatic but inspirational, and, when it suited him, charming character, long after Wilson had turned away from him.

The Political Riot of 1912

Politics in 1912 raised "a sharp and divisive struggle over impending major changes in the Constitution which would determine not only how, but also, and more importantly, in whose interest, the nation was to be governed," writes historian George Mowry. The cry for democracy was loose in the land, in reaction to a growing popular sense that the ruling elites, political and corporate, sheltered behind the barriers of checked and balanced constitutional indirections, were milking the system for their own power and profit. Bosses in the state legislatures chose bosses for the Senate, who saw to the appointment of their own kind to federal judgeships. Behind the scenes the giant corporations wove their own webs of genteel bribery and pilferage, enlisting the government for the grinding of the poor. The Populists and Progressives urged reform: direct election of senators, recall of judges, the income tax, federal control of trusts, regulation of working conditions, a better break for unions. The J. P. Morgans felt otherwise. The newspapers roared their pro and con thunderations.

These fissures of policy crisscrossed widening regional splits in the dominant Republican party in which insurgents of the West and urbanizing East strained the patience of the moneyed regulars. Yet another tear was the unraveling relationship between Theodore Roosevelt and the complaisant hero of happiness he had picked to succeed him, William Howard Taft; their supporters egged on their estrangement. Four years of Taftian stolidity had paved the way for a national electoral fight.

The combative surge boiled up inside the Democratic party, as well. The Democrats had gained substantially in 1908, taking over the Congress in 1910. But that same year, Bryan went down to defeat in his homestate convention, Wilson outmaneuvered his party's bosses in New Jersey, and, in New York State, a young Democrat named Franklin Delano Roosevelt joined twenty other insurgents in walking out of the Democratic legislative caucus in protest over Tammany's Senate choice. Bryan was puzzled about the unlikely professor in politics, Woodrow Wilson, and where he stood on issues—somewhere along the road, he said, "Saul had become Paul"—but he included him in a list of four Presidential possibilities.

At the Democratic national convention of 1912, chaos reigned. Half a dozen eager and plausible contenders, scattered across the ideological spectrum, contended for the two-thirds vote it then took to nominate. Despite his at-home defeat that year, Bryan was a force, though not himself a candidate. He held back on any endorsement. The conservatives were still strong; many of the Democrats newly elected in 1910 were of their persuasion. On the liberal end of the scale, Wilson faced Champ Clark of Missouri, another ex-college president, now Speaker of the House, who had come to the convention with more delegates than anyone else. Harvey was there, predicting a Wilson victory but dutifully standing aside from the intense wheeling and dealing, as ballot after ballot failed to produce a winner.

After the tenth vote, Wilson sent his managers a private message to release his delegates—but they pocketed the missive and stubbornly dealt on. On the fourteenth ballot, Bryan released his Nebraska delegation from their preference for Clark. The weary bosses endlessly intrigued. At last, on the *forty-sixth* ballot, a passel of Southern delegates swallowed their doubts and shifted to Wilson. After all, he was a son of Georgia and Virginia. Thus, as in his nomination for governor of New Jersey, Wilson came to the fore through well-publicized oratory and then took his party's banner through the earthiest kind of inside combination.

A week after the convention, Wilson's name reappeared in *Harper's Weekly* after an absence of seven months. Harvey wrote of the Democrats' "admiration of his exceptional intellectual capacity, consideration of his freedom from entanglements, and respect for his moral courage." But in that year of the politics of conflict, the Democrats went into the election frayed and frazzled, a patchwork of factions tentatively knit together around Woodrow Wilson. Harvey's judgment—"If the Democrats cannot elect Woodrow Wilson, they could not elect anyone"—could be read two ways.

Even the Socialist party fell into disarray. Led by gentle Eugene Debs, the Socialists had elected more than twelve hundred of their own members to public office between 1910 and 1912. But the bomb throwers in the party could not get along with the meliorists, so the latter expelled the former by a two-to-one vote.

In the Republican camp, Taft and Roosevelt floundered to disunity and defeat. Taft shocked the conservatives by starting an antitrust suit against U.S. Steel, but he was far from progressive enough for Roosevelt, who now leaped leftward, calling for "pure democracy," including initiative, referendum, and recall. The two former friends took to the preconvention hustings and released their pent-up invectives. TR said, "The fight is on and I am stripped to the buff." Riotous state conventions and stormy national committee sessions led up to a national convention, where, reported the *Washington Post*, "Passions have been unloosed, anger has been unbridled, and prejudice permitted a free rein." A furious Roosevelt marched his forces from the hall to form the Progressive party, whose mission, he declared, lacked ambiguity: "We stand at Armageddon and we battle for the Lord." With Roosevelt in the race, said the *Post*, "women and children should be removed from the scene before the carnage begins."

Taft, hurt and confused, said privately that the Progressive party was nothing but "a religious cult with a fakir at the head of it." Roosevelt called him "a dead cock in a pit." But as the election campaign itself opened, Taft could not find it in himself to lash out at Roosevelt personally in public. His party, hopelessly split by the mayhem of the nomination battle, was headed for defeat. Wilson's own message to the voters that fall of 1912 carefully tiptoed around the sensibilities of his conservative backers. He was for free enterprise, but not "illicit competition," for human rights as superior to property rights, but against "paternalism." He went his enigmatic way, ignoring the platform, invoking the past, emitting vague attractions of such uncertain import that even today historians are not sure whether he was standing on his left foot or his right. Not one conservative journal hit him as a threat to the going order. Harvey continued to beat the Wilsonian drum in the pages of *Harper's Weekly*. Three weeks before the election, Wilson's manager, McCombs, asked Harvey to let bygones be bygones and come aboard to manage publicity for the first Democratic President-to-be in twenty years. Harvey accepted, and went to work.

As in the summer, the excitement of the fall focused on Roosevelt. His program startled the country: subject the judiciary to popular control, put industry under a regulatory commission, make government the active protector of the victims of industrial enterprise. Every "fossilized wrong" oppressing the weak and downtrodden should be eradicated—by the people's government. In short, as historian George E. Mowry puts it, "Roosevelt's 1912 campaign was one of the most radical campaigns ever made by a major American political figure and deserves to rank along with Franklin Roosevelt's in 1936 and Harry Truman's in 1948." The conservative press leaped into the fray. Roosevelt's program resembled "the inspiration of a thousand tyrants," said the *World*; the *Times* predicted dictatorship followed by monarchy if TR won; the *Sun* called him "Theodorus Rex." The *North American Review* pulled out all the stops: Roosevelt "was the first President whose chief personal characteristic was mendacity, the first to glory in duplicity, the first braggart, the first bully, the first betrayer of a friend who ever occupied the White House." In Milwaukee on October 14, a maddened gunman shot Roosevelt in the chest as he was about to make a speech. TR clapped his hand over the wound and spoke on, near the end waving his bloodied handkerchief in the air.

With equal intensity, in this year of combat, newspaperman William Randolph Hearst took out after Wilson. Wilson had applied to the Carnegie Foundation for a study grant—a crime in Hearst's view, because it appealed for money from an outfit "steeped in the blood of Carnegie's workers." Wilson's thoughtless libels on the new immigrants in his *History of the American People* were exhumed and hurled at him. Hearst called him "a perfect jackrabbit of politics, perched upon his little hillock of expediency, with ears erect and nostrils distended, keenly alert to every scent and sound and ready to run and double in any direction."

The week before the voting Harvey reviewed in *Harper's Weekly* six predictions he had made over the years about Wilson, all of which had come true, and added to them a seventh estimate that Wilson would win the Presidency with more than a 300-vote majority in the electoral college. The night before the election, confident of the result, he wrote Wilson: "My congratulations go to the country. To my mind, it is probably unnecessary to say, your election is the greatest thing that has happened since Lincoln's. Nor am I sure that it *was not as essential* as his was." Wilson won 435 electoral votes, TR 88, Taft only 8. Wilson won with a minority of the popular vote, polling fewer votes than Bryan had as a loser in 1896, 1900, or 1908. In that year of the politics of conflict, the only noncombatant was swept into office. Harvey put out a special edition of *Harper's*, celebrating "The Triumph of an Idea," and tracing his own ten-year effort to make Wilson President. The *New York Times* prophesied Wilson would turn out to be a "conservative President."

But they did not know their Wilson. Coming into the presidency of Princeton as a conservative, he had surprised the professors by suddenly offering a complete reformation of the place. Coming into the governorship of New Jersey, he had turned his back on the conservative bosses and his heart to progressive causes. Throughout his political history, Wilson displayed a remarkable ability to shift his ground, once in power, and then, when the next high opportunity for advancement offered itself, to wipe out the memory of his record by bedazzling moralistic rhetoric. Now, as President of the United States, he left Harvey and his conservative friends in the lurch ideologically and personally. Not until September 1914, after war had broken out, would Harvey be invited to the White House. As a significant influence on Wilson, his role was over, with the victory at the polls. A new Wilson, the Wilson of the New Freedom, moved with the country, relegating to the sidelines the mentor who had made it all possible.

The New Wilson of 1916

Taking power, Wilson called Congress into special session and proceeded to ram through in eighteen months of hard legislative labor a remarkable program of reform—the New Freedom. It was as if Theodore Roosevelt had won the election after all; by 1916 Wilson boasted that the Democrats had "come very near to carrying out the platform of the Progressive party." The tariff was comprehensively reduced, the whole banking system reorganized by the Federal Reserve System, strong antitrust measures passed, and a Federal Trade Commission promised to put some administrative teeth into the law. After the Democrats picked up Progressive support in the midterm elections of 1914, Wilson got a Federal Farm Loan Act and a Child Labor Act through; in 1916 he ordered Congress to establish the eight-hour day at ten-hour wages, and they obeyed. The Democratic party, last represented in the White House by Grover Cleveland (1893–97), rapidly redefined itself as the dominant liberal force in twentieth-century American politics. To the chagrin of his conservative backers—including George Harvey—Wilson emerged as the national champion of progressivism.

Wilson the moralist was as quick to emerge. His inaugural address in 1913 set his purpose "to lift everything that concerns our life as a nation to the light that shines from the hearthfire of every man's conscience and vision of the right." Even after the May 1915 sinking of the British liner *Lusitania* with many Americans aboard, Wilson declared, "There is such a thing as a man being too proud to fight" and "There is such a thing as a nation being so right that it does not need to convince others by force that it is right." That September, speaking on "The Faith America Lives By," he said, "The law that will work is merely the summing up in legislative form of the moral judgment that the community had already reached." In front of the League to Enforce Peace in May 1916, Wilson performed a great moral leap: "It is clear that nations must in the future be governed by the same high code of honor that we demand of individuals," and he informed New York's Press Club the following month that he had "not read history without observing that the greatest forces in the world are moral forces."

In 1916, the Republican party, chastened by the fitful memory of 1912, met and, said one observer, "proceeded steadily and stolidly upon its appointed course," drafting a reluctant but dutiful Charles Evans Hughes from the quiet dignity of the Supreme Court bench. Theodore Roosevelt groused but refused to accept another disastrous Progressive party nomination. He backed Hughes as an alternative to Wilson, who lacked the patriotic militancy to stand up to the Germans. But Hughes was no Roosevelt. His speeches sounded like a man reading from a thesaurus. Hughes opened his campaign with a rumbling, hour-and-a-half mesmerization on "Americanism":

I mean America conscious of power, awake to obligation, erect in self-respect, prepared for every emergency, devoted to the ideals of peace, instinct with the spirit of human brotherhood, safeguarding both individual opportunity and the public interest, maintaining a well-ordered Constitutional system adapted to local self-government without the sacrifice of essential national authority, appreciating the necessity of stability, expert knowledge, and thorough organization as the indispensable conditions of security and progress; a country loved by its citizens with a patriotic fervor permitting no division in their allegiance and no rivals in their affection —I mean America first and America efficient.*

Wilson, underestimating the impact of such sonorous goo, was reminded of "the rule never to murder a man who is committing suicide." He was very busy being President.

The Great War was on its way. Wilson narrowly avoided war with Mexico when American troops crossed the border to pursue Pancho Villa, who had raided New Mexico; Wilson insisted on a negotiated settlement. The British, two years into their desperate struggle with Germany, forbade trade with eighty-seven American firms they thought were trading with the enemy. Wilson said he was "about at the end of my patience" and "this black list business is the last straw." Wilson got through legislation enabling him to retaliate by closing American ports to British ships—demonstrating that he could stand up to the British and was not about to pitch American power into battle.

* Quoted in Arthur S. Link and William M. Leary, Jr., "Election of 1916," in Schlesinger et al., eds., *History of American Presidential Elections*, vol. 3, p. 2256.

When the Democratic delegates gathered in the St. Louis Coliseum on June 14, they found the arena draped with flags, resounding with patriotic anthems, electric with "Americanism." The keynoter, New York's Governor Martin Glynn, recited instance after instance of Wilsonian war resistance, to interrupting shouts of "Hit him Again! Hit him Again!" which cued him to a camp-meeting litany of rhythmic response: at each example of a challenge to peace, the delegates roared "What did we do? What did we do?" and the speaker roared back, "We didn't go to war." Glynn soared on:

> This policy does not satisfy those who revel in destruction and find pleasure in despair. It may not satisfy the fire-eater and the swashbuckler. But it does satisfy the mothers of the land . . . at whose hearth and fireside no jingoistic war has placed an empty chair. It does satisfy the daughters of this land, from whom brag and bluster have sent no husband, no sweetheart and no brother to the mouldering dissolution of the grave. It does satisfy the fathers of this land, and the sons of this land, who will fight for our flag, and die for our flag, when Reason primes the rifle . . . when Honor draws the sword, when Justice breathes a blessing on the standards they uphold.*

In the press box, Bryan, the lifelong pacifist, wept.

Wilson's renomination was a foregone conclusion. Accepting it at his home in New Jersey, he pledged "our ungrudging moral and practical support to the establishment of peace throughout the world." The rallying cry of the campaign became "He kept us out of war," the persistent slogan, "Peace with Honor." The Democratic platform called it "the duty of the United States to join the other nations of the world in any feasible association" for international security—the seed of the League of Nations.

In the campaign of conscience that followed, the press was crucial. Hughes, the stern-visaged conservative legalist, did his failing best to attract attention, pumping hands and kissing babies. Wilson, consumed with the gathering war crisis, could not campaign extensively, contented himself with a few front-porch sermons addressed to the Republican opposition: "All our present foreign policy is wrong, they say, and if it is wrong and they are men of conscience, they must change it; and if they are going to change it in what direction are they going to change it?" Wilson's labile moralistic rhetoric fastened itself to domestic reform and international responsibility. And there it found and enlisted unprecedented journalistic energies.

In marked contrast to TR, Wilson never got along with newspaper reporters. Biographer Arthur S. Link writes, "Few Presidents in American history have better understood the importance of good press relations and failed more miserably to get on with newspapermen than Woodrow Wilson." At his first Presidential press conference he announced to the two hundred Washington correspondents, "I sent for you . . . to ask that you get into partnership with me." But his attitude of haughty disdain sent the reporters away indignantly blaspheming. He really disliked them and thought he did

---

* Quoted in ibid., pp. 2253–54.

not need them. *Vox populi* joined with *vox dei* in *vox Wilson*, he thought, whatever the papers said:

> With all due respect to editors of great newspapers, I have to say to them that I seldom take my opinion of the American people from their editorials. So that when some great dailies not very far from where I am temporarily residing thundered with rising scorn at watchful waiting, Woodrow sat back in his chair and chuckled, knowing that he laughs best who laughs last—knowing, in short, what were the temper and principles of the American people. If I did not at least think I knew, I would emigrate, because I would not be satisfied to stay where I am.*

By September 1913 he was writing a friend, "Do not believe anything you read in the newspapers. If you read the papers I see, they are utterly untrustworthy. . . . The lying shameless and colossal!" In 1915 he wrote to the *New York Herald* to denounce one of their stories as "an invention out of whole cloth." He hated reporters also for intruding on his family's privacy: "I am a public character for the time being, but the ladies of my household are not servants of the Government and they are not public characters. I deeply resent the treatment they are receiving at the hands of the newspapers at this time. . . . The thing is intolerable. Every day I pick up the paper and see some flat lie, some entire invention, things represented as having happened to my daughters where they were not present, and all sorts of insinuations." A few papers showed sense (including, he thought, Pulitzer's *World*), "but the rest are a tissue of inventions and speculations and of versions of what they would like to believe to be true. I never imagined anything like it. And most of the newspapers are owned or controlled by men who fear and would discredit the present administration." Wilson's press manager, Joe Tumulty (1910: "Thank God! At last a leader has come!"), cozened the reporters as best he could, got Wilson to send flowers when a *New York Times* correspondent's wife died, persuaded him to write nice letters when he did get good coverage. Tumulty was the one who convinced Wilson to give personal interviews to a few of the muckrakers in 1916, including Ray Stannard Baker and Ida M. Tarbell.

And it was there, among the progressives of the left, that Wilson in 1916 found new moral sustenance. Harvey and the conservative press wavered as war approached, backing The President in Crisis, though wishing him more militant. But the new fervor came from the left. Baker wrote him up as infusing the White House with "a great quietude, steadiness, confidence. . . . It all came to me that night—the undisturbed home, the peaceful surroundings, the thoughtful man at his desk—curiously but deeply as a symbol of immense strength." Ida Tarbell gloried in his liberalism: "Here at last we have a President whose real interest in life centers around the common man, and on whom we can count to serve that man so far as his ability goes." Wilson quoted Tennyson to her, as she reported:

---

*Quoted in George and George, *Woodrow Wilson and Colonel House*, p. 149.

> A nation yet, the rulers and the ruled—
> Some sense of duty, something of a faith,
> Some reverence for the laws ourselves have made,
> Some patient force to change them when we will,
> Some civic manhood firm against the crowd.*

Wilson told her that "the reactionaries, those who call themselves conservatives, are the real destroyers. All life is positive and must change and enlarge to keep itself in health. You cannot conserve liberty by letting liberty alone." He said he had no personal desire for reelection, that "it would be an unspeakable relief to be excused" but asked, "Is it wise that the country should change now, leaving so much at loose ends?" Miss Tarbell suggested he "stood about where Lincoln stood in August, 1864," and Wilson said "Exactly."

The Republicans bought full-page ads to counter Wilson's claim of monopoly on morality in politics. A typical effort was Theodore Roosevelt's insistence that "America Needs Hughes":

Since 1912 we have had four years of a policy which has been an opiate to the spirit of idealism.

It has meant a relaxation of our moral fibre.

A sordid appeal to self-interest and fear has paralyzed the nation's conscience. . . .

Not once has President Wilson squarely placed before the American people the question which Abraham Lincoln put before the American people in 1860: what is our duty?

Not once has he appealed to moral idealism, to the stern enthusiasm of strong men to do the right.

On the contrary, he has employed every elocutionary device to lull to sleep our sense of duty, to make us content with words, instead of deeds, to make our moral idealism and enthusiasm evaporate in empty phrases, instead of being reduced to concrete action.†

But it was no use. Wilson, obscure and mysterious in the election of 1912 compared to Roosevelt, Taft, Bryan, and Debs, in 1916 had emerged as the moralist of progress and reform. He captured the liberal impulse. Walter Lippmann praised the "extraordinary growth" of this President, "remaking his philosophy," and "creating, out of the reactionary, parochial fragments of the Democracy, the only party which at this moment is national in scope, liberal in purpose, and effective in action." Influential Herbert Croly wrote in the New Republic that the "moral integrity" of the Republican party was "destroyed," and if "public opinion is still far from being morally or mentally prepared to act wisely and decisively in world politics . . . it is better prepared for action than it was two years ago," thanks to Wilson. By election day, the New York Times, the New York Evening Post, the Nation, the New Republic, and nearly all the other independent newspapers and magazines

*Tennyson's "The Princess," quoted in Ida Tarbell, "A Talk with the President," Collier's, 28 October 1916.
†Collier's, 14 October 1916.

came out for Wilson. The campaign's moralistic theme hit home with the journalistic conscience-keepers as rarely before, this time with the moralists of the center and left.

George Harvey, disillusioned at last, voted for Hughes in 1916, though he came around to back Wilson in the Great War. Despite the customary Republican majority in the country, reunited after the 1912 split, Wilson won by a narrow margin. Six months later the nation went to war—a course Woodrow Wilson's conscience told him was absolutely right.

Wilson's mark on Presidential history is not to be denied. Had the Republicans been able to unify with Taft in 1912 or if Hughes had been able to seize the imagination of the country in 1916, the course of the century might have taken a very different tack. Wilson set in place a program of humanistic reform from which, in dark days yet to come, progressives would draw their inspiration. He won in 1916 on the slogan "Peace with Honor" and then he led the nation into war, as another reformer, Franklin Roosevelt, would be compelled to do a score of years later, lest an isolated America wake up to discover itself the lone surviving outpost of Western civilization. In the end, in his tragic quest for the League of Nations, in just the precise form his narrow conscience demanded, Wilson killed his own dream and the hope of mankind for a world without war. His character did him in—that childborn drive to make his power perfect—and he failed to achieve his heart's desire.

George Harvey spearheaded the attack on Wilson's cherished league. As Wilson's reign drew toward its end, *Harvey's Weekly*, as now it was called, celebrated "Only SIX Days More!"

But Woodrow Wilson, abetted by the moralists of his age, left a legacy his successors would cleave to again and again, the legacy of the politics of conscience, a vision of a nation with a holy mission. Wilson called the League of Nations "the only hope for mankind"; rejecting it would "break the heart of mankind." Then he put aside his notes and spoke his faith:

> The stage is set, the destiny disclosed. It has come about by no plan for our conceiving, but by the hand of God who led us into this way. We cannot turn back. We can only go forward, with lifted eyes and freshened spirit, to follow the vision. It was of this that we dreamed at our birth. America shall in truth show the way. The light streams upon the path ahead, and nowhere else.*

Wilson's own sea change from conservativism to liberalism, supported now by the Harveys, now by the muckrakers, showed that the vision of the politics of conscience dictated no particular ideological path. Rather that theme was attachable, available to infuse with moral fervor opposite political points of view. The campaign of 1916 portrayed a progressive version; twelve years later the pulse of politics would bring on a conservative version. Then Herbert Hoover the Republican, a devotee of Democrat Wilson, would revive for a very different time Wilson's high-minded sense of virtue in the White House.

* Quoted in George and George, *Woodrow Wilson and Colonel House*, p. 273.

Wilson, stumping the country for the league, collapsed with fatigue in Colorado in September, 1919; in 1920, he waited for a draft that never came. A broken wreck of a man, Woodrow Wilson died in early 1924. But he lived again each time the national need for moral restoration surged up again.

Wilson's Heir Advanced by Harvey's Heir

The uplift of 1916 was followed by the letdown of 1920, the century's classic case of the politics of conciliation, Harding's election. That summer at the Republican convention, it was George Harvey, now a Republican, who, in a smoke-filled Chicago hotel room, asked Senator Harding to swear his past was clean. Harding died in 1923, making Calvin Coolidge President. 1924, on schedule, returned to another rock-'em-sock-'em fight: it took the Democrats 103 ballots and three weeks to land on John W. Davis. The Progressives, with Robert La Follette, sailed into the battle. Coolidge neatly capsized them both, using his Vice-Presidential candidate, "Hell 'n Maria" Dawes, as torpedo, while Coolidge sat and rocked and stared out the White House window. George Harvey, now editor of the *Washington Post*, having supported Harding in 1920, lent his pal and fellow Vermonter Coolidge a hand with articles on "Coolidge or Chaos" and the like. Coolidge's staffers wrote Harvey admiring notes about those efforts: "one of the greatest achievements in political history" and "the rare skill with which you have steered the campaign." Harvey died as he was gearing up for 1928. Among the condolences came one from another fellow moralist: "The country has lost a great constructive leader, and I have lost a friend. Herbert Hoover."

It was Woodrow Wilson who brought Herbert Hoover into Presidential politics. Trapped in London by the hostilities in September 1914 (and thus luckily unable to take up his long-standing reservation to sail home on the *Lusitania*), Hoover organized relief for some 120,000 American refugees pouring into London. Wilson wrote him a note of congratulation; Hoover expanded his incredible relief activities into Belgium and, eventually, to millions of suffering people on both sides of the battle lines. He wrote to Wilson recommending "a strong line of constructive character" to help along "the ultimate redemption of Europe from the barbarism into which it is slowly drifting from all sides." He added, "We all of us count our country as being most fortunate in possessing at this critical time, in its President, a man of such lofty ideals and in whose wisdom we are prepared so implicitly to trust. We have no doubt whatever that the course which is taken will be the wisest course that could have been adopted." He urged Wilson to correct the Germans with moral rhetoric: "The enunciation of a high ideal, or in effect a correction of their ideals from an exalted source such as yourself is bound to penetrate the whole of Germany and through their own public opinion in itself act as a deterrent to future transgressions." Wilson, impressed, brought Hoover back to head up the food program, and throughout the war, turned to Hoover again and again for counsel on a wide range of issues.

Like Wilson, Hoover was a moralist carrying the flag of principle. Like Wilson he came to public view as an outlander sprung from incontestably American soil (Iowa), a non- (perhaps anti-) politician, and exceedingly smart. But he added a dimension suited to the new age: he became a titan of industry who had made it on his own, a "Great Engineer." And like Wilson, Hoover had a politicking editor of his own, George Horace Lorimer, editor of the *Saturday Evening Post*, the organ Will Rogers called "America's greatest nickelodeon."

Lorimer looked like a chunk of granite and his Americanistic morality was rock hard. He turned the *Saturday Evening Post* into a plinth of patriotism, rising above the moral and political degradations of the twenties and thirties, unmovable in witness to firm foundations, adamantly resistant to foreign-born ideologies and their chiseling agents. He was the son of a Scotch actor who deserted the stage for the pulpit, where he shone as a church-packing evangelist, married a deacon's daughter, and edited the Boston Baptist paper, the *Watchman*. George went to Yale, but in the summer after his freshman year he met his father's parishioner P. D. Armour, the Napoleon of meatpacking, who grumped about the "anarchists" and told him Yale was a waste of time—"Give up that nonsense and come to work for me. I'll make you a millionaire." George took the job and in true Horatio Alger style rose through the ranks; business became his pleasure, businessmen his mentors and models. He developed a biographical theory "that great men are most interesting in the years before their greatness is recognized." But then ambition drew him away from Armour and he took an unsuccessful flier in the wholesale grocery business, concentrating on a liquid coffee extract he thought was about to be discovered. Then consecutively he became a reporter for the *Boston Standard*, went to Colby College for a year, wrote a novel, went to work for the *Boston Post*, then the *Boston Herald*, then saw a notice that the publishing magnate Cyrus H. K. Curtis had bought the sagging *Saturday Evening Post* and was looking for an editor and got the job, as "literary editor."

Curtis went to Europe leaving Lorimer in charge of a magazine with little money and no reputation. Lorimer worked like a galley slave, often writing most of the copy himself. By the end of 1900, circulation reached 250,000. By 1909, the *Saturday Evening Post* was America's leading magazine. Woodrow Wilson was glad to see a piece of his, "Cut Out Privilege," in the *Post* in 1912. Lorimer discerned what the new middle-class male was looking for: a sense of adventure in the life he led, a sense of respect for the things he valued. The symbol of the *Post* was Norman Rockwell's cover pictures, showing the individual just-above-average American as a character of hope and vigor, in warm touch with the objects and persons of his familiar home places. The appeal of the idea of "business" in those days was like that of the "craft" in an earlier time, like "profession" today, when "professional trucker" sounds all right. The *Post* would make of business not only a drama, but an ethic, an American ethic. "We are not crusaders or uplifters or muckrakers in our editorial policy," wrote Lorimer, "but we are trying to follow the dictates of ordinary business common sense and to work for the best interests of all America over a term of years." The man of ordinary business common sense found in the *Post* a pleasure better than the vicarious titillations of scandal among the rich and criminal classes; he found affirmation. What he was up to was interesting—and Meaningful. From his early years as an editor, Lorimer had the sense that politics could help education, nudge the public along a bit toward improvement in the quality of national life, supplementing journalistic infiltration. Presidents had written for the *Post*, from Grover Cleveland light ("The Mission of Fishing and Fishermen") to heavy ("Strength and Needs of Civil Service Reform"). Taft, Roosevelt, and Wilson all wrote *Post* articles in 1912. Wilson delayed a message to Congress until his *Post* interview on the topic could run, and Harding, no doubt calling on special sensitivities, put in a piece on "The Conscience of the Republic." After early backing for the Progressives, the *Post* became primarily a resistance movement—against Henry Ford's Peace Ship, the Great War, the League of Nations, immigration, government ownership, Bolsheviks, Europe, and "the pinks, the preachers and the professors" propounding propaganda.

As early as 1919, Lorimer had an eye out for some businessman who might make a President and, in its New Year's issue for 1920, the *Post* asked readers to "consider Mr. Hoover," intimating that because his partisan affiliation, if any, was unknown, he could somehow be drafted directly by the people. Hoover and Lorimer hit it off; by 1925 they were reviewing political manuscripts together. As 1928 approached, Lorimer had his scouts out to test—as all the Presidential journalists were doing—what Coolidge's enigmatic pronouncements meant and, if they meant no, how Hoover might be brought along. First, though, Hoover himself had to be brought around; like Hughes and Wilson and other moralistic Presidential types yet to come, Hoover shied from any public appearance of ambition and dodged a flat answer. A friend wrote: "Hoover is very anxious that you know his position with regard to the Presidency. He therefore talked to me on Saturday with great frankness. Hoover said that he would make no effort to get the nomination. He declared that, in his opinion, the scramble for delegates is 'a degradation of the office.' " Lorimer dispatched a man to advise Hoover on press relations, telling him to accentuate the positive and that he was "shooting an editorial and a couple of articles that ought to help." The *Post* became a Hoover publicity machine; the flow of advice about publicity went all one way, as Hoover—"our peerless but somewhat gun-shy candidate"—still suffered from the rhetorical rheumatism that had led him to fail English four years running at Stanford. Lorimer backed him as the better man, but kept his personal distance. When Hoover got the nomination, the *Post* saw him as "a man, not a formula—a man of capacity, experience, and leadership conversant with large problems." The *Post* drummed on through the campaign.

Hoover stalked into the Presidency in a circus of morals played in the shelter of prosperity. To Americans then, "depressions" were over for good, though a minority of farmers could not seem to get with the national upswing. New millions each year acquired electricity, telephones, radios, automobiles, stocks, bonds. *"Is your bread buttered?"* asked the Republican ads. Times were looking good. The campaign news would have to develop themes beyond the economic. Themes of interest grew out of the revolution in manners and morals the Roaring Twenties came to symbolize. Even then, the Lost Generation and their jazzy, uncynical, liberated imitators formed a minority bulge in the demographic flow. Eventually their aimless pleasure-seeking lost its piquancy and the Great American Mass turned from entertaining tales to tales of enterprise, from prurience to principle. As would happen again in the early 1950s, against the baseline of prosperity the American propensity for political moralizing played out fast and loose.

Neither convention offered excitement. Hoover won on the first ballot, 837 votes to 72 for Senator Charles Curtis, who quickly accepted the Vice-Presidential nomination. The Democrats sleepily nominated their "Happy Warrior," Governor Al Smith of New York, also on the first ballot. Then the whirlwind struck. Smith was a wet, Catholic, New York, Irish politician. His nomination revitalized the waning Ku Klux Klan and the wider national paranoia about aliens with secret allegiances. Within a week some ten million pieces of anti-Catholic propaganda were passed out—"Popery in the Public Schools," "Convent Life Unveiled," "Convent Horrors," "Crimes of the Pope." The equation Catholic = Tammany = foreign = liquor = Bolshevik = un-American summed itself up in the person of Al Smith. Smith tried not to notice it. But when at last the "issue" would not go away, he came flat out for "absolute freedom of conscience for all men" and "the equality of all churches" and "the law of the land"—the Constitution's plain separation of God's organizations from man's governments. Hoover stood aside from the matter, mildly reminding voters that he, as a Quaker, came from persecuted stock and that he hoped Americans would respect religious freedom. He refused to debate Smith and did not once mention his name. Other Republican leaders said Smith himself was responsible for injecting the religious issue into the campaign. But it seemed nothing could stop the flood of accusation and suspicion and righteous indignation. The political reality of Al Smith—a competent, progressive governor, with a flair for organization—got blanked out by a symbolic reality freighted with moral meaning. Hoover beat him with more than 58 percent of the vote. Clearly journalism had fed, and fed upon, an emotional surge that rapidly outran reasonable calculation from moral principles. Smith came on as an alien invader of the American Eden, where rural-rooted Protestant values held sway. The rest period after 1920, the fight of 1924, had cleared the agenda of political feelings for an election in which questions of right and wrong consumed the national attention.

8

Wendell Willkie 1940

A DECADE AFTER the bottom fell out of American prosperity, a vast new magazine enterprise, Time, Inc., invented Wendell Willkie. Actually Willkie, like Wilson and Hoover, used journalism just as journalism was using him. But he comes closer to exemplifying the candidate "made" by the media than any contender before or since. His mentors in *Time* brought to bear on that inventive task a new mode of moral instruction, the news as parable, that would transform the way Americans experienced the politics of conscience. Harvey of *Harper's* had argued. The muckrakers of *McClure's* had exposed. Lorimer of the *Saturday Evening Post* had celebrated. Henry Luce's *Time* magazine discovered how to enlist the tremendous psychological power of the week's news as a narrative story to the cause of ethical uplift. *Time* became the most popular newsmagazine in the Western world; to this day it shapes the thinking of millions of middle-class Americans—many of whom are hardly aware that they are being influenced. As the election of 1940 approached, *Time* had reason to believe its time had come to make a President.

President Franklin Delano Roosevelt was in trouble. Elected in 1932 as an alternative to Hoover's hard times, Roosevelt proceeded to play every card in his New Deal. In the fighting election of 1936, he overwhelmed his Republican opponent, Alfred Landon, the Kansas sunflower. No sooner was he back in the White House than he began to make a series of mistakes that, by 1940, would add up to a series of charges of political moral turpitude. Frustrated by rulings of the Supreme Court, he came up with a cute plan to increase their number and thus enhance his chances at saving certain legislative and executive programs. Indignant reaction to this assault on the Constitution's sanctum sanctorum led to open rejection of the plan by the Senate. Then a new recession hit. At first FDR stuck to conservative balance-budgeting principles, but then suddenly reversed himself and went in for big spending—"pump-priming." Economically it worked; philosophically, it looked like a slippery trick. As the 1938 midterm elections loomed on the horizon, Roosevelt set out to "purge" the Democratic ranks in Congress of mossback obstructionists, intervening publicly in selected primaries. That flopped. Most of the mossbacks won, and came back to Washington feeling betrayed by their party's leader. In the election, the Republicans did better than they had in ten years, gaining eight new Senate seats, eighty-one House seats, and thirteen governorships. Southern Democrats joined Republican conservatives to frustrate the Presidential will, but the big trouble was in Europe. On September 1, 1939, the Nazis swept into Poland. "This nation must remain a neutral nation," Roosevelt advised, "but I cannot ask that every American remain neutral in thought as well," a statement that seemed to advertise a gap between conviction and performance.

Speculation arose that Roosevelt might shatter the ancient tradition, started by George Washington, barring a President from a third term. Roosevelt, very busy with international affairs, let that rumor run right on into the Democratic convention in Chicago. There Mayor Ed Kelly broke another tradition by welcoming the delegates with a flat-out endorsement for Roosevelt, posed in the standard moralistic formula:

> The salvation of the nation rests in one man, because of his experience and great humanitarian thinking. I think I know that the President has no wish to labor longer under the burden of this office. He has discouraged every advance that I have made toward his becoming a candidate. He is not a candidate.
> But this convention faces a world condition that surmounts any man's convenience. We must overrule his comfort and convenience and draft Roosevelt.*

He was drafted by a big margin on the first ballot. From Washington, he accepted in a radio broadcast, echoing the moral theme: "It is with a very full heart that I speak tonight," he said, "I must confess that I do so with mixed feelings—because I find myself, as almost everyone does sooner or later in his lifetime, in a conflict between deep personal desire for retirement on the one hand, and that quiet, invisible thing called 'conscience' on the other." He said he would "not have time or the inclination to engage in purely political debate" that year, though he would not let lies pass unremarked. Not until September 11 did he make a clearly political speech, not until the last two weeks did he let loose with five speeches defending his record and excoriating the Republicans.

The editorial press, as earlier, was not impressed. The *Washington Post* saw a "Messianic complex" apparently "possessing Mr. Roosevelt even more firmly." In 1937, the editorialists of the *New York Times* had launched that paper's most intensive editorial attack ever, against Roosevelt's court-packing plan, a series of fifty pieces running over six months. In 1940, with few exceptions, the columnists (fixed as a branch of newspaper journalism by Pulitzer's *New York World*) had long been savaging Roosevelt. Pundit Walter Lippmann damned his "dictatorial tendencies." Raymond Clapper,

---

* Quoted in Robert E. Burke, "Election of 1940," in Schlesinger et al., eds., *History of American Presidential Elections*, vol. 4, p. 2933.

disappointed at FDR's acceptance of nomination for a third term wrote, "Up to the time of that message I have had faith in Mr. Roosevelt. I have none now." Westbrook Pegler kept up his running diatribe against Roosevelt as either a fascist or a communist—in any case evil incarnate. Columnist David Lawrence even wrote a book accusing Roosevelt of *Stumbling into Socialism.* A rare supporter, columnist Dorothy Thompson, was eased off the pages of the *New York Herald-Tribune* when she put out a column endorsing the President.

In contrast to publishers and columnists, reporters liked Roosevelt— personally, but also professionally. He used to sit with them out in the Rose Garden and read aloud from the most damning of the columns, laughing all the way. In 1938, the president of the National Press Club greeted him as "a newspaperman's President," saying, "You have made historic news, and you have served it hot and steaming." Reporters responded with raucous approval when he appeared in a skit before the Gridiron Club in 1939, asking, "Is there nothing to be said for a man who does what he can every day in every way for the welfare of the world? Is there nothing to be said for a man who is willing to take the burden of the world on his shoulders? Is there nothing to be said for a man who daily shares the wisdom of the ages with all men? Can a man help it if he is omniscient? Is it fair to pillory such a man merely because he is—*a newspaper columnist?*"*

In 1933, Henry Luce found Roosevelt in person stunning: "What a man! What a *man!*" But in time doubt set in. Roosevelt could only succeed if business succeeded, and business had lost confidence in a President who implied they were "anti-social, unpatriotic, vulgar and corruptive." *Time* turned to Willkie.

The Hoosier Hero

The Willkie idea looked bizarre. *Who's Who* listed him as a Democrat. He confessed to having contributed money to FDR's 1932 campaign. He had spoken of Roosevelt as "one of the greatest Presidents." His public office experience was zero, elected or appointed, and he had served on a Tammany Hall committee. He was a Wall Street lawyer (though, as he pointed out, his office was actually around the corner on Pine Street). He was a rich utilities tycoon. He was a mere forty-eight years old and of German extraction on both sides of the family—a matter thought relevant in that season when Hitler's armies were out border smashing. Physically, Willkie was a big and bushy-haired bear of a man; his style was loquacious candor, the near-opposite of the politician's ambiguous art. And he was up against three Republican regulars—Robert Taft, Thomas Dewey, and Arthur Vandenberg—set

* Quoted in Harold Brayman, *The President Speaks . . . off the Record* (Princeton: Dow Jones Books, 1976), pp. 345–46.

to fight for the nomination against the best politicians of the century. A seasoned Old Guardsman tried to warn him off, telling Willkie that it was "all right if the town whore joins the church, but they don't let her lead the choir the first night." When at last the party did nominate him, he jarred the convention by addressing them as "you Republicans."

Willkie thus met none of the standard political criteria for "availability." That fact made him attractive to the moralists looking for someone free of the political taint who was as clean as Wilson and Hoover had been, and able to be offered as a champion against "that man" in the White House who dared to break precedent to run for a third term. Luce enlisted his entire empire in Willkie's behalf—*Time, Life, Fortune.* Back in 1892 when Wendell was born, said *Life,* "Elwood, Ind. was the kind of town that young Americans of spirit flocked to, sure of making fortunes," thanks to an abundant supply of natural gas. *Life's* pictures showed that "hollyhocks now grow high"; the main street ran "flat and straight and smells of frying meat at noon. Hardly anyone wears coat or tie in summer." There was the Willkie birthplace, a "big frame house" with a porch and trees out front. His four grandparents, it turned out, had "fled German autocracy." His father, H. F. Willkie (nicknamed "Hell Fire"), "bawled Shakespearean quotations up the stairwell to wake his children in the morning." He was a great reader and "made their home a midland athenaeum. Intellectual visitors flocked to it. Dinner at the Willkies was a perpetual debate." Only fifteen, "red-sweatered 'Win' Willkie" took off for Indiana University, where he "was soon famed as a campus radical and orator"—the radicalism amounting to leading the campus "barbarians" (later he joined a fraternity), criticizing the faculty, the Bible, and inheritances, and preaching "socialism one day and Jeffersonaian Democracy the next." "Inspired by a family hatred of Prussianism," *Life* reported, "Willkie enlisted the day after the U.S. entered the first world War."

Thus the Americanism, born and bred and demonstrated in the heartland. Willkie is portrayed in images that link back to the traditional American contrast with fancy-pants European sophisticates. He has a "partiality for double-breasted coats that he persists in wearing unbuttoned." His wife and secretary keep trying to spruce him up, but "he wears ineradicably the stamp of small-town Indiana. The twang in his voice, the eagerness of his round friendly face, his love of cracker-barrel debate, and the way he props his feet on a desk or drapes a leg over a chair arm while engaged in one are a giveaway of his midland origin." But he is no hayseed patsy: "Privately . . . New Dealers who have battled with him complain that he is not above slipping a rabbit punch or even a pair of brass knucks into a tough fight." He is an up-and-coming, go-getting, plain-speaking, unabashed American, personifying themes that trace back to George Washington the frontiersman vs. the gloriously dandified George III.

But was he too ambitious? The moralist's ideal candidate should be no

shrinking violet, but neither should he lust after the Presidency. *Life's* judgment on the ambition question shines through this "balanced" paragraph:

> Wendell Willkie presents the engrossing psychological spectacle of a man who
> had admittedly made himself "virtual czar" of his own corporation, yet appears by his
> lifelong record to have a genuine passion for democratic freedom. This phenomenon
> admits of two possible explanations: 1) Willkie cannot bear to have anybody be boss
> but himself; 2) he understands, as only a man who craves and has won it can, the
> temptations of power, and has become fired with the conviction that a democracy
> must be forever alert to keep any man from getting too much of it. Each conclusion
> would bear, and assuredly would receive plenty of public examination if Mr. Willkie
> should happen to receive the Republican nomination.*

"Plainly delighted with the attention he is getting," *Life* observed, "Willkie
likes to insist that it is not a personal tribute, but a public trend." Public
opinion was swinging back: Willkie said, "They want business to have a
chance again, but they want to keep the social controls over it. That's the
idea I symbolize. That's why there's all the fuss about me." Cincinnatus
could not have said it better.

Life found also in Willkie the final attitudinal qualification—an emphasis on moral idealism as distinguished from "politics." *Life* reprinted from
Fortune Willkie's "Petition to Politicians," in which he identified the politicians throughout as "you." He asked of the weary and despairing pols, "Give
up this vested interest that you have in depression, open your eyes to the future, help us build a New World." The politicians, "under the banners of
reform, . . . have usurped our sovereign power by curtailing the Bill of
Rights, by short-circuiting the states, and by placing in the hands of a few
men in executive commissions all the powers requisite to tyranny. . . . Give
us back the powers that our forefathers declared to be ours; liberate us to
govern ourselves by *law*." Willkie's petition climaxed in an italicized section
declaring that these views would not interest the social experimenters, people who see the United States as *"a free-lunch counter"* or *"a somewhat impoverished gold mine."* Rather, *"it will interest only those who think of the
United States as their land—a land that they know and love—a land that became rich through the industry, thrift, and enterprise of its people, and will
never regain its prosperity in any other way."* Thus the high, long principles
that were to guide and govern Willkie's choices—principles specifically
counterpoised to "social experiments," principles prior to experience.

That was Willkie as *Life* had him in the spring of 1940. But three years
earlier, the Luce magazines had introduced him through *Fortune*, which gave
him a long profile stressing the genius behind his unaffected exterior. He
was a new-breed businessman, it said, free of outworn habits and prejudices,
scrappily struggling to reward the customers and stockholders of his mammoth Commonwealth and Southern utilities empire. The moralist's problem

Life, 13 May 1940.

with goodness is to distinguish it from dumbness. *Fortune* stressed Willkie's savvy, his "quick-witted and resourceful legal mind," while maintaining his innocence:

> Finally, he is so manifestly candid, sharp, and unaffected that many Congressmen have probably been reminded unconsciously of the traditional American type they like to think they are representing—the Mississippi Yankee, the clever bumpkin, the homespun, rail-splitting, soil-eared, cracker-barrel simplifier of national issues in the style of Abe Martin and Will Rogers. . . . There is at any rate nothing bogus or staged about Willkie's picturesque Americanism.*

And *Time* had put Willkie on its cover on July 31, 1939, the news peg being TVA's purchase of Commonwealth and Southern's Tennessee subsidiary for a whopping $78,600,000. Not yet pictured as a potential President, Willkie was "resourceful, informed, more publicly articulate than any big U.S. businessman today," a man who "turned committee hearings into promotion for his own political-economic doctrines." *Time* saw Willkie as "an Indiana crackerbox debater in store clothes, and full of intellectual hops." His eyes, "blue, humor-flecked" in repose, "get hawk-like" in argument.

Willkie had what it took to attract the moralizing journalists: a maverick personality, a slightly offbeat articulateness, and a new slant on the nation's current crisis. The speaking invitations poured in. He argued the case for private utilities specifically and liberated business generally in various public statements for the *Atlantic Monthly* on "Political Power: The TVA," and "Brace up America"; a radio speech on "The Town Meeting of the Air"; a commencement address at Indiana University; a *Saturday Evening Post* article on "Idle Men, Idle Money"; in a Washington speech on "The New Fear"; a *Reader's Digest* essay on "The Faith That Is America." Meanwhile, the Great Mentioners began to notice his Presidential qualities. Apparently the first was Arthur Krock of the *New York Times*, who was told at little dinner parties that Willkie's farmbelt roots might well give him "a strong appeal to the folks back home." Krock let his readers know Willkie might be just the man, and the floodgates opened. Every Tom, Dick, and Harry with access to Republican-oriented print learned how to spell his name and drop the Presidential hint. Out on the West Coast, a young enthusiast clipped Willkie's "petition" from *Life* and sent it hither and yon for signatures, with amazing results: by convention time some five million had signed, seven hundred Willkie clubs had been formed, and half a million buttons (e.g., "Win With Willkie") were fastened upon American breasts.

In the sunny Washington April of 1939, Willkie, a nondriver of automobiles, asked a friend to drive him around. They paused at the Lincoln Memorial. It is written that the friend said to him there, "Now that we are approaching conclusion of the Tennessee Valley controversy, with all the publicity that you have been receiving, you had better be careful or you will

Fortune, May 1937.

suddenly find yourself a candidate for the presidency." Willkie promptly replied, the report goes, "They will never drag me into anything like that." He called to mind some campaign help he had given an Ohio candidate who made much of his honesty and wound up disgraced.

The 1939 *Time* story featured him on the cover, asking, "Wouldn't I be a sucker to say 'Yes'?" But several thousand encouraging letters later, he told badgering newsmen: "I am not running for President. Of course, it is not going to happen, but if the nomination were given to me without strings, I would accept it. But I couldn't go out and seek delegates and make two-sided statements. I value my independence." To an importuning capitalist who asked what was being done to advance his campaign, Willkie said, "Nothing." In March of 1940 Willkie's mother died; after the funeral, one report has it, he told his three brothers he was in the race. But in April, when Sinclair Weeks said he had heard the Willkie name mentioned for the Presidency, Willkie is said to have responded, "What do you think I am, a Goddamn fool?"—which could be interpreted several ways. Perhaps he turned the corner when, in May, the managing editor of *Fortune* threw up his job and took on the management of his campaign. He said to the National Press Club on June 12, "People keep asking me if I am a candidate. Of course I am a candidate," and he named his nominator and seconder. But then a few days before the Republican convention opened that month in Philadelphia, Willkie said, "I'm not running for anything, and I'm not running away from anything. But I would be a liar if I said I wouldn't like to be President or wouldn't accept the nomination." A case could be made that his very acceptance speech—to "you Republicans"—showed a certain retention of uncertainty.

Well before then, the magazine moralists had made their own minds up. Russell Davenport, *Fortune*'s managing editor, had Willkie to one of his "Round Tables" shortly after the *Time* cover story. Davenport came away saying, "I have just met the man who ought to be the President of the United States," and invited him for a long, intensive talk at his summer place. He introduced Willkie to Henry Luce, monarch of Time, Inc., who wrote in a memo: "I think of Willkie as a force of Nature. I think of Davenport as a force of Spirit. When the two met—the chemical reaction produced an event of political history."

Magazine journalists had been mixing the ingredients for the reaction since the twenties. Two very different publications helped set a style and technique that much more directly political magazines would exploit from then to now—especially *Time*. The *New Yorker* pranced onto the scene in 1925, birthed on a Round Table in the lobby of the Algonquin Hotel by Harold Ross and a gang of pals who had put out *Stars and Stripes* during the Great War. These fellows used to sit around trading witticisms and mild insults. They read a lot. Above all, they were Clever. They dreamed up a magazine aimed not at "the old lady in Dubuque" but at the urban sophisticate. Ross himself, with his upstanding shock of straw-thatch, his tooth-fraught mouth, and rawboned body, looked and sounded like a bumpkin from Dubuque. His voice was raucous, his sentences structureless. He cussed. He hated crowds. He had come along from Colorado and Utah and as a tramp reporter had been known to wear yellow shoes. He was innocent of Higher Education. In short, he was just the fellow to discover romance in the parlors of Manhattan—an excitement the locals were too close to see.

The *New Yorker*'s cardinal rule was Not to be Excited. It covered the market panic of 1926 with the same aplomb and panache as it covered Earl Carroll's adventures with a naked girl in a bathtub of ginger ale. The *New Yorker* was paid to be funny, but to grin, not guffaw—sacred cows were not gored; they were pricked—it was wise and sly and cute. And it appealed— enough for long-lasting solvency—to the insider mentality, the in-the-knows, the "person who knows his way about or wants to," as its creators claimed. Weighing down the other end of the sincerity scale came the *Reader's Digest*, offspring of a deep-dyed Presbyterian, DeWitt Wallace, whose preacher father sent him off "to do as much good in the world as possible," as the son put it. Severely wounded at the Meuse-Argonne, he spent months in the hospital reading magazines. He liked that, but felt the authors stalked their points too prolixly. He got out a pencil and went to work on them. In January 1920, he mocked up a sample *Reader's Digest*, in pocket-size, thirty-one pieces for the month, one a day, "each article of enduring value and interest." They ranged widely: "Is Honesty the Best Policy?" "The Shortest Route to the Top," "How to Regulate Your Weight." After failing tries, the first real issue appeared in February 1922, printed in a garage; several decades later, the *Digest* emanated from a magnificent feudal barony near Pleasantville, N.Y., some 30 million copies, in thirteen languages, each and every month. *The Reader's Digest* took up a political issue now and then, but the tone was not readily distinguishable from that of the *Saturday Evening Post*. Slickly homely, the *Digest*'s simplified, determinedly upbeat celebrations of free enterprise and the American way gave the moral essay a fresh cast. It proved that old news could sell and that busy people would read tightly digested versions of it.

Time put it all together. Like Sarah Hale, *Time*'s inventors set out to improve life by schooling the citizenry, not only in the facts but in the national proprieties. Like Ida Tarbell and the muckrackers, they peered behind the facades for the realities and portrayed the dramatic personalities at the levers of the social machines. Like George Lorimer's *Saturday Evening Post*, they took aim at middle-class Americans, whose pretensions were less literary than enterprising. Like Harold Ross of the *New Yorker*, they punched out a new language that let the reader feel smart as well as wise, and like DeWitt Wallace, they condensed from the gaseous fog of reportage the simple clear essences a harried reader could imbibe in flight. And like

Harvey of *Harper's Weekly*, *Time's* inventors saw the Presidency as the ultimate national platform—and took it upon themselves to see the right man
there ensconced. By *Time's* time, it seemed natural for the progressive
businessmen-publishers to exercise their energies among the Republicans,
who, convinced of the correctness of their principles, saw selling them as the
crucial task.

Like all of the above, the titans of *Time* were moralists and their story
was a moral tale. Like Diogenes, they searched the American landscape for
an honest man they could make a leader of, a clean-limbed purifier, innocent
and knowing, righteous and attractive, a visceral American nationalist at ease
in the parlors of diplomacy. Along the way, they bent and shaped the thinking of their times.

Preaching by Parable

Time was set going by an unlikely pair of Yalies, Briton Hadden and
Henry Luce, in their and the century's early twenties. Hadden was a tough-
talking, hell-raising son of a Brooklyn stockbroker, out to make a million
dollars before he was thirty. Luce was a shy and stuttering, heaven-longing
son of Presbyterian missionaries in China, out to make the world safe for
God and man. They had in common enormous energies, galloping intelligence, and a very high opinion of themselves.

Hadden and Luce suddenly appeared on each other's horizons in prep
school, as rival journalists and eventually rival editors, Hadden of the school
news organ, Luce of the literary magazine. At Yale they continued to fight
and admire one another. Hadden barely beat out Luce in the vote for chairman (editor) of the *Yale Daily News* and Luce became managing editor. As
the Great War heated up, they came together in castigating Kaiser Wilhelm.
But they kept score. Luce wrote home that "I have written 40% of the editorials and Hadden 30%"; later, as fledgling reporters on the *Baltimore News*,
they competed in the number of front-page lines each could get into print.
They left Yale for a brief stint in the army, where they took walks together,
shared their judgment that the world was grossly underinformed, and talked
tentatively about a new publication to solve that problem. Back at Yale after
the war, in the class of 1920, Luce was "most brilliant," Hadden "most likely
to succeed."

Then Luce spent a year at Oxford, reading and thinking, and Hadden
put on a tie and went to New York. Luce wrote his parents: "My desire is to
go into public life and whatever I do in the next ten years is preparatory to
that . . . publishing? . . . business? . . . financial independence so I can go
into politics without being entirely dependent upon the boss for my bread
and butter." His first "real" journalistic job was as a leg man for columnist
Ben Hecht of the *Chicago Daily News*. Fortunately for his future, Luce was
fired after five weeks. Hadden talked himself into a job at the *World* by accusing the reluctant editor of "interfering with my destiny."

They joined fortunes again when Walter Millis of the *Baltimore News* needed two new reporters and turned to his Yale classmates. Hadden wrote Luce, "If we are ever going to start that paper, this looks like our chance." The two took up lodging in Millis's attic, *News* reporters by day, incessant plotters of the new publication by night. Briton Hadden led the talk.

Hadden of the *World*, frustrated at not being immediately assigned to cover Big Stories—or, for hours on end, *any* stories—confronted the city editor. They had a man to meet ships; why couldn't he meet trains? Permission was granted; he chased important if reluctant interviewees through Grand Central and Penn stations. Between trains he slowly turned a frustration into a creative opportunity. The reporter at the next desk remembered Hadden picking up a *New York Times* one day and saying:

See this? Full of wonderful news, tell you everything going on in the world, but you haven't got time to read it all every day. You're a rich millionaire. You live at Glen Cove. You get on the train in the morning. You pick up the *Times*. Maybe you get only half-way through by the time you reach Penn Station. I have an idea for a magazine that comes out every Friday with all the news condensed so you and all the other rich millionaires commuting home for the weekend can catch up on the news that they have missed. How's that?*

Hadden's working title was *Facts*, but Luce came up with a better one. Riding the subway under Manhattan, he saw an ad slogan, "Time to Retire or Time for a Change." Next morning, he told Hadden they ought to call it *Time* and Hadden agreed at once. (A symbolic transition of subsequent import: from *Facts* to *Time*, from item to sequence, from event to story.) They wrote up a brave prospectus for "Time: The Weekly News-Magazine." It said, among other confident assertions,

People are misinformed BECAUSE NO PUBLICATION HAS ADAPTED IT-SELF TO THE TIME WHICH BUSY MEN ARE ABLE TO SPEND ON SIMPLY KEEPING INFORMED. . . .

Time is interested—not in how much it includes between its covers—but in HOW MUCH IT GETS ITS PAGES INTO THE MINDS OF ITS READERS. . . .

There will be no editorial page in *Time*.

No article will be written to prove any special case.

But the editors recognize that complete neutrality on public questions and important news is probably as undesirable as it is impossible, and are therefore ready to acknowledge certain prejudices which may in varying measure predetermine their opinion on the news.

A catalogue of these prejudices would include such phrases as:

1. A belief that the world is round and an admiration of the statesman's "view of the world."
2. A general distrust of the present tendency toward increasing interference by government.
3. A prejudice against the rising cost of government.

* Quoted in Noel F. Busch, *Briton Hadden* (New York: Farrar, Straus & Company, 1949), pp. 63–64.

4. Faith in the things which money cannot buy.

5. A respect for the old, particularly in manners.

6. An interest in the new, particularly in ideas.

But this magazine is not founded to promulgate prejudices, liberal or conservative. "To keep me well-informed"—that, first and last, is the only axe this magazine has to grind.*

Hadden and Luce took a leave from the *News* and the first issue of *Time* appeared, dated March 3, 1923. The two publishers were not yet twenty-five years old, the new circulation manager, Roy Larsen, hired three giddy debutantes to do the mailing; they so mucked it up that many *Time* triers got three copies, many none. (Later, when *Time* headquarters moved to Cleveland, Larsen hired parolees from the Ohio State female reformatory to open trial subscription orders. They pocketed the five-dollar bills and threw away the coupons.) Circulation was 25,000 in 1923, over 100,000 in 1926, 140,000 in 1927. By 1928 *Time* showed the first substantial net profit, $125,000. Hadden and Luce were rich.

Luce and Hadden listed themselves as editors on the masthead, but from the start they decided Hadden would edit and Luce would take care of the business end. Five years later they would switch roles. Luce wrote pieces for the Religion section from time to time, and took over editing when on rare occasion Hadden was away. But if any hand shaped the genesis of *Time*, it was Hadden's. He invented a new manner of speaking in print. The form imposed terseness: no story would run over about seven inches of type, the prospectus said, but "every happening of importance" would be covered. The raw material was a great pile of newspaper clippings, largely from the *New York Times* and the *World*, backed up with a twenty-year *Times* file. Thus the task—every week—was like pushing camels through the eye of a needle, camels freighted with moral baggage on top of their cargo of fact. Artfulness was not an option, it was a necessity.

Hadden sat at a big rolltop desk, in shirt sleeves, his mustache bristling and his habitual green eyeshade cocked over one eyebrow, grunting and jutting out his jaw as he chopped every inessential word with his great big red lead pencil. "In the nick of time"—no, "in time's nick." Most "the's" had to go, and most "and's" and "on the other hand's" and "neverthelesses." Copy-cutting knifed down inside the very words to save a letter or syllable here and there. Not "famous"—"famed." Not "powerful"—"potent." When Hadden could not find a short word to replace a long one, he would hurl his thesaurus at the wall. Latinate endings gave way to abrupt Anglo-Saxon. Hadden sparked up the copy with his own new words and constructions—a kind of Englishese, actually reaching back past Anglo-Saxon to the sparest of languages, Greek, a legacy of Hadden's and Luce's Greek classes at Hotchkiss and Yale. Hadden took the language into his life. Homer en-

* Quoted in Robert T. Elson, *Time Inc.: The Intimate History of a Publishing Enterprise 1923–1941* (New York: Atheneum, 1968), pp. 49–50.

chanted him. He read the *Iliad* again and again, underlining phrase after phrase: "rolling-eyed Greeks," "far-darting Apollo." He loaded such hyphenations into *Time*—gently at first: "gray-thatched," "many-towered," "custard-piety," then more abrasively: "bald-domed," "moose-tall," "snaggle-toothed," "rat-faced," "hog-fat." Verbs slid toward the end of sentences: "Forth from the White House followed by innumerable attendants, Mr. and Mrs. Warren G. Harding set out. . . ." *Time* layered adjective on adjective, like a collage, and *Time's* alliterations dinged in the ear. George Bernard Shaw was (all at once) "mocking, mordant, misanthropic." Remembering another of his professors' aversion for weak verbs, Hadden refused to let *Time* people merely *say* something—they "barked" or "burbled"; nor could they *go* here and there—they "ambled" or "dashed" or "lumbered." Old words were resurrected—"moppet," "tosspot"—new ones quickly adopted—"oldster," "ecdysiast"—foreign ones imported— "tycoon," "pundit," "marmeluke," "kudos." When extant vocabularies gave out, *Time* invented its own—"cinemalefactor," "nudancer," "paradoxhund," "socialite," eventually even "lemoncholy" and "führious." Hadden kept his *Iliad* on his desk and a black notebook in which his favorite phrases were delightedly scrawled. *Time's* new words and upside-down constructions strung out into mini-dramas composed in classic Aristotelian beginning-middle-end form and acted by vivid characters.

Hadden had no use for abstractions or anticlimatic qualifications. "One hears" and "on the highest authority" got chopped; if *Time* could not name a source, *Time* itself would assert the facts. Hadden also had a sense of the ridiculous. He got an asbestos suit so he could snuff out cigarettes on his sleeve. He was forever inventing games; he liked to play a shifty-ruled combination of hearts, blackjack, and old maid at raucous parties in his bachelor digs. Hadden played with *Time*, blurring the boundary between the real and the plausible, employing a trick he had played with the Yale *Daily News*— the fake letter. Hadden at Yale entertained readers with a virulent controversy between "Divinity Student," writing to complain about dormitory noise, and "Old Hatchet Face," his vituperative answerer. Hadden wrote all the letters himself. *Time's* letters from real readers were not as good as Hadden's were. His writers joined the fun, each adopting several pseudonyms and venting their repressed spleens. An early invention was the old lady from Dubuque writing haughtily, "They should learn that there is no provincialism so blatant as that of the metropolitan who lacks urbanity." Hadden's playful fakery served its purpose. The letters poured in, including a minor correction from his own mother. Before long there were plenty of satisfactorily *Time*-like real letters; many that *Time* lacked space for were printed in a separate publication, which reached a paid circulation of 35,000.

Briton Hadden died of septicemia in 1929 when he was thirty-one years old. He had made his million and more before he was thirty and he had marked a new style of reporting into magazine journalism. He let the air out of interpretative newswriting and replaced it with an irreverent sparkle and rancor and jest. Hadden's *Time* caught the attention of a generation. And from then to now—from *Time* to *Newsweek* and *New York, Esquire* and *Playboy, Harper's* and the *New Republic, Rolling Stone,* and *National Review*—the summarizers and interpreters have been peppering their sermonettes with snatches of dashing doggerel, hokey verbal inventions, and literary handstands.

Time under Luce had a point of view with a vengeance. Hadden could not resist calling some blacks "blackamorons" or "blackamoors," but men of both races were called "Mr." (to the horror of some readers), and a lynched black was portrayed as "put to death by the premeditated violence of yokels who believed in their gross way that they were maintaining the honor of the race that bred them." Luce's *Time* reported the Ethiopians, then under attack by Mussolini's Italy, as "savage and illiterate," "screaming savages," "mud-wallowing savages," who lived in the "hell-hole of creation" amid "fleas, flies and filth," their men "squalling for protection," their women "fashionably tallowed with Ethiopian grease." Mussolini, by contrast, appeared five times on *Time*'s cover, a "buoyant empire-builder." Praise of Hitler was comparatively restrained, but his early depredations were treated as inevitable—"Even to intelligent Germans it began to seem that the Hitler regime might be useful in getting Germany's necessary international dirty work done"—or amusing—"Germany has been naughty but is not to be spanked." Winston Churchill's warnings about the Nazi menace were mere "verbal postures," and *Time* suggested, "Perhaps it was the intuition of Adolf Hitler to let this windy provocation pass. . . ." Franco was a "humorous and carefree" fellow, "soft-spoken, studious," a man of "soldierly simplicity" and strong in "caution, thoroughness, quick decision, forehandedness," while his enemies were "largely composed of ill-trained, ill-disciplined showmakers, cab-drivers and waiters who were only prevented from scattering in despair by their officers standing behind them with cocked firearms." Most of *Time*'s racist and fascist trash in these years was hauled into print by one Laird Goldsborough. Luce kept him on a long leash, though eventually, as Hitler's crimes emerged, his virulent anti-Semitism got toned down. (In 1950, Goldsborough went out a skyscraper window to his death, in bowler hat and carrying a cane.) Luce took a more direct hand in domestic affairs: *Time* raised the question whether Mrs. Roosevelt was a "publicity-glutton" or a "genuine, warm-hearted woman," and freely scathed such New Deal officials as Rexford Tugwell and Hugh Johnson. When Governor Alf Landon came along to oppose Roosevelt in the election of 1936, *Time* pictured him as a "husky, broad-shouldered" man with an "honest, cracker-barrel voice" who had made a fortune "by enterprise, hard work, fair dealing and stiff bargaining," then, as the dimensions of Landon's impending loss loomed, turned querulous, reporting his bored and booing audiences. In any one issue, *Time*'s judgmental vision was abundantly one-sided. As last week's judgments faded into obscurity, *Time* could change its moral mind. When politics in the real world got really more serious—much more so than in the easy-speaking twenties—*Time* glowered where it had glimmered. Luce's soul was attuned to that mood, as Hadden's had been to the Jazz Age.

Henry Luce's Pilgrimage

Henry Luce was conceived in America but born in Tenchow, China, the child of newly arrived Presbyterian missionaries. His father—former editor of the *Yale Courant*—burned with Christian zeal; he got across to the boy his belief that "character means destiny," that willpower—"Lucepower" he called it—was the key to success, and that someplace called "America" was the greatest place in the world and someone called "Theodore Roosevelt" its greatest citizen. Mother was the disciplinarian and homebody. Day began at 6:00 with a cold bath and Bible study before breakfast. From mother and father, little Harry heard again and again the glorious tale of the liberation of Peking by American troops in the Boxer Rebellion. By the time he was four, the boy was propounding sermons to his mother, in imitation of the thunderous diatribes the mission elders delivered; at five he was preaching to the neighbor children. His mother copied down some of these declamations: "He has established the earth and he founded it upon the seas. For the tower of Babel, it was a wicked thing that man should do, and Jehovah smashed it. . . ." At six he expanded the message beyond Isaiah and Paul to other saints, telling his mother, "I have the globe ready to teach the history of George Washington." Despite a bad stutter, he helped found the school debating society and was first editor of a school paper. He excelled in his studies, but was already, as a teenager, fascinated with power. "I would like to be Alexander if I were not Socrates," he wrote. And he had a powerful Ally, who answered his prayers in the most practical fashion—"Just take my 100% in Algebra," he wrote home. "It was all God." From the fragments of his experience, Luce like every man built his personal myth. He had grown up with people of mission who had taken on an enormous burden to bear forward in a hostile world. The quiet excitements of religious devotion were not enough for him. Nor was the spectator's excitement of seeing and sensing the world's strange places—the pleasure of the scout, the discoverer, as distinguished from the pioneer. The load of purpose was an essential piece of life's equipment, a load to be borne on up the mountain. Much of Luce's life was spent traveling, but never as an idling jet-setter, always as a burdened quester for whom the sense of earnest effort was the core of the drama. From school he had written his parents, who would appreciate his feeling, of just that sense as he struggled for promotion: "I do not care if I die for it. I must get inside. I must. I will." When he did die, the minister ended the funeral eulogy with the hymn beginning:

Who would true valor see
Let him come hither;
One here will constant be,
Come wind, come weather;
There's no discouragement
Shall make him once relent
His first avowed intent
To be a pilgrim.

Luce once remembered that the people "I grew up with—all of them—were good people," and the fact that they were Americans was where "the idealistic view of America came from." The actual Americans, as he experienced them, were "good Christian people." Mythical America had loomed, he later thought, "too romantic, too idealistic" in his young consciousness. "I never went through any special period of disillusionment," he remembered, "but I was, from my earliest manhood, dissatisfied with America. America was not being as great and as good as I knew she could be, as I believe she was intended to be. The Intender of American and Lucean betterment was God Himself. But God had not turned mankind loose in Eden with a mere encouraging Word: "God rules the world," he believed; by contrast, "men cannot achieve wisdom by their own efforts, nor goodness. Only a great Event can change man—an event in their personal life (Nicodemus had to be born again) or their collective life (the Assyrians coming down like the wolf on the fold)." The God of the Old Testament—guiding, leading, punishing, rewarding—was alive and well in *this* world, "not annulled but fulfilled by the New." A God of spirit, yes, but also of power; a God above and beyond history, but also in and of history. A God at once invisible and manifest, an ordering God. Thus *Time* announced on its thirtieth birthday: "That God's order in man's world includes a moral code, based upon man's unchanging nature and not subject to man's repeal, suspension or amendment." As God was the founder and foundation of that moral code, so He was of the human arrangement it impelled: "equality before the law is based on each man's dignity in God's sight" and "political liberty is based on the soul's freedom to accept or reject the good." Thus the meaning of God's will was not abstract but tangible, discoverable in history. And "no nation in history," Luce said, "except ancient Israel, was so obviously designed for some special phase of God's eternal purpose" as America was. "In His Providence, He calls this nation now to be a principal instrument of His will on earth."

Luce had the Bible forever in his mind and speech. America "must undertake now to be the Good Samaritan of the entire world." At *Time*, "if there is any gospel around here it is the Postwar Memos." And "pending a new Messiah and a fresh conversion, we are *for* Private Capitalism." When the Chinese Communists were said to claim "sanctuaries" from which to bomb Korea, Luce blew up: "Sanctuary! How blasphemous can you get!" Exhorting *Time* executives, he identified God's Opposite: "For the first time

America has a Capital E-Enemy—huge, brainy, implacable, our self-avowed Enemy. . . . Gentlemen, I say the time has come . . . to begin to make the Enemy hurt—and hurt bad." But it was more than language. In a kind of Presbyterian paradox, Luce saw success and power in this world with a double vision: on the one hand, God willed the world as Inventor and Sustainer, which made worldly power seem a sign of grace; on the other hand, the Implacable Enemy seemed to have his own sanctions and sanctuaries, unblessed, but also undestroyed, and only the most intense possible mobilization of human will could root them out.

Not much of Luce's personal theologizing got directly onto *Time*'s pages. *Time* was stories, and he was no storyteller: "If a parable is any good," a memo told an editor, "it needs no expository moralizing. But being a poor parable-sayer, you will have to bear with me while I moralize." Luce's moralizing was always pronounced with an air of noblesse. "I do not conceive of myself as having to be the continual Moral Schoolmaster of this place," he wrote in a long, schoolmasterish memo, "But I think I cannot escape being the custodian or depository of '*Time*'s conscience.' " "God's classmate," as one ex-editor called Luce, had little patience with intellectual celebrators of moral ambivalence. *Time* had turned itself into a power; of necessity that meant action: "Our great job from now on is not to create power but to use it," he wrote. "Furthermore the use of power and the creation of it are not separate things—they are inevitably bound up together. . . . To see Time Inc. in perspective is to realize its tremendous potential power. . . . I don't particularly like it . . . but there it is." Luce's original name for what was to become *Fortune* was "Power." He had created for himself a position of power from which he could define, from week to week, where in the storm of life the compass of God must point. Such an attitude came to pervade magazine journalism—left and right—for instance in the *New Republic* as Henry Wallace ran it or the *National Review* under William F. Buckley's hand. It led *Time* through long stretches of misconception and misinformation: on early fascism and nazism, on China, on the nature of the post–World War II communist threat, on McCarthyism, Vietnam, and the wonders of Richard Nixon. When, eventually, the historical realities caught up with *Time*, the moral ground could be shifted relatively suddenly, as *Time*, and *Time*-trained readers, closed the book of history each week and started again. Rarely did some obsessive journalist dig back into the old issues and point out the massive reorientations that had taken place.

The puzzle about Henry Luce is that people put up with him. Among the adjectives *Time* might have applied to him were rude, tasteless, arrogant, inarticulate, insensitive, uninterruptible, prejudiced, condemning, intrusive, demanding, and humorless. Yet Theodore White, who broke with Luce in an angry fight about China coverage, said, "If you loved magazine writing, you had to love Luce." Whenever *Time* was criticized for shoddy journalism, Luce simply responded that he and Hadden, having founded the thing, had a right to make it what they wished, and that if *Time* was so bad, why was it so successful?

One reason top-notch writers stayed with *Time* as long as they did was that *Time* paid well. That helped compensate for anonymity—*Time* had no use for by-lines, though platoons of writers were listed as editors of one sort or another. But they also stayed and labored on because Henry Luce was a magazining genius with an incredible sensitivity to soon-to-break waves of popular sentiment, a vision confirmed in the success of *Fortune* just as the Great Depression hit, the success of *Life* launched in that depression's depths. Occasionally *Time* made those waves, telling readers what "most" or "many" of them were thinking—thus seducing them into thinking that.

Luce's access to the councils of the mighty let *Time* get by with a great deal of bald assertion about the moods and anticipations of topside insiders. Franklin Roosevelt detested Luce and laughed at his wife; once he wrote a long letter to Luce, itemizing scores of errors and saying, "I hate to see an educated group of people doing things to their country which their very education, in the better sense of the word, should keep them from doing." But FDR had an assistant send a briefer plaint instead. *Time* raked and blasted Truman for years, but in 1956 Luce had him to dinner and the ex-President played a Paderewski minuet for him. Kennedy would rage to Hugh Sidey, *Time*'s wise and thoughtful Washington man, about *Time*'s derelictions, but he said, "I like Luce. He is like a cricket, always chirping away" and sent his brother Edward with a message to *Time*'s fortieth birthday party calling Luce "one of the creative editors of our age." Yale would not let Luce fulfill his ambition to become a member of the Corporation, but gave him honorary degrees in 1926, "in recognition of distinguished accomplishments in a novel and worthy field of journalism," and in 1966, announced, "With all its risks, your zestful journalism has bolstered the capacity of the citizens of the republic to cope with domestic complications and world responsibilities." Somehow Luce managed to make it seem unsporting for high news sources to complain about their coverage in *Time*.

Luce made *Time* editors and writers feel they were involved in titanic endeavors and sacred searches. His unending "reexaminations" of the magazines, though they seldom made much practical difference, did make life at *Time* seem worth living, meaningful, responsible. Even his more outrageous sophomorisms, such as the *Life* editorials that reminded a London writer of "an Archbishop giving a service in a super-cinema," furnished propositions for discussion, invited improvement by tutoring editors. He rarely issued direct commands; he ruled by a kind of climate control—savvy editors learned to sense his meaning. So did savvy readers. Luce's power was thus in a large sense the power of persuasion, of agenda setting and attention guiding, the most powerful kind of power in politics, the power to compose a culture. *Time* addressed the reader as if describing objective events, not as an advocate, but Luce told staffers, "*Time* will not allow the stuffed dummy of impartiality to stand in the way of telling the truth as it sees it." *Time's* story-editorials, conveying values through factual narrative, included no such disclaimer.

Time for Willkie

Hitler's blitzkrieg tore into Poland on September 1, 1939 and then into country after country. Luce saw a new world war arraying the forces of light against the forces of darkness. He cabled his editors from Europe that "if you were here today, remembering 1914, you would be sad but also you would be plenty, plenty mad. The word Boche is the only word used on the streets today to describe the enemy, and no other word would sound right. I deeply wish all priggish, pious pacifists could be here today." Along the way he wrote a brief introduction for Ambassador Joseph Kennedy's son's book, *Why England Slept*. To Luce, Hitler's evil deeds pointed with absolute clarity to the American course:

> Sober and long experienced observers say it is utterly irrelevant to discuss right and wrong in connection with the present German regime. The simple fact is that the Germans will stop at nothing to get what they want and there is utterly no evidence that they want anything less than all they can get by the most ruthless means. . . .
>
> The United States is indulging in complete and criminal folly unless it proceeds at once to build every single military airplane it can possibly make in the next six months. Never mind who uses them, never mind who pays, but for God's sake, make them. Similarly, all possible military equipment of every sort should be ordered at once, regardless of cost.
>
> If Life and Time fail to sell this idea now, it probably won't matter much what these estimable publications say in years to come. . . . The Germans have one weapon greater than all their army and that is the blindness and stultification of those in every country who are too fat to fight.*

Luce decided to back Willkie for President by a somewhat Jesuitical process. Roosevelt, while expressing his shock and horror at European events, "can't believe we are ever going to fight," Luce wrote. Willkie was also "a prime keep-out-of-war man"—but "may reasonably be pardoned." That is, Willkie, a political freshman, might prove more instructable than Roosevelt, already a two-time winner.

Time observed in early June 1940: "While Tom Dewey, with bravado, was fumbling with the topic of foreign affairs, while Taft appeared to be running toward the wrong goal posts, Willkie seized the ball, flatly declared: '. . . England and France constitute our first line of defense against Hitler. . . . It must therefore be to our advantage to help them in every way we can, short of declaring war.' It was what many a U.S. citizen believed." Luce went to the Republican convention and did what he could for the cause.

* Quoted in W. A. Swanberg, *Luce and His Empire* (New York: Charles Scribner's Sons, 1972), pp. 174–75.

Willkie, as ever the tradition breaker, personally set up shop in Philadelphia two days before the convention met on June 24. Herbert Hoover spoke that evening, a righteous condemnation of the New Deal. Then the Republican insiders, Thomas Dewey of New York, Robert Taft of Ohio, and Arthur Vandenberg of Michigan, wheeled into action with their inside strategies, strangely disconnected from Willkie's public onslaught. Dewey shot for a big vote on the first ballot, seeking to go over the top to the nomination. Taft moved to start small and impress everyone with his growing strength as the balloting proceeded. Vandenberg would stand back and wait for a Dewey-Taft deadlock, at which point the delegates would rally to him. But the Willkie onslaught, fueled by publicity, slammed those old-timey calculations into irrelevance. His nominator, Representative Charles Halleck of Indiana, noted that the regular candidates kept stressing their own long service to the Grand Old Party, but he asked, "Is the Republican party a closed corporation? Do you have to be born in it?" The convention chairman, Representative Joseph Martin, privately a Willkie man, recessed the convention to allow Halleck's challenge to get into the newspapers. The next night, as the packed galleries echoed with "We Want Willkie!" he won on the sixth ballot. The outsider was now on top. A disgruntled delegate complained that Willkie was "unfair to organized politics."

Life's coverage of Willkie's convention progress was a prime illustration of Time, Inc. atmospherics: strong mood-attributions spiced with fact and incident. Thus Willkie was becoming "the political sensation . . . starting from nowhere . . . swept into the front rank of Republican contenders by a mass wave of spontaneous, volunteer, amateur enthusiasm." The Gallup poll showed him up from 1 percent to 17 percent in one month, a boom "the like of which few politicians have seen in their lifetimes." *Life* discovered that "G.O.P. professionals who dismissed Willkie as 'politically impossible' two months ago began to reconsider their convention commitments." Pictures showed vast crowds turned out to hear him, but:

> More significant than their size was their spirit. By some sixth sense these American voters seemed to appreciate the extraordinary quality of this election. To them this was no routine Presidential contest, with routine issues and routine politicians; instead it was a great and important referendum the like of which the U.S. had not experienced in its 164 years.*

Willkie and *Life* called it Willkie's "crusade."

At the convention, *Life* reported, "the American people played out a political drama unique in their history." Seldom in American magazine writing had the moralizing story been told more trenchantly than in these paragraphs:

> Act I was dreary. Across the Atlantic, the world as living men and their fathers and grandfathers had known it was crumbling fast. But in Philadelphia things looked

Life, 24 June 1940.

and sounded pretty much as they had at any political convention in the past 20 or 40 years—except more confused and dispirited. In streets and hotels there were the same old jostling crowds, the same stunts and signs and gadgets, the same well-whiskyed bedroom conniving, the same desperate finagling to write a platform that would please everybody and offend nobody. The familiar pattern was broken only in six small rooms on the top floor of the Benjamin Franklin Hotel, where delegates, reporters and visitors were crowding in morning, noon and night to see and hear a new kind of leader named Wendell Willkie, an amateur whose campaign had been largely managed by amateurs. But the professionals still seemed to be running the show, and by Tuesday night everybody agreed it was a dull one.

Act II was depressing. In petitions, letters, telegrams by the hundreds of thousands the people were demanding that the Republican Party meet the challenge of the new times by nominating Willkie. But the Party elders, to a man, still held back, still strove to nominate a safe-and-sound Party Regular. The high-powered professional machine of Senator Robert A. Taft rolled into action with a barrage of attacks on Willkie as a "Democrat" and "Wall Streeter." By Wednesday night, when the Willkie opposition broke into boos and physical fighting on the convention floor, progressive observers were about ready to write the G.O.P. off as hopeless.

Act III provided the happy and inspiring ending. Thursday night, with the galleries cheering every Willkie vote and the delegates breaking away from their leaders, a tidal wave of popular demand crumbled the opposition, swept the old bosses out and Wendell Willkie and his young followers in to the leadership of the Republican Party.*

The grand climax of the drama happened after the voting: "Striding like a champion down the center aisle with pretty, shy Mrs. Willkie on Friday afternoon, a picture of power and confidence, he mounted the rostrum amid showers of confetti, balloons, cheers and cried in a fighter's voice: 'I stand before you without a single pledge or promise or understanding of any kind except for the advancement of your cause and the preservation of American democracy.' " Thus the classic themes and sequences appeared once again: America in trouble, the politicians conniving, the yeoman amateur, the righteous people, the hero at last, free and clean and dedicated.

The Time, Inc. talent went into high gear. Russell Davenport struggled to get Willkie's chaotic amateur campaign in some semblance of order; he drafted editorial-like speeches the spontaneous Willkie had trouble reciting and frequently departed from. Luce himself swung into action. Luce would telephone his secretary in the middle of the night with some hot speech idea and she would dash to the office to dispatch it to the Willkie campaign train on Luce's private wire. Willkie would stride into Luce's office unannounced (not even Luce's father could do that) and put his feet up on the desk for long strategy sessions. Luce raged at *Time*'s occasional lapses into balance, as when a Willkie crowd was said to have come to see "a dead whale on a flatcar" and when Republican professionals were said to be worrying that Willkie was "only a fatter, louder Alf Landon." A *Time* correspondent cabled

Life, 8 July 1940.

from the campaign train, "Take me off this train. All I can do is sit at my typewriter and write, 'Wendell Willkie is a wonderful man. Wendell Willkie is a wonderful man.' " Luce threatened to "exile himself" from the editorial offices—to the editors' relief—but could not stay away for long.

As the campaign progressed, moral issues predominated over the details of practical alternatives. Luce saw Roosevelt as violating a fine old tradition, writing that it was only the horror of the Hitler threat "which (in his eyes, not mine) justified Franklin Delano Roosevelt in seeking a third term—thereby shattering an honorable precedent established by George Washington." In his introduction to young John F. Kennedy's new book, *Why England Slept*, he hit FDR for slighting the sacrificial necessity: "how can he so glibly guarantee that we will not need to sacrifice one tiniest bit of our 'social gains,' " he asked, "or is he just playing politics?" When in September the President, all on his own, announced a deal to furnish used destroyers to Britain, Willkie hit him as "dictatorial" and "arbitrary." Luce agreed, writing Willkie, "I want nothing more done for Britain on the personal and exclusive authority of Franklin D. Roosevelt."

Willkie flailed away, flatly charging at one point that Roosevelt "telephoned Mussolini and Hitler and urged them to sell Czechoslovakia down the river at Munich." (He had "misspoken," his press secretary explained.) *Life* printed a shortened version of a Willkie speech, titled "American Faith" and circled by thirty-six head shots of Willkie looking dire and dazzling: "This campaign is a crusade to preserve American democracy." He rejected the counsel of "the corrupt political machines of Boss Kelly, Hague, Pendergast and Flynn." He urged mothers to "gather your family together on our great national holidays. Read to your children the sacred words of the Declaration of Independence or the Gettysburg Address. They are the living creed of our creed of our American faith." He capped it off with the pledge of allegiance.

As the campaign drew to a close, *Life* printed pieces on "The Case against Roosevelt" and "The Case against Willkie," balanced around a signed editorial by Luce called "This Great Moment." Luce reported that "many readers" had been writing in to complain that a (supposedly different) "many citizens" were not taking the election seriously enough. Indeed, said Luce, "this is the most important election since 1860," in part "because this *may* be the last time in this century that free men will determine what men and what principles shall govern them." Indeed, "the highest values in human life are at stake." The voters, who should "stand in the polling booth as if we stood on holy ground," must decide *which man is more likely to contribute to the achievement of a mighty efficiency in this mighty land?*" Luce did not come right out and say which man that was. He didn't need to. He ended praying, "May God help us to be wise and brave in order that we and our children may be forever free."

Willkie's opponent had *become*, one might say, by 1940 the national

Democratic party. James Farley, his old friend and Presidential campaign manager was now national party chairman; Farley wanted the nomination for himself, ran in one primary, and refused FDR's plea that he step aside. At the convention Roosevelt's forces simply ran right over Farley. Roosevelt had but to declare his willingness to be drafted again to set aside a rule of the game—the two-term limit—solidly in effect since Washington went back to Mount Vernon. "That man," as the Republicans called him, had become in the minds of millions of Americans synonymous with the Presidency.

That moralizing year Roosevelt also claimed the blessing of the Almighty. "The spirit of the common man is the spirit of peace and good will," he said as he wound up his campaign in Cleveland. "It is the spirit of God. And in his faith is the strength of all America." Through that season, he had hardly seemed to campaign at all, in the direct political sense. He never mentioned Willkie's name. Through the first part of the season his "nonpolitical" talks had concentrated on a much graver threat to the principles of Western civilization than Willkie posed: the threat of Nazi totalitarianism. He never said so, but as his adviser Rexford Tugwell remembered, Roosevelt "spoke as though the Republican party were a branch of the National Socialist organization." It was FDR running against Hitler. Near the end of the campaign he also ran against Hoover—reborn in such mossback Republicans as "Martin, Barton, and Fish." He won with a margin of nearly five million votes.

Luce's disillusionment with Willkie did not take long. Like Harvey's and Lorimer's, his hero had clay feet, in Willkie's case, a disturbing independence of mind. By the time of the 1944 election he was memoing his colleagues not to get stuck in a "Willkie-or-else" position, and when Willkie came out of the Wisconsin primary—after forty speeches in thirteen days—with zero delegates, Luce felt "a certain sense of relief from a long and painful situation." *Time*, in an issue Luce edited, said the Wisconsinites had voted "against a crusade which had never been clearly defined." His hope had been that Willkie would take the lead in revitalizing the Republican party, which Willkie did not. Willkie blew up at him at dinner: "Harry, you may be the world's best editor, but you are certainly the world's worst politician." Willkie had emerged as an advocate of "One World," presaging the United Nations approach, and he had reached such an understanding with Roosevelt that FDR had considered him a conceivable running mate for 1944. Willkie died of a heart attack on October 8, 1944.

Willkie's story can be seen in retrospect as marking a key transition in American politics: the decline of the parties as nominators. Moralizing candidates—coming in from the outside with their guns blazing at the "politicians"—undercut rhetorically the public's confidence in the parties as groomers, winnowers, and endorsers of candidates. Organizationally, Willkie owed nothing but trouble to the Republican powers-that-were; such organization as he had going into the convention was independent, amateur, unbeholden. It was a Willkie organization, not a Republican faction. Its focus was a man, not a clear-cut cause. Its support was the fundamental product of mass publicity, not party elite approval. If Willkie was not invented by the magazines, he was at least discovered and advanced by them. The party organization as a tiered pyramid linking Joe Republican at the bottom with the national chairman at the top was simply bypassed. Whereas Wilson had used party elements to get in and then turned aside from them, Willkie never bothered with them in the first place. Their vulnerability was demonstrated when a young fellow out West, mailing copies of a petition from *Life*, could spark an enormous and sudden proliferation of volunteer campaigners who put themselves together in clubs. Thus, long before there were many primaries, the Willkie race showed that a personalized endeavor of national scope could cut clean across the elaborate party network. That strategy would work again, for Eisenhower, then for Kennedy, for Barry Goldwater, Richard Nixon, and Jimmy Carter, until what had once seemed an exception became the rule.

9

Barry Goldwater 1964

As ever when a President dies in office, the nation was reeling in shock. Camelot was over; Lyndon Baines Johnson—Merlin of the inside deal—moved into the White House. No one knew quite what he would conjure up. John F. Kennedy, shot dead in Dallas, had not yet been buried when the new President took an oath that would shape the politics of the next dozen years. "I am not going to lose Vietnam," Johnson told Henry Cabot Lodge, Jr., "I am not going to be the President who saw Southeast Asia go the way China went."

Johnson came out of Texas in the Roosevelt years—FDR was his political "Daddy," he said—first as a wet-behind-the-ears congressman, then as a senator of extraordinary coordinative power, elevated by his Democratic colleagues to be their chief. In 1960, he had thought himself ready for the Presidency, especially because the alternative was young Senator Kennedy. To the surprise of nearly everyone, Kennedy first capsized him at the convention and then turned around and chose him as his Vice-Presidential running mate. Now Johnson had gotten what he had wanted, though not as he wanted to get it. A bullet made him President. A cloud hung over his title to the office. He would have to find legitimacy before he could use power.

Taking over closer to the next election than any other "accidental" President in history, he would have to move quickly. The election of 1964 would focus again on the relation of righteousness to power. A national newcomer from Arizona, Senator Barry Goldwater, would pose that challenge in stark black and white. The contest would throw into clear relief the major—and divergent—branches of the politics of conscience in their modern ideological configurations. In that test, the moralistic version of politics in America would exhibit most luxuriantly its capacity to drift beyond political sanity.

Lyndon Johnson's Hope

Johnson addressed his erstwhile comrades of the Congress on November 27, 1963, four days after the assassination—the Court, the cabinet, the nation in hushed and expectant hope. His first words set the tone.

All I have I would have given gladly not to be standing here today.

The greatest leader of our time has been struck down by the foulest deed of our time. Today John Fitzgerald Kennedy lives on in the immortal words he left behind. He lives in the mind and memories of mankind. He lives in the hearts of his countrymen.

No words are sad enough to express our sense of loss. No words are strong enough to express our determination to continue the forward thrust of America that he began. . . .

And now the ideas and the ideals which he so nobly represented must and will be translated into effective action. . . .

We will serve all the Nation, not one section or one sector, or one group, but all Americans. These are the United States—a united people with a united purpose. . . .

For 32 years Capitol Hill has been my home. I have shared many moments of pride with you, pride in the ability of the Congress of the United States to act, to meet any crisis, to distill from our differences strong programs of national action. . . .

On the 20th day of January, in 1961, John F. Kennedy told his countrymen that our national work would not be finished "in the first thousand days, nor in the life of this administration, nor even perhaps in our lifetime on this planet. But," he said, "let us begin."

Today, in this moment of new resolve, I would say to all my fellow Americans, let us continue.

The audience perked its ears. Johnson was not introducing an era of healing recovery or vindictive revenge. His rhetoric built toward constructive action. Johnson the doer was about to implement the Kennedy vision with specifics.

Action-forcing had long been his strength. Never a visionary himself, he understood the art of personal persuasion better than any other politician in the Senate. There he made himself master of the rules, then master of the chamber, memorizing the preferences (and the peccadilloes) of his fellows, alternating between cajolery and insistence, patching together ad hoc alliances for whatever President happened to be in office. Critics called him a "wheeler-dealer"; admirers called him the essential Senate professional. What they agreed on was his hound-dog persistence and ability to sniff out the traces of an emerging majority.

"Our most immediate tasks," they heard him say, "are here on this Hill."

First, no memorial oration or eulogy could more eloquently honor President Kennedy's memory than the earliest possible passage of the civil rights bill for which he fought so long. We have talked long enough in this country about equal rights. We have talked for one hundred years or more. It is time now to write the next chapter, and to write it in the books of law.

By the time Lincoln had been dead a century, Congress, in the emotional backwash of the Kennedy assassination, would enact laws to make it safe for a black man or woman to ask for a ballot, for a black family to check into a highway motel. A hope long deferred found fruition at last. Johnson the Texan, formerly not above disdainment of the "nigras," translated a mourning into a dawning. He ended his speech in a long reach for the American heart and soul. In the chamber not many eyes were dry as he said,

I profoundly hope that the tragedy and the torment of these terrible days will bind us together in new fellowship, making us one people in our hour of sorrow. So let us here resolve that John Fitzgerald Kennedy did not live—or die—in vain. And on this Thanksgiving eve, as we gather together to ask the Lord's blessing, and give Him our thanks, let us unite in those familiar and cherished words:

> America, America
> God shed his grace on thee,
> And crown thy good
> With brotherhood
> From sea to shining sea.

Johnson's motives were obscure—not because he hid them but because he threw out so many. Few questioned his purpose, though one struck a sour note, speculating, "I don't think he's motivated by any greater desire than to please the *New York Times* and get a pat on the back from [Georgia Senator] Dick Russell—both at the same time." Maybe the civil-rights revolution would have happened anyway, whoever had taken over. But that election-year springtime, Johnson came on as prophet and producer of the nation's deepest moral issue, justice for black Americans. His accent strengthened the cause. Here was a southerner, of a fading generation, quoting Martin Luther King, Jr., putting teeth into the promise, "We shall overcome."

If he was seen at first as a transitional, custodial, figure, he soon dispelled any such doubt. He would run on his own in 1964. His strategy was clear: "stay Presidential," above the furor of the primaries, in Washington vigorously attending to the nation's business, advocating a "war on poverty" to produce "a Great Society." He was nominated in one of history's dullest conventions. Not until October would his visceral inclination to get out among the people send "Preacher Lyndon" into the Midwest for a last-minute whirlwind circuit riding. To the large liberal wing of the press and public, Lyndon Johnson now seemed to have turned out to be one of them. If his style—overwhelming by personal dramatics—grated the sensibilities of those who remembered Kennedy's low-keyed grace, his fierce determination and concrete achievement promised a time of the fulfillment of long-held hopes, redemption. "Rising expectations" was a key phrase in describing the national mood.

Goldwater's Secret Plot

Republican conservatives had hopes and expectations of their own. In 1964 they sought and found a champion who really seemed to believe in their principles. Unlike Dewey, Eisenhower, and Nixon, he did not represent a surrender to eastern domination and compromise of heartfelt conservative convictions. If Johnson appeared in 1964 in the guise of Saint Paul, Barry Goldwater played Ezekiel, a prophet from the wilderness (Arizona) with a vision of political perfection, a rebuke to the liberal consensus.

Retrospective writers depict the Goldwater nomination as the product of a "cabal" holding "secret" meetings and plotting "sinister" plots; the Doctor Moriarty behind this conspiracy was one F. Clifton White. White was a business consultant who had worked for Nixon in 1960, a genius of manipulative technique, his dark purposes cleverly concealed behind a sunny smile, twinkling china-blue eyes, and jaunty bow tie. White had already "seized" the national Young Republicans, presumably while no one was looking, as chairman from 1950 to 1960; on October 8, 1961, White gathered to him twenty-two coconspirators for an "absolutely secret" meeting at the Avenue Motel on South Michigan Avenue in Chicago, to plan how "to seize control of the national Republican Party" and grab the Presidential nomination for a conservative. Carefully expanding the group to twenty-seven (including the governor of Montana), White convened a second secret meeting at the same out-of-the-way place on December 10, 1961; as Christmas shoppers wandered Michigan Avenue, the plotters divided America into nine regions. White would contact key figures in each, working out of a headquarters in New York City. Sixty thousand dollars would be assembled. In April 1962 the White group came by different routes to a hunting lodge in Minnesota for two days of intense but quiet deliberation, interspersed with the drinking of whisky. On August 24, 1962, White sent a "confidential" (and unsigned) memo to selected conservatives around the country, advising that time was running out and said, "We must be prepared to move into high gear in January of 1963." Some had not reported in since April; the anonymous message said, "I am anxiously awaiting word as to the state of your health." White's group brashly forgathered again at the Avenue Motel in Chicago to hold "a meeting so secret that White did not mention it in his confidential memos." They then decided to bring together "the entire underground organization" on December 1 and 2 at Chicago's Essex Motor Inn, to "determine where we go—whether we are serious or dilettantes," as a White confidential memo of October 18 put it. One hundred undergrounders attended—and disaster struck. The proceedings were leaked to the press. Indeed, the press account had such detail that White was convinced someone had smuggled in a tape recorder. Dismayed but not defeated, the "inner circle" of conspirators held another "highly secret" meeting at the O'Hare Inn in Chicago some time in early 1963. It was decided to go public, but to keep White behind the scenes. On April 9, 1963, Peter O'Donnell, Texas Republican chairman, at a press conference in the Mayflower Hotel, Washington, D.C., announced the formation of the National Draft Goldwater Committee.

George Harvey would have smiled. It is hard to imagine any candidacy born without a fair amount of private consultation and indeed it is an open question whether, had White pleaded with the press to cover his early motel machinations, they would have come. Americans (particularly American journalists) vastly overrate the power of secrecy, as if a potion mixed in private somehow acquires therefrom an arcane force. In no segment of politics was that inference more rampant than among "conservatives," that is, revolutionists of the right who wanted to dismantle the federal government.

The man White sought to be President was approximately as secretive as a first-time grandfather. "Covering Goldwater," wrote Theodore White, "was like shooting fish in a barrel." He was forever popping off. He had no appetite at all for ambiguity. He tossed out pithy opinions and true confessions with apparent abandon at the drop of a reporter's pencil. His opinions expressed over the years were so various and contradictory that not even a computer hired for the purpose could sort them out. In the large his proposals had two common characteristics: he did not like the way things were and his proposals for making them better stood very little chance of happening. His typical pattern was to make some shocking statement, stand amazed that it shocked people, and then explain that he only meant part of what he had said. Clifton White had a tiger by the tail. White may have seen Goldwater as a guidable missile. The senator's record was neither extensive nor well defined.

Barry Goldwater was descended from merchant pioneers who went West with the Gold Rush, back when that was a dangerous crowd to join. He grew up in boom times; his family succeeded in the department store business. Some of them went for public office: "There's always been one and sometimes two Goldwaters damned fool enough to get into politics," he remembered, and added, "It ain't for life and it may be fun." Barry was a popular student, though no scholar, at Staunton Military Academy in Virginia. He dropped out of the University of Arizona after one year when his father died and he was needed in the department store. In World War II, he ferried bombers over the Hump into India, dangerous business, and came home a lieutenant colonel. Phoenix was booming again—free enterprise in action—but corruption reigned in its government, so in 1949, Goldwater won a seat on the city council as a nonpartisan reform candidate. The next year he managed a winning campaign that put a popular radio announcer in the governor's office. He became a popular luncheon-club speaker throughout the state and enough of a Republican activist to get himself nominated for the U.S. Senate in 1952. At the Republican convention he backed Eisenhower over Taft and campaigned as a middle-of-the-road Eisenhower Republican, in favor of fiscal responsibility and such New Deal advances as Social Security, unemployment insurance, and civil rights. He won by 7,000 votes while Eisenhower was carrying Arizona by 42,000. In the Senate he voted to outlaw the filibuster, proposed a cutoff of U.S. aid to

France unless she let go of Vietnam, Laos, and Cambodia, and introduced bills to help American Indians.

Up to 1957, Goldwater seemed a middling Eisenhower Republican of no particular note. That year he broke with his party's main line: Ike's appropriation requests were "abominably high," Republican fiscal policies constituted a "betrayal of the people's trust." Goldwater became a ready font of controversial quotation. He began to emerge as spokesman for the discontented—particularly conservative heavy thinkers, some of them in the magazine press, who, unlike Eisenhower, had never made peace with the New Deal and were given to apocalyptic visions and political fundamentalism. Goldwater was reelected in 1958. Two years more of Eisenhowerism led him to publish *The Conscience of a Conservative*, which ran through fifteen printings in a year and a half and became the political Bible of the "Goldwater movement."

Goldwater the Senator had little in the way of concrete achievement to boast about. But then, Clif White may have thought, John F. Kennedy had nothing much to his credit when he ran for and won the Presidency in 1960. He made it on what he said, not what he had done, and perhaps Goldwater could do the same.

White's choice of Goldwater was no stranger than many another alliance between a backstager and an onstager. Their roots, though distant, were analogous. Clif White's mother went West in a covered wagon when she was ten, then came back to upstate New York, where her husband farmed and ran a gas station. Unlike Goldwater, White excelled at school, graduating from Colgate with a major in social science and returning for graduate work. Like Goldwater, in the war he flew many a desperate mission as a bomber pilot in Europe, way out beyond fighter cover. Back home he too took up reform, becoming chairman of the local American Veterans Committee, battling for veteran housing. Goldwater went on to candidacy; White went in for political management—mastering the complexities of petitions and lists and maps and rules, which had proliferated as politics became more and more scientific, translating for new circumstances and into workable strategies the arts of meetings and media, canvassing, and conventioneering. Big companies hired him to teach their junior executives how to get their oars into politics. The more he taught about it, the more he thought he could do it. Direct experience in the Nixon campaign of 1960 made him think he could do it better than *that*. "I'd always been interested in back-room politics," White said later, "I've probably elected more presidents of more organizations than any other man in America. But after a while you get to think about the dimensions of the room. What's going on in the country?" The country seemed to be going to hell in a handbasket. Liberal as a young man, White now saw the only solution in the conservative cause. Maybe it was time for someone like him—and why not he himself—to get hold of a candidate and lead him into the limelight.

Thus the secret meetings. But it was not White's secrecy or technical agility that created and gave force to the "Goldwater movement." The energies were steaming up from popular experience, crying out to be organized. A patchy cloud of resentments lay on the land, making the sentries of patriotism tense with suspicion. Joe McCarthy may have gone too far, but there *had* turned out to be some Communists high up in the government, hadn't there? These Negroes—"blacks" or whatever—had rights but where did they get the right to riot and demonstrate and force themselves into white neighborhood schools? What had happened to nice young kids who went off to college and then came home with beards and see-through blouses and wacky ideas? There were other, darker questions: Why had Roosevelt been so quick to recognize Russia? Truman to treat with Stalin? Eisenhower to back the United Nations? And why was it so hard for the government to get to the bottom of the Kennedy assassination? To increasing factions among the long-distance families in their scattered new suburbias—relatively few of whom had ever seen a Communist, a black mob, or a genuine beatnik except on television—the answers they heard rang false. This side of the lunatic fringe of the Minutemen, the John Birch Society, and the Ku Klux Klan, millions were looking for better answers than they had seen.

Goldwater's Public Surprises

Barry Goldwater seemed to have an answer for everything—or more precisely for each thing as it came up. At various times and places, Goldwater advocated on matters of foreign policy: dropping "a low-yield nuclear bomb on Chinese supply lines in North Vietnam," "defoliating" the Vietnam forests with "low-yield atomic weapons," giving "the NATO command the right to use nuclear weapons—tactical weapons—when they are attacked," getting the U.S. out of the UN, stopping foreign economic aid, blockading Cuba, working to "train and equip the Cuban refugees and help put them ashore with adequate air cover," "withdrawing recognition from Russia," and unilaterally resuming nuclear testing. As for the views foreigners might have on such matters, "Frankly, I do not care what the rest of the world thinks of us," he said, and "I don't give a tinker's dam what the rest of the world thinks about the United States, as long as we keep strong militarily."

But the real threat was not foreign. "I fear Washington and centralized government more than I do Moscow," Goldwater said. Walter Reuther and the United Auto Workers were "a more dangerous menace than the Sputniks or anything else Russia might do." His home policies included making Social Security payments "voluntary," letting "welfare be a private concern," and fixing the income tax at "an equal percentage of each man's wealth, but no more." He thought, "We have no right to tell the Southern states what they must do about school integration and segregation." He was against "any form of Federal grant-in-aid program to the states" for educa-

tion. The Tennessee Valley Authority "should be turned over to private enterprise, even if they only get one dollar for it."

In other words, he favored a massive turnabout in the direction of
American policy at home and abroad. From time to time he modified this or
that detail in response to the shock and dismay his proposals stimulated. But
the main drift was clear enough. As he wrote in *The Conscience of a Conservative,* it was time to reverse the liberal tide:

The turn will come when we entrust the conduct of our affairs to men who understand that their first duty as public officials is to divest themselves of the power
they have been given. It will come when Americans, in hundreds of communities
throughout the nation, decide to put the man in office who is pledged to enforce the
Constitution and restore the Republic. Who will proclaim in a campaign speech: "I
have little interest in streamlining government or in making it more efficient, for I
mean to reduce its size. I do not undertake to promote welfare, for I propose to extend freedom. My aim is not to pass laws, but to repeal them. It is not to inaugurate
new programs, but to cancel old ones that do violence to the Constitution, or that
have failed in their purpose, or that impose on the people an unwarranted financial
burden. I will not attempt to discover whether legislation is "needed" before I have
first determined whether it is constitutionally permissible. And if I should later be attacked for neglecting my constituents' interests, I shall reply that I was informed
their main interest is liberty and that in that cause I am doing the very best I can."*

Traveling around the country, Goldwater wrote, "I find that America is
fundamentally a Conservative nation" whose "preponderant judgment" was
"that the radical, or Liberal, approach has not worked and is not working.
They yearn for a return to Conservative principles." But he was quick to
explain that his proposals derived, not from the pragmatics of what "worked"
but from a source high above the ebb and flow of human experience. The
people were being misled in that respect:

Perhaps we suffer from an over-sensitivity to the judgments of those who rule
the mass communications media. We are daily consigned by "enlightened" commentators to political oblivion: Conservatism, we are told, is out-of-date. The charge is
preposterous and we ought boldly to say so. The laws of God, and of nature, have no
dateline. The principles on which the Conservative political position is based have
been established by a process that has nothing to do with the social, economic and
political landscape that changes from decade to decade and from century to century.
These principles are derived from the nature of man, and from the truths that God
has revealed about his creation. Circumstances do change. So do the problems that
are shaped by circumstances. But the principles that govern the solution of the
problems do not. To suggest that the Conservative philosophy is out of date is akin to
saying that the Golden Rule, or the Ten Commandments or Aristotle's *Politics* are
out of date.

The core content of that transcendent law was evident:

* Barry Goldwater, *The Conscience of a Conservative* (New York: Hillmann Books, 1960), pp.
23–24.

The Conservative believes that man is, in part, an economic, an animal creature; but that he is also a spiritual creature with spiritual needs and spiritual desires. What is more, these needs and desires reflect the *superior* side of man's nature, and thus take precedence over his economic wants. Conservatism therefore looks upon the enhancement of man's spiritual nature as the primary concern of political philosophy. Liberals, on the other hand—in the name of a concern for "human beings"—regard the satisfaction of economic wants as the dominant mission of society. They are, moreover, in a hurry. So that their characteristic approach is to harness the society's political and economic forces into a collective effort to *compel* "progress." In this approach, I believe they fight against Nature.*

That philosophy—not Goldwater's concrete proposals—stamped the 1964 contest with its peculiar moral cast. One could argue about when and where to drop what bombs, whether or not to sell TVA. One might even take a shot at Aristotle. But "fight against Nature"? Deny "the truths that God has revealed"? Take on the Golden Rule and the Ten Commandments? The effect of posing the matter that way was to render political argument illegitimate, to make of practical opposition a kind of blasphemy. Opponents were not merely mistaken, they were apostates whose devious commentaries concealed a grave moral flaw. Politics was translated from a discussion about preferences to the pronouncement of a faith, the force of which sprang directly from its assertion. Lyndon Johnson used to claim to like Isaiah's invitation, "Come, let us reason together." The Goldwater motto was "In Your Heart You Know He's Right."

Goldwater would have been a much more satisfactory villain had he not been such a nice guy. Standing tall and tan before the Rotarians, joshing with his senatorial pals, he came across as a natural man—easy, open, smiling, and spontaneous. He was so plausible. One had to listen hard to realize what he was actually saying. Clearly he was no obsessed seeker after personal power, burning with ambition to be President, and that gave Clif White trouble, though Goldwater's indifference to power served to advance the moralizing story. Goldwater had talked randomly in private about the Presidency as early as 1961, not so much about winning it as about using a campaign to straighten out the Republican party. News of White's meetings failed to thrill him: "I don't know who the group was, where they met or what it's all about." He might have some Presidential interest, but, he said a little later, "I'd rather stay in a fluid position for the rest of this year and see how the situation looks." The Republican liberals were scrapping already—"You might say, 'let them fight it out for awhile.'" When White went public to "draft the son of a bitch," Goldwater said, "It's their time and their money. But they are going to have to get along without any help from me." By April 27, 1963, he was available; the draft movement had got so strong that he had "given up trying to stop it. It's like trying to stamp out a forest fire with your feet. It's coming up too many places, too often," he said.

*Ibid., p. 3.

White's initial strategy, designed in 1963, was astounding. It rested on three prongs. Prong one was Goldwater's collection of grass-roots contacts developed in his endless rounds of the creamed-chicken circuit—all those folks angry at assaults on their freedom—to be organized into a network of cadres. Prong two was the "southern strategy." The South, angry at Kennedy over desegregation, would troop en masse to the Republican column: "Barry Goldwater will take all 128 electoral votes of the eleven Southern States!" shouted White's pamphlet. "In 1964 Goldwater will give 'the solid South' dramatic new meaning! *This is the key to Republican success!*" Kennedy could be conceded much of the rest of the nation; a Republican South would form the core of the 270 electoral votes Goldwater needed to win. The third White prong was a mysterious entity that came to be known as "the great silent majority." Goldwater would appeal across the board to millions of potential voters among the indignant inarticulate—blanked out of notice by the press, but waiting for a sure voice that did not merely echo the liberal pieties.

There were three great obstacles: New York's popular Governor Nelson Rockefeller, incumbent President Kennedy, and Elder Statesman Eisenhower. Rockefeller undercut his chances when he divorced his wife of thirty-one years and a year later, in May 1963, married the mother of four young children whose custody had not been settled. As with the marital troubles of Stevenson, exploited in the 1952 and 1956 elections, this was a personal tragedy of no real significance to the governor's official performance—but as Theodore White noted, "One was to hear more of 'morality' in the campaign of 1964 than ever before in American life" and the more the press decried "hysteria" over the "issue," the more hysteria was generated. Rockefeller plummeted in the Gallup poll of Republicans, from 43 percent in April to 30 percent a month later, as Goldwater moved up from 26 to 35 percent.

Kennedy was murdered in November 1963; a Goldwater-Johnson struggle would be a whole new enterprise. As for Eisenhower, he stood staunchly on the peak of his popularity, refusing to designate which Goldwater-stopper had his blessing. Nixon had yet to shed his loser image, having struck out in 1960 and again in the 1962 California governor race; he moved to New York and started a law practice. Governor George Romney's thrust petered out. Ambassador Henry Cabot Lodge and Governor William Scranton no sooner thought they had been tapped by Ike than he forswore commitment.

By the New Hampshire primary, Goldwater's identity as a "conservative" had stimulated pleasant anticipations in the Granite State, where he had strong organizational backing and the support of the state's largest newspaper, the archreactionary *Manchester Union-Leader.* No sooner had he arrived than he began peppering wide-eyed Hampshiremen with his deductions from natural law, in re "voluntary" social security, the causes of joblessness ("low intelligence or ambition"), America's "undependable" missiles, "carrying the war to North Vietnam," and the like. When Castro cut off the water supply for the American base at Guantanamo, Goldwater said Johnson should say, "Turn the water on or we are going to march out with a detachment of Marines and turn it on." Newsmen who wanted to be fair kept trying to figure out how to report him without continually calling for the two-inch headline. New Hampshire, conservative but not radically right, re-coiled. A dignified New Englander, Ambassador Henry Cabot Lodge, whose name had to be written on the ballot and who spent the campaign in Saigon, won with 35 percent of the vote; Goldwater and Rockefeller got about 23 percent each. Goldwater trailed the other two in Oregon, but won in Califor-nia with more than half the vote, in Texas with 75 percent, in Indiana with 67 percent, and in Illinois with 62 percent. Out in the precinct meetings and state conventions Clifton White's amateur cadremen slaved away. By June 1964, the Associated Press gave Goldwater 647 pledged or favorable votes; only 8 more were needed to nominate.

Henry Luce did not know quite what to make of Goldwater, though his wife had become an ardent Goldwater champion. She worked diligently on his behalf and seconded his nomination at the convention. But Luce himself stood aside, perhaps to give Hedley Donovan, his new editor and Rhodes scholar, freedom of action, perhaps because Lyndon Johnson had looked him square in the eye and promised he would not be the President to let South-east Asia go the way of China. *Life* eventually endorsed Johnson. But in 1964, *Time*'s regular coverage wobbled. They had backed one maverick in 1940 and lost, had backed centrist Eisenhower in 1952 and won; though much of Goldwater's philosophy read like early Luce—all that about the con-junction of God's will and natural law—Goldwater's policy peregrinations may have fluctuated too wildly for an older Luce's sense of stability. Then there may have been a real question as to whether even Henry Luce could by then have brought off an all-out *Time* drive for Goldwater. *Time*'s blatant booming for Eisenhower in 1952 had opened up deep splits within the Time, Inc. organization, a near-rebellion by staffers who favored Stevenson. Proba-bly for some combination of these reasons, *Time* let 1964 pass by in a collage of mixed impressions.

Lyndon Johnson, President of the United States, also seemed to let the campaign pass. "I gave good thought to what my course of conduct should be and concluded that I would not enter any primaries," he said. "I would do the very best job I could as President for all the people up to convention time and then let the delegates at the convention make their choice freely. Then my conduct would be determined after they made their choice." In fact, Johnson was running full throttle—but *as* President, not *for* President. While Goldwater plucked deductions from natural law, Johnson rammed through the Civil Rights Act of 1964, a massive if long-delayed recognition of the rights of blacks in voting, education, jobs, and public accommodations. He proposed—demanded—enlistment in his "war on poverty" to create a

"Great Society." He settled a rail dispute and a flap in Panama, cut taxes and instituted a food stamp program, toured a flood disaster area and opened the World's Fair in New York, eased relations with the Soviet Union and rocked on the front porch with an Appalachian family. Along the way he proposed putting up a "memorial to God" in Washington. Prosperity reigned. Aside from some naggingly worrisome developments way off in Vietnam, "Preacher Lyndon" seemed invulnerable. The June 1964 Gallup poll gave him 81 percent of the vote against Goldwater.

Yet the pollsters had difficulty finding voters who were enthusiastic for Johnson. If Goldwater's political morality seemed weird, Johnson's personal morality seemed flawed—it was a contest between "a kook and a crook," said some cynics. Stories critical of Johnson the person, taboo in the immediate aftermath of the Kennedy assassination, began to crop up: about the fortune he had reaped from a Texas television station, about his aide Bobby Baker's rapid climb to wealth, about Johnson picking up his beagle dogs by the ears, swimming nude in the White House pool, roaring around the Texas countryside in his white Cadillac while swilling beer and flirting with a pretty reporter—all that got added to the image of Johnson as a wheeler-dealer politician and tasteless cornpone presuming to take the place of the sainted President Kennedy. And as newsmen knew, Johnson could be a rough customer—a punishing arm-twister when his purposes required that. Goldwater, by contrast, was an abstemious nondrinking, nonsmoking fellow and in person as nice a fellow as you would want to meet.

The contradiction between personal and political morals thus got its share of attention in 1964, but a larger contrast was of more lasting interest, the contrast between Goldwater's missionary zeal—presaged in Luce's version of the American calling—and the moral sentiments of those columnists and commentators who came in for such a lashing at the Republican convention. Prime among the latter were the pronouncers of moral guidance working for the New York Times, the nation's newspaper of record. Although the New York Herald-Tribune in 1964 broke a 124-year tradition by recommending Johnson over Goldwater, and Herald-Tribune columnist Walter Lippmann, who had ventured to suggest that Goldwater was not above calculation, came in for special knocks from the Republican convention delegates (one of whom was heard to shout "Down with Walter Lippmann! Down with Walter Lippmann!"), it was the Times that came to symbolize for the Goldwaterites all that was evil about the eastern establishment press. And in the larger framework of the story of politics as morals, the New York Times represents a strain different from and as important as that of Henry Luce's Time.

The Times for Moderate Johnson

The New York Times, founded by Henry Raymond in 1851, took on its modern definition when Adolph Ochs bought it in 1896, at the nadir of its fortunes, and set out to beat Hearst and Pultizer—not by beating them at their own game but by producing another game, a different kind of paper. Ochs was a middle-roader born and bred on the border: his father joined the Union Army and his mother smuggled quinine to the Confederates; they were buried with their respective flags. Adolph worked himself up in the newspaper business in Tennessee, becoming owner of the *Chattanooga Times* at age twenty. He turned that *Times* into a newspaper stressing *news*—the more of it the better—presented accurately, reliably, comprehensively, in contrast to the lurid sheets typical of the period. So he did with the *New York Times*, establishing a tradition reexperienced daily by modern *Times* readers, who turn to that paper for all the news they can bear to consume. But precisely because they could count on the *Times* for the full and accurate story, readers also came to count on its editorial page for sober and reliable opinion. Adolph Ochs had decreed that the *Times* speak "in language that is parliamentary in good society." His first illustrated Sunday magazine section was a sixteen-page photographic presentation of Queen Victoria's jubilee of 1897. When his nephew John Oakes took over the editorial page in 1961, Oakes also considered that page the "soul" of the paper. He sent a memo to a young fellow using the by-line Tom Wicker to suggest that he should sign himself Thomas Wicker or Thomas G. Wicker, remembering, perhaps, that his uncle had always called *Times*men "Mister."

Tom Wicker (so he insisted) became Washington bureau chief of the *New York Times* in 1964, tapped for that job by his predecessor and mentor James Reston. Through the political season, Wicker saw to the news, expressing an occasional opinion, but it was Reston, in his column and through his pervasive spirit, who set the tone, then and in the decade preceding. Reston was a moralist from birth. His parents brought him to Ohio from Scotland when he was eleven; his mother, hoping he might become a preacher, turned him from a teenage passion for golf with her insistence that he "make something" of himself. Like immigrant Henry Luce, Reston fell in love with America. A war correspondent in London during the Blitz, with his midwestern wife and infant son in tow, Reston came to fame as author of a 1942 book, *Prelude to Victory*, arguing, "We cannot win this War until it ceases to be a struggle for personal aims and material things and becomes a national crusade for America and the American Dream." But if Presbyterian Luce, with his missionary zeal and passionate devotion to America as the expunger of worldly sin, was the godfather of Goldwaterism, Presbyterian Reston drew from his experience a lighter, more rational, lesson, inductively derived. What Luce had read about, Reston had lived through—the reality of life in mid-America, the actual warp and woof of American pragmatism. Eisenhower once asked, "Who the hell does Reston think he is, telling me how to run the country?" Reston could answer that he had been there, in the middle of it, knew it in his bones. In 1964, Reston and the reporters he inspired saw the jeopardy Goldwater posed to the America he revered, and the need to find an alternative.

The *Times* had come to represent a brand of American political Puritanism antithetical to the Luce-Goldwater version. Luce had preached the American mission: America as the new Zion, Americans as a chosen people, the American as an ideal type. The essential problem of politics was a problem of will, of mobilizing the passions for the war against sin. At its worst, that strain of Puritanism could degenerate into an indignant and self-righteous censoriousness, a narrow restrictive covenant with conscience, an urge to justify the self by correcting the other. Impatient and perfectionistic, the crusading Puritan celebrated principle and neglected circumstance, his argument a demand for instant conversion to the Pure Truth. When that failed, as it had to in the real world, the frustration turned to rage and the search for devils. But Puritanism had another root and branch. If the Pilgrims at first congratulated themselves when, as they saw it, God rescued them from the desperation of their early years, they also came to see their prosperity as a sign of obligation. Mastery called for servanthood, wealth for stewardship, security for duty. They were to be "other-regarding." They felt a sense of responsibility in history. A man would have to answer for his deeds—for all of them—at a hearing to take place after the record was complete. That meant he had better serve and that he had better be careful what he did. The tradition called for energy, but especially for restraint, self-restraint. For the Puritan knew that alongside the Kingdom of Heaven in each of us, the Prince of Darkness stalks his realm. The *Times*'s Reston was that kind of Puritan; so was John Oakes, and both less stuffy than the venerable Krock. From the start, the *New York Times* had taken pride in what it would *not* say. It was "not a School for Scandal," an early slogan claimed, and "would not soil the breakfast cloth." The politicians the *Times* admired were sober progressives, not revolutionaries, men of energy but restraint. John Oakes endorsed John F. Kennedy in 1960; his disillusionment with him came not because Kennedy had deviated from some orthodox canon but because the President failed to produce a federal aid to education bill.

The *Times* celebrated complexity, recognized and appreciated moral variety. At its doorstep were crowds of foreigners and immigrants, including blacks from the South, though for decades the *Times* barely noticed these native neighbors. The city had long practiced compromise in a mixed polity. The eastern sophisticate found it easier than did the culturally isolated to discriminate between diet and destiny, color and character, faith and fidelity. Life is rich in differences and the different have their claims. The political order exists not so much to resolve them as to contain them, in a state of variegated nature this side of war. Politics thus inevitably becomes patchwork, its art consisting of stitching, out of scraps of more or less plausible and creditable principles, some more or less progressive and sensible pattern to more or less satisfy the Great American Middle. Above all the Puritans of the *Times* believed in reason, and thus in the overriding importance of maintaining rational political discourse. The essence of politics was the great conversation, forever threatening to degenerate into the bark and howl of passion. The *Times* might be dull; it was determined to be rational and to keep politics sane, and sanity *was* a little dull.

Goldwater threatened the core values, as the *Times* made clear. Commenting on the early development of the Goldwater movement, however, Wicker took rational pains to point out that "the nuts and kooks" were "a small, if vocal, part of his troops," backed by "a greater army of the discontented and frustrated—men and women angry and disenchanted with the Cold War, Big Government, Big Unions, even with Big Business," and that Goldwater himself, far from being a fascist beast, came on "handsome, informal, friendly, a man without pomp." Nor was he an innocent surrounded by "right-wing ogres," according to Charles Mohr of the *Times;* the Goldwater staff, Mohr wrote, "show more intellectual tolerance than any men in politics that I have ever met. They can be joked with and joked about without losing their tempers."

The primary trouble with Goldwater was that he would not behave in such a way as to make the campaign a rational debate. At the start of the year a *Times* editorial took him to task for failing to reveal what policies he was for, though his againstness was clear as a bell. In New Hampshire, the Boston *Times* correspondent John Fenton reported Goldwater was refusing to answer questions voters asked. Mohr complained that he spoke "with great imprecision and often obviously has not done his homework," and that his "innate honesty" led him to condemn government programs he knew could not be abolished, which "leaves his hearers nowhere." In California, noted Gladwin Hill of the *Times*, Goldwaterites and backers of Governor Rockefeller could not converse: "A Goldwater crowd seems as unmotivated by specifics as a bunch of Beatle fans. Similarly, the Rockefeller-oriented are as dogmatic as a group of Catholic seminarians passing a Holy Roller meeting." James Reston summed up the primary season this way:

The 1964 Presidential primary campaign was remarkable in at least one respect. It lasted for three months without really coming to grips with a single major national issue or producing a single memorable speech.

Goldwater and Rockefeller in California ended merely by dramatizing the deep divisions within the Republican party about how to deal with the major problems of the day. They did not strengthen their party but weakened it for the campaign against the Democrats just ahead.

What dominated the debate through this long, strange campaign was a bedlam of obscurities about whether Goldwater was reckless about the Communists and heartless about the old and the poor; whether Eisenhower was for Goldwater or against him; whether Goldwater was "in the mainstream of the Republican party"—whatever that is—and whether Rockefeller and the "Eastern Liberal Establishment" were trying to "buy" or "kidnap" the Republican party.*

---

* Quoted in Harold Faber, ed., *The Road to the White House: The Story of the 1964 Election by the Staff of the New York Times* (New York: McGraw-Hill, 1965), p. 43.

To "a Goldwater lady from Indiana" who wrote him to complain of press bias against her man, Reston replied in his column, "We simply read what Barry and his spokesman say, and then pass on the results. Or we compare what the Senator says one day with what he or his aides say on another, and the thing comes out anti-Goldwater almost every time." For all the noble sentiments he invoked, Goldwater's wildly illogical combinations could not be ignored.

In the same speech, the Senator calls for more military strength, and "a slowdown in the expansion in Federal spending," and the end of the military draft—all within a few paragraphs of one another!

In one paragraph he condemns the Democrats for suggesting his policies might lead to war, and a few minutes later condemns the Democrats for drifting "closer to war on an ebbing tide of military strength."*

Thus to Reston and the *Times*, Barry Goldwater was a political adolescent throwing around "serious charges, based on wildly inaccurate information," such as that President Kennedy had got into the Cuban missile crisis on purpose, to jack up his popularity at home. The *Times* condemned him out of his own mouth, restraining its own vocabulary; in contrast, the *Saturday Evening Post*, in a startling break with tradition, turned on Goldwater as "a grotesque burlesque of the conservative he pretends to be . . . a wild man, a stray, an unprincipled and ruthless jujitsu artist like Joe McCarthy." The *Times* did not talk that way. But the message came across.

The picture the *Times* painted of the Democratic configuration was much simpler and starker. By the end of Johnson's first week in office, James Reston was writing that the new President had emerged as "a commanding figure," and at the end of his first month, Wicker wrote, "With considerable force and skill, he has established the continuity of the Government in the face of a disaster of which no one had conceived." On March 2, 1964, President for one hundred days, Johnson was interviewed on television by reporters. Reston celebrated his performance: in contrast to Johnson's wheeler-dealer image he had appeared as

the quiet, philosophic, almost fatherly Johnson who never has a bad word for anybody. . . . He is charged with vanity; he was, in contrast, the very soul of modesty. . . . As nonpartisan as the Ten Commandments. . . . If the commanding ground of American politics is the center, President Johnson captured it this evening. . . . Militarily, he made Barry Goldwater's suggestion about landing Marines in Cuba sound like the proposal of an impulsive boy. . . . The President was even detached, almost indifferent, about himself.†

Reston quoted approvingly Johnson's description of himself as "a progressive who is prudent." Later in the spring, when Johnson succeeded in settling an apparently interminable rail dispute, Reston applauded his skill in "making

* Ibid., p. 162.
† Ibid., pp. 9–10.

stubborn men put the general interest above their special interests," his "total absence of ideology, the passionate insistence on the general welfare, the willingness to talk endlessly." Reston concluded,

He has that rare gift in a small room of antagonists, not only of telling men how he thinks they should feel, but of making them feel it, of forcing them to face the larger problems, as if they were sitting in his chair.

In a vast continental Federal Union, with inevitable conflicts between regions, parties, classes and institutions, this is a personal force of immense value to the nation.*

In foreign policy, *Times*man Max Frankel noted, Johnson "is giving about equal weight to gestures of conciliation and defiance toward the Communist world. . . . The Democrats' basic theme, in the face of Mr. Goldwater's charge that they 'cringe before the bully of Communism,' will continue to be that different Communist countries must be treated differently."

On through the spring, the summer convention, and during Johnson's fall foray into explicit campaigning, the *Times*, while dutifully reporting the charges against him, found Lyndon Johnson an exceptionally admirable political creature. Reston took note that Johnson "does not want to inflame or envenom the almost theological issues between Republicans and Democrats," of how well he performed the "intricate, delicate and positive art" of politics, of his success as "a whirlwind who wants to calm the waves," and, after the election, of how Johnson, though yet unproved in foreign policy, "is a shrewd and knowledgeable man, an elemental force of nature who commands respect and even a certain amount of fear." *Times* columnist Arthur Krock applauded "his brilliant virtuosity in the technique of politics" at the convention; a *Times* editorial spoke of "the depth and variety of his political experience . . . which will guide and caution him," of his "vast and unillusioned knowledge of human nature." To the moralists of the *Times*, Johnson, the restrained, tolerant, rational progressive, appeared uniquely qualified to lead the nation safely past the alarming temptations of Goldwaterism.

Eisenhower arrived at the July Republican convention in a state of amorphous indefiniteness. A few days before, he had been bonked on the head with a Goldwater placard. His brother Milton, president of Johns Hopkins University, was scheduled to second the nomination of Pennsylvania Governor Scranton for President. Shortly before the California primary in June, Eisenhower had contributed a long article to the Republican *New York Herald-Tribune*, mentioning no names but Lincoln's, laying out the principles he thought should govern the Republican choice: someone "vigorous in the furtherance of civil rights," ardent for "the maintenance of peace while protecting and extending freedom," devoted to "loyal support for the United Nations" and to "calm, painstaking study of all the infinitely complex situations that confront us." "In today's nuclear-age diplomacy," the General

* Ibid., p. 51.

counseled, "there is no time for indecision, but neither is there room for impulsiveness." The piece was widely interpreted as defining Goldwater out of the contest. But Eisenhower, employed as a commentator for ABC television at the convention, insisted that was not the case.

Q.: Mr. President, have you changed your mind, sir, about remaining neutral among the major candidates for the Republican nomination?

A.: I don't know whether you should say I am neutral. I said that fourteen months ago I took the position that I thought that it was necessary in view of the conditions then developing, and to every individual that I spoke who I thought had a chance of becoming a candidate, or a potential candidate, I made one pledge: that if he would get into the list to continue and promote the dialogue, that it would give us a broad spectrum of Republican thinking, I would applaud it, I would welcome him into that group. I would not support anybody but I would be against nobody. . . . After fourteen months of saying this to individuals and publicly I don't see how I can change now.*

Left in that limbo, the liberals of the Republican party gathered around Scranton, in a last-ditch fight against Goldwater; Rockefeller had been virtually eliminated in the California primary. Scranton visited Eisenhower, hoping for a definite endorsement, but came away disappointed. Henry Cabot Lodge, Rockefeller, Milton Eisenhower, Governor Romney of Michigan, and Ike's son John, collectively appalled at the prospect of a Goldwater nomination, had their hopes for the Scranton alternative dashed when Ike refused to back him and said the Goldwater platform was all right.

Melee in San Francisco

At the convention, Eisenhower set off an unexpected drama. Though the press and television had done yeoman service in helping him win two Presidential elections, Eisenhower had never had much use for them. He was a child of the rural Midwest, lacking in the slick style of Manhattan. His military experience made him wary of free-floating newsmongers and his Presidential experience taught him what a bother they could be, intruding on *his* freedom of movement, demanding answers he was not ready to issue, mocking his wandering verbal peregrinations. In the midst of his speech to the delegates came a line of chagrin: "Let us particularly scorn the divisive efforts of those outside our family, including sensation-seeking columnists and commentators"—and suddenly the galleries and the delegates on the floor erupted in an enormous and unstoppable roar of angry agreement. When the noise at last subsided, Ike finished his sentence: "—because, my friends, I assure you that these are people who couldn't care less about the good of our party," at which the roars rolled forth again. It was an incredible scene. Whatever Eisenhower may have had in mind, the furious delegates

* Quoted in Charles McDowell, Jr., *Campaign Fever: The National Folk Festival from New Hampshire to November, 1964* (New York: William Morrow & Co., 1965), p. 117.

and guests gave his words their meaning—a convention raging against editorial journalism. A few weeks later, a smiling Lyndon Baines Johnson would begin his address to the Democratic convention with, "My fellow Democrats, columnists and commentators. . . ." But to the assembled Republicans there was nothing funny about it. They were mad.

The uproar Ike's comment triggered took reporters by surprise. As it continued unabated, they reacted in mock horror. One turned to another: "Do you suppose they are coming in here after us?" They remembered the fury of the Goldwaterites in earlier days, when one excited partisan had shouted at them, "Don't quote what he says, say what he means!" and the time another rushed up to a Goldwater aide and gasped, "You've got to warn the Senator right away. There are men out there taking down every word he says." They recalled the mimeographed instructions to Goldwater delegates, item #2 of which advised, "DO be very thoughtful and careful when talking to anyone representing the press." They agreed that if the delegates rushed them, they would throw themselves on the mercy of the *Chicago Tribune*.

When at last the furor died down, the reading of the platform went forward. NBC's David Brinkley took note of that, but it was dull stuff; Brinkley switched to his colleague John Chancellor, on the floor of the convention. Chancellor loomed up on the screen, saying, "Well, I'd try if I could, David, but I wonder if I may be under arrest." The television audience saw Chancellor, in respectable suit and tie, being forcibly carried out of the hall, reporting as he went, "This is John Chancellor, somewhere in custody."

About midnight, Nelson Rockefeller, scion of the eastern establishment, took the podium to speak for a platform amendment condemning extremism. Jeers and boos greeted his appearance. Extremist tactics, he said, "have no place in America"—the "anonymous midnight and early morning telephone calls, unsigned threatening letters, smear and hate literature, strong-arm and goon tactics, bomb threats and bombings, infiltration and take-over of established political organizations by Communist and Nazi methods." This vigorous message was repeatedly drowned out by the indignant delegates. Rockefeller struggled to continue. "It's a free country, ladies and gentlemen," he said. "Some of you don't like to hear it, ladies and gentlemen but it's the truth"—and the roaring jeers erupted again, accompanied by a booming bass drum and shouts of "We want Barry! We want Barry!"

The demonstrations next day, nomination time, were flossier and better organized. Mellifluous Senator Everett Dirksen of Illinois, Senate minority leader and erstwhile GOP TV commentator, placed in contention "the peddler's grandson," Barry Goldwater. The roll call rolled on to its predictable conclusion: Goldwater on the first ballot defeating Scranton 883 to 214 votes. The following day, Richard M. Nixon ("a simple soldier in the ranks," he called himself) introduced Goldwater to the predictable hullabaloo. The band blared "The Battle Hymn of the Republic," and Goldwater appeared. "The Good Lord raised this mighty Republic," he intoned, but "our people have followed false prophets." The longed-for truth came down to one word:

This Party, with its every action, every word, every breath and every heartbeat, has but a single resolve and that is:

Freedom!

Freedom—made orderly for this nation by our Constitutional government.

Freedom under a government limited by the laws of nature and of nature's God.

The Democratic administration had failed: their "failures proclaim lost leadership, obscure purpose, weakening wills and the risk of inciting our sworn enemies to new aggressions and to new excesses." The failure was essentially moral:

Tonight there is violence in our streets, corruption in our highest offices, aimlessness among our youth, anxiety among our elderly, and there's a virtual despair among the many who look beyond material success toward the inner meaning of their lives. And where examples of morality should be set, the opposite is seen. Small men seeking great wealth or power have too often and too long turned even the highest levels of public service into mere personal opportunity.

Now, certainly simple honesty is not too much to demand of men in government. We find it in most. Republicans demand it from everyone.

They demand it from everyone no matter how exalted or protected his position might be. . . .

Now we Republicans see all this as more—much more—than the result of mere political differences, or mere political mistakes. We see this as the result of a fundamentally and absolutely wrong view of man, his nature and his destiny.

Those who seek to live your lives for you, to take your liberty in return for relieving you of yours; those who elevate the state and downgrade the citizen, must see ultimately a world in which earthly power can be substituted for Divine Will. And this nation was founded upon the rejection of that notion and upon the acceptance of God as the author of freedom. . . .

And then the peroration so often to be quoted back to the candidate:

Anyone who joins us in all sincerity we welcome. Those, those who do not care for our cause, we don't expect to enter our ranks in any case. And let our Republicanism so focused and so dedicated not be made fuzzy and futile by unthinking and stupid labels.

I would remind you that extremism in the defense of liberty is no vice!

And let me remind you also that moderation in the pursuit of justice is no virtue!*

Halfway through, one reporter looked to another and said, "My God, he's going to run as Barry Goldwater."

Goldwater thus turned his back on the American Middle. The morning

---

*John Bartlow Martin, "Election of 1964," in Schlesinger et al., eds., *History of American Presidential Elections*, vol. 4.

after Goldwater's nomination, Eisenhower told Theodore White it meant disaster for the Republican party. Lyndon Johnson had only to hang Goldwater's indiscretions firmly around his neck—about bomb dropping and an end to Social Security, for example—while invoking Kennedy ("up there in Heaven watching us") and the awesome authority of the Presidency. But one by one: Rockefeller, Nixon, Scranton, and the rest, the leaders of Lincoln's party, rallied round to endorse Barry Goldwater, whose views, each of them knew, marked a revolutionary departure from what each of them believed.

James Reston wrote:

> It is a remarkable situation: for here is the party of "respectability," of "responsibility," of "equality," and of "peace" handing leadership in a cold war and a racial revolution to a militant man who wants to leave war to the soldiers, and the Negro to the states. They are giving us a choice . . . but what a choice!*

The choices of the nation's daily newspaper editors, most of them traditionally Republican, piled up steadily against Goldwater as the season wore on. From The *New York Herald-Tribune* to the *Rocky Mountain News*, editors swallowed their old loyalties and dis-endorsed Goldwater. Only three major dailies stuck with him, the *Los Angeles Times*, the *Chicago Tribune* and the *Cincinnati Enquirer*.

Halfway through the summer, Johnson profited from an attack, real or supposed, by North Vietnamese boats against Americans in the South Pacific Tonkin Gulf. With only two dissenting votes, the Senate handed the President a virtual blank check to do as he pleased militarily in Southeast Asia. In October, the press learned that an aide to President Johnson had been arrested on a morals charge. There was much scurrying about at the White House, but the next day, Moscow announced that Nikita Khrushchev had been displaced and London announced that the Conservatives had lost to Labour in the British election. And one day later, the Chinese Communists exploded their first nuclear bomb. Reston commented that

> The world has done the American people a favor this week. It has startled us out of our preoccupation with secondary issues in the Presidential election, and clarified the primary issue of the campaign. Who is best qualified to sit in the White House and deal with a world in which Communist China is setting off nuclear explosions, the Soviet Union is moving to unite Communist parties and Britain has established a weak Labor Government?†

Not, Reston thought, Senator Goldwater: "The world has not been kind to the Senator. For, in a few strokes of lightning, it has illuminated the facts, and the facts have always been his downfall."

Goldwater agreed that he had not been treated kindly, but it was not the world's fault. After the election, he let his feelings show. Reporters had

---

* Faber, *Road to the White House*, p. 57.
† Ibid., p. 246.

done all right, but he had only bitter disdain for the columnists. "I have never in my life seen such inflammatory language as has been used by some men who should know better, who should write better, who should have enough decency, common ordinary manners about them," he sputtered. "I think these people should, frankly, hang their heads in shame because I think they have made the fourth estate a rather sad, sorry mess."

On October 21, 1964, shortly before his electoral victory, President Johnson declared, "We are not going to send American boys nine or ten thousand miles away from home to do what Asian boys ought to be doing for themselves." On October 27, 1964, the President said, "There can be and will be, as long as I am President, peace for all Americans." The Preacher would hold his pulpit against the lonely prophet from the desert in an election of conscience that preferred the moralist it knew to one it knew not of.

He won with an incredible 61 percent of the popular vote, the all-time record, an electoral college margin.

Aftermath

In a postelection commentary, Reston wrote, "the voters answered the major questions of the election quite clearly":

Would the United States reject the policy of trying to reach an honorable accommodation with the Communist world, despite all their disappointments since the last world war, and accept instead a more aggressive policy toward the Communist world? They said "No."*

President Eisenhower had authorized some three hundred United States military "advisers" in Vietnam. President Kennedy had raised that to fourteen thousand. President Johnson, the "dove" of 1964, would thereafter dispatch thereto more than half a million young Americans, some fifty thousand of whom never came home.

Partway through the campaign, Reston had let himself think there might be some virtue in the kind of contest Goldwater was trying to strike up. "A savage conflict between the parties on ideological grounds cannot be avoided now, but it can have some advantages," he wrote. "Ideally, the purpose of an election is to clarify and not to confuse the issues, to destroy and not to perpetuate illusion, to make a little clearer what we are and where we are. Senator Goldwater has set the stage for this." The Democrats should "stop moaning . . . and start dealing with his arguments." But at the end, Reston verged on despair:

Anything that stains the reputation of America, or weakens the confidence of the people or the world in her institutions, injures mankind. And this election campaign has done just that.

No matter who wins on Tuesday, the nation has lost something. For the cam-

* Ibid., p. 274.

paign has disillusioned and divided the people, revived their ancient feelings that politics is a dirty business, raised doubts about the integrity of the press, and even cast a shadow on the White House.

This could not possibly have happened at a worse time.*

Thus to the *Times*, the essential problem was that a sacred process had gone awry, a process of reasoned deliberation on the issues, from which a rational consensus should emerge. But there was a different diagnosis of the same sorry result, a diagnosis focusing not on what the candidates said or the policy territory they fought over, but on who they were. Woodrow Wilson's grandson, the Very Reverend Francis B. Sayre, Jr., preached it this way in the Washington Cathedral on September 13, 1964:

This summer, we beheld a pair of gatherings at the summit of political power, each of which was completely dominated by a single man; the one a man of dangerous ignorance and devastating uncertainty, the other a man whose public house is splendid in its every appearance but whose private lack of ethics must inevitably introduce termites at the very foundation. The electorate of this mighty nation is left homeless, then, by such a pair of nominees. It knows not where to turn, it stares fascinated at the forces that have produced such a sterile choice—frustration and a federation of hostilities in one party; and, in the other, only a cynical manipulation of power.†

1964, in other words, would stand as a prime example of the politics of conscience gone awry. Goldwater exemplified the political moralist cut loose from the moorings of political reality. Johnson would come to illustrate most starkly the lock-step perseveration of the "practical" President, immersed in intense dutiful effort, who loses sight of the purpose and meaning of his labors. The Presidency was on its way to its twentieth-century nadir, the downhill slide to Nixon in 1968. Barry Goldwater's conscience-fraught crusade greased the skids. The party of Lincoln was about to be taken over by a crew of political gangsters.

* Ibid., p. 257.
† Ibid., p. 181.

10

Jimmy Carter 1976

W HEN JIMMY CARTER, after much soul-searching, told his mother he had decided to run for President, she said, "President of what?" At least from that time forward to the White House, Carter was continually being asked to explain what he was doing, and why, and who was he, anyway? The theme that would emerge from his answers to dominate the campaign of 1976 was the politics of conscience. He ran because he thought he ought to. He was a go-getter of a moralist: "I believe that the essence of a worthwhile life is the striving. I do not fear failure, but I do fear the resigned acceptance of what is mean or mediocre or wrong." His purpose was rooted deep in the religion that had come to mean more to him than anything else: "I have never felt that the Lord required me to run for President, or that I'm ordained to be President," he said, but "I have the feeling, without any doubt at all, that what I am doing is compatible with God's will, whether I should win or lose. There's no doubt in my mind that my campaign for the Presidency is what God wants me to do."

Woodrow Wilson would have amened that. Carter set off on a mission, a crusade he had been called to. But his moral quest would gather and move in modern style, beginning early with the vigorous pursuit of media coverage. He would not wait to be drafted, would not even pretend that. His would be no Eisenhower amateur enterprise, no chaotic Goldwater hip-shooting foray, no McGovern-like exploitation of accidental situations. Carter and his managers studied Kennedy's rise to power and aspired to match its efficiency. Like a Billy Graham revival, Jimmy Carter's crusade for decent government would combine evangelism with systematic planning. If he was to reach the Jerusalem on the Potomac, he would have to plot the route.

In 1972, Carter adviser Gerald Rafshoon, a professional advertising man, laid out in writing a stage-by-stage plan of attack toward ultimate victory: "Each of these phases runs into the succeeding phase and is an integral part of the overall buildup. They all cannot be accomplished at the same time but they all must be accomplished at the time allotted in order to evolve into the next phase. Phase I must be accomplished early enough to make the others work."* Hamilton Jordan elaborated this theme three days before McGovern lost to Nixon:

The sequence or chronological order of primaries are important for obvious reasons. Good or poor showings can have a profound and irrevocable impact on succeeding primaries and a candidate's abilities to raise funds and recruit workers. The press shows an exaggerated interest in the early primaries as they represent the first confrontation between candidates, their contrasting strategies, and styles, which the press has been writing and speculating about for two years. We would do well to understand the very special and powerful role the press plays in interpreting the primary results for the rest of the nation. What is actually accomplished in the New Hampshire primary is less important than how the press interprets it for the nation. Handled properly, a defeat can be interpreted as a holding action and a mediocre showing as a victory.†

Jordan invented a numerical calculus, allocating points to states on the basis of delegation size and the sequence of the contests. The sequence or "strategy" factor he estimated as half as important as the size factor. Thus each state was first assigned one point per delegate, a total of 3,071 of them as then expected. Since 73 percent of the delegates would be selected in primaries, 73 percent of the sequence points went to primary states, distributed in declining magnitude from primary to primary, as scheduled—thus New Hampshire got 150 sequence points, then Florida 125, then Illinois 100. Out of all this arithmetic was to come an allocation of time, effort, and money. No one seems to have audited the figures retrospectively, but the major strategic inference was effected.

No serious candidate will have the luxury of picking and choosing among the early primaries. To propose such a strategy would cost that candidate votes and increase the possibility of being lost in the crowd. I think we have to assume that everybody will be running in the first five or six primaries. The crowded field enhances the possibility of several inconclusive primaries, with four or five candidates separated by only a few percentage points. Such a muddled picture will not continue long, as the press will begin to make "winners" of some and "losers" of others. The intense press coverage which naturally focuses on the early primaries plus the decent time intervals which separate the March and mid-April primaries dictates a serious effort in all the first five primaries.‡

Such were the early secret calculations—not that anyone else cared to know. But an important real calculation was how to orchestrate the interplay of private and public estimates, as Carter emerged in the news. The goal was

---

* Quoted in Martin Schram, *Running for President: A Journal of the Carter Campaign* (New York: Pocket Books, 1976), pp. 64–65.
† Quoted in Jules Witcover, *Marathon: The Pursuit of the Presidency 1972–1976* (New York: Viking Press, 1977), p. 135.
‡ Quoted in ibid., p. 136.

surprise, Jordan thought: "Our public strategy would probably be that Florida was the first and real test of the Carter campaign and that New Hampshire would be just a warmup." But "in fact, a strong surprise in New Hampshire should be our goal, which would have a tremendous impact on successive primaries."

Other candidates set their march routes for 1976 differently. Senator Birch Bayh of Indiana, for example, looked for ambiguity in the early primaries followed by his startling primary victory in New York in April. Senator Frank Church of Idaho planned to hold back until the Massachusetts primary (eventually scheduled second, after New Hampshire). Senator Henry ("Win the big ones") Jackson of Washington decided *he* would take Massachusetts—after staying out of New Hampshire entirely. George Wallace of Alabama consulted his instincts and came to the same conclusion. Senator Hubert Humphrey of Minnesota would wait for some clarion call, remembering that he had lost the nomination by the primary route in 1960 and 1972, inherited it in the 1968 national convention without that effort. And Senator Edward Kennedy kept saying, implausibly to many, that he would sit out the race. What was special about the Carter calculations was the realization the campaign was not a set of isolated battles over large and small chunks of political territory, but a connected drama, rewritten for each new act to reflect what happened in the last one.

Equally important was the Carter team's understanding that the campaign would begin long before the New Hampshire primary. They weren't the only ones. In August 1975, a *Chicago Tribune* headline announced "The Epic Struggle Begins." But as early as February 1975, a *Tribune* story led, "With serious warfare for the party's 1976 nomination already underway. . . ." Newsmen right and left swore off the expectations game—notably including those who had set the thing going in 1972. But in fact, all through the year preceding New Hampshire, the scenarios and speculations spun across the print and broadcast media. Who would have to beat Wallace, by how much, where? Would Edward Kennedy change his mind and come in? Could Henry Jackson (running "like a bowl of old, cold oatmeal," "sounding like a carbon copy of himself," as arresting as "a pane of glass," according to various newsmen in private) yet develop "charisma"? Could it be true that Senator Birch Bayh was "looking more and more like the party's best hope to beat George Wallace," as another *Tribune* story suggested in June? Had Senator Morris Udall as of six months into 1975, actually "tentatively established himself as the leading liberal candidate?" and would he, as "many Democratic politicians" were said to think, "quickly lose his perch on the catbird seat" if challenged by various others?

And so on. Harry Kelly, a Washington reporter for the *Chicago Tribune*, confessed to "that awful foreboding that nothing exciting will happen." After the thrills of Watergate, reporting the campaign was "like coming back from a war unable to find any gainful employment nearly as stimulating as flying a bomber thru flak." The favorite excitement generator was the "brokered convention" scenario: none of the running pigmies would come through in the primaries and the nomination would be decided in a knockdown, dragout, story-spawning national convention.

Carter one-upped them all. Steadily building notice through the year, he concentrated in Iowa, where party caucuses would vote for delegates more than a month before the New Hampshire primary. "We were seeing if we could find a place to surprise before New Hampshire," said Carter's press secretary Jody Powell, "and the people of Iowa seemed to be our kind of folks." A year in advance, Carter started cultivating Iowa. Carter aide Tim Kraft, a devotee of "politics as theater," discovered that a straw poll was to be conducted in a series of precaucus caucuses; Kraft got out a mailing and Carter won—with 9.9 percent. Being "the only hard bit of political information looking to the 1976 race availble for the press and television to latch onto," wrote reporter Jules Witcover, "it made news in Iowa." The next poll, at a Jefferson-Jackson Day dinner in October 1975, was even more carefully prepared for. R. W. Apple's front page *New York Times* story was headlined "Carter Appears to Hold a Solid Lead in Iowa as the Campaign's First Test Approaches." Carter went on to win the Iowa vote on January 19, corralling twice as many votes (27 percent) as runner-up Bayh—though 37 percent were "uncommitted." "Uncommitted" was the real winner. The *Tribune* nevertheless called it "a victory in the first voter test of 1976 presidential support in the nation." Carter himself knew the place to be as the Iowa returns rolled in—in New York. The day after the voting he appeared on all three network morning news shows. Not quite 14,000 people had voted for him. But he was the hottest property in politics, sprinting out ahead of the pack.

The story of who Carter was, and what he stood for, and why, and what sort of President he might make, came later, as the election of 1976 defined itself away from its battle phase to higher concerns. 1976 was the year for a moralist and Carter turned out to be the one to make that very different story work.

The Question of Character

Americans long ago realized that they were electing a man, not a philosophy, and that the character of the President, as he wrestled with the challenges of his time, shapes the quality of political life. Indeed the Presidency itself was designed by the Constitution makers in part to suit a certain man, George Washington, who could be counted on to make of its loosely defined powers a strong and steady force. In our century, the moralists in journalism looked beyond the issues and platforms to the person: Wilson's highmindedness, Hoover's granite integrity, Willkie's homespun vigor, Eisenhower's simple heroism. Hiroshima cast the question of character in a new, stark light and the intercontinental ballistic missile cut the time for consultation to a matter of minutes, placing in the hands of the President the instant power to trigger a holocaust. In the 1964 campaign, Lyndon Johnson had dramatically raised his thumb in the air, inching it toward a imagined nuclear button, and asked his audience whose hand they would trust for that risk. In 1974, Richard Nixon, resigning, reminded his dwindling crew that the black box with the button in it would be in his hands right up to the moment his authority ended. It was a dangerous time; the need for sanity in the White House, important in McKinley's era, now became an urgent necessity.

Lyndon Johnson the old reliable of 1964 had transformed a minor mission in Vietnam into a titanic national tragedy; Richard Nixon demonstrated how far off the deep end of tyranny and corruption a President could go, hiding his secret crimes behind a mask of propriety and patriotism. Their stories made it clearer than ever before that candidates and Presidents could fool The People, that we had better be careful whom we crowned as The Most Powerful Person in the World.

Hope for Presidential decency surged up again after a dismal time when Gerald R. Ford, forced on a reluctant Nixon as his Vice-President by insistent congressmen when Spiro Agnew resigned in disgrace, moved up into the White House in 1974. Ford seemed as honest as a good piece of furniture from his hometown of Grand Rapids. Three hundred FBI agents had been unable to find a flaw in his background. Eagle Scout, football star, navy officer, Yale man, and "Congressman's Congressman," Ford seemed just the straight shooter the country needed. He himself said that "our long national nightmare is over" and that "truth is the glue that holds government together." But then, a month into his Presidency, Ford suddenly and all on his own issued a complete pardon for Nixon, cutting off the legal process then in train to bring him to trial. Confidence plummeted. Speculation spread that Ford, for all his honest demeanor, had made a deal with Nixon to get the Presidency, a contract now paid in full. Struggling to recover trust, Ford explained the pardon as an act of charity to a beaten man and the only way to clear the national agenda for progress on other issues. Back in 1964, despite the theory of the great hidden curdled majority, 76 percent of the public went along with the pollster's alternative that officials in Washington could be trusted "to do what is right most of the time." After the years of betrayal, that proportion dropped to a mere 33 percent in 1976.

Ford came off as calm and Presidential in crisis when he saw to the rescue of forty American merchant seamen captured by Cambodians. He was seen regularly on the television evening news speaking from the Rose Garden behind the White House—and slowly Americans began to think of him as President after all. He pressed on Congress a comprehensive energy and economic package and he vetoed bills left and right. In the summer of 1975, his wife shocked staid traditionalists by casually telling a television interviewer she "wouldn't be surprised" if her eighteen-year-old daughter told her she was having an affair and suggesting that premarital sex might help cut the divorce rate. But that passed and Ford's prospects for 1976 picked up.

When Ford had become Vice-President, the *Washington Post* columnist David Broder had spoken for most observers when he speculated that the prospect of Ford as candidate in 1976 could "probably be safely ignored." Now, in 1975, James Reston was writing that the notion that the Republican nomination could be wrested away from Ford by Ronald Reagan "is patently ridiculous unless you suspect the Republicans of suicidal tendencies." Ford decided to run. His advertising adviser wrote a memo for him on "The Mood of the Country":

The issues that people feel most deeply about concern traditional American values. These are emotional issues. Love of family and love of God. Pride in their country and pride in themselves. Morality, freedom, independence, individual achievement are among the things that are most important to people today.

People want a more honest government, and a far higher morality in every walk of life. In their leaders, they look for moral leadership, strength of character, religious conviction, love of family, and great personal integrity above all else. They also look for compassion in their leaders. . . . They want a conservative government, but one tempered with compassion for all the people.

It is particularly important to note that the people are far more influenced by their own feelings about the candidates' personal traits than by the candidates' positions on issues.*

The slogan for Ford would be "The Man Who Made Us Proud Again."

Still, the campaign for the Republican nomination was chaotic and Ford beat Reagan by a whisker, 1,187 to 1,070, and entered the general election contest with only a badly divided party. His managers, assessing the damage, decided on a "no-campaign campaign"—the Rose Garden, "I am your President" approach. As for the Democratic opponent, Georgia Governor Jimmy Carter, the Republicans would portray him as another Nixon. "Carter's campaign must be linked to Nixon's '68 and '72 campaigns—very slick, media-oriented," said Ford's advisers. Carter would be shown to be "a candidate that takes positions based on polls, not principles. . . . A candidate who tries to be all things to all people. Avoids specifics on issues. Driven by personal ambition—harsh and manipulative. Secretive and surrounded by a protective and fiercely loyal staff . . . one who uses religion for political purposes." Driven themselves by the ghost of Nixon, they tried to project the image of the ghost on the opposing candidate.

Carter, of course, had a different vision of himself and his mission. He was destined to play out what William Lee Miller called "the old American story," in which "a lonely achiever and outsider, with a simple moral

* Malcolm D. MacDougall, *We Almost Made It* (New York: Crown Publishers, 1977), p. 70.

earnestness and a limited political and social understanding, moves out into a larger world that is not so simple, not perhaps as earnest, and much more 'realistic,' perhaps excessively so." Miller noted that "America regularly needs to recover its moral bearings." The pulse of politics was beating again for 1976.

The Press as Moral Psychologists

Jimmy Carter's earliest national notice was a *Time* cover story on May 31, 1971, bannered "Dixie Whistles a Different Tune." An epigraph highlighted three sentences from his inaugural address as governor of Georgia: "I say to you quite frankly that the time for racial discrimination is over. Our people have already made this major and difficult decision. No poor, rural, weak or black person should ever have to bear the additional burden of being deprived of the opportunity of an education, a job or simple justice." *Time* was enthusiastic. "A promise so long coming," *Time*'s lead said, "spoken at last." Carter's observation "heralded the end of that final Southern extravagance, the classic rhetoric of 'never.' " Down there were "new political voices, new images, new goals," behind the politics a new emerging spirit: "William Faulkner's South—heavy with ghostly Spanish moss, penumbral myths, and morbid attachment to the past—is giving way to a South that has discovered it does not need fable to shore up its pride or the past to cloud its future." The story featured more of Dixie than of Jimmy, a Dixie of "fresh alignments and priorities," thanks largely to "strong business leadership." But there was Jimmy in his shirt-sleeves, waving from his tractor. "Straddling this varied state is Governor Jimmy Carter, a South Georgia peanut farmer who is both product and destroyer of the old myths. Soft-voiced, assured, looking eerily like John Kennedy from certain angles, Carter is a man as contradictory as Georgia itself, but determined to resolve some of the paradoxes." There followed a relatively adjective-free account of his birth and rise, noting up front the very small place he was from and his old American roots. Emphasis fell on his business success, the ways his ten years of extrasouthern travel and education "had changed Carter," his daring "impassioned speech against excluding blacks from church membership," how he was given to "poring over old Georgia budgets, and at the other extreme, stretching his mind on the likes of Reinhold Niebuhr and Dylan Thomas." The zip of the story was race vs. progress—the ironic reversal of the Goldwater-Nixon southern strategy, which *Time* had long disdained.

But *Time*'s story did not present Carter in a Presidential context; it was soon forgotten, except by Carter himself, who found it encouraging. With his permission his young aides Jerry Rafshoon and Hamilton Jordan went to the Democratic convention of 1972 to get him picked for Vice-President. They could not even get in to see McGovern's twenty-two-year-old pollster, Pat Cadell. The experience was sobering. When Carter began to run for

President—almost immediately thereafter—he knew it would take all-out, carefully planned effort. The resulting strategy, suited to the new politics, focused strongly on winning the press. Rafshoon understood that the race for the Presidency had been transformed into a long, running story in which "each . . . phase runs into the succeeding phase and is an integral part of the overall buildup." Jordan understood "the very special and powerful role the press plays in interpreting the primary results for the rest of the nation. What is actually accomplished in the New Hampshire primary is less important than how the press interprets it," he wrote. "Handled properly, a defeat can be interpreted as a holding action and a mediocre showing as a victory." The "eastern liberal news establishment," whose views "are noted and imitated by other columnists and newspapers throughout the country and the world," had to be convinced of Carter's "candidacy as a viable force." Carter's breakthrough came in Iowa, where his manager Tim Kraft (a devotee of "politics as theater") got his people to the Jefferson-Jackson Day dinner in October 1975, sparking that surprising story in the *New York Times* noting Carter's "dramatic progress." Carter was on his way to front-runnership, a status confirmed when he did best in the New Hampshire primary with 29.3 percent of the votes.

Carter's campaign theme held steady from first to last, as he endlessly repeated his call for "a government as good and as honest and as decent and as competent and as compassionate and as filled with love as are the American people." But in spring of 1976, as he dashed from primary to primary, new questions, questions of character, hit him full force. "The electorate was interested in character in 1976," wrote reporter Jules Witcover, "—not surprising, in light of the fact that the voters had bought experience at the expense of character in 1968 and 1972," and added, "The press, too, no doubt in large measure because it had been burned so badly by Nixon, was taking an extra-close look at character."

The question for journalism was *how* to go about plumbing character. Academic speculators had offered some suggestions of promising techniques of assessment; journalism itself had grown much more intellectual and speculative—a far cry from the old days of narrow concentration on the obvious happenings of the day. At *Time*, for example, in 1968, intellectual Hedley Donovan named as managing editor Henry Anatole Grunwald, a heavy thinker who looked and spoke like a professor drafted into deanship. Essays and "Op Ed" pages and magazines of every conceivable variety welcomed varieties of prose poems George Harvey could not have imagined. But still journalists, including the very best of them, hung back from the task of delving into the souls of politicians. David Broder found the prospect of "journalists as amateur psychologists" a "terrifying" one. R. W. Apple said the whole business "makes us nervous, because most of us feel incompetent to try to do much psychological interpretation." Jules Witcover of the *Washington Post* thought it true that "we don't do enough looking at a candidate and finding out what makes him tick," but he was loath to "draw psychoanalytical conclusions."

Standing back from the immediacies of 1976, one can see why journalists tend to resist the urge to inferences about character and psychic health. In the largest sense it seems somehow un-American: we are a nation of beginners-again, a nation of immigrants and pioneers and class climbers who put the past behind us and took on new identities. As *Times*'s Bonnie Angelo put it, "The American way is that a man can rise above his background." At the other end of a scale of significance, soul-probing can lapse into trashy gossip and character assassination. Furthermore, it often involves "old news"—a contradiction in terms—and long copy too cumbersome and complicated to get past most editors. But in fact, for better or for worse, journalists are psychologists of the day-to-day; they judge what a candidate means, what he is likely to do, where in his past his present behavior comes from. Jimmy Carter's candidacy—"Jimmy Who?" they called him—made character work imperative and journalists groped for an approach to an answer.

Carter-as-Nixon confronted four important challenges to his image as a champion of decency and compassion:

Was he just another con man manufacturing an image, a liar hoping to fake his way through?

Was his toothsome smile but a mask for hidden hate? The suspicion that Carter, the southerner, was a secret racist raised that hypothesis.

Did he bear within him secret moral idiosyncrasies? He claimed to be a Christian—seriously—and thus was suspected of marching to a Drummer different from those who cadenced most politicians.

And could it be that Carter, for all his pious idealism and appearance of health and happiness, was really just another hyped-up, superambitious politician?

By 1976, the story of the politics of conscience had spread from its early base in magazines to every sort of medium. *Time* still led the way, challenged by feistier *Newsweek* and supplemented by the essay magazines like *Harper's* and the *New Republic*. But in the newspapers, columns of moral import abounded and gurus from David Broder to George Will got in their licks for the national betterment. And on television, viewers could find instruction with respect to proper principles from stern Sevareid to sardonic Brinkley, issuing their mini-editorials on the day's declines and falls. What they shared was not only a sense that virtue, while down, was not out, but also a much wider repertoire of analytic approaches than had been readily available in Wilson's day. The Victorian consensus was done with. The new moralism in journalism combined psychology, literary sensibility, historical comparison, and the analysis of style. Responding to the Carter crusade, journalists of every school and stripe sought to find the news in the character of the man.

In its early coverage, *Time* had a friendly view of Carter the campaigner, "smiling his down-home peanut-farmer grin," exuding "folksy charm," a "genial campaigner." He had outgrown a parochial rhetoric:

He won election by appealing to the down-home, antibusing inclinations of his rural constituents and to the antibusing sentiments that they share with Georgia's urban working-class whites. Only 7% of the state's blacks voted for him in the primary, but 61% supported him in the general election. He set the tone for his governorship in his inaugural speech to Georgians: "I say to you quite frankly that the time for racial discrimination is over."*

Through 1975, *Time*'s Carter coverage seesawed along, first a con, then a pro:

Carter has an image elusive enough
To qualify as that "new face" many voters seem to be seeking. . . .

Physically, the Carter face looks younger than his 51 years,
But it also bears some hard lines from a strenuous rural past.

Though he often seems flat and pedantic in front of large crowds,
Carter effectively conveys a soft-spoken reasonableness and decency in face-to-face talks.†

By *Time*'s December 1, 1975, issue the going political rumor may have reached it: *Harper's*, insiders said, was about to publish a devastating attack on Carter's pretense to honesty. *Time* then saw criticism of Carter as "a sure sign of progress. . . . They are taking him seriously." On January 19, Christopher Lydon of the *New York Times* reported "Carter Now a Target." Carter's press secretary, Jody Powell, got an advance copy and issued a twenty-two-page rebuttal of the *Harper's* piece on February 2. The next day *Time* appeared with a large box titled "Carter and His Critics." "Overall," the piece concluded, "Carter's rebuttal to his critics sounds reasonable—or at least well within the reasonable bounds of political expediency." On February 3, Carter himself said on television that the as-yet-unpublished *Harper's* article was "the most remarkable piece of fiction I've ever seen." *Harper's* sent advance copies to newspapers; eventually about one hundred of them printed parts of it. A *Village Voice* columnist found the release "well-researched" and "a devastating piece of work." But the *Washington Star*'s respected columnist Jack Germond called it "but the latest round in what has become a liberal assault on Carter perhaps unmatched in harshness and intensity in any presidential campaign of the postwar period." Before *Harper's* threw its stone, *Time*'s press section featured the *Harper's* author Steven Brill "Doing a Job on Jimmy," with pictures of a smiling Carter and a cold-eyed Brill captioned, "During open season, a visit from the hit man." "Carter has already rebutted (*Time*, February 2) many of the charges, and hedged some," said *Time*, but so had "other candidates."

*Time, 23 December 1974.
†Time, 13 October 1975.

It was a remarkable buildup, complete with "momentum" (the primary season's buzz word), that no doubt sent many a reader scurrying to the newsstands for *Harper's* March issue. There it was: "Jimmy Carter's Pathetic Lies"—accompanied by editor Lewis Lapham's "Easy Chair" column suggesting that *Time* had set out to do a "hatchet job" on Brill. Henry Grunwald wrote a chilling reply, denying the charge as "totally and offensively untrue."

The article's subtitle—"The Heroic Image is Made of Brass"—posed the general point. *Harper's* was long past George Harvey's enthusiastic hyperbole, so such a blast of smoke seemed a symptom of real fire. Actually Brill did find this and that to like about Carter, "a good governor," with "many qualities that could make him a good president." The negative evidence consisted mainly of ways in which Carter cozied up to segregationists like Wallace and Lester Maddox during his 1970 campaign for governor. Brill's main point was not that Carter was a racist, but that Carter was running a "pious antipolitics campaign," claiming never to lie, conducting a long-shot con game, a "personality pitch," hypnotizing his audience with "tantalizing promises, . . . potentially more disillusioning than the myths he is floating about his past record," so that "it is difficult to tell if he really means what he says," leaving "one wondering who he really is." Brill concluded, "Jimmy Carter's campaign—hungry, no philosophy, and brilliantly packaged—*is* Jimmy Carter."

TRB of the *New Republic* announced that "the greatest manhunt in political history now begins as an aftermath of the New Hampshire primary; the press has set itself to finding the 'real' Jimmy Carter."

"Harper's harpooning," as *Time* called the Brill article, showed one mode of approach to character analysis: attack. For all its faults, the *Harper's* piece did raise and dramatize serious questions about the Carter record, particularly his 1970 campaign, and forced a review of the evidence. But the prosecution-defense exchange sparked a good deal more heat than light. The press came out of it about where they went in: Carter was a politician who had changed some of his stands in the past, was now interpreting his record in its best light. It was a small advance on a large problem, preceded by such momentous huffing and puffing as to raise expectations of a good deal more. Thus TRB had it right; the search for the Carter reality was just beginning.

The Great "Ethnic Purity" Crisis

Carter the surpriser went on winning key primaries. But before long another crisis sent up new flags of doubt. Two little words "almost overnight burgeoned into the first major *gaffe* of the 1976 campaign," writes Jules Witcover. On April 2, 1976, as the New York and Wisconsin primaries approached, Jimmy Carter gave a long interview to a reporter for the *New York Daily News*. The reporter got around to asking how Carter felt about government's locating low-income housing projects in suburbs. Carter said such housing ought to go mainly "where the housing is needed most—downtown areas of deteriorating cities." The reporter followed: "Well, can a black central city survive surrounded by all-white neighborhoods?" Carter thought so—"provided you give people the freedom to decide for themselves where to live. But to artificially inject another racial group in a community? I see nothing wrong with ethnic purity being maintained. I would not force racial integration of a neighborhood by government action. But I would not permit discrimination against a family moving into a neighborhood."

Carter's comment appeared in the sixteenth paragraph of a story nineteen paragraphs long, on page 134 of the *New York Daily News*'s Sunday edition. The substance was not big news. He was saying what all sorts of Democrats had concluded—notably Morris Udall and Henry Jackson—on a sticky issue of the contemporary American community. The language was made big news. The political editor of CBS News, Marty Plissner, spotted "ethnic purity" and passed word to his correspondent Ed Rabel to ask Carter what that meant. Carter explained, repeating the phrase "ethnic purity" in his reply. On the way to the next campaign stop, reporters, noting that CBS found the phrase interesting, played back their tape recordings of Carter's answer. Carter staffer Greg Schneiders told Powell, "Jody, wee Jimmy stuck his foot in his mouth." At the South Bend airport, more "ethnic purity" questions popped up. "Tired, agitated, perspiring," Witcover wrote later of Carter at that moment, "he offered a rare contrast to the alert, cool, at times almost icy demeanor he customarily displayed." The reporters smelled blood. Schneiders wrote a memo to Carter; the press was picking up on the language—too emotional and controversial. Carter told Schneiders he intended no offense, and thought none would be taken. The issue itself might help or hurt. Unpersuaded, Schneiders phoned Powell. Another staffer called Jordan. "I thought it would pass," he said later, "I felt that it was a serious mistake, but that it wouldn't last."

The press, now tuned up for verbal nuances, returned to the topic; Carter tried to explain again, and they wrote down his new phrases: "a diametrically opposite kind of family" and "the intrusion of alien groups" and "a different kind of person." Carter went on to say that at first "ethnic purity," caused no stir: "none of you noticed it. There was nothing notable about it. Now, in retrospect, you are trying to make something out of it and there's nothing to be made out of it."

Carter nevertheless won the Wisconsin primary, by a narrow margin, to the chagrin and dismay of NBC, ABC, and several newspapers who prematurely awarded Udall the victory; recalling a famous Truman scene, Carter held aloft a newspaper headlining his loss. But at Pittsburgh, ABC's intrepid Sam Donaldson asked Carter, "Are such terms as 'ethnic purity' and 'alien group' almost Hitlerian?" Carter, by Witcover's report, "blinked and his facial muscles tensed a bit." He explained again where he stood on the issue

of neighborhood integration, carefully employing an uninteresting vocabulary. He added, "If anyone derived from my statement the connotation that I
have an inclination toward racism, then I would resent that because it's certainly not true." It was too late. Carter's verbal crime splashed all over the
campaign coverage. Enterprising reporters sought reactions. Morris Udall
declared, "A mistake is revealing. There is no place in this land for thinly
veiled hints of the politics of racial division." Henry Jackson was variously reported as "amazed," "shocked," and/or "appalled." Reaction from black
leaders was far worse. Atlanta's Mayor Maynard Jackson pounded his desk:
"Is there no white politician I can trust?" Chicago's black leader Jesse Jackson saw "a throw-back to Hitlerian racism." Mayor Richard Hatcher of Gary
said, "We've created a Frankenstein's monster with a Southern drawl, a
more cultured version of the old Confederate at the schoolhouse door." New
York's Bayard Rustin said Carter had "a big smile with no heart." Worst of
all, Carter's strongest black ally, Congressman Andrew Young of Atlanta,
calling the phrases "a disaster," said, "I don't think he understood the loaded
connotations of the words. They summoned up memories of Hitler and Nazi
Germany. I can't defend him on this." Young and sixteen other members of
the Congressional Black Caucus sent Carter a telegram denouncing his
words.

The fat was in the fire. Carter's support among blacks and liberals—
crucial to his victory—seemed to be rapidly melting away just as his prospects were peaking. Carter kept trying to deal with the substance, reiterating and illustrating what the government should and should not do to help
preserve or variegate neighborhoods. On a related front, he reexamined his
opposition to one of the Black Caucus's favorite proposals, the Humphrey-
Hawkins bill, which would make the government an employer of last resort,
declaring he could see merit in an amended version. Some of his critics gave
his now famous remarks a political interpretation: he was trying to send a
message to Pennsylvania bigots, just before that state's crucial primary, that
their ethnic enclaves would be safe with him.

"Ethnic purity" had acquired a life of its own—a symbolic life. Brill had
raised suspicion about his past performance; "ethnic purity" raised the suspicion that all his liberal talk was a mere mask, a wink and a dodge to cover up
his real reactionary nature. The key question became not what Carter had
done or would do but who he *was*.

At first Carter's staff thought the thing would blow over. Then they noticed how the reporters stared at him, how they took note of his sweat, his
expression, the throb of the vein in his forehead. Jody Powell thought the
press was "more interested in how, whether he could handle the problem
than they were in whether he was a racist or not." The staff got busy on strategy. Carter's seasoned Atlanta friend Charles Kirbo thought he had better
say he was sorry; the press would not let him alone until he took it back. In
Philadelphia on April 8, Carter made this statement:

I think most of the problem has been caused by my ill-chosen agreement to use the word ethnic purity. I think that was a very serious mistake on my part. I think it should have been the word "ethnic character" or "ethnic heritage," and I think that unanimously my black supporters with whom I discussed this question agree that my position is the correct one. . . . I do want to apologize to all those who have been concerned about the unfortunate use of the term "ethnic purity." I don't think there are any ethnically pure neighborhoods in this country, but in response to a question and without adequate thought on my part, I used a phrase that was unfortunate . . . I was careless in the words I used. . . . I have apologized for it. It was an improper choice of words. . . .*

But apology was not enough. "Was this one of those fatal slips that can destroy a candidate?" *Time* asked. "For the first time in what had been a near faultless campaign to reach the White House, the candidate had stumbled badly." *Newsweek*, noticing shifts toward Humphrey invisible to the proverbial "Many Others," treated "ethnic purity" rather more lightly and briefly. The April 19 issue headlined "Carter's Trip of the Tongue" and called it his campaign's "first serious case of the stumbles," a "blooper," a "self-inflicted wound," a "brouhaha," a "flap."

Carter arranged a dramatic ceremony of redemption: a rally in Atlanta with the Reverend Martin Luther King, Sr., in the noonday bright of April. Carter spoke of America growing up in slavery, then throwing off that yoke. Then "Daddy King" addressed the crowd.

I've always been able to let my religion and politics work together. And I've always fitted in somewhere a statement for this man who I love and believe in. I want to find that man who has lived so perfect that he's never made a mistake. I know I have; it may well be that I'll make some more mistakes before the day's out. But if there is a forgiving heart and one who stands to apologize, then this nation, this state and everyone else, has no choice but to accept. Further, and I preach it everywhere I go, I refuse to hate any man. I refuse to step low enough to have any envy or strife in my heart against anybody. I have a forgiving heart. So, Governor, I'm with you all the way.†

The people exploded in applause.

The mainline press revealed its own forgiving heart. James Reston wrote it would be bad "if they beat him on the slip of the tongue and on phony charges that his record refutes," and "it would be ironic if 'purity' were turned into a dirty word." The *Washington Star* editor reproached "the lurking sentinels poised to spear candidates on verbal slipups," and in a second editorial noted that "Dr. Freud was not the first to alert us to the deeper significance of verbal lapses, but he probably made our suspicions permanent." Jackson, wrote the editor, and Udall had fallen into "noxious sanctimony and hypocrisy." The *Washington Post* hit the same unforgiving pair for "feigning shock and horror" over a policy they really shared. David

---

* Quoted in Witcover, *Marathon*, p. 306 (italics and interpolations omitted).
† Quoted in ibid., p. 272.

Broder reasoned that his impure language was "disturbing, distasteful" but his larger "record . . . should not be forgotten." James J. Kilpatrick put it more colorfully. "What a flap!" he wrote. "It was like a sneeze in a brooder house. Seldom have we witnessed such a beating of wings, such a chorus of yelps, yawps and adenoidal cackles, such a wringing of hands and a rolling of eyes." Carter seemed to *Time* "to have weathered that mistake." By May 17, "ethnic purity" had sunk without a trace—not even a story on "Mobilizing the Black Bloc," featuring pictures of recent purity denouncers Richard Hatcher and Jesse Jackson and dealing *in extenso* with Carter's relations with blacks, mentioned the phrase or the "disaster." Carter would go on to win 94 percent of the black vote in the general election. The whole sorry episode represented character exploration at its worst—the psychology of the "gaffe"—though not for the first or last time.

As far back as 1884, James G. Blaine virtually sank his candidacy merely by *listening* without protest while a speaker condemned the Democrats as the party of "rum, Romanism, and rebellion." But in the age of the long campaign, the dash from primary to primary, and media-saturated politics, the odds that an exhausted and loquacious candidate would say something silly had risen radically. So had the odds that the press, bleary-eyed with boredom from listening to the same old speeches, would pick up on any markedly unusual turn of phrase. And perhaps the public, too, confused by the complexity of it all as too many candidates took too many positions on too many complicated issues, would welcome some simplifying signal to clarify character once and for all. But the assumption behind gaffe-grabbing was psychologically daring to the point of folly: that a single phrase could represent a personality. George Romney's confession that he had been "brainwashed" in Vietnam, George McGovern's ripped-out-of-context "$1,000 for every American," Ed Muskie's choked-back rage at family insult—none of that amounted to a hill of historical beans. Mr. Loquacious himself, Hubert Humphrey, decided not to run in 1976 for many reasons, but one was, "All I gotta do is stumble just one place and the media will jump on me; old Humphrey lousing things up."

The gaffe story now had a plot of its own. The extraction of the slip. The shocked reactions of opponents and friends. The candidate's inadequate explanations. The demand for an apology. The candidate's repentance. The forgiveness of the offended. The press's own judicious absolution. It was a running story capable of spawning news for weeks at a stretch. The candidate who refused to play it out did so at substantial risk. Nor was Carter through gaffing.

From the editorial commentary after the "ethnic purity" flap one might have hoped that gaffe-grabbing as a journalistic sport would fade away. But no. In September, *Playboy* magazine published a long interview in which Carter, trying to explain that he was not holier than thou, admitted to occasional "lust in the heart" and reached out for a connection with *Playboy* readers by saying "screw" and "shack up," setting off the whole racy drama all over again.

The moralists' search for "a real American" ran into trouble with Jimmy Carter. Obviously his stress on goodness and love rang a bell with the popular sentiments of 1976. Here was a man who accentuated the positive, who talked about doing one's best, and who took his moral bearings from the fundamental goodness of The People. They knew, and they heard him say, that even though they fell far short of perfection day by day, many of the Americans they knew personally were good people—sacrificing for their children, caring for the old folks, sticking with their wives and husbands, passing up chances to make a crooked dollar, and reaching out to lend a hand to those less lucky than they had been. They seldom made the news. What they read of the sleazy behavior of their elected representatives did not represent what *their* lives were all about. Carter spoke past the skeptical press to that public understanding. And he was heard. Coinciding with his rise, and possibly reflecting it in part, polls on public confidence began to pick up.

Carter's Bizarre Religion

But doubts remained. America had grown up as a nation of strangers, an experience that left in the culture a residue of suspicion, not only of the sly flimflam man, but also of the new arrival. Did he really share their values? Was he really one of them? Or was there in him some secret faith or passion that might, on some crucial occasion, emerge and distort and destroy the common assumptions? The moralizing story in Presidential politics had sought to allay those fears by finding a natural son of the undeniably American soil. Recognizing their own deviation from that norm, the eastern establishment moralists (many of them born outlanders) reached out to the midsection, the gut, the heartland of the nation for an Iowan or Indianian or Kansan, who, though he had left home long ago, still carried in his breast the breath and blood of his breeding. Wilson the native southerner had to be shown as not dumb, not provincial, not a stranger. Al Smith and John F. Kennedy had to deal not only with their foreign religion but also with their eccentric urbanity. The Roosevelts had to work past their funny accents, which sounded English to midland ears. Lyndon Johnson the Texan and Richard Nixon the rootless Californian kept trying to allay those disadvantages by out-Americaning everybody else. Carter came on as an alien intrusion in the national neighborhood. He lacked the right kind of ethnic purity. People who could forgive his lapses of language—for they, too, could resent the tyranny of the superarticulate—might still wonder where he was coming from. Carter was odd. He was a Christian—not in the easy, arm's-length sense in which most Americans are "Christian," but deeply and seriously committed to his faith as the crux and guide of his life, including his political life. Worse yet, he was a Southern Baptist, conjuring up shades of

Elmer Gantry and the preacher in *The Grapes of Wrath*. And he came from
Georgia; people knew about that from such movies as *I Was A Prisoner on a
Georgia Chain Gang* and *Gone with the Wind*. As *Time* pointed out, he
came stepping onto the national scene right out of Atlanta, the city General
Sherman had burned down.

What turned out to be "the Carter election" stimulated a marvelous
outpouring of literature on The South—America's storyland. Reynolds
Price, the distinguished southern novelist, reported, "Critical organs which
have long since blown Taps over 'exhausted' Southern writers are imploring
those same writers now for guidance through the ticking underbrush of dark
Dixie—as though we were nimble scouts, not the sad sclerotics we so recently seemed." Biographer Robert Sam Anson "decided that if I were to
know Jimmy Carter and what we were about to become, I had to know his
land. The South had the answers. The mystery of him was here in Dixie."
Sadly or proudly, southerners testified, "We're all getting to be Yankees"
and, "We're coming back into the country." Harvard psychiatrist Robert
Coles wrote on "The Southern Paradox—Jimmy Carter: Agrarian Rebel?"
analyzing with his usual perceptiveness how Carter's history did and did not
link to the populist tradition of the likes of Tom Watson. Some assayed
prediction: Johnny Greene wrote in *Harper's* that "Good Ole Boy" Carter
"will have an entire region behind him, unquestioning, at each moment of
his four-year term," and *Washingtonian* magazine forecast "The Southern-
ization of Washington," advertising that "if Carter comes, here's what to
look for in fashion, food, jokes, talk, music—plus a peanut-butter tasting."
The Old South groping out of defeat, the New South straining against the ills
of modernization, the southern land and sky, river and forest, the South of
feud and family, soul and sin—all that spilled across the pages of the magazines. Never since Lee's surrender had so much been written, and maybe
even read, about the American South. What counted for understanding
Carter was the South he himself had experienced and what that had come to
mean for him. Nervous northerners got only hints of that in stories about
coon hunts and cotton chopping. The effort was roughly analogous to seeking
the souls of Birch Bayh and Everett Dirksen, Hubert Humphrey and William Jenner, in the spirit of the Midwest. Somehow one senses there is
something there, but like the smoke from a leaf-fire, no sooner does it form
than it wafts away. Carter was southern, and proud of it, but he was also a
"Yankee from Georgia," as William Lee Miller called him: Puritan, given to
efficiency.

Carter's religious identification had a finer focus than his southernism.
Voters slowly picking up on the Carter personality as the primaries rolled on
could not help but read of his preacherlike style, his moralizing emphasis,
and his special affinity with black religious leaders and congregations. But
not until the North Carolina primary in March 1976, did his faith arouse
special concern. Myra McPherson of the *Washington Post*, in an interview
with Carter's sister, Ruth Stapleton, a full-time charismatic Christian evan-

gelist, uncovered a poignant drama. One day ten years ago, Mrs. Stapleton said, she and brother Jimmy took a long walk and talk in the piny woods near their home in Plains. Jimmy was depressed; he had run flat out for governor and lost to none other than Lester Maddox. As they paced along, his sister's serenity dawned on Carter. "You and I are both Baptists," he said, "but what is it that you have that I haven't got?" Ruth said, "Jimmy, through my hurt and pain I finally got so bad off I had to forget everything I was. What it amounts to in religious terms is total commitment. I belong to Jesus, everything I am." He said, "Ruth, that's what I want." They talked on about the sacrifices the Christian life required—a letting go, a giving up of all the lesser wantings and needings for one great want and need. Carter wept, his sister said. And from the ashes of his political failure, he changed his life that day.

The people at the *Post* thought the story controversial and asked Jules Witcover, on the road with Carter in North Carolina, to check it out. On the way to a reception in a home in Winston-Salem, Carter told Witcover that Ruth's memory was "accurate, basically," though he did not remember the tears. He confirmed that he took to praying—"There was no wave of revelation that came over me, no blinding flash of light or voices of God or anything. I just had a quiet feeling that was reassuring. But I wouldn't want it connoted as a mystical set of events. It's a typical experience among Christians." He said he had spent several periods of a week or more, in the midst of his Georgia politicking, up North doing missionary work. Later when he was governor, "I spent more time on my knees . . . than I did in all the rest of my life put together." At the reception, a question about his faith came up. Carter confirmed the "profound religious experience that changed my life dramatically." He said, "I recognized for the first time that I lacked something very precious—a complete commitment to Christ, a presence of the Holy Spirit in my life in a more profound and personal way, and since then I've had an inner peace and inner conviction and assurance that transformed my life for the better."

No Presidential politician in modern memory had talked that way. The next day at a press conference in Wake Forest, a reporter predictably wanted to know more about this "profound religious experience" business. Sensing something, Carter carefully explained what it was *not*:

It was not a profound stroke or miracle. . . . It wasn't a voice of God from heaven. It was not anything of that kind. It wasn't mysterious. . . . I don't feel I'm ordained by God to win an election or to be President of the United States. And I would be perfectly at ease if I won or lost. I don't intend to lose, but I don't think God is going to make me President, by any means.*

Discussion of the piny woods drama spread through the press, more gently than "ethnic purity" but insistently. Witcover thought it "brought to the forefront a sort of whispered issue concerning Carter that had bothered

* Quoted in ibid.

many people outside the South unfamiliar with the ways of the Baptist faith. It was not something specific, but rather a general uneasiness about this rather strange man who had strode so boldly onto the political landscape, speaking unabashedly about love and compassion and being influenced in his conduct of public office by God's word and guidance." His comments "only served to create more talk about Carter's religiosity, especially outside the South." The press had neither space nor patience for extensive elaborations of Carter's religious heritage and experience, or for his interesting theological thinking (he was a Niebuhrian activist—a combination Luce would have called a contradiction). Instead, concern centered on whether or not Carter's Christianity might wrench his political thinking in destructively deviant ways.

Back when he announced his candidacy in December 1974, *Time*'s story did not even mention his religion. A paragraph-long note about him in February 1975 mentioned that he was "a Baptist who taught Sunday school as a midshipman at Annapolis and conducted religious services on wartime submarines." A longer *Time* profile on October 13, 1975, added that he was "a Baptist church deacon," mentioned his missionary work, and quoted him as enjoying "witnessing among people who don't know about Christ." A December 1, 1975 story, "Taking Jimmy Seriously" ("Suddenly he is no longer Jimmy *Who?*"), went on for nearly a page without a religious grace note. But by March 8, 1976, *Time* took note of his unusual motivation and of the reaction that was beginning to arouse: Carter "is an earnest Baptist who says that religion is the most important thing in his life. His Southern-style evangelism, showing up in so many of his speeches, irritates the less devout. They are uneasy about a man who uses the word God so easily, so often." On April 5, a story stressed how well his "unashamed evocations of love and compassion, his Baptist fundamentalist evangelism" were going over with blacks. On April 12, "Carter: The Deacon" was featured reading the Bible morning and evening, telling one television interviewer calmly that no, he did not take pep pills, telling another that while he prayed about twenty-five times a day, "I have never asked God to let me succeed . . . but I do ask God to help me do the right thing." The picture alongside showed him preaching, stern-visaged, under a shining cross. On April 26, *Time*'s Religion section had a basically sympathetic account of Ruth Stapleton's work as a healer, noting along the way her unorthodox but successful methods, her history of despair and conversion, and her experience in "speaking in tongues"; virtually nothing was said of her famous brother.

"Jimmy's Breakthrough" was *Time*'s cover story on May 10; after his win in the Pennsylvania primary, "Suddenly, only a third of the way through the obstacle course, the race was all but over." His "call for a moral revival of sorts seems to have struck home in the American psyche, vintage 1976." On the other hand: "Nothing arouses more fascination, suspicion and questions than Carter's deep-seated religious convictions. He contends that he does

not inject them into his campaigning. But the two are inescapably in-
tertwined, producing a blend of William Jennings Bryan's religious fervor
and Woodrow Wilson's moral idealism." *Time* said that Protestant Evangelicals, now numbering 40 million, were the country's fastest growing Christian
grouping, constituting "a natural constituency for Carter." But:

> To skeptics, Carter's language often sounds like a pious facade. That, decidedly,
> is not the case. To Carter, his religion had always been a central and natural part of
> his life—"like breathing," as he says. Like many Southerners, he finds no contra-
> diction in mixing an earthy appreciation of the good, secular life with the harder
> demands of Evangelicalism.

Time issued a series of refutations: Carter was a missionary and a praying
governor, but "claims no 'special relationship' with God." As governor he
took the heat when the fundamentalists faulted him for opposing Sunday
liquor bans and eliminating Maddox's daily statehouse service. The Bible
was his "prime source" but he disagreed with some of it, and he had "read
deeply" Niebuhr, Barth, Tillich, and Kierkegaard, liking specially Niebuhr's
epigram, "The sad duty of politics is to establish justice in a sinful world." To
the fears of "some critics" that his religion might intrude on his Presidency,
"Carter vows a strict separation of church and state," quoting Christ with respect to what should be rendered unto whom.

The Carter campaign, recalling the mass defection of Jewish voters from
McGovern's cause in 1972, "has mounted a determined effort to woo Jews,"
Time said. The President of the American Union of Hebrew Congregations
noted that "historically, anti-Semitism had its roots in fundamentalist religion"—but quickly added that it "is unjust and paradoxical for religious
Jews to look askance at a man because he is deeply religious." Carter
stressed the sameness of the God of Israel and of Christendom and the
American "system of religious pluralism . . . that is precious to me." And
"the survival of Israel," he declared, "is not a political issue. It is a moral imperative."

Newsweek saw approximately the same series of revelations, though
from a rather more skeptical perspective. As early as December 1, 1975,
Newsweek said, "Out on the stump, the Carter message is as mellow as a
Baptist sermon," and, that "Carter admits proudly to being 'a born-again
Christian Baptist Sunday-school-teacher-deacon.' But he has some other,
more worldly credentials as well." Yet "his born-again faith gives him a born-
yesterday air from time to time." A long piece on March 8, 1976, said that he
had "begun toning down the more floridly godly passages in his spiel, on the
advice of various well-wishers including his own mother. . . . But his meetings retain the flavor of a devotional, to God, love, morality, hard work and
not incidentally himself, and it all cuts—just as intended—across ideological
lines." On April 5, *Newsweek* analyzed "Carter and the God Issue." He had
"aroused misgivings" and "at least part of the stir over Carter's shirtsleeve

religiosity is that he seems to practice what he preaches." His "smug moral tone" and "his openness about religion" made various categories of Americans "uneasy," but "more and more it seems, churchgoing Americans see Carter not as a shrewd, ambitious politician but as a man who can heal the spiritual wounds of America." Recounting Carter's religious history in brief, *Newsweek* concluded: "With a discerning combination of piety and politics, Jimmy Carter has set out to make himself both a party leader for the Democrats and a faith healer for the nation." In June 1976, *Newsweek* wrote of "Carter's Cross to Bear." A Jewish leader said, "Jimmy Carter is the focus of the most anxious political debate in the Jewish community. . . . Many Jews still think of evangelicals as spiritual headhunters out to nail Jewish scalps on the wall like coonskins." A northern Catholic thinker thought "the evangelical tradition" lacked a "thought-out political morality," and a liberal Protestant protested that he wanted "political answers to political questions." But, "as a matter of fact," *Newsweek* discerned, "Carter's evangelical piety comes as close as any style to being the folk religion of the nation." Indeed some evangelicals felt, as one said, "concern about one of ours being tainted by politics," though another thought a President of his persuasion "would be an improvement over what we've had recently." Carter's media director said, "We're reassuring people Jimmy won't turn the White House into a Billy Graham Bible class."

Thus by the time the Democratic convention met in July, the Carter faith was public. *Time* headlined a July 12 account, "Shall We Gather at the Hudson River?" and led, "The Democratic Party fairly shines with the inner peace of the born-again." When the convention met, *Time* said, "One could almost hear shouts of 'Hallelujah!' "

In the essay magazines of smaller circulation—*New York, Harper's, Atlantic, New Republic,* and the like—Carter's version of Christianity came in for all sorts of philosophical peregrinations, some by authors who had actually walked the streets of Plains or dropped in on a Sunday school class. Garry Wills, with unintended comedy, let himself be amazed that Carter had not read Rudolf Bultmann. Norman Mailer, in the *New York Times Magazine,* let himself write, "A man running for President could comment about Christ, he could comment a little, but he could hardly afford to be enthusiastic. Religion had become as indecent a topic to many a contemporary American as sex must have been in the 19th century." Lewis Lapham, editor of *Harper's,* put to print his view: "If Mr. Carter believes himself rescued by Jesus (a figure somewhat comparable to a Southern banker who lends unlimited amounts of money without charging interest), then I can well imagine he would find it difficult to take much of an interest in a world elsewhere."

Journalism's commentaries on Carter the Christian show how deeply the acids of skepticism had eaten into the story of politics as morals since Ida Tarbell's day. Johnson with his proposed "Monument to God," Nixon with Billy Graham at White House Sunday services, Eisenhower with his cosmetic prayer breakfasts, had undercut faith in faith. Carter's religion had to be handled not as a virtue but as a worry. The worry that he did not mean it (the faker) alternated with the worry that he did (the fanatic). Slowly but steadily the magazines helped allay those concerns. Carter came to seem what he most probably was: a person of prayer, a God-searcher, whose form of faith connected with themes millions of his countrymen had found life-sustaining and life-enhancing, a man of politics who understood—and felt —how partial and perverse could be the temptation to claim a special revelation.

But the accounts of Carter's struggle with what Hamilton Jordan called "the weirdo factor" also illustrates the broader difficulty journalism encounters in a suspicious age in analyzing politically relevant beliefs. Carter's stands on particular issues were noticed, though late in the game and then mostly to point out contradictions. What was hard to handle was his political philosophy. He stressed The People's goodness—but how would that vision connect with his strategy as President? He spoke of the need to establish justice in a sinful world—but what large lines of intervention in the flow of history did that imply? He stressed his decency—but which broad directions of policy did decency demand? Simply placing him on a left-right ideological scale would not answer those questions.

Who Is Jimmy Who?

But there was yet a deeper, vaguer worry about Jimmy Carter that pervaded the 1976 campaign. The more he won, the more the suspicion grew that winning might mean too much to him—that Carter might really be another Nixon, mouthing pieties as he calculated, step by step, the path an inordinate ambition forced upon him. An old enemy, Reg Murphy, longtime editor of the *Atlanta Constitution,* saw Carter as "absolutely ruthless." An old friend, Charles Kirbo, said, "It's not that often you see someone that gentle who is tough as nails inside." His own mother saw that "he has a look of steel if you do anything he doesn't like." That sense of a man "wearing a brick in a velvet glove," as Bill Moyers put it, could not help but haunt the citizenry after the Johnson and Nixon years.

That fear could hardly be allayed by quoting on the one hand some who shared it and on the other some who denied it. Nor—after "ethnic purity"— was there some conveniently sharp symbolic event on which to hang a decisive interpretation. If the question of Carter as Nixon was to be addressed in any convincing manner, there was only one place to look: to Carter's past.

And there, at long last, the magazine moralists searched him out. After his nomination in New York's Madison Square Garden, in the dog days of August, *Time* and *Newsweek* turned to the task of recounting, not just the external items of The Jimmy Carter Story, but the person-shaping and person-showing history that produced him as he was in 1976. The most incisive and clarifying biography during the campaign appeared in the *Washington Post,* in a long, three-article series by William Greider, beginning on October 24, 1976 and titled "A Carter Album." Greider worked into the Carter life history from an independent perspective, standing back and looking hard at how so many of his friends in the President-assessing business were going about that task.

Plains, Ga.—People have a right to worry about Jimmy Carter's smile. He smiles so often, so engagingly, sometimes in the wrong places, sometimes even when he is suffering.

In Washington they gossip about the man behind the smile. They trade anecdotes and insights and make troublesome comparisons with other men who have been President and turned out to be so different from appearances. This uneasiness reflects our own experience more than it says anything about Jimmy Carter. We have been so deeply deceived in the recent past. . . .

How is anyone supposed to know about Carter, if the campaign images, the rhetoric, the filtered wisdom of the news media can be so wrong?

The terrible answer, of course, is that we can't know, not with certainty. It is not given with the human condition that people will understand one another fully, not on this earth anyway, certainly not in newspaper articles. The best we get are glimpses, a few clear snapshots which freeze a man in action, a sense of his direction, maybe some modest suggestions of his probabilities. That's all. . . .

So we are looking for clues to impossible questions. Is the Jimmy Carter behind the smile another Nixon? Glib comparisons between the two men are in vogue among politicians and the press, based on Carter's uptight spurts and splashes, as a candidate. It is almost a matter of scent: Carter does not have that funky give-and-take among politicians that they find reassuring. Neither did Nixon. Carter distrusts the press, so did Nixon. Carter listens to a tight circle of young and untested advisers, people from outside the ranks of regular politicians, just like Nixon's palace guard. Reporters and politicians smell "stranger," and it reminds them with embarrassment of how poorly they understood Nixon. . . .

Jimmy Carter is a politician, whatever that implies to different people. He is also human, as he keeps reminding us. Voters are not choosing an idealized creature to be loving father or loyal husband or dutiful son or even to be a good friend. They are selecting someone to be given awesome political power, to lead the nation and the national government. The question is not how Jimmy Carter will do when the roll is called up yonder, but how he might behave if he becomes President.*

Greider proceeded then to review Carter's life, selecting from the material for special examination those experiences and relationships and attitudes most apposite for assessing Carter as a potential President. *Time,* in a striking cover story, applied "The Character Test" in the October 25 issue, and *Newsweek* devoted a full twenty-two pages, on September 13, to "Sizing Up Carter: The Question of Character," a history-packed, artfully composed review by Senior Editor Peter Goldman. Even television came through, with a long, sensitively incisive interview with Carter by Bill Moyers.

* William Greider, "A Carter Album," *Washington Post,* 24 October 1976.

Thus very late in the game, long after the "Jimmy Who?" question had been posed and reposed dozens of times, Carter emerged for those who cared to read about him as a three-dimensional man with a present and a past. It turned out there was far more material available than readers might have supposed as they skimmed along through the primaries. Carter himself had published his story, *Why Not The Best?*, way back; not much had been done with that. When Greider went to Plains—representing the newspaper that had done more than any other to reveal the Nixon scandals—Carter's mother casually let him rummage through her son's old school papers while she went off to run errands. People who had known Carter, pro and con, since his Day One turned out to have reportable memories, not only of this or that little incident, but also of the way he was, the human context of his life, the meanings that had slowly shown themselves as he developed and emerged.

Was Carter a con man? He had been presenting himself to publics at least since, as a child of five, he toddled into Plains to sell bags of peanuts. In school his act got the close perusal of teachers like Miss Julia Coleman, who set him to reading Tolstoy and debating and reciting. At Annapolis other teachers, and his classmates, could compare his words with his deeds, as could his navy boss Admiral Hyman Rickover—an assessor not given to naïve or casual evaluations. Back home, he served six years with his neighbors on the school board, two of them as chairman, then at thirty-seven ran for and won a state senate seat, ran again and won again, ran for governor and lost, ran again and won. Along the way he spoke at nearly every Georgia crossroads town and as governor got out of the mansion and around to the courthouses at every opportunity. Current hopes and suspicions could be checked against that past. Now that happened, in depth and at length. The upshot was that he had indeed trimmed and dodged from time to time, but that no reasonable review could make him out a Georgia Nixon, devoted to masking what he thought and felt and meant behind a facade of fakery.

Was he a closet racist? There the record reached back even farther, to his mother's father, for instance, who used to boom out hymnal harmonies in the living room with the local black bishop, to his own father, who would not let the bishop's son use the front door, and to his mother, who as a nurse treated babies and mothers of whatever color. Some of his black childhood playmates and longtime neighbors were still around to testify how it had been with Mr. Earl's boy. In the navy came other tests of racial liberalism and back home a series of encounters with racists in his church, the Klan, and the White Citizens' Council. The school board took up issues of school integration, as did the state legislature, and race issues, express and implied, ran through his winning campaign for governor. Then there was the actual record—with respect to appointments, for example—that followed his startling inaugural announcement that segregation was dead. One could find out what such longtime Carter watchers as Lester Maddox and Julian Bond had said and thought of his stands on blacks and whites. One need not stop at symbolic gestures such as Carter having portraits of Martin Luther King, Jr., and two other black Georgians put up in the statehouse; there was a record to be compared with what his critics and competitors advocated, what his predecessors and fellow southern governors had done.

Was Deacon Carter's God-talk indicative of a private prejudice that might distort his Presidential performance? He had done his share of reciting and witnessing and scripture-reading and preaching from the pulpit. Church had occupied much of his—and nearly everybody else's—life in Plains; as his mother explained, "there was nothing else to do," though often enough she would scare the children out of bed on Sunday morning and then stay home herself while Mr. Earl taxied them to church and left them there while he walked downtown to chat with his friends. Again in the navy and during the Plains years afterward, Carter spoke out again and again about what he believed and why. Nor need one rely too much on sister Ruth's recall of the woods walk varying in minor ways from Carter's. He had voted with his feet when he went North on his missionary ventures. The Reverend Eloy Cruz, who took him house to house in the Puerto Rican barrio of Springfield, Massachusetts, could describe what Carter said, what made him weep, what his reaction was when Cruz told him, "Our Savior has hands which are very gentle, and he cannot do much with a man who is hard." And then there were all those years of political standtaking and policymaking, to show if or how Carter's Christian vision had affected his uses of authority in the public realm.

But deeper down, was Jimmy Carter really some kind of "authoritarian personality," a "compulsive-obsessive," an "active-negative" type so consumed by ambition that he would drive on to a Nixonian tragedy? A plausible start was his family life. One need not make of that a psychoanalytic mystery or accept arcane interpretations from inexplicable premises. Carter seemed to invite psychiatric speculation, and psychiatrists and psychohistorians by the bushel accepted the invitation, too often substituting the fancies of speculation for the facts of his upbringing.

How had the boy learned to be, as he met the inevitable hurts and hopes of life? What had *he* made of the mother who nursed him out of early illness, the father who worked him and switched him when he was bad? What was *his* way of getting along with Gloria and Ruth and Billy? Much of that might be obscure, since he was not then known as a future President. But the surviving playmates and teachers could testify, and there were even documents such as "Jimmy Carter's Health Report" ("Take happy thoughts to bed with you") and "Healthy Mental Habits" ("1. The habit of expecting to accomplish what you attempt") composed for his teacher when he was twelve. His adolescent cruising around with girls, his navy terrors and triumphs, his marriage, homecoming, his feelings at his father's death—there were people around who had seen and heard at least the edges of those personal experiences. And in his much more open and public later life, he had exhibited what those old times had taught him, so that people could see whether he worked much or little, liked it or complained about it, laughed at himself or only at others, and how he reacted to defeat and victory, sorrow and solace, confusion and clarity. An enterprising reporter could even check the facts against his earliest memories, as when he said, "When I grew up on the farm and when I got hurt, my Mamma and Daddy were always there—on the edge of the field or not too far away from the creek. If I got thrown off a mule, my Daddy was close by to pick me up."

Thus haltingly and unevenly—and only when the campaign was nearly over—Henry Luce's inheritors found their man. His character was in his history, whatever his destiny might be. Carter's history, as evidence, had a clear advantage: it had happened and it could be discovered. That process of discovery was by no means over when *Time* and *Newsweek* produced their long and novel biographies in 1976. To this day, academics of various psychological persuasions are at work recombing the material for more critical assessment. But even in 1976, editors were pondering how much sense it made to send their best reporters chasing after candidates and nervously noting their verbal twitches. As early as 1975, David Broder got off the bus and systematically explored the hometown sentiments behind ten of the contenders (though he did not include Carter). R. W. Apple, Jr., made his campaign flash about Carter's early victory in Iowa into a new start for the horserace, but he also went out to Everett, Washington, to prepare a revealing biographical portrait of Henry Jackson. 1976 sapped journalism's confidence in the Great Campaign Stress Test as *the* examination Presidents had to pass, because, as it turned out, the gaffes and slips and waffles—seemingly so "disastrous" at the time—bore little relation to either the electoral outcome or the performance of Presidents.

The nation came out of the Johnson-Nixon years with its trust busted. Carter set out to restore that essential element of democratic politics. Over and over, in the snows of New Hampshire and in the heat of Southern California, he posed his promise: "If I ever lie to you, if I ever mislead you, if I ever avoid a controversial issue, then don't vote for me, because I won't be worthy of your vote if I'm not worthy of your trust." After his nomination, his pollster Pat Cadell said, "Without the trust thing, he couldn't have made it." As the campaign drew to a close, his opponent came out with the same moral message, claiming trust as *his* essential virtue. His last newspaper ad, headed, "One final thought," had the word in every sentence:

It is not enough for anyone to say "trust me."
Trust is not having to guess what a candidate means.
Trust is not being all things to all people, but being the same to all people.
Trust is leveling with the people before the election about what you're going to do after the election.

Trust is saying plainly and simply what you mean—and meaning what you
   say.
Trust must be earned.

President Gerald R. Ford*

By an electoral eyelash, 1,682,970 votes of a total of 81,555,889, a bare
majority invested Carter with their highest political trust. He continued to
pray his way through crisis after crisis, his finest hour arriving with the
agreement he arranged between the Israeli Prime Minister and the President of Egypt—peace, albeit shaky, in the Holy Land at last. But by the time
in the summer of 1979 when candidates were gearing up to challenge his
confident claim to another term, troubles gathered around him. The energy
problem translated into an energy crisis of sorts, as gas stations piddled out
their waning supplies. The rate of inflation escalated; expert economists of
various schools continued to predict a dark recession ahead. Soviet troops
stationed in Cuba for a long time turned out to be a "combat brigade" to the
shock and horror of senators. Washington insiders scathed Carter for political ineptitude; his intentions to prune and reshape the bureaucracy were
postponed once more. In the polls, his job-performance rating took a heavy
beating, down to the lowest ever for any President since that game began,
though at the same time four out of five Americans rated him high as a
decent and well-intentioned character. Carter responded, not by isolating
himself or by freezing onto a failing line of policy or by caving in to the
strongest pressures, but by opening up an extensive examination of what the
trouble was and why his works were not working. Platoons of critics were invited to give him their candid assessments; they did, and he wrote down
what they said. The speeches that followed publicly admitted failure and announced reorientation: a comprehensive energy plan, followed by a cabinet
shuffle in hopes of getting action on it. His troubles were far from over, but
he had demonstrated a readiness to grow and learn in office.

He had to cope quickly when Iran seized American hostages, when the
Soviets suddenly invaded Afghanistan. His reputation in the polls shot upward as the nation rallied around their leader.

As the new Presidential season opened the call went out for "leadership." Convinced of Carter's personal goodness, people asked for a sure
sense of direction, a firm hand on the tiller, even perhaps a little charisma
again. But few offered clear counsel as to which path they wanted to be led
along. In a milder version of 1932, the nation was looking for the President to
"do something" to allay the popular anxieties. Through it all, Carter the
Conscientious spoke the language of moral revival. In 1976, the nation had
taken that theme for its own—for a time. Once again, that theme faded, and
the mythic rhythm picked up new music for the next march to the White
House.

---

* MacDougall, *We Almost Made It*, p. 195.

III

THE POLITICS OF
CONCILIATION

AFTER THE BATTLE OF 1796 and the moral trial of 1800, the spirit of forgive and forget gave us a nation family reunion in the election of 1804. Jefferson shone as its warmhearted celebrity; in a troubled world, America seemed for a moment a blessed place to live.

Jefferson began his Presidency in 1801 by extending the hand of peace to the politicians who had so recently been condemning him as an atheist and a foreign agent. "Let us, then, fellow-citizens, unite with one heart and one mind," he said in his inaugural address. "Let us restore to social intercourse that harmony and affection without which liberty and even life itself are but dreary things." The "throes and convulsions of the ancient world" had reached "even this distant and peaceful shore," Jefferson said, "but every difference of opinion is not a difference of principle. We have called by different names brethren of the same principle. We are all Republicans, we are all Federalists."

The hated Alien and Sedition Acts were allowed to lapse and Jefferson pardoned those convicted under them. He cut federal spending, reduced military expenditures, resolved the disputes with France. Even the mountaineers were comforted when the federal whisky tax was wiped off the books. And Sunday after Sunday went by with no Bibles confiscated, no altars overturned.

Jefferson continued to suffer under the lash of the predominantly Federalist press. But the Republicans were growing a press of their own; the *National Intelligencer* sang Jefferson's praises so harmoniously that critics called it "Mr. Silky-Milky Smith's National Smoothing Plane." Hamilton scoffed at Jefferson's little lullabies to Congress, rhetorical versions of the counsel the President wrote privately to his children: "It is a charming thing to be loved by everybody; and the way to obtain it is, never to quarrel or be angry with anybody." A man of wide learning, infinite curiosity, and exceptional eloquence, Jefferson attracted the interest of those who wanted to exercise their minds. But as Henry Adams saw, he attracted hearts as well: "The leadership he sought was one of sympathy and of love, not of command." The election result was consensual: Republicans 162 electoral votes, Federalists 14.

Even Massachusetts and New Hampshire went for Jefferson. Jefferson wrote
a friend in France, "The two parties . . . are almost wholly melted into one."
At his inauguration the following March, he struck a happy note: "Con-
templating the union of sentiment now manifested so generally as auguring
harmony and happiness to our future course, I offer our country sincere congratulations."

That was the first election of conciliation. The hunger for harmony has
from time to time distorted and distracted American political thinking. But
that theme, like the others, serves a key democratic purpose. For as Lincoln
understood, the plenitude of malice in our politics makes of charity an element essential to the continuance of the national story. The politics of conciliation is an antidote to uplift, a relaxation of the tension between life as it is
and life as it ought to be. It is a romance of restoration. Its heroes are politicians who manage to get themselves perceived as representing *all* Americans, not just this or that faction or region or interest. The great conciliators
accentuate the positive, and the common, reinforcing the "ordinary"
citizen's sense of himself as a pretty good fellow after all. It sets aside the
strain of salvation, celebrates instead the pleasure of national friendship.

The characters who star in the dramas to follow are as various as we are
likely to find in politics. What their stories share are the themes of relief and
reconciliation.

Warren Harding's road to the White House was pioneered by William
Jennings Bryan, with his balmy free silver nostrum, and Big Bill Taft with his
"Smile, Smile, Smile." But Harding in 1920 preferred conciliation: no election illustrates the theme more clearly than the descent to "normalcy" following Wilson's holy crusade. Harding seemed to suit exactly the nation's
need for solace. Then as the Jazz Age jarred into the Great Depression,
another master reliever, Franklin Delano Roosevelt, appeared—not as the
heroic statesman he would eventually become, but as a charmingly confident
alternative to Hoover's helpless rectitude. After the war, the easer was Eisenhower, swept in in 1952 on a wave of righteous indignation against Truman,
but by 1956 evolving into a kind of uncle figure for an anxious people,
millions of whom resolved their doubts in simple affection—"I like Ike." Not
so many liked Dick Nixon, but in the chaotic context of 1968, Nixon role-
played the healer who would "Bring Us Together." Thus each in his own way
and for his own time whistled us through the graveyard of despair.

Broadcasting carried the tune. Unlike newspapers and magazines,
broadcasting is primarily a medium of entertainment. People turn it on to escape from the wrangles of reality. There they find politics as a branch of show
business. That combination grew out of Chautauqua, the late nineteenth-
century's favorite form of community entertainment: traveling troupes of entertainers and lecturers. That enterprise furnished hundreds of platforms in
American towns from which the Bryans and Hardings could expound their
harmonious sentiments. Radio picked up that mode and passed it on to tele-

vision. From the start, government set the boundaries of broadcasting—not only the frequencies and ranges, but also the limits of allowable content. Then in the 1920s and 1930s, radio's incredible commercial success fixed its easygoing style. The market was immense, far beyond what any print publication could hope to reach. Market research began to show what did and did not hit the target, confirming the appeal of the lighter side of life, particularly when, in the thirties, real life looked grim.

Television took off suddenly, in the middle 1950s, the age of Eisenhower—and of anxiety and Joe McCarthy and Sputnik. With few exceptions, television dodged the tough issues, reflecting instead that era's dominant desire for a time of peace and quiet. Today, television touches nearly every American home; would-be Presidents study it obsessively and hire at outrageous sums experts in making its magic work for them. Its hypnotic power is grossly exaggerated by those who run it, and those who fear it, but its influential place in political journalism is evident. It can show whatever the camera catches—the battles in the primaries, the moral fulminations of evangelists real and political. But as our prime purveyor of entertainment, television shines most brightly when concilation is called for, the celebration of the sentiments we share.

Of the elections described here, Harding's is the pure case. He had almost nothing to offer but his soothing presence, which turned out to be formidable. The Presidency killed him, but running for President was the highpoint of his life as a bloviating orator and friend of all. Franklin Roosevelt, no intellectual giant but certainly no Harding, shows how powerful could become the conjunction between a talented actor and broadcasting's special style of intimate, conversational reassurance. Roosevelt responded to the changing phases of national need; he played the leading role in all three stories, a political tour de force yet to be matched. In his waning years, broadcast news began to diverge from a casual adjunct of entertainment to a more distinctively journalistic and independent endeavor. But politicians learned to exploit it. In the fifties, Eisenhower's luck was Adlai Stevenson's misfortune; the good General's managers learned how to turn their telegenic candidate into a commercial product. Nixon, Eisenhower's legacy, carried it a giant step forward. Apparently politically dead in the water after his 1960 defeat and sunk to the bottom when he lost the California governorship in 1962, Nixon did what he had to do to win in 1968. That fascinating campaign, tragic in its eventual result, illustrates as no other how in the modern context a candidate can reconstruct his image by carefully controlling its exposure, not only in commercials but in the campaign as a whole. The "New Nixon" elected in that grand act of American amnesia turned out to be an old wolf in the guise of a new sheep.

The story of the politics of conciliation harps back into the national music when, after a time of conflict, "We the people of the United States, in Order to form a more perfect Union," tire of our discords and yearn, once again, to "insure domestic Tranquility."

11

Warren Harding 1920

ARLY ONE MORNING in October 1899, a mildly hung-over Harry Micajah Daugherty walked out into the sunlit yard behind the ramshackle Globe Hotel in Richmond, Ohio. A safe distance from the two-hole privy in the corner stood a rusty pump, to which he made his way, worked up the water, and filled the tin dipper. As he slowly sipped that restoring libation, the outhouse door opened. A stranger stepped therefrom into Daugherty's field of vision, stretched, and strolled over to say good morning. The man made a striking appearance, Daugherty thought. Tall, muscular, with white hair crowning his bronzed, firm-jawed face, he had a regal air about him. He introduced himself affably as Warren Harding, editor of the *Marion Star*. They shared a plug of chewing tobacco and had a little slow-moving chat. Harding excused himself; watching him walk away, Daugherty mused, "Gee, what a great-looking President he'd make!"

Two decades passed. In the dead heat of a June night, Daugherty sat and smoked with a clutch of nervous politicians in George Harvey's suite at Chicago's Blackstone Hotel, trying to figure out whom the Republicans could nominate for 1920. The convention seemed hopelessly deadlocked. "There ain't any first-raters this year," explained Connecticut's Senator Brandegee. One after another, the hypothetical possibilities were raised and dashed. Finally, at 3:30 in the morning, Kansas Senator Curtis came out. A sleepy reporter asked him what was up. Curtis said, "We are going to try to put Warren Harding over."

Daugherty's determination to get his man "into the big circus" was at last paying off. It had taken years of backstairs maneuvering. Not the least of his problems had been Harding's own doubt that he had the stuff to be President. Daugherty finally persuaded him with the argument that "greatness in the presidential chair is largely an illusion of the people."

Harding's rise to power and the election campaign of 1920 illustrates best of all the story of politics as conciliation. Harding's character fit the role he played when he followed frowning Wilson with a smile. The audience he appealed to was attracted to political entertainment as an easing, unifying experience; it learned to appreciate his type of rhetoric in the popular theater of his day. Later, with the spread of radio and television, that type of appeal would draw audiences of enormous proportions. At least since Ben Franklin, there has been a market in America for politics as fun—a theme that sets us apart from the world's stern aristocracies, dismal dictatorships, and grieving slumlands. Again and again in our modern history the aftermath of a period of moral crusading has been a time for restoration and romance. It is easy to see why we needed that.

Imagine our political drama as nothing but fighting and moralizing. We would have fallen apart long ago. The wide stretch of North America would have broken up into a patchwork of mini-nations, like the banana republics to the south, each exhausting itself in defensive maneuvers and ethnocentric posturing. California would disdain Kentucky; New York would spy out Pennsylvania's aggressive intentions; Texas would send tense ambassadors to Minnesota. A balkanized America would be the playground of foreign intrigue and depredation, as each little satrapy jockeyed for advantageous alliance. The "United States" would be remembered as some vague passing mythic hope, like the Holy Roman Empire. Instead, we have union, love, and laughter. With one horrible exception—the Civil War—we have somehow managed to reach reunion on this side of the appeal to arms. Even the cynics and the ironists, depending as they do on the firm presence of mockable naïveté, can be wooed and won to the comforts of tolerance and the pleasures of good cheer. Even the mordant moralists—recently so adamantly condemning—will be found when the smoke clears, joshing with their "enemies." After a time of combat, we are ready for a truce; after a season of uplift, we could use a little relaxation. The story of conciliation is a tale of peacemaking, of forgiving and forgetting.

The roots of that story run back to an enterprise called "Chautauqua," which, in the flickering gaslight, gave rough form to many of the features of today's way of making politics a pleasure.

Bring the Family

In the woods of northwestern New York, a summer enterprise got underway that eventually, married to business enterprise, would define a whole new mode of religious-political-entertainment experience on the American scene. At Chautauqua Lake, a Methodist camp meeting drew farmers and their families from miles around for a few summer days of swimming and salvation each year. In the 1870s, a program to enliven Christian education brought Sunday school teachers from near and far to study and sing and learn about the Holy Land from a mammoth sand relief map of Palestine. Before long, in that Victorian age, the founders of the program worried that the Devil might be lurking among the young people who were strolling at their leisure along the twilight shore. To fill their time, lecturers—not all of them ordained—were brought in. As night follows day, the founders progressed from modesty to ambition: they sought a star speaker. Already in the theater the star system was rampant. People who cared little about Shakespeare would flock to watch handsome Edwin Booth moan and declaim his way through Hamlet. The founders recruited none other than the President of the United States. Not notably religious, a known cigar smoker and bourbon sipper, Grant's office made up for his person.

Grant arrived in all his Presidential glory, churning up the lake in the sidewheeler *Josie Bell*, which was so draped in red, white, and blue bunting that "it looked like something out of fairyland," a reporter wrote, trailing behind other floating craft "gaily bedecked and carrying thousands of cheering enthusiastic watchers." New York State Republicans turned out their faithful; New York newspapers estimated the crowd at 30,000. Grant's speech hit just the right note. Instead of talking about his troubled Presidency, he called to mind the good old days back home in Galena, Illinois, before his fall into power. The response was most pleasingly positive. The national press covered the event. Chautauqua got on the map of the nation's attention. Unconscious of the symbolism of his act, a visitor one night just off the lake steamer and searching for quarters—perhaps a "traveling salesman" fortified for the trip—stumbled onto the great sand map, staggered up the mountains of Judaea, and fell on his face into the Dead Sea.

But Chautauqua was, and for years remained, a religious gathering. At least until 1880, when a daring performer played Weber's *Invitation to the Dance*, all the music was sacred. The stars were extra; the stress was on the Bible. The whole atmosphere was restrained and respectful. Uncertain whether they were hearing a sermon or a show, the people refrained from clapping and yelling, instead, when the spirit moved them, rising in silence and waving their handkerchiefs in a "Chautauqua salute." Only rarely did their constraint break down and the cheers roll forth. Once was in 1880, when Presidential candidate James A. Garfield came and heard the Fisk University Jubilee Singers herald his prospects:

> This is the Year of Jubilee,
> You shall gain the victory,
> The Lord has set His People Free,
> And you shall gain the day.

at which the crowd whooped out and waved their hankies so high that "the fluttering linens made the lake shore look as if a magical snowstorm had fallen on the forest." Other Presidential candidates and ex-Presidents made their way to the lakefront over the years: winners Harrison, Cleveland, McKinley, Theodore Roosevelt (five summers), Taft, Wilson, Harding, Coolidge, Franklin D. Roosevelt (four times), and losers Parker, Hughes, Cox, Debs, La Follette, Smith, and Wallace—not to mention that perennial loser and wonder of the Chautauquan world, William Jennings Bryan. But when they came, they adapted as need be their style to that setting, their message to the spirit of the place.

Until the turn of the century, most popular oratory in the United States had been of the sermon variety—including political sermons from many a stump in a clearing. For the pioneering poor in the nineteenth century, that and a little music was the available entertainment. Few could read. Fewer yet had room for books in their packs and wagons. To the long New England sermons—often spiced up with gossip in the guise of corrective examples— the circuit-riding preachers added the fiery zest of the Book of Revelation. But in many a community some uplifting soul would organize a literary society where the more articulate could address their neighbors. Then, having run through the local talent, they would seek out visiting enlighteners. Before long speakers were seeking invitations and some even hired agents. Not long thereafter, as the railroads improved, lighter fare began to appear on the programs. Phineas Barnum brought around the midget "General Tom Thumb" and the beautiful singer Jenny Lind. When Barnum got to Cincinnati, he spoke on "The Philosophy of Humbug." The audiences ate it up. People tired of being railed at by convinced divines. Rather they flocked to hear—and see—the likes of dashing Mark Twain, in his cream-colored formal silk evening suit, chuckling at life and at himself in an easygoing, living-room style.

In the land of enterprise it did not take long for an organizer to see the profit potential in putting audiences and performers together. The first of consequence was a reporter, James Redpath, a fiery Scotsman hired by the great Horace Greeley for the New York Tribune. One night in 1867, Redpath was in the audience at Boston's Tremont Temple when Charles Dickens spoke. Dickens was at that time an enormously popular celebrity; speculators bought tickets for his talks at three dollars and scalped them for fifteen. He made sixty-seven appearances in 1867 and 1868, and may have earned as much as $228,000, or an average of $3,000 a gig. But as Redpath learned from Dickens's manager and then from the man himself, the great author detested what he had to go through to get his message around in primitive America. He said he had "caught American catarrh," found rail travel "truly alarming" as "the train either banged up hill or banged down hill." He ran into fire in Boston, flood in Albany, blizzard in New York. The way his baggage was handled was "outrageous." All in all, he was "much disgusted." And he let his audience know it. Redpath pondered overnight and at breakfast laid out his idea. "There should be a general headquarters, a bureau for the welcoming of literary men and women coming to our country for the purpose of lecturing," he said. "They should be made to feel at home among us and the business of arranging routes of travel and dates for lectures should be in charge of competent workers and an established fee agreed upon." Thus the Boston Lyceum Bureau came to be.

By 1871, Charles Sumner, Edward Everett Hale, James G. Blaine, and such feminists as Lucy Stone had signed on. Year by year, Redpath jacked up his clients' fees. Ralph Waldo Emerson, for example, once spoke for five dollars and three quarts of oats for his horse; Redpath eventually got him up to $500 a night. Gauging the market, Redpath quickly discovered which kinds of speakers went over, which fell flat. "The Lyceum lecture is a failure," he concluded, "if it succeeds in imparting instruction alone. It should afford pleasure as well." Edward Everett Hale hit it right with his motto, "Look up and not down, look forward and not back, look out and not in, and lend a hand." To add spice to such encouragements there were speakers like Ann Eliza Young, who claimed to be Brigham Young's nineteenth wife and recounted to wide-eyed innocents the secret affairs of the "Mormon harems."

Chautauqua brought the Lyceum out of the stuffy halls of winter to the fresh summer air. As the fame of the lectures by the lake spread, "Chautauqua Literary and Scientific Circles" sprang up all over the country; at one point Des Moines had thirty of them. By 1900, there were at least two hundred such Circles, from Maine to California, mostly next to bodies of water. For nearly three decades, traveling-tent Chautauquas spread culture, fun, and knowledge from sea to shining sea. No other popular medium could match it in engaging and extending mass sentiment in America. Chautauqua refined an approach to public enlightenment and titillation that would be broadcasting's inheritance, television's teacher.

A typical week of Chautauqua entertainment began with a parade from the train station to an immense tent, where the band played "Put on Your Old Gray Bonnet" as the men in their Sunday collars and the women in their voluminous skirts found their seats. The stage lights went up and the superintendent, handsome in his white pants and blue coat, asked: Wasn't this the greatest town? and Weren't they going to have the finest time? Then onto the stage marched the "World Famous Bohemian Orchestra" in their colorful costumes, led by Mr. Giuseppi Bartolotta, sporting a large dark mustache, to sing "Silver Threads among the Gold." Then perhaps after a rousing xylophone rendition of "Funiculi, Funicula," came the lecture, the educational centerpiece. Chautauqua managers practiced what might be called a strategy of least objectionable programming: nothing risqué, nothing vulgar, nothing too disturbing. They generally avoided such dangerous topics as female suffrage, prohibition, and attacks on Christianity or the Constitution—not because they invited criticism but because they drove away patronage. When reformers spoke, the sins they decried usually ran rampant far away—Bolshevism, the harems of Araby, the brutalities of New York City, the giant trusts of the East. The political message from the Roosevelts and La Follettes touted democracy: The People—people just like you folks here in this tent tonight—should run the country, not the bloated bosses. People came to Chautauqua as an audience, not a congregation; they could use some uplift, but they did not arrive in a mood to be railed at. The most popular themes by far were "Take the Sunny Side," "Silver Lining," "How to be Happy," and the like. A speech called "Tallow Dips" with its theme of "Let your light shine" was delivered 7,000 times. Perhaps that was the topic the night young Dale Carnegie was won to the platform, long before he wrote *How to Win Friends and Influence People*. The Reverend Russell H. Conwell (skeptics thought him aptly named) lifted hearts by delivering, thousands upon thousands of times, his "Acres of Diamonds," with its happy revelation that "wherever there is human need, there is always a fortune." Conwell got so rich making his speech that he was able to found Temple University and endow thousands of fellowships.

The lecturers were valued as performers—in tough competition with the likes of a girl playing the piano and the trombone simultaneously, or the "Anvil Chorus" performed on real anvils in the dark, as electric sparks showered around. A speaker waiting in the wings might be asked by the master of ceremonies, "Shall I put you on now, or let them enjoy themselves awhile longer?" The managers discovered, through their own rough, experimental market research, how short the audience's attention span was. One star who beat that was "the Billy Sunday of Business," also known as "Gatling Gun Fogelman," because he could speak at the rate of three hundred words per minute. They learned to appreciate the varied talents of "Fiddlin' Bob" Taylor, three times governor of Tennessee, who in 1900 ran as a Democrat against his brother on the Republican ticket and his father on the Republican ticket, touted as "the Paganini among politicians and the Patrick Henry among fiddlers"—but whose most popular specialty was purple prose, which he "scattered like fireflies over a clover field." Children were attracted to the "Mother Goose Festival" and brought along their mothers.

Politicians learned how to exploit this new mass medium. By all odds the most popular Chautauquan ever, sustaining crowds for thirty years, was "The Great Commoner," "The Boy Orator of the Platte," Bryan. The tent and baggage crews called him "The Old Dependable." No crowd was too small, no night too dismal, no train too jostling, no schedule too demanding for Bryan on the circuit. Long before his famous "Cross of Gold" speech, he discovered, "I had power over an audience. I could move them as I chose," and he prayed, "God grant that I may use it wisely." In 1896, he broke the world's record by speaking nineteen times in one day—then in 1908 raised that to twenty-one, and in 1908 actually spoke thirty-six times in twenty-four hours. On the road he ate six meals a day, at night rubbed himself down with gin (though he took no alcohol internally), and after three hours of sleep was up, smiling, ready for another go at the next engagement. Mrs. Bryan explained that "when Mr. Bryan stood in the Chautauqua tent at night under the electric lights and the starlight, with practically every adult and most of the children from miles around within sound of his voice, he could forget the hardships and weariness of travel. His voice would grow deep and solemn, for he knew he was speaking to the heart of America." What he spoke about, almost always, had nothing directly to do with political controversy or the irate critics who were forever castigating him. He spoke of peace and of the miracle of the ordinary wonders of life. By far his most famous speech was "The Prince of Peace," the hopeful side of Jesus' message, with its homely word pictures of seeds and stalks, its skepticism about skepticism, its eloquence of "heart speaking to heart," as Bryan put it. People sat silent, as if hypnotized, and that clear, melodious heart-warming voice flowed over them. Across America, they spread an antidote to the poisonous suspicions and jarring conflicts the nation suffered as it struggled to define democracy at home and a new role for the United States in the world.

Bryan never won the Presidency, but another ardent Chautauquan, William Howard Taft, did—beating Bryan himself in 1908. Big, bluff, good-natured Will Taft exuded political love and fed on the affection politics brought to him. William Allen White noted the "easy gurgle of his laugh and the sweet insouciance of his answers," and a senator described him as "a large, amiable island surrounded entirely by persons who knew exactly what they wanted." Calling on his experience in amateur theatricals, Taft dutifully stood and beamed from platforms. His campaign motto was "Smile, Smile, Smile," his campaign song was of "the man worthwhile with the big glad smile." When Taft left office, Will Rogers gave his benediction: "We are parting with three hundred pounds of solid charity to everybody, and love and affection for all his fellow men." The season Taft retired, Chautauqua offered among its orators the former lieutenant governor of Ohio, speaking on "Hamilton, Prophet of American Destiny." By then Warren G. Harding was already a practiced Chautauquan, having signed on with the Redpath Bureau in 1904, following a glorious "hit of the day" speech at the Republican state convention, an effort that "made the delegates believe the word *harmony* had been written with indelible ink," a reporter wrote. From then right on up to his Presidency, Harding was an extraordinarily popular Chautauqua regular. In 1920, handsome Harding and the national need for a surcease of anxiety would merge our century's classic example of a harmonizing election.

Harding Our Friend

Warren Gamaliel Harding was born on November 2, 1865—which would give an extra fillip of pleasure to being elected President on November 2, 1920. His mother thought the baby's head was "beautifully shaped" and she noted that "it attracts a great deal of attention." As a boy he loved to declaim at school; in college his favorite subjects were "debating, writing, and making friends," his roommate said. No great shakes at anything occupational, he and two friends eventually bought the *Marion Star* for $100. The *Star* hewed closely to the middle of the road and Harding saw to it that the name of every man, woman, and child in Marion appeared at least once a year. "W. G." stressed reconciliation: "We are a common people with common interests and the idea that political differences, so essential to our perpetuity, must make us bitter enemies is one that comes from minds warped by prejudice and schooled in hatred." He joined the clubs and played the helicon bass in The People's Band. At twenty-five he married the rich girl in town, Florence Kling, who soon took over the newspaper and with a firm hand put it on a paying basis. W. G. thus had more time for speechmaking, at which he was becoming a minor celebrity. "We want an up-to-date young man who can make a rattling good 30-minute speech," read a typical invitation. "From what our people saw of you at Bellefontaine two years ago we believe you are the man." In 1899 he became the man for the state senate, announcing his candidacy at length in the paper, sounding the harmonious note: "I have not thought the senatorial contest serious enough to involve a bitter fight. My own candidacy shall not be promoted by any plan that involves a conscienceless attack on other aspirations." He won. In the legislature he proved adept at "oiling the machinery." Reporters liked him as "a regular he-man . . . a great poker player, and not at all adverse to putting a foot on the brass rail." He spoke easily, "rich in eulogy, sparing in denunciation." It was not long before members looked forward to his shows. "Senator Harding added much to his reputation as an orator," said a newspaper of one of his triumphs. "The speaker's address was rich in grace of diction, and his manner, earnest and forceful throughout, rose to the dignity of true oratory. He was heartily applauded when he rose, and he was repeatedly interrupted by the clapping of hands on both sides of the chamber and he was cheered to the echo when he resumed his seat."

Harding was nominated and elected lieutenant governor of Ohio in 1904, on a ticket of "Hanna, Herrick, Harding and Harmony." Out on the Chautauqua circuit that summer he urged the people to "preach the gospel of American optimism while preaching and practicing the gospel of Jesus Christ," and advised them that "pessimism never inspired an efficient endeavor or lighted a human pathway." In 1910 he lost a race for the governorship and in 1914 was elected United States senator. In the Senate as in his other offices, Harding rarely appeared as the advocate of particular measures and more rarely still as a contender in debate. Indeed, in seven sessions of the Senate, he never stood on the floor to champion a piece of legislation. He introduced 134 bills—122 of them on such local matters as changing the name of a lake steamer. The dozen public bills he brought forward were uniformly trivial. He missed 43 percent of the roll call votes and was specially careful to be absent when issues potentially divisive in Ohio came up. Yet for all his irrelevancy, Harding was well-liked—even by the Democrats. Wilson's secretary of war, Newton Baker, kept "a grateful and affectionate memory" of Harding, who "sought to be helpful in every possible way, and refrained from any partisan criticism at a time when partisan feeling ran very high." Secretary of the Navy Josephus Daniels found him "one of the most

agreeable men with whom I ever came in contact, courteous and cordial."
And his occasional golfing partner, young Assistant Secretary of the Navy
Franklin D. Roosevelt, found him "most agreeable, a good sport, whether
he won or lost." Thus Harding among the rulers was not a complete nothing;
if he made no waves, he was an artist in smoothing them over.

Harding became a national celebrity only after he was nominated for
President. His public strength was his ability to appeal to popular sentiments and obfuscate differences. Harding's message, reduced to print, was
elusive. He wanted "an America to continue where childhood had a right to
happiness, motherhood to health, everyone to education, and all Americans
the right to equal opportunity . . . an example of a government always responsive, always understanding, always humane." Such material was for
Harding not filler, but the main substance. He was a Presidential candidate
when he told the Richland County Harding and Coolidge Club:

> We need to cultivate friendliness and neighborliness. I sometimes think in this
> busy, work-a-day world we are neglecting those little acts of neighborliness that make
> life sweet and worth while. It is well enough for one to strive to get ahead in a mate-
> rial sense, for through that ambition progress is wrought. To acquire and accumulate
> honestly is laudable, but we should not forget that life's greatest joys lie in the social
> intercourse of friends and neighbors. Out of such relations grow mutual respect, mu-
> tual sympathy and mutual interest, without which life holds little of real enjoyment.*

His most famous contribution to the English language was noticed in this
fantastic alliterative sally:

> . . . not heroism but healing, not nostrums but normalcy, not revolution but res-
> toration, not agitation but adjustment, not surgery but serenity, not the dramatic but
> the dispassionate, not experiment but equipoise, not submergence in internationality
> but sustainment in triumphant nationality. †

Close study might reveal a theme in that mélange of epigrams, but without
doubt it was the rhythm and the ping-ping-ping of echoing initials that rang
in the ears of Harding's audiences.

Harding was a presence—one of those remarkable beings who captures
half the audience with his entrance and the other half with his style of delivery. If Taft, with his big body and walrus moustache, would have made a
good model for a beer ad, Harding could have posed as Your Model President. William Allen White sensed him as "vigorous, self-contained almost to
the point of self-repression, but not quite; handling himself, as to gestures,
the tilt of the shoulder and the set of the head, like an actor. His clarion voice
filled the hall and he was obviously putting on a parade with the calm, assured, gracious manner of the delegate from some grand lodge exemplifying

---

* Quoted in Donald R. McCoy, "Election of 1920," in Schlesinger et al., *History of American
Presidential Elections*, vol. 3, p. 2379.
† Quoted in Samuel Hopkins Adams, *Incredible Era: The Life and Times of Warren Gamaliel
Harding* (New York: Capricorn Books, 1964), p. 117.

the work to the local chapter." Skeptics wondered whether there was a man behind that mask. H. L. Mencken called a typical Harding speech "a string of wet sponges." Woodrow Wilson said he had "a bungalow mind." All in all, Harding stands out as a star who winged it—flew way out beyond his capabilities on the strength of an uncanny talent for personal showmanship. But that could only work, as it finally did, when the times were right.

The Harmonizer in a Harmonizing Time

Harding on the way to his rendezvous with destiny appeared twice with his peaceable palaver in Presidential politics at times out of sync with that theme. Those times illustrate precisely how a personality attuned to one of the phases of the Presidential story gets shunted aside when another phase is playing. At the national Republican convention of 1912, Harding rose to place in nomination for the President of the United States his fellow genius of geniality, William Howard Taft. But that was the year the Democrats fought through forty-six ballots before they nominated Wilson. It was the year Roosevelt marched his forces out of the Republican party to "battle for the Lord." The combative spirit was loose in the land, ripping up unities, trampling the common ground into a battlefield of furious factions. The country had had enough of Taftian stolidity. The convention itself was in an uproar before Harding could open his mouth. Rough Riders in uniform prowled the streets of Chicago looking for Taft delegates to intimidate. It was rumored that Roosevelt supporters planned to occupy the hall and prevent the Taft delegates from entering. Some said the entire Oklahoma Roosevelt delegation carried pistols. The night before the convention, Roosevelt whipped to a frenzy five thousand of his devotees, attacking Taft as a thief and betrayer. Deliberations got underway the next morning with hard fights over which delegates had a right to be there, and every time the chairman ruled in favor of the Taft forces, raucous jeers rolled up from the floor.

Harding strode out to the rostrum, a geranium in his buttonhole. At the very sight of him, TR's backers booed and hissed. The People, he said, "a plain people and a sane people are ruling today"—"Where?" bellowed a heckler—"ruling with unwavering faith and increased confidence in that fine embodiment of honesty, that fearless executor of the law, that inspiring personification of courage, that matchless exemplar of justice, that glorious apostle of peace and amity"—"We want Teddy!" they yelled, and spun their noisemakers. Harding had not even got to his nominee's name when two fistfights broke out on the floor. Startled and dismayed, Harding marshaled his full alliterative artillery:

Progress is not proclamation nor palaver. It is not pretence nor play on prejudice. It is not perturbation of a people passion-wrought, not a promise proposed. Progression is everlastingly lifting the standards that marked the end of the world's march yesterday and planting them on new and advanced heights today. Tested by such a standard, President Taft is the greatest Progressive of the age.*

Roosevelt's Progressives would have none of that. Such an angry roar went up that it seemed Harding might have to step down. Somehow he finished, as the balconies jeered and disgusted delegates clattered their wooden chairs as they stomped out of the hall.

So much for Harding the conciliator. After the disaster on election day, Harding's *Marion Star* explained, in the Harding style, what had happened: "Torn through ingratitude, rended by the rule or ruin faction, the Republican party could not successfully appeal to a people grown restless in the reign of good fortune." Harding seemed finished. He had a friend sound out Taft on the possibility of his being appointed ambassador to Japan, but the place was taken. He went with some pals to Texas on a hunting trip. He came home for Christmas, restless and discouraged; he rambled around Marion; he endured the laments of his sick wife. Spring came and he played golf. Then blessed summer—and the Chautauqua circuit again, with all those enthralled and respectful audiences soaking up his liquid phrases. "It is always a delight to me to be on the Circuit," Harding said.

Four years later, in 1916, Harding had the honor to deliver the keynote address at the Republican national convention. But again he and the national mood of conscience diverged, and again, for a different reason, his sonorous rhetorical oil failed to satisfy. Wilson's Presbyterian politics had infused the culture with its moralistic language of virtuous adamance. "Principle" ruled the roost of national debate and politicians rushed to judge one another. The tattered remnant of Roosevelt's Progressive party—minus Roosevelt— gathered in rain-drenched Chicago for one more try at resurrecting their champion. By then the whole Rough Rider bit had an air of nostalgia about it. They nominated Roosevelt by acclamation—but he sent a telegram declining the honor and, to the astonishment of one and all, recommended instead that archreactionary Henry Cabot Lodge, one of the "staunchest fighters for different measures of economic reform in the direction of justice." When the chairman read that message to the delegates, they sat for a moment in stunned silence; then a buzzing, angry murmuring spread through the hall. Sensing trouble, the chairman had the band strike up "America," but delegates everywhere were tearing off their Roosevelt badges and raging out of the room. Thus the Bull Moose party, like an aging animal left behind by evolution, staggered and died.

Down the street in the Coliseum, the pure, non-Progressive Republicans were meeting amid patriotic bunting before a rostrum backed with a large, flag-draped portrait of Lincoln. The affair lacked luster. The delegates seemed to share not much but their disdain for TR. What they needed from

*Quoted in Francis Russell, *The Shadow of Blooming Grove: Warren G. Harding in His Times* (New York: McGraw-Hill, 1968), p. 230.

a speaker—what a Lincoln might have given them—was a moral vision, a depiction of some Holy Grail worth crusading for. Instead, the party bosses turned to Harding, who might conceivably be able to woo back the Progressive-leaning members of the wayward flock, since no one knew what he believed in. Some of the leaders were worried that Harding's oratory might swing the nomination to *him*, of all people, but they took the chance.

This time, as handsome W. G. strode to the rostrum, no jeers beleaguered him. The delegates sat sullen and silent, waiting to see what he might have to offer. He tried to diminish the great fights of the past: "We did not divide over fundamental principles," he said. "We did not disagree over a national policy. We split over methods of party procedure and preferred personalities. Let us forget our differences, and find new inspiration and new compensation in a united endeavor to restore our country." On and on he went, through the lunch hour, shuffling through his well-practiced collection of classic gestures and gelatinous generalities. When at last he finished, there was only polite applause. Hughes, the "bearded iceberg," was offered as the Republican sacrifice to Wilson. Harding got but one vote on one ballot. "Since the roasting I received at Chicago," Harding told a friend, "I no longer harbor any great self-confidence in the matter of speechmaking."

Two weeks later, harmonizing Harding wrote a flattering letter to Theodore Roosevelt, praising him for his determination "to serve our common country." Then he went off Chautauquaing again. The natural American politician starts living into the next election as soon as the last one is over. But Harding seemed done for. Then the scene began to shift. Theodore Roosevelt died on January 6, 1919, leaving an enormous invigoration gap. Hughes's campaign and defeat in 1916 had revealed his wooden tongue. Poor Will Taft had become anathema to many in his party. Bryan, having gone down three times, was counted out. President Wilson suffered a paralyzing stroke and subsequent breakdown in the fall of 1919.

In the brief space since Wilson's reelection in 1916, the American soul and body had been battered into nervous exhaustion. He who "kept us out of war" led us into war. Wilson defined it as a holy mission, a "last war," a war to "make the world safe for democracy." Five million men went into the armed forces; fifty thousand of them died in France—each a mother's son, a would-be father. Peace came on November 11, 1918. Then came Wilson's crusade for the League of Nations, another national moral high followed by the letdown when that hope was smashed in the Senate. Peace brought no peace of mind, rather labor war—steel strikes, coal strikes, a police strike in Boston—and race strife—massive riots in Washington and Chicago, a reborn Ku Klux Klan of 100,000 members. Unexplained bombings set off a Red scare; on New Year's Day, 1920, some six thousand suspects were arrested in a nationwide raid. Inflation hit the American family like a ton of bricks: the cost of living surged in 1919 to 77 percent above prewar levels, and in 1920 alone went up another 28 percent. Taxes in 1919 were raised higher than they had been in the war. Returning veterans had a hard time getting jobs and those they bounced naturally resented it. To add insult to injury, not even the narcotic balm of alcohol was as easily available as it had been: the Eighteenth Amendment was ratified in January 1919.

It was time for a change—not just any change, but a change toward harmony and ease. Harding was nominated in the famous "smoke-filled-room" convention, as pure a case as we are likely to get of least-common-denominator politics. A reporter, hearing the Columbus Glee Club warbling "We sing with hearts on fire, O Harding, salute!" thought, "When you get hearts on fire for Harding, you have generated enough heat to set Lake Michigan boiling and turn the Chicago River into a pot roast." Even when Harding's name was placed in nomination—"What we want is not brilliant maneuvers but safe and sane seamanship by a captain who knows the way, by a captain who as he walks the deck working with the officers and men in these troubling times can say, 'Steady boys, steady' "—the perfunctory demonstration was short and confined mainly to the Ohio section. Thirteen candidates received votes on the first ballot; Harding ranked sixth. There followed days and nights of tortuous confabulation as a deadlock developed among the leading contenders. At last on the tenth ballot, in the sweltering heat, the word was passed and the much-relieved delegates went for Harding. Harding was elated. "We drew to a pair of deuces and filled," he said. On the way out of town, the Republican candidate for President stopped off at a friend's apartment for an amorous hour or so with his mistress, Nan Britton.

The Democrats met in San Francisco, their deliberations helped along by forty barrels of illegal whisky the National Committee obtained. They were split six ways to Sunday. Wilson, ill and reclusive, would not make clear either his own intentions or his preferred successor. Into that gap galloped troops of lead and dark horses. After eight days and forty-four ballots, they compromised on Governor James M. Cox, like Harding a newspaperman and Ohioan. Though he was a millionaire and divorced, Cox seemed a safe enough bet: mild and moderate on all the issues from the League to prohibition, he had a reputation as a friend of all. The Vice-Presidential candidate, thirty-eight-year-old Franklin Roosevelt, seemed equally safe. The *Washington Post* found him "genial and companionable" and Henry Cabot Lodge judged him "a well-meaning, nice young fellow, but light."

Harding had gone home to wait for the official committee that would come and break the news to him that he had been nominated. Like McKinley in 1896, it was announced, Harding would wage a Front Porch Campaign. Marion got set for Notification Day. A "Victory Way," guarded by white columns with gold eagles atop them, extended from the depot to Harding's house, with arches of bunting and flags and big pictures of the hero in every window. The town barber put HARDING in large shaving-soap letters on his window. Little Marion prepared for more than 100,000 visitors. The sunshine beamed on the great day, July 22, as delegation after delegation poured into town, led off by the Hamilton Club of Chicago, with their ribbons, canes, and gray top hats, escorting Senator Lodge and the committee. Four abreast they marched through the business district and the Marion Marching Band let forth with "Good Morning, Mr. Har-Har-Harding," which everyone sang right up to Harding's front porch.

Two thousand were waiting inside the Chautauqua Auditorium—thirty thousand more crowded about outside—while the Republican Glee Club regaled them with song. There good old W. G. at last appeared to celebrate "preserved nationality as the first essential to the continued progress of the Republic." They cheered and cheered. Thereafter, morning after morning the bands blared new delegations and celebrities down the Victory Way. Civil War veterans, the Ohio Dental Association, Elks, Moose, and Knights of Pythias—by the thousands they trooped to his door and whooped his glory. An Indian chief took the Hardings into his tribe and named his wife "Snow Bird." The Masons fulfilled Harding's long ambition by making him a member. He said, "There is not an atom of hatred in my heart." The celebrities of the entertainment world—Al Jolson, Texas Guinan, and forty-odd actors and actresses—marched with a band of one hundred pieces. Harding told them how he had been moved by a great performance of "Shakespeare's *Charles the Fifth,*" especially that "camp scene on the night before a crucial battle" and, he recalled, "the King put aside his regal garb and, clad as a simple soldier, went among his armed forces to learn their feelings, their confidences, their fears, and ascertained on terms of equality and intimacy what a monarch might never have learned in any other way." Jolson then led the singing of "Harding, You're the Man for Us." Politicians came and urged their pro and con solutions for the world's ills. Harding said, "My whole job as President will be first to get the people of the United States together in better understanding of a workable world league."

Harding stuck to his front porch until September, then announced a whirlwind speaking tour. He released two pigeons with a goodwill message for a druggists' convention in Saint Louis. In Oklahoma City the newspaper called his arrival "the noisiest, gladdest, maddest day" ever. He put on an engineer's cap and took the throttle of a train for a fast twenty miles. It was a glorious progress. Everywhere people longing for the peaceable kingdom greeted him as their hope and joy. When his old friends of the *Marion Star* presented him with a "golden rule" of the kind printers used in those days, Harding thanked them with the tears rolling down his cheeks.

Harding got important backing from another local paper, the *Washington Post,* run by a pal of his, Ned McLean. During the campaign the *Post* found Harding "an American of the finest type" and later greeted the ascension of this man who "brings high character and strong mental equipment to solve the nation's problems."

Meanwhile, Cox and Roosevelt, radically misreading the national mood, decided to conduct a hard-fighting campaign. They figured something had to be done, something vigorous, to counteract the obviously growing unpopularity of Wilson, their party's high chieftain. Instead of taking a blurred position on the League of Nations, Cox visited the ailing President and promised: "We are going to be a million percent with you, and your Administration, and that means the League of Nations." Then he and Roosevelt stumped the country, Cox especially castigating Harding as a "Happy Hooligan," Lodge as the "archconspirator of the ages," and, at the end, shouting, "Every traitor in America will vote tomorrow for Warren G. Harding." On election day—Harding's birthday—W. G. refused to be put at the head of the line and waited in the cold for fifteen minutes. To accommodate the photographers, some with motion picture cameras, he repeated the gesture of putting in his ballot. Someone joked about his voting twice. Everyone laughed.

Harding won in an incredible landslide—the best margin in a century. He got 16,152,200 votes to Cox's 9,147,343, the highest percentage of the popular vote ever recorded. A little melodrama of love captured the sense and style of Harding's victory: the night of the day after the election, Warren and Nan rendezvoused secretly in an empty house in Marion. "Oh, sweetheart," she whispered as he held her close, "isn't it *wonderful* that you are President!"

A Voice for the People

The mellifluous music of Warren G. Harding played out over the airwaves on June 14, 1922, as he dedicated a memorial to the composer of our national anthem. Easygoing Harding thus inaugurated Chautauqua at a distance. Coolidge followed. His quacking voice, irritating close up, came across surprisingly well on radio; the machinery made him sound natural, even intimate, and listeners could hear him turning the pages of his manuscript. Even his taciturnity appealed in that age of ballyhoo. When H. V. Kaltenborn arrived in the Oval Office to interview him, Coolidge said, "Sit down (pause) for a minute." Kaltenborn asked about possible American cooperation with the League of Nations. Coolidge said, "I think we are very snug as we are."

Radio at first was a gimmick, a toy for amateurs. Serious futurologists thought not much would come of it. Others, echoing Thoreau's opinion of the telegraph, doubted that the power to talk at however far a remove would improve the quality of conversation. A few determined engineers and business visionaries saw a revolution in the making. They were right. But as late as 1930, when scientists sent the song "I Love You Truly" around the world and even got a dog in Australia to bark at the cry of a cat in Schenectady, New York, radio seemed mainly an intriguing trick on geography.

From the first, broadcasting depended on government. When young

Guglielmo Marconi arrived in England in 1896 with a suspicious-looking black box strung inside with wires and dials, British customs officers smashed it. But before long, the British Navy began installing wirelesses on battleships. Marconi's arrival in America in 1899 happened to coincide with Admiral Dewey's victorious return from Manila Bay and with an America vigorously flexing its manifestly destined military muscle. Soon all sorts of ships at sea had some form of radio equipment. Then on Christmas Eve, 1906, came the breakthrough from dots and dashes to transmitted speech. Lonesome wireless operators bobbing about in the Atlantic suddenly heard a human voice. But the gaggle of talk and the sound of music began to scramble, confusing the essential military messages. President Taft signed a law in 1912 that began the process of government regulation. The Secretary of Commerce and Labor could assign wave lengths and broadcast times. Operators had to be licensed.

Taft's 1912 law had a little clause saying that the President, "in time of war or public peril or disaster" could close down or seize any radio apparatus. But war seemed far away. The day America declared war on Germany, April 6, 1917, the government ordered all amateur stations not only shut down, but dismantled and sealed. Within a few days, almost all other stations, such as commercial ship-to-shore operations, were taken over by the navy or army. Radio went to war. Newspapers and magazines were needed as instruments of propaganda, but radio was itself a military instrument. That fact—along with continuing and complex battles over corporate responsibilities and patent rights—gave radio pioneers an accommodating cast of mind different from that of the Hearsts and the Tarbells: the right to speak through radio depended essentially on government permission. Radio could report a fight; it was not itself a crusader.

The attitude thus engendered shone forth when H. V. Kaltenborn was dismissed—in 1924, long after the Great War—for suggesting that our government erred. The Soviet foreign minister had written what Kaltenborn told his radio audience was a "tactful and carefully phrased note" proposing U.S.–USSR diplomatic relations. Secretary of State Hughes said no and said it in a way Kaltenborn called overly abrupt. Hughes happened to be listening with "a number of prominent guests." Chagrined and appalled, he telephoned the Washington representative of the telphone company, AT&T, upon whose facilities the offending radio station depended, and "laid down the law." His view that "this fellow Kaltenborn should not be allowed to criticize a cabinet member over the facilities of the New York Telephone Company" was rapidly conveyed to New York. The station manager took Kaltenborn off the air. The telephone company's "fundamental policy," wrote their public relations man, was one "of constant and complete cooperation with every government institution that was concerned with communications."

From the start, radio, like television later, defined itself as essentially a purveyor of entertainment. Enterprising David Sarnoff, rising in the ranks on his way to moguldom, wrote a prescient memorandum to his boss in 1916: "I have in mind a plan of development which would make radio a 'household utility' in the same sense as the piano or phonograph . . ." Sarnoff's "Radio Music Box" caught on. Celebrities paraded to the studios—Madame Schumann-Heink, Jolson, Rudolph Valentino—performing free of charge. Curious listeners could hear what the silent movie stars sounded like. In the early years, "potted palm music" filled almost all the time: softened and shortened renditions by concert singers and hotel orchestras, with a dignified little talk or reading thrown in occasionally. The mode was theatrical. Only slowly did performers catch on to the fact that their listeners were in a living room, and begin to picture an audience of one or two—to be chatted with, not lectured at, to croon to, not to blast with a full-force aria.

On November 15, 1926, NBC announced its existence, broadcasting a grand inaugural bash from the ballroom of the Waldorf-Astoria, with remote pickups from here and there, to an estimated twelve million listeners, featuring music and comedy such as Will Rogers's takeoff on President Coolidge, from Kansas City. And so it went. Radio was for fun, for relaxing fun. When the crash fell in on President Hoover, he told crooner Rudy Vallee, "If you can sing a song that would make people forget their troubles and the Depression, I'll give you a medal." Even the commercials were upbeat: "When you're feeling kinda blue/And you wonder what to do,/ Che-e-ew Chiclets, and/Chee-ee--eer up!" And then there was Kate Smith with her moon coming over the mountain—"every beam/brings a dream/dear, of you"—and sentimental Eddie Cantor—"I love to spend/this hour with you/as friend to friend/ believe me it's true." Through high times, on into low times, radio was balm, mostly musical balm, a medium like Chautauqua that most people turned to in order to turn away from the realities of life. Harding would have loved it, had he lived. The British politician Winston Churchill detested it. The BBC, he complained, was trying to *"lull . . .* to chloroform . . .* the British people into a state of apathy."

Balm or chloroform, radio sold like boxed cereal. By 1924, Americans spent 358 million dollars on radio equipment. By 1927, 732 stations were broadcasting. Sparking that incredible effulgence was the organizing genius of David Sarnoff and his ilk—big businessmen, out to make big money, fascinated by corporate arrangements and technical innovations. They themselves were not entertainers—and certainly not politicians. Sarnoff, like his network of inheritors down to this day, was very much interested in what sold. Broadcasting thus got its cast of mind from commerce and its driving force from perpetual experiments in popularity. More listeners was the goal, whatever it took to attract them was the means. Commerical radio, like Chautauqua, learned banality. The desire to please large numbers of different people—plus fear of government regulation—made for caution. It was built into the business. In 1921, Olga Petrova, then performing at a nearby theater, went over to Newark's new station to help it get going. The managers were nervous: Petrova was a fanatic on birth control. Might she say something "red"? She said no, much to their relief, she just wanted to read some of her own versions of nursery rhymes. She went on the air:

> There was an old woman who lived in a shoe,
> She had so many children because she didn't know what to do.

The managers were terrified. They installed an emergency switch to cut off other risky recitations. Station WGY in Schenectady, advertising a drama contest, specified "PLOTS MUST BE CLEAN with no attempt at questionable situations. . . . No 'sex dramas' will be considered."

Commercials came in when music publishers got announcers to mention their companies, then "plug" their songs. Straight-out commercial appeals were delicately deliberated upon at first, lest they offend. Should so intimate a matter as toothbrushing be mentioned? A vacuum cleaner company was prevented from using the phrase "sweep no more, my lady," lest Stephen Foster lovers take umbrage. Commercial announcements could not be broadcast between seven and eleven P.M. But by the turn of the decade the dikes of decorum had been radically eroded. Commercial interruptions during the presentations of 208 stations on one day in 1932 numbered 12,546 and took up more time than all that devoted to news, education, lectures, and religion put together. The big-time broadcasting advertising agency was born and flourished. Nor were they content with interruptions. By 1931, advertisers were themselves producing virtually all sponsored network programs. The content of commercials, after that early period of dignity, settled down to a comfortable middling vulgarity. Typical was old Chautauquan Tony Wons, whispering into the microphone, while violins played, of Camel cigarettes, "as fresh as the dew that spills on a field of clover." The quintessential symbolic product was Ovaltine—warm chocolate milk. To get their pictures of Little Orphan Annie, 418,000 people sent in the little slip in the Ovaltine can. Occasional lapses into controversy, such as George Bernard Shaw's calling "Hello America! Hello, all my friends in America! How are all you dear old boobs . . ." evoked the predictable outrage and balancing response.

Early radio announcers and performers were mysteriously anonymous: managers did not want them turning themselves into uppity celebrities with inflated ideas of reasonable compensation. But people started writing in to ask who those charming voices belonged to. One station replied by form letter: "Dear Madam: It is against the rules of this radio station to divulge the name of our announcer. With deep regret, I am ———." It was a losing battle. "Each announcer," wrote one of them, "knew in his heart that he was God's gift to radio"—and many a listener agreed, such as the woman who wrote in to Ted Husing asking, "Would you like to thrill a lady in person?" An early silverthroat who escaped anonymity was Norman Brokenshire, who could charm the leaves from the trees. He covered Coolidge's inauguration in 1925, ad-libbing for over two hours about Silent Cal's scene, no doubt a hard test for any wordsmith. That day he made sure the UPI photographer got his picture for the next day's papers. "I used my name at every decent opportunity," he said, and "for the nice listeners I think I even spelled it several times." Brokenshire's station manager tried to hold up his voluminous mail—station property, he said. Brokenshire got his own post office box and put in a change-of-address card. Listeners sent him all kinds of gifts, material and spiritual, including speaking invitations. Thus celebrification set in.

People began to discover radio could help them; then they idolized the helpers. The gladdest of the helping hands was attached to the great Dr. John Romulus Brinkley, who came to radio from a Kansas City diploma mill, specializing in transplanting buck goat glands into gentlemen who detected their powers waning. In 1923, with $40,000 garnered in the California gland market, he set up a powerful radio station in Milford, Kansas, where he lectured every weekday night. "Don't let your doctor two-dollar you to death," he said, "Come to Dr. Brinkley." "Are you a manly man full of vigor?" the doctor asked. If not, you needed his "compound operation," or one of his numerous specifics for other ailments. Listeners wrote by the thousands. By 1930, Brinkley's station was declared the most popular radio station in America by *Radio Digest*, winning with 356,827 votes, despite hearings and court cases in which such eminences as Dr. Morris Fishbein of the American Medical Association cast doubt upon his medical ethics. Fishbein won, at last: the station license was lifted. Brinkley went to the U.S. Court of Appeals. The 1927 Radio Act forbade "censorship." Was it not "censorship" to throw him off the air for what he said? The court ruled otherwise: to determine whether "the public interest, convenience, or necessity" had been served by a station, the Federal Radio Commission had to consider "the nature of the program broadcast"—a landmark decision opening the way for a long train of cases in which officials of the United States government decided what could and could not be spoken and shown through the air, and how much of what kinds of sayings by whom. Brinkley simply opened up a powerful station across the border in Mexico, transmitted his programming by telephone from Kansas. In 1930 he got 183,278 write-in votes for governor of Kansas—even after thousands of misspelled ballots were thrown out —threatening the winner who got 217,171. In 1932, he got on the gubernatorial ballot and took a healthy 244,607 votes of Alf Landon's 278,581. The potential of radio for politics was beginning to emerge.

Before long the airwaves were awash with stories—not "Great Moments in History" or "Biblical Dramas," but stories about ordinary folks, folks who had families, folks caring about one another through the endless hassles and clashes of life. They tutored a generation. When it came to continued stories, "Amos 'n' Andy" put all the rest in the shade. "Amos 'n' Andy" sounded forth (after some preliminary experiments) on the NBC network two months before the stock market crash in 1929. That fall it must have seemed the only funny thing around. Before long it was a national obsession, an addiction. Telephone use dropped by half when "Amos 'n' Andy" went on; street traffic fell off, cows went unmilked, papers lay unshuffled. In Charlotte, North Carolina, forty factories agreed to shift their closing time from 6:00 to 5:45 P.M. when daylight saving time shifted the program from 7:00 to 6:00. President Hoover entertained Gosden and Correll at the White House for more than an hour—listening to their jokes and, it is written, telling some of his own.

Amos and Andy (Freeman Gosden and Charles Correll) were a couple of blacks from Atlanta who had found their way to Chicago. They were ignorant. They spoke in dialect. The show would stand about as much chance of playing today as a comedy about the Holocaust. Obviously a piece of its appeal was to comfort the conscience of the white majority, only beginning to sense the pain and injustice of racial repression. But they offered other comforts. For one thing, they were very funny, at a time when the laughter of everyday life was in markedly short supply. For another, they kept running up against just the kinds of confusions and frustrations the American adventure was handing millions of Americans, black and white. In the early years, the soaps featured life among the ethnic outsiders—blacks, Jews, the Irish, hillbillies—as if to provide the Wasp majority with a vicarious experience of the warmth and ease their Calvinist heritage had progressively shredded. The soap operas had their chuckling moments, but their strength was love, not laughter. People fought on the soaps, but it was a fight of emotions the drama of which inhered in the promise of reconciliation. People preached on the soaps, but the stress of the sermons was on Jesus' second great commandment, the one about love, not a demand for moral heroism.

As late as 1934, the largest network, NBC-blue, presented Lowell Thomas, the wandering wonderfinder, whose "news" did not pretend to convey the harsh events grinding into his time. Thomas explained that "talks should be sprinkled with nonsense, with here and there a thrill, perhaps a sob. My talks are planned as entertainment, not education." CBS got across the same feeling with Edwin C. Hill's "The Human Side of the News." CBS did also put on—for five minutes twice a day—a controversialist named Boake Carter, who included scattered facts among his free-swinging aspersions of State Department conduct. But in 1938, Carter was first intimidated into triviality (stories on whether night baseball would pay, the death of a seeing-eye dog) and then yanked off the network. Sponsors avoided news programs like the plague; when they bought a newscast they expected to own it. Radio came through with dramatic reports of special events such as the 1924 Democratic convention and Lindbergh's flight to Paris. The thing was a business, an entertainment business harvesting huge profits when nearly everything else was wilting on the vine.

By far the most important factor in setting radio's style was its nature as a money-making relaxer. The government's sensitivities frayed broadcasters' nerves from time to time; the President had shown he could wipe them all off the air. In 1927, a new law, much affected by that year's concerns with conserving natural resources (following the Teapot Dome scandal), with avoiding censorship (following the *Gitlow* case extending free speech guarantees against abridgements by the states), and preventing monopoly (following a decade of agitation), established the government's right to regulate broadcasting for the "public interest, convenience or necessity," prohibited "censorship over the material broadcast" about candidates for public office provided rivals were treated equally, and outlawed monopoly and "unfair methods of competition" in broadcasting. The law left unclear who would decide when any of these things had happened. And the language was vague enough to brighten the employment prospects of legions of lawyers.

But the major inhibitors were right there in the studios and living rooms. Long before news was a significant feature, those who controlled and composed that medium's message had got rich with the light touch, the soft touch, the voice of a friend. That antidote to the turmoil and challenge of politics passed down the broadcasting generations. Soon it would ease into politics itself, as politicians learned how to talk past the equipment to that soap opera fan at the other end of the air wave.

The Presidential master of radio, soon to appear, was waiting in the wings.

12

Franklin Roosevelt 1932

FRANKLIN ROOSEVELT ran through the whole repertoire of basic campaign themes—history's example *par excellence* of a flexible, responsive President, capable not only of sensing the pulse of politics but of adjusting his own tempo to its beat. In 1932, he was a hopeful alternative to Hoover, a conciliator; in 1936, Roosevelt the fighter emerged; in 1940, he carried a moralizing election; and in 1944, he returned to the unifying role. His history demonstrates the independence of the electoral rhythm from changing personalities. For he was the same man throughout, a President with a remarkable capacity for growth in office.

Particularly with Roosevelt, the hardest historical task is to see past what we know now to what we saw then. Back in 1932, no one could foresee his checkered future. Founder of the New Deal, modern American democracy's closest approximation to a common political philosophy, Roosevelt came on the national scene as the least philosophical of men—"a chameleon on plaid," Hoover called him. Firm fighter of yet another Great War, Roosevelt appeared to H. L. Mencken in 1932 as "far too feeble and wishy-washy a fellow to make a really effective fight." Architect of world organization, he introduced himself as almost totally concerned with America's domestic drama. His name is inseparable from the story of his generation's great social revolution; in 1932, nearly all the heavy thinkers scoffed at him as just another placebo politician—"a pill to cure an earthquake," said Professor Laski. Now the most famous of modern Presidents, Roosevelt then was a virtual stranger to millions who voted for him the first time—many under the mistaken impression that he was TR's boy and thus could be counted on to *do* something about the bad times. They had the genealogy wrong but the import right.

The election that ushered in The Age of Roosevelt, like Harding's election, played to the public's need for an end to trouble. Unlike such battle elections as 1912 and 1924, the result in 1932 was a foregone conclusion before a single ballot was cast. Harding himself, running as a Democrat, could have won in 1932. It was a quiet rout. A frightened people, given the choice between two touters of confidence, pushed aside the one they knew had let them down and went for the one they prayed might not.

Collapse of Confidence

The odds flipped over in the gap between elections. When Herbert Hoover won in 1928, he seemed a sure bet for 1932. Times were good. Hoover took the Republican nomination anticipating "the final triumph over poverty"; he took office as President with "no fears for the future of our country. It is bright with hope." That same season Roosevelt went in as governor of New York and was judged the likely front-runner for the empty honor of the next Democratic Presidential nomination. But by election day in 1932, hardly a bookie in the country would have held money bet on a Roosevelt victory, so certain had that come to seem. In the interim, feelings of depression became widespread among Amos and Andy's audience. Just half a year after Hoover the virtuous took the oath, stock values fell in one day by nearly the cost to the United States of fighting the First World War. Within a few months, wages began to slide down all over the country. A few months more and thousands upon thousands of American workers opened their pay envelopes to discover the pink slip of dismissal. In October 1931 an ad for 6,000 jobs in the Soviet Union brought more than 100,000 American applications. Twelve million were out of work on Labor Day in 1932; by the time Hoover left office the following March, one out of three American workers was jobless. In Chicago, hundreds of women were sleeping in the public parks. In New York, seven hundred families a day, seeking relief funds, were told to look elsewhere because the money had run out. In upstate Iowa, farmers dragged barricades of spiked logs across the highways; two thousand of them, wielding pitchforks and clubs, patrolled the roads around Sioux City, halting cattle shipments and dumping fresh milk on the roadside. Businesses went out of business at the rate of thousands per month—3,458 of them in the one month of January 1932. Banks closed their doors to customers bent on withdrawal—2,298 banks in 1931 alone. At the beginning edge of the troubles, embarrassed white-collar workers tried to get relief money without giving their names; by early 1931 they were joining hunger riots in Oklahoma City, Minneapolis, and New York. That spring, ex-President Coolidge made it official. "This country is not in good condition," he said.

"Worst of all," writes Allan Nevins, "was the fear which gripped the nerves of the nation." As election time approached, both Hoover and Roosevelt agreed with that diagnosis.

An extraordinarily talented and intelligent administrator, Hoover had not the faintest idea how to stir the public heart. The press got hold of him after the Great War and made him a hero in spite of himself, dramatizing his incredible achievements as organizer of relief for millions of starving Europeans. But he hated political razzle-dazzle. Up close, Hoover typically came on as a gloomy gus in a high white collar—long before the depression hit. As for public relations, Hoover proved approximately as adroit as Ulysses Grant. Abstractly he realized that the Presidency "is an inspiring symbol of all that is highest in American purpose and ideals," but personally he simply could not do "a showman's job." "I will not step out of character," he said. "You can't make a Teddy Roosevelt out of me." The list of the aspects of ordinary democratic politics that he intensely disliked runs on and on. Politics is talk; "A conversation with Hoover," said Henry Stimson, "is like sitting in a bath of ink." The endless round of handshakes and backpats nauseated him—"I intensely dislike superficial human contacts." Your typical American politician will rise up to speak at the drop of an invitation. Hoover said, "I made no pretensions to oratory and I was terrorized at the opening of every speech." Nothing suits a real pol better than sweet praise at a dinner party. Hoover used to dodge in and find a place after the celebrities had been introduced, hoping not to be noticed. Even the servants in the White House made him nervous. Learning that he disliked encountering them in the hallways, butlers and maids would take shelter in the nearest available closet at his approach.

Hoover would have none of the new ghostwriting techniques; he laboriously scrawled out his speeches in longhand and then picked over draft after draft, changing a word here, a phrase there. The result demonstrates the limits of industry as an aid to rhetoric. Whatever zest and spontaneity may have colored his first drafts, Hoover doggedly diluted, like a novice painter who does not know when to stop improving his picture. To the average radio fan, after a hard day's work, the thud-thud-thud of an average Hoover speech sounded like someone reading from a dictionary. Hoover's press relations scuttled rapidly downhill shortly after he became President, but his use of radio was even worse. He could not get it through his head that there were people at the other end of those contraptions and connections. He spoke to those he saw; his twenty-one radio addresses were mainly "greetings" to special group, or, in the campaign, laundry lists of abstractions. In short, as various friends of Hoover noted, he seemed "not to have the least appreciation of the poetry, the music, and the drama of politics."

Hoover was not alone, at the start of what was to become the Great Depression, in seeing it as an unfortunate blip in a rising curve. He tried to yank hope up again with increasingly implausible prophesies. The stock market crash left "the fundamental business of the country . . . on a sound and prosperous basis," indicating "a healthy condition." In December 1929 he said a great deal of suffering had been prevented. In January he saw the unemployment trend reversed, in March he found "employment had been slowly increasing," in May his program had "succeeded to a remarkable degree," so that "we have now passed the worst and with continued unity of effort we shall rapidly recover." In June he said flatly, "The depression is over." On October, a year after the crash, Hoover told his countrymen: "No one can occupy the high office of President and be other than completely confident of the future of the United States. . . . Perhaps as to no other place does the cheerful courage and power of a confident people reflect as to his office." The worse things got, the harder Hoover clung to his cracking crystal ball. At first, a number of people—especially the hometown boosters who had been riding the boom—joined Hoover's graveyard whistling. Billboards in 1930 asked, "Wasn't the Depression Terrible?" and audiences sang along with "Life Is Just a Bowl of Cherries." Amos and Andy even joked about suicide, as the Empire State Building quietly stopped running its elevators to the upper floors; a hotel clerk asked a room-seeking guest whether he wanted it "fur sleepin' or jumpin', suh?" But amusement deepened to irony as the hard times ground on, and irony to cynicism. By 1932, America was singing "Brother, Can You Spare a Dime?" Nearly half of the country's factory workers were unemployed.

Hoover nearly worked himself to death fighting the depression—endlessly structuring complex plans and conferences, existing on three hours of sleep a night. Because he was who he was and believed what he believed with a fierce Wilsonian adamance, he could not bring himself to open the coffers of the government to buy food for hungry people. Worse yet, he sounded either cruel or deluded. As community after community ran right through available resources for relief, there was Hoover on the radio: "No governmental action, no economic doctrine, no economic plan or project can replace that God-imposed responsibility of the individual man and woman to their neighbors." Fathers, suddenly cast aside by their employers, staring at the prospect of giving up their homes and rationing food to their children, were supposed to take comfort from the fact that at least their characters were uncorrupted by government coddling. Hoover's secretary of war, Patrick Hurley, had a suggestion: restaurants should save their scraps to feed the hungry. It sounded like a joke. Scavenging the leftovers was already common practice, starting with the waiters and ending with the waifs in the alley, picking the garbage from the trash.

Thus Hoover the public figure, recognizing fear, sought to allay it with denials and hopes and the high appeals to principles that had worked for him before. As late as October 1932, Hoover was moralizing and prophesying in Cleveland: "There should be no fear at any deserving American fireside that starvation or cold will creep within their doors this winter." That might have been the year of a second American revolution. Hoover could see the mobs he so disdained as his limousine zipped past block after block of them in Detroit, past tens of thousands of silent, grim-faced men and women lining the curbs, punctuated with an occasional shaken fist and unheard curse. "Hang Hoover!" yelled another Detroit crowd surging against lines of armed mounted police. On Halloween night he made his way into Madison Square Garden through a crowd of thousands shouting, "We want bread."

Hoover was renominated in June in a dismal, issueless, air-conditioned convention in Chicago. The delegates swallowed the largely negative Republican platform whole, except that they voted an amendment to phase out Prohibition. The following month, twenty thousand angry veterans made their way to Washington from all over the country—the "Bonus Expeditionary Force"—determined to force early payment of the bonus due them in 1945. Hoover absolutely refused to see them or their spokesmen. Most stayed on, sweltering in their tarpaper and packing-crate camp. By July 28, Hoover had had enough. General Douglas MacArthur, with troops and tanks and tear gas (and junior officers Dwight D. Eisenhower and George B. Patton) marched down Pennsylvania Avenue. The veterans saw them coming— and cheered, but before they knew what was happening, a cavalary contingent drew their sabers and charged, scattering men, women, and children in a wild rush. Tear gas was tossed into a booing crowd; the shacks were set afire. A three-month-old child was killed by the gas. The *Washington News* called it "a pitiful spectacle" and concluded, "If the Army must be called out to make war on unarmed citizens, this is no longer America"—but most newspapers, coast to coast, backed their stalwart President. MacArthur saw un-Americanism in the crowd, not the troops; the Bonus Army was "animated by the essence of revolution." His old comrades in arms were "insurrectionists." Hoover gravely agreed: "A challenge to the authority of the United States Government has been met, swiftly and firmly."

Thinkers of the MacArthur persuasion began to suppose the European fascists, who knew how to deal with mobs, might have something after all. Dictatorship for America was being discussed—even openly predicted "by many sober-minded people—including not a few members of Congress," wrote political scientist Frederic A. Ogg. Muscular Bernarr MacFadden interrupted his calisthenics to declare, in the magazine *Liberty*, "What we need now is martial law; this is no time for civil law. The President should have dictatorial powers." Henry Hazlitt wrote in *Scribner's* that it was time to jettison Congress and elect instead twelve directors of the nation. Thinkers of the opposite ideology—such as Theodore Dreiser, Sherwood Anderson, John Dos Passos, Erskine Caldwell, Sidney Hook, and Lincoln Steffens—came out for the Communist party as the only hope for "the overthrow of the system which is responsible for all crises" and "a practical and realizable ideal, as is being proved in the Soviet Union." Thousands more who were not about to go fascist or communist—under those labels—looked around in desperation for some alternative to a system that seemed to hold no hope for them.

The Smiling Bus Driver

The answer turned out to be, of all people, Franklin D. Roosevelt. Here the country was, flat on its collective rear end, and along comes this rich marshmallow from the country-club set. H. L. Mencken, who had little use for any politician, puzzled over Roosevelt. "He is one of the most charming of men," Mencken wrote, "but like many another very charming man he is also somewhat shallow and futile. It is hard to say how that impression is produced: maybe his Christian Science smile is to blame, or the tenor over-

tones in his voice. Whatever the cause, the fact is patent that he fails somehow to measure up to the common concept of a first-rate man." Columnist
Heywood Broun called him "Feather Duster" Roosevelt, "the cork-screw
candidate." Reporter Ernest Lindley judged, "the country yearned for a
Messiah . . . Mr. Roosevelt did not look or sound like a Messiah." Henry
Stimson, Hoover's secretary of state, observed that Roosevelt "is not a strong
character himself," and early in the season Hoover saw him as "the easiest
man to beat." Quintessential pundit Walter Lippmann composed a picture,
which was soon widely quoted:

Franklin D. Roosevelt is a highly impressionable person, without a firm grasp of
public affairs and without very strong convictions . . . an amiable man with many
philanthropic impulses, but he is not the dangerous enemy of anything. He is too
eager to please . . . Franklin D. Roosevelt is no crusader. He is no tribune of the
people. He is no enemy of entrenched privilege. He is a pleasant man who, without
any important qualifications for the office, would very much like to be President.*

In other words, Roosevelt seemed to many a resurrected Warren G. Harding.

   In a negative sense, Roosevelt's contemporary critics were right. In
1932, the substance of the "new deal" was as obscure as the hole card in a
blackjack game. Thus 1932 was to be a no clear-cut contest of rival programs,
no Calvinistic crusade against moral malefactors. If Harding had been sooth-
ingly common, Roosevelt came on as "A man so various he seem'd to be/Not
one, but all mankind's epitome," in John Dryden's words. Party platforms
left him cold. So did political philosophy. As governor of New York in 1929,
he had pushed through substantively liberal legislation—aid for farmers,
reform of public utilities. But the ideological coloration was obscure. Roosevelt helped obscure it further by his now-this-now-that rhetoric in 1932. His
campaign speech to the Commonwealth Club in San Francisco in October
1932 is a favorite of historical Rooseveltists as, in retrospect, it seemed to
presage the shape of liberal government interventions to come. "Every man
has a right to life," Roosevelt intoned, "and this means that he has also a
right to make a comfortable living." But if his close adviser Rexford Tugwell,
who helped write the speech, is to be believed, Roosevelt "never saw that
speech until he opened it on the lectern." And soon thereafter he delivered
the product of another ghost—calling for a 25 percent reduction in the federal budget and criticizing the Hoover administration for living beyond its
means. When two of his writers brought him contrasting drafts advocating
higher and lower tariffs, Roosevelt instructed them to take the drafts and
"weave them together."

   Thus Roosevelt disappointed the ideologues in their search for consistency and system. He got on better with the politicians, though some found
him devious to a fault. It was hard to tell where he stood. He would nod and

* Quoted in Frank Freidel, *Franklin D. Roosevelt: The Triumph* (Boston: Little, Brown, 1956),
pp. 248–49.

smile, "Well, there may be something in what you say." One of his best friends found that "his greatest defect is that he seldom explained himself when he changed position. He was never frank about a switch." He told Frances Perkins·how he got on with the middling pols: "They'd rather have a nice jolly understanding of their problems than lots of patronage. A little patronage, a lot of pleasure, and public signs of friendship and prestige—that's what makes a political leader secure with his people and that's what he wants anyhow." With politicians at the top, he was ever prepared to compromise and (especially if he won) to forgive.

Approaching the Democratic convention as the clear front-runner, Roosevelt ran up against fighting William Randolph Hearst, adamant enemy of Wilson's League of Nations. Roosevelt had come into national politics as a Wilson man, appointed assistant secretary of the navy; as Vice-Presidential candidate in 1920, he had campaigned hard for the league. But when Hearst took out after him in his *New York American* as an un-American internationalist, FDR danced and dodged. As long as he could he said nothing. Then he sent his manager James Farley to see Hearst, but Hearst told Farley that Roosevelt could only cleanse himself by a statement in public. Three days later Roosevelt declared in a speech that "the League of Nations today is not the League conceived by Woodrow Wilson," and "therefore, I do not favor American participation." Even his wife was flabbergasted—but Hearst's attack ended. "Let's concentrate on one thing," Roosevelt once said. "Save the people and the nation and, if we have to change our minds twice a day to accomplish that end, we should do it." That is how Roosevelt put together what Tugwell called "the most miscellaneous coalition in history," and stepped into office virtually free of clear commitments—other than to Do Something.

Roosevelt's managers, gnomelike Louis Howe and genial James Farley, sweated through the Democratic convention in Chicago, wheeling and dealing to stave off various moves by the Old Guard. When Roosevelt's name was placed in nomination, Howe got the organist to play "Happy Days Are Here Again." When deadlock loomed, they threw in their trump card: crusty maverick Texan Jack Garner got the Vice-Presidential nomination and swung over the needed votes. Their man got 666¼ votes on the first ballot to runner-up Al Smith's 201¾. It took only one long night of machinations to put him over the top, partly because the delegates remembered 1924, when the party had nearly fought itself to death. Back in Albany, Roosevelt listened to the returns on the radio and prepared to fly to Chicago—a dramatic, precedent-shattering act in that era when the candidate was supposed to wait at home, in all apparent innocence, until the official committee came by to notify him. It was an athletic event in those days of jiggly little low-flying aeroplanes, a demonstration that he was no invalid. After a hat-waving progress through the streets of Chicago, he came into the Chicago Stadium to thunderous applause.

Tipping up his chin jauntily, Franklin Roosevelt addressed "My Friends of the Democratic National Convention of 1932," beginning with a typical warm note of sympathy and identification: "I appreciate your willingness after these six arduous days to remain here, for I know well the sleepless hours which you and I have had." The microphones on the podium carried that same sentiment to attentive listeners throughout the country. "Wild radicalism has made few converts," he said, "and the greatest tribute that I can pay to my countrymen is that in these days of crushing want there persists an orderly and hopeful spirit on the part of the millions of our people who have suffered so much. To fail to offer them a new chance is not only to betray their hopes but to misunderstand their patience." He sketched out the broad dimensions of what he hoped to do. His climax was a promise: "I pledge you, I pledge myself, to a new deal for the American people." The applause rang loud and long. The next day a cartoonist showed a farmer looking up from his field at a plane flying over, "NEW DEAL" blazoned on its side. Thus the campaign found its slogan. Whatever else it meant, it meant change.

Roosevelt handshook his way out of the stadium and continued the gripping, patting, and hugging for hours at the Congress Hotel, apparently recharged by every encounter. At dinner he poured the balm of forgiveness on the heads of yesterday's bitter rivals—"my very good and old friend, John Raskob," "my old friend Jouett Shouse." Later on, even Al Smith was won over and joined in the campaign. FDR's friends, the Democratic senators, told him with one voice exactly what to do: stay home, make talks on the radio and speak at a few well organized rallies in the East. Texas Jack Garner sent a message: "Tell the Governor that he is the boss and we will all follow him to hell if we have to, but if he goes too far with some of these wildeyed ideas we are going to have the shit kicked out of us." Jack told Franklin, "All you have got to do is to stay alive until election day." Roosevelt smiled and nodded. But it was Garner who stayed home, beached in Uvalde, Texas, while Roosevelt traveled 23,000 miles, to all but seven states.

On the road, Roosevelt came on as a warmhearted, energetic, supremely hopeful, and confident person—a presence, not an argument. He delivered his major addresses with an actor's gusto, totally unfazed by their blatant contradictions. At a thousand whistlestops, he was a reborn William Howard Taft. "Roosevelt smiles and smiles and smiles and it doesn't get tiresome," wrote a reporter. "He can smile more than any man in American politics without being insipid." He and his audience wrapped their arms around each other. "The calls and cheers of the crowd came up to him and he seemed to absorb the good will as a thirsty man drinks, capaciously and eagerly," Tugwell observed. "The sealing of the leader and the crowd was a kind of mystic rite whose ceremony was celebrated in these gatherings." Another reporter put it more mundanely, remembering Roosevelt as "a kind of smiling bus driver" who "loved the passengers." *That* was his contrast with Hoover. It would have taken a Jesuitical scholar his full sabbatical year to sort out their policy differences. Indeed for most of the campaign, Roosevelt did little more than "shadow-box" with the issues, as Jim Farley put it—"He ignored the enemy and gave the country a picture of a confident man who knew what he intended to do when the reins of government were passed into his hands." Only near the end, with Hoover on the hustings intimating that Roosevelt represented some kind of foreign heresy, did FDR take out after "the Republican administration"—and even then he identified the opposition not as a set of guilty persons but as an alliterated quartet of anxiety-generators: "Destruction, Delay, Deceit, Despair."

Radio Roosevelt

But even in those days, those who heard and saw Roosevelt could occasionally catch a sense of his rhetorical eptness. Ghostwriters aside, Roosevelt had a gift for putting things in a way people who had not gone to Harvard could grasp. Once Frances Perkins wrote a speech for him that included the sentence, "We are trying to construct a more inclusive society." Some weeks later she heard what Roosevelt made of that for the radio audience: "We are going to make a country in which no one is left out." Which directional alternative was more viable—systemic restructuralization or capitalistic preservationism? Roosevelt invited his listeners to "say that civilization is a tree which, as it grows, continually produces rot and deadwood. The radical says: 'Cut it down.' The conservative says: 'Don't touch it.' The liberal compromises: 'Let's prune, so that we lose neither the old trunk nor the new branches.'" No Chautauquan could have done that better. Roosevelt—no great shakes as an intellectual anyhow—had an incredible talent for turning lectures into parables. He was a dramatist born and bred; as a child he impressed his governess (a lady not easily impressed) with his flair for enlivening history, as in his composition on the sufferings of Israel in Egypt: "The Kings made them work so hard and gave them so little that by wingo! they nearly starved and by jinks! they had hardly any clothes so they died in quadrillions."

As early as January 1929, Roosevelt estimated that "whereas five years ago ninety-nine out of one hundred people took their arguments from the editorials and the news columns of the daily press, today at least half of the voters sitting at their own firesides listen to the actual words of the political leaders on both sides and make their decision on what they hear rather than what they read." In 1932, both parties would spend more for radio time than for any other item.

While most politicians came crashing into the living room with their bombastic effusions, Roosevelt had quickly caught on to radio's conversational style. "In the olden days," he said in a radio talk in July 1932, "campaigns were conducted amid surroundings of brass bands and red lights," and "oratory was an appeal primarily to the emotions and sometimes to the passions." Instead, he would speak "in this quiet of common sense and friendliness." A radio executive noted that FDR's delivery was first class—clear, well pronounced. "But above all," he said, "it has a tone of perfect sincerity, a quality that we consider supremely essential."

With the great majority of editors and publishers against him, Roosevelt won over the reporters with his instinctive appreciation of their problems and his close-up charm. But it was radio that brought him home to the public as never before, particularly after he assumed office as President, but beginning back when he was governor in Albany. As early as 1931, FDR instructed the networks to pronounce his name "RO-se-velt." His genius with that medium was not a mere trick; it was an act of imagination, an attitude, a mode of sharing experience exactly suited to what the broadcasting audience had learned to expect from that vibrating box. Secretary of Labor Frances Perkins sensitively perceived Roosevelt's way of appreciating the listeners:

He did not and could not know them all individually, but he thought of them individually. He thought of them in family groups. He thought of them sitting around on a suburban porch after supper of a summer evening. He thought of them gathered around a dinner table at a family meal. He never thought of them as "the masses." . . .

His voice and his facial expression as he spoke were those of an intimate friend. After he became President, I often was at the White House when he broadcast, and I realized how unconscious he was of the twenty or thirty of us in that room and how clearly his mind was focused on the people listening at the other end. As he talked his head would nod and his hands would move in simple, natural, comfortable gestures. His face would smile and light up as though he were actually sitting on the front porch or in the parlor with them. People felt this, and it bound them to him in affection.

I have sat in those little parlors and on those porches myself during some of the speeches, and I have seen men and women gathered around the radio, even those who didn't like him or were opposed to him politically, listening with a pleasant, happy feeling of association and friendship. The exchange between them and him through the medium of the radio was very real. I have seen tears come to their eyes as he told them of some tragic episode, of the sufferings of the persecuted people in Europe, of the poverty during unemployment, of the sufferings of the homeless, of the sufferings of people whose sons had been killed in the war, and they were tears of sincerity and recognition and sympathy.

I have also seem them laugh. . . .

He wanted to talk to them about the things he thought they cared about. In particular, he wanted to talk everywhere about what could be done to make this a better, more beautiful, and more sustaining country.*

Roosevelt told a friend how he felt about his countrymen, having "looked into the faces of thousands of Americans": "They have the frightened look of lost children. . . . Now they are saying: 'We're caught in something we don't understand; perhaps this fellow can help us out.'"

* Frances Perkins, *The Roosevelt I Knew* (New York: Harper & Row, 1946), pp. 71–73.

Near the end of the campaign, he spoke directly to the radio audience: "You may not have universally agreed with me, but you have universally been kind and friendly to me. The great understanding and tolerance of America came out to meet me everywhere; for all this you have my heartfelt gratitude. . . . Out of this unity that I have seen, we may build the strongest strand to lift ourselves out of this depression." To nobody's great surprise, Roosevelt swept in on election day. He carried forty-two of the forty-eight states, beating Hoover 472 to 59 in the electoral vote and 22,809,000 to 15,758,000 in the popular vote. The Communist party polled a mere 103,000 votes.

Thus once again America cast its collective ballot for an end to troubling times. Perhaps Roosevelt was inevitable, but another alternative to Hoover might, like Bryan, have blown away his opportunity on some panacean cloud, or like Debs, have read the crisis as a call for revolutionary change. Instead they passed the cards to a new dealer who, for all his seeming softness, might yet hand them a straight or a flush—even just three of a kind. Odds are the great majority of votes "for Roosevelt" were really votes against Hoover. But those who cared enough to pay attention saw and heard in Roosevelt himself the nurturing, caring sympathy and hopefulness their ragged nerves called out for. Roosevelt eased in as the nation crossed its fingers and knocked on wood.

In fact, they had tapped for Presidential power the man who would rule that roost until he dropped dead in the spring of 1945. He was a man of mystery—which helped; mystery is clearly a major ingredient in the chemistry of charisma. The aspect of his complicated public character most significant at his first election was just that spark of intimacy Frances Perkins caught in his radio speaking. That, too, was mysterious. For while everyone who knew Roosevelt saw how much he loved company, loved talk, loved and fed upon the affectionate response he stimulated, many of his closer friends also perceived in Roosevelt a passion for privacy. For all his laughing chatter, Franklin Roosevelt was not an intimate man. Raymond Moley sensed in him "always the suggestion of some inner watchfulness, some subtle incompleteness that makes intimacy impossible." Speechwriter Sam Rosenman saw him as "friendly, but there was about his bearing an unspoken dignity which held off any undue familiarity." Felix Frankfurter called it "that mystical touch of grace, a charismatic quality that stirs comfortable awe, that keeps a distance between man and a leader." FDR's own son thought, "His greatest lack in life . . . was that, while he had lots of persons to whom he could talk, he had no real confidants. . . . Of what was inside him, of what really drove him, Father talked with no one." Not even with his wife. "I don't think I was his confidante either," she said.

The roots of Roosevelt the intimate stranger may have traced back to a childhood in which his nearest friend lived a mile and a half away, his playmate and brother Archibald died when Franklin was eight, and the boy spent much time in the company of adults. Bernard Asbell, in his fascinatingly imaginative construction of *The F.D.R. Memoirs*, asks, "Can it be that this loneliness, a never fulfilled yearning to be 'one of the boys,' underlies his getting on the radio to say, as no political leader has ever so effectively said: Let me be one of you. I will speak to you intimately, not as an orator but a friend. I will declare to you my most intimate trust if you will repay me with yours?" Perhaps. What is certain is that Roosevelt had—and sustained—just that quality of friendship at a distance the newest of the mass media demanded.

"I Never Heard of a President Like You"

The depression did not end between election day in November and inauguration day in March. But then the bands played "Happy Days Are Here Again." A vast radio audience heard Roosevelt "assert my firm belief that the only thing we have to fear is fear itself—nameless, unreasoning, unjustified terror." As he spoke, fear was running through the crowd in front of him, right there before the Capitol. "Capitol Crowd in Wild Rush to Find Cash" headlined the morning paper—because hotels and banks would not honor checks. Suddenly all over the country, the phrase "solid as a bank" became a mock, as bank after bank locked out anxious withdrawers. Panic was born and multiplied. Anxious politicians grabbed at radical solutions, such as Senator Burton K. Wheeler's suggestion that "the best way to restore confidence in the banks would be to take these crooked bank presidents out and treat them the same way we treated Al Capone when he failed to pay his income tax." Other senators thought it just the right time to nationalize the whole banking system. Special money for the emergency—scrip—was contemplated. On the Monday after his Saturday inauguration, Roosevelt closed the nation's banks. On Tuesday a solution formed in the brain of the secretary of the Treasury, Will Woodin, ex-manufacturer of railway equipment and guitar-playing composer of the popular "Raggedy Ann's Sunny Songs" for children, such as "Let us be like bluebirds,/Happy all day long,/Forgetting all our troubles,/In a sunny song." In the middle of the night it dawned on Woodin that currency—U.S. dollars, not scrip—could be issued against the sound assets of the banks. Thus the core of the Emergency Banking Act took form—a bill passed the following Thursday by both houses of Congress in one afternoon and signed that night by the President in the White House, surrounded by unopened packing crates. But what would happen when, as must happen soon, the banks reopened their doors?

Roosevelt went on the radio the next Sunday night at 10:00. Down in the basement of the White House, workers removed James Monroe's gold dinner service and other stored items to make room for all the wires and mikes and switchboxes. Ready for the first "Fireside Chat"—a fireplace was nearby, but no fire in it—at the last moment no one could find the President's reading copy, so he borrowed a mimeographed copy from a reporter. Roosevelt chatted easily with the radio men, asking, "What's the CBS for?"

Mrs. Roosevelt sat nearby, quietly knitting. Then the NBC man tapped him on the shoulder and some sixty million Americans heard their President call them "My Friends."

It was decidedly a first. Presidents made addresses. Brokenshires and Kaltenborns made chats. Cool as a cucumber, Roosevelt began as if he had dropped in for a cup of coffee:

I want to talk for a few minutes with the people of the United States about banking—with the comparatively few who understand the mechanics of banking, but more particularly with the overwhelming majority who use banks for the making of deposits and the drawing of checks. . . . I know that when you understand what we in Washington have been about, I shall continue to have your co-operation as fully as I have had your sympathy and help during the past week.

"First of all," he said, "let me state the simple fact that when you deposit money in a bank, the bank does not put the money into a safe deposit vault. It invests your money in many different forms. . . ." He went right on through a short and simple course in Introduction to Banking, told what "we in Washington" had been up to, and gently advised; "It needs no prophet to tell you that when the people find that they can get their money—that they can get it when they want it for all legitimate purposes—the phantom of fear will soon be laid. . . . I can assure you that it is safer to keep your money in a reopened bank than under a mattress." And that was that. The President confessed, "It has been wonderful to me to catch the note of confidence from all over the country"—from whom he did not say—and said, "Confidence and courage are the essentials of success in carrying out our plan." With that, "together we cannot fail."

He stopped talking. The engineer signaled he was off the air. The President turned and asked, "Was I all right?"

The answer was yes. In the next three days, 4,507 national and 567 state banks reopened. Kansas City wired in: "BANKS REOPENED HERE IN AMAZINGLY QUIET FASHION PUBLIC HYSTERIA SEEMS OVER"; San Francisco reported "NORMAL BANKING CONDITIONS PREVAIL EVERYWHERE . . . DEPOSITORS CHEERFUL AND MOST WILLING TO COOPERATE IN THE PRESIDENT'S POLICIES."

Harvard Professor Felix Frankfurter wrote Roosevelt that with "simplicity and lucidity you are making known to the nation what you are doing. But you are also making the people feel—and nothing is more important for a democracy—that in a true sense of the word it is *their* government, and that *their* interests and *their* feelings are actively engaged."

That same month, the Bonus Army tramped back into Washington. Roosevelt asked his Eleanor to go see them for him. He told her, "Above all, be sure there is plenty of good coffee. No questions asked. Just let free coffee flow all the time. There is nothing like it to make people feel better and feel welcome." Eleanor and Louis Howe went over and talked with them, about the World War days; she wondered if any of them had come through Washington back then, when she was doing volunteer work in the railroad yards. "I never want to see another war," she said. "I would like to see fair consideration for everyone, and I shall always be grateful to those who served their country." She led them in singing "There's a Long, Long Trail." They cheered her goodbye. "Hoover sent the army," they said. "Roosevelt sent his wife."

The mail poured in to the White House. One distant citizen wrote:

Dear Mr. President:

This is just to tell you that everything is all right now. The man you sent found our house all right, and we went down to the bank with him and the mortgage can go on for a while longer. You remember I wrote you about losing the furniture too. Well, your man got it back for us. I never heard of a President like you. . . .*

That month, half a million Americans wrote to their President. People clipped his picture from magazines and tacked it up on the wall like a saint. He had come in and tried something and it worked. He had found in radio a medium to conjure his confident spirit into the national psyche—for the time being, anyway. Though he hardly needed it in 1933, when Congress was whooping through whatever legislation he sent them, Roosevelt had also found a shortcut right past the Washington thicket to his friends in the living rooms. Later on it was said that he had but to glance at a microphone to strike electoral terror into the hearts of recalcitrant congressmen. The radio men called him "a real pro." In his second Fireside Chat, in July of 1933, well into a conversation on relief, he stopped and asked for a glass of water; listeners heard it being poured and sipped. "My friends, it's very hot here in Washington tonight," he said. But he had sense enough not to overdo it: he rationed his radio chats, four the first year, two the next, one in each of the following two years.

The Flexible Flyer

The New Deal scattered its cards in every conceivable direction, gambling that if the government tried enough different moves some of them might take hold and help. The important thing was first to get money into the hands of the impoverished, second to create the atmosphere of forward action that would inspire a revival of confidence. The checks were mailed, the action got reported, the image was established. Broadcasting helped bring home Roosevelt's concern for the forgotten Americans.

If 1932 was a time for allaying fear, 1936 was a battle royal. By then the reaction against Roosevelt was no longer exotic or intellectual; spellbinders other than Roosevelt seemed to be succeeding in drawing fame from popular anxieties. After four years of Democratic experiments, the Republicans mobilized an all-out attack on the record. Had Roosevelt come on in 1936 as he

* Quoted in Richard Harrity and Ralph G. Martin, *The Human Side of FDR* (New York: Duell, Sloan and Pearce, 1960), unpaged.

had in 1932—as a pleasant fellow with a heart of gold—his first term would have been his last.

Fulminating Father Charles E. Coughlin, man of the cloth, revived Bryan's free silver nostrum, railed against the "red serpent" of communism, and fell upon the selfish wealthy "dulled by the opiate of their own contentedness." The networks eased him off their air, but radio had already given Coughlin an enormous audience—it took a hundred secretaries to answer his mail—and they sent him enough money to buy his own time on twenty-six stations in 1932. He was all for Roosevelt that year but dropped off the bandwagon when the secretary of the Treasury revealed Coughlin's substantial investments in silver and, a few months later, FDR proposed joining the World Court—that nest of scheming international bankers, as Coughlin saw them. As the depression deepened, the good father, with his "National Union for Social Justice," seemed a real menace. As the 1936 election approached, Coughlin traveled the land diatribing against "Franklin Double-crossing Roosevelt."

Huey Long, flamboyant grand sachem of Louisiana, got himself elected to the Senate in 1932 on the Roosevelt ticket. Unlike Coughlin, Long came over on the radio as a warmhearted fellow like Roosevelt though without the Harvard accent:

Hello friends, this is Huey Long speaking. And I have some important things to tell you. Before I begin I want you to do me a favor. I am going to talk along for four or five minutes, just to keep things going. While I'm doing it I want you to go to the telephone and call up five of your friends, and tell them Huey is on the air.*

He did not sound dangerous. The broadcasters welcomed him to the air. He called himself "Kingfish" after the head of "Amos 'n' Andy's" lodge. He built up a fantastic audience with his Share-Our-Wealth scheme; by the middle of 1935 there were said to be Share-Our-Wealth clubs in eight thousand communities, with a membership of seven million. The idea in substance was a ludicrous fraud—cut down the big fortunes and by some financial magic produce enough to give everybody $5,000 and an annual income of $2,000, plus pensions. But the time was ripe for radical visionaries. Asked to explain Share-Our-Wealth, Long told a reporter, "It's all in Plato. You know—the Greek philosopher."

Long and Coughlin were pondering an alliance for 1936 when, in September of the preceding year, a gunman slew the Kingfish. Even so, a coalition was formed, bringing in Dr. Francis E. Townsend of California with *his* weird potion for economic security.

The Republicans, encouraged by the apparent splintering of their left wing of the polity, nominated a centrist, Kansas Governor Alfred Landon. Landon was picked up and borne forward by the newspapers, who promoted him as a "liberal Coolidge" who might beat That Man in the White House.

---

* Quoted in Erik Barnouw, *A History of Broadcasting in the United States*, vol. 2, *The Golden Web* (New York, Oxford University Press, 1968), p. 49.

The *Kansas City Star* got him regional fame. Then William Randolph Hearst had his newspaper chain puff him up and featured him in Hearst's *Cosmopolitan* and *Good Housekeeping* magazines. He took Cissy Patterson, publisher of the *Washington Herald* to visit Landon. "I think he is marvelous!" said Hearst. "I thought of Lincoln," said Patterson. By the time the Republicans gathered in Cleveland on June 9, the press build-up had squashed a vestigial challenge by Idaho Senator William Borah. Landon took it on the first ballot, the delegates uniting around one overriding purpose: "stop Roosevelt."

There was no stopping Roosevelt at the Democratic convention in Philadelphia opening on June 27. Some 100,000 people greeted him at the airport in the rain. His acceptance speech rang with fighting rhetoric, calling for war against the "new industrial dictatorship." "There is a mysterious cycle in human events," he said. "To some generations much is given. Of other generations much is expected. This generation of Americans has a rendezvous with destiny."

Landon's rhetoric reached no such heights. His most memorable pronouncement was, "Wherever I have gone in this country, I have found Americans." To compensate for his uninspiring style, the Republicans hired the best advertising agencies to prepare snappy little radio dramas featuring downhome Americans and a "debate" between Senator Arthur Vandenberg and snippets culled from old Roosevelt speeches. *Variety* complained that "political parties are being reduced to merchandise which can be exchanged for votes in accordance with a well-conceived marketing plan, taking stock of income levels, race, local problems, exactly as does a commercial sponsor. This differs no whit from the tactics employed by Lifebuoy, Chase and Sanborn, or any other of a thousand commercial commodities."

The campaign between the candidates was a roughhouse, a battle election to the last. Historian William E. Leuchtenburg testifies that "the parties divided on issues in 1936 as they had at no previous time in this century." Landon hit Roosevelt for using "relief rolls as modern reservations on which the great colored race is to be confined forever as a ward of the federal government," blasted the Social Security Act as "unjust, unworkable, stupidly drafted and wastefully financed," asked whether Roosevelt "intends to change the form of our government," and intimated that the New Deal would lead straight to the guillotine. Gerald L. K. Smith joined with Coughlin and Townsend in the "Union party" with their own candidate, vowed "to drive that cripple out of the White House." Coughlin raged that the New Deal was not only "bent on communistic revolution" but had also sold out to the "international bankers." Townsend called the President a "political savage." Roosevelt's "dear friends" Al Smith and John J. Raskob stalked out of the Democratic party and backed Landon. The "Happy Warrior" growled, "It is all right with me if they want to disguise themselves as Norman Thomas or Karl Marx, or Lenin, or any of the rest of that bunch, but what I won't stand for is allowing them to march under the banner of Jefferson,

Jackson and Cleveland." Roosevelt's administration would take anybody, said Smith, "even a communist with wire whiskers and a torch in his hands is welcome so long as he signs on the dotted line."

A Republican put in the *Congressional Record* a rhyme against the Roosevelt of 1932:

> I'm tired, oh, so tired, of the whole New Deal,
> Of the juggler's smile and the barker's spiel,
> Of the mushy speech and the loud bassoon,
> And tiredest of all of our leader's croon.*

But the FDR of 1936 was no patsy. By election eve he was wound up tight:

> For twelve years this Nation was afflicted with hear-nothing, see-nothing, do-nothing Government. The Nation looked to Government but the Government looked away. Nine mocking years with the golden calf and three long years of the scourge! Nine crazy years at the ticker and three long years in the breadlines! Nine mad years of mirage and three long years of despair! Powerful influences strive today to restore that kind of Government with its doctrine that that Government is best which is most indifferent. . . .
>
> They had begun to consider the Government of the United States as a mere appendage to their own affairs. We know now that Government by organized *money* is just as dangerous as Government by organized *mob*.
>
> Never before in all our history have these forces been so united against one candidate as they stand today. They are unanimous in their *hate* for *me—and I welcome their hatred*.
>
> I should like to have it said of my first Administration that in it the forces of selfishness and of lust for power met their match. I should like it said of my second Administration that in it these forces met their master.†

Right down to the wire, pundits and pollsters foresaw a close finish. Fourteen of them met for lunch two weeks before the election and decided Landon would win narrowly. A newspaper drew together results of some three thousand different straw votes and predicted a Landon landslide, as did the *Literary Digest* at the end.

By then much of the press, dominated by Republican publishers, had had enough of FDR and his New Deal. The *Washington Post* (which had not bothered to send a reporter to the Democratic national convention of 1932) in 1936 puffed Landon, noting his "easy stance of the skilled prize-fighter who does not waste an ounce of energy." Roosevelt's acceptance speech was all the more dangerous for being "very moving and eloquent"—it was "the sort of speech which paves the way for fascism," said the *Post*. Henry Luce, who had greeted FDR's election in 1932 with relief—"The country will feel better and that's fine," he said—in 1936 did what he could to build up Lan-

---

*Quoted in William E. Leuchtenburg, "Election of 1936," in Schlesinger et al., eds., *History of American Presidential Elections*, vol. 4, p. 2819.
†Quoted in ibid., p. 2839.

don ("the Governor went for a brisk seven-mile canter. . . ."), but gave up on him late in the season; the time for a Lucean candidate was four years away. The *Chicago Tribune* experienced no such hesitations. On August 6 it reported that "Moscow has ordered Reds in the United States to back Roosevelt against Landon." To reach past the hostile press, Roosevelt again turned to radio, broadcasting "non-political" talks, turning issues into stories. The Republicans reminded him of the old gentleman in a silk hat who fell off a pier into the water. A friend dived in and saved him, but the hat floated off. "Three years later the old gentleman is still berating his friend because the silk hat was lost." One could hear the audience roar with laughter.

FDR's win was history's greatest landslide. The electoral vote was 523 to 8. Roosevelt got a record-smashing 60.8 percent of the popular vote, carrying forty-six of the forty-eight states, all but Maine and Vermont—he laughingly blamed that on Farley. "I knew I should have gone to Maine and Vermont, but Jim wouldn't let me." It was Roosevelt's high point as a partisan. That year he made being a Democrat mean something; the election divided the electorate into clear-cut party camps. Roosevelt would go down as the last great party President, master of a firm coalition that would never again attain that degree of unity and coherence. By the end of his reign, he would have contributed to its eventual dispersion; in the fighting election of 1948, Harry Truman would enjoy no such unified backing.

Roosevelt overpowered the charismatic characters who competed with him for mass popularity. But after his mammoth win in 1936, he overreached himself, continuing the battle long after the election, trying to purge senators in 1936 and pack the Supreme Court in 1937. The rhythm of action and reaction beat forward through those years. Willkie, and the moralizing election of 1940, formed the predictable aftermath of the combat of 1936.

The News Over the Air

Through the Roosevelt years, radio news was coming into its own, emerging as a separate—though hardly equal—enterprise in a medium of entertainment. By 1940, fifty million Americans had radios and H. V. Kaltenborn, the "Dean of News Commentators," had become the medium's most popular news voice, a mind-blowing hailstorm of fact and opinion, sometimes rattling forth at the rate of two hundred words per minute of real-life drama about the real world.

As a schoolboy, H. V. learned juggling and went on the stage but when TR's war came he joined the army, having persuaded the local editor to take him on as a war correspondent. The war was over before he could get overseas. He signed on as a reporter for the *Brooklyn Daily Eagle*, got himself accepted at age twenty-seven as a special student at Harvard, where he won an oratorical prize, acted in plays, made Phi Beta Kappa, and graduated, in

1909, with honors. He set off after college for a long cruise in John Jacob Astor's long yacht, as tutor to his son. In 1914 he went to Paris to shape up the *Eagle*'s bureau there; after the war, the *Eagle* made him an associate editor and encouraged him to go on the radio—it might help circulation. In two years, he had his own weekly half hour.

The radio audience is like a blind man, the commentator like a sighted friend looking around for what, in the flux of the surrounding, lends itself to verbal portraiture. Clinging to a haystack in the midst of the Spanish Civil War, Kaltenborn broadcast the boom of the guns, the swoosh of the planes overhead. He seldom failed to let his listeners know that he was where the action was: "Now, I stood alongside the desk of the President of the United States at a press conference last week, where he said definitely that he believed in the Civil Service, and I believe he does. . . ."

But the climax that made Kaltenborn famous and radio news the focus of mass attention played out of Studio 9 at 485 Madison Avenue, New York City. In March 1938, Hitler's troops crossed the border into Austria, followed shortly by the triumphal entry of Hitler himself into Vienna. From over there, CBSers William L. Shirer and Edward R. Murrow transmitted their observations to New York. As the crisis got hot that September, with Hitler fulminating against Czechoslovakia to an immense rally at Nuremberg, President Roosevelt and Prime Minister Chamberlain pleaded for peace. That month, Kaltenborn made 102 broadcasts from New York in eighteen days. A bulletin would come in, H. V. would take it and read it over the air, and then launch into an ad-lib analysis for as long as two hours at a stretch. Fifty thousand people wrote to thank him. When it was over—or seemed to be, with Chamberlain returning from Munich to London declaring "peace in our time"—a survey showed Americans for the first time preferring radio to newspapers as a news source on the European crisis.

Hitler's diatribes, relayed in their original Germanic expectoration, sounded hysterical. Kaltenborn had learned how to play off that, back when he used to broadcast faked-up "interviews" between himself-as-commentator and himself-as-Hitler. He was comparatively cool, comfortingly didactic. Furthermore, he virtually reveled in complexity, analyzing the threat into so many fragments that somehow none seemed fatal. For example, what must the audience, attuned to the leisurely pace of soap opera, have made of this randomly selected passage, delivered from Kaltenborn's oral machine gun?

From every capital I have news in front of me here which indicates the tightening of the situation. In Italy, the press insists on Mussolini's desire to make this a general dividing up of Czechoslovakia. That is something which the British and French are apparently determined to resist. In Warsaw, the controlled press and the Government are both acting in such a way as to indicate that they are determined that Poland is to have the Teschen district at this time. Recruiting offices have been opened in Warsaw for the organization of volunteer corps similar to the Sudeten Corps. Of course that's the Government's way of covering up aggressive intentions against Czechoslovakia. It organizes these so-called corps of people supposedly native in the Teschen District who have fled because of alleged persecution and who are only going back to claim some territory for the homeland Poland. That's the idea as it is underscored and emphasized in Poland.

Kaltenborn—like almost all informed observers except Winston Churchill—kept perceiving hopeful signs:

> The way has been opened which must bring a solution of the crisis . . . the prospects for peace have improved immeasurably. . . . As I survey the Press Radio bulletins that are placed before me, as they come in, I can see that almost everyone promises a peaceful solution of the European conflict. . . . There is to be no European war, after all. There is to be peace. . . . It's all settled.*

After the crisis seemed over, Kaltenborn took air time to tell his listeners he felt "very humble and very grateful in view of the response that has come to me from Columbia's vast radio audience."

But for all his inability to see the hell to come, and for all his self-advertisement and obfuscation, Kaltenborn did stake out a territory for the broadcast newsman that extended beyond entertainment to the real world. It was hard to hold that territory. The president of CBS, William Paley, insisted, "We must never have an editorial page," and, "We must never try to further either side of any debatable question." Kaltenborn recounts how that affected practice:

> Vice President Edward Klauber would call me up to his office for a friendly heart-to-heart talk. . . . "Just don't be so personal," he'd say to me. "Use such phrases as 'is said,' 'there are those who believe,' 'the opinion is held in well-informed quarters,' 'some experts have come to the conclusion. . . .' Why keep on saying 'I think' and 'I believe' when you can put over the same idea much more persuasively by quoting someone else?"†

In 1940, he wrote for his broadcast, "I listened to Wendell Willkie's speech last night. It was wholly admirable." But upon reflection he changed that to: "Millions of Americans of both parties listened to Wendell Willkie's speech last night. Most of them agreed that it was a wholly admirable speech." Kaltenborn left CBS for NBC—but the same number was running there:

> News analysts are at all times to be confined strictly to explaining and evaluating such fact, rumor, propaganda, and so on, as are available. No news analyst or news broadcaster of any kind is to be allowed to express personal editorial judgment or . . . to say anything in an effort to influence action or opinion of others one way or the other.‡

The FCC and the National Association of Broadcasters issued similar prohibitions, which could only have the effect of encouraging false attributions. When the Munich crisis hit, things moved too fast for calculated fakery. Kaltenborn became the first president of the Association of Radio News Ana-

---

*H. V. Kaltenborn, *I Broadcast the Crisis* (New York: Random House, 1938), p. 149.
†Quoted in Barnouw, *The Golden Web*, p. 136.
‡Ibid.

lysts; he refused to do commercials; he talked back to worried sponsors. As important, he established in the public mind the sense of the sentient reporter as his own man. Not long thereafter, Mr. Klauber passed the word that "we don't want people around here with beards," and a doughty CBSer threw a dinner party at which he ceremoniously shaved.

Edward R. Murrow—the best in broadcasting, the standard setter—began in the Kaltenborn mode, discovering calm where one might have expected terror. When Murrow left Warsaw that March of 1938, he broadcast, "There was very little excitement apparent . . . people went quietly about their work." In Vienna, "There isn't a great deal of hilarity, but at the same time there doesn't seem to be much feeling of tension. Young storm troopers are riding about the streets, riding about in trucks and vehicles of all sorts, singing and tossing oranges out to the crowd." Back in London five days later, Murrow reviewed what had happened:

Later Herr Hitler arrived, made a speech, took the salute of the big parade, and Austria ceased to exist. Vienna became a provincial town; faithful party members, most of them Germans, were placed in all the important posts. It was called a bloodless conquest and in some ways it was—

And at that point, Murrow himself stepped into the aural picture. The night before this broadcast he had gone out for a drink. "A Jewish-looking fellow was standing at that bar," he told Shirer. "After a while he took an old-fashioned razor from his pocket and slashed his throat." The broadcast continued:

—but I'd like to be able to forget the haunted look on the faces of those long lines of people outside the banks and travel offices. People trying to get away. I'd like to forget the tired futile look of the Austrian army officers, and the thud of hobnail boots and the crash of light tanks in the early hours of the morning on the Ringstrasse, and the pitiful uncertainty and bewilderment of those forced to lift the right hand and shout "Heil Hitler" for the first time. I'd like to forget the sound of the smashing glass as the Jewish shop streets were raided; the hoots and jeers at those forced to scrub the sidewalk.*

It was a whole new manner of speaking—of sensing, thinking, writing—for radio. Murrow's baritone voice cast a shadow. His pronunciation was precise, his timing verged on the Shakespearean. He entered the living room like a survivor of a shipwreck, who, carefully husbanding what is left of his self-control, is at last persuaded to tell what he has been through.

Murrow was a shy young man who found courage. He was born not far from Polecat Creek, North Carolina, in 1908, to a mother who must have given a lot of thought to naming her children: he was Egbert Roscoe, his brothers were Lacey Van Buren and Dewey Joshua Murrow. His father was a big, strong, silent, but restless man, not doing too well at farming. When

* Quoted in ibid., p. 78.

the boy was five, the family moved across the continent to the State of Washington, where father Murrow found work as a locomotive engineer at a logging camp seventy miles north of Seattle. His little mother was religious—he remembered that in answering the telephone she would not say "hello," "because one syllable of that tells the name of Satan's home. She says 'hey-yo.'" Every night she had the boys read one chapter of the Bible. At Washington State College, Egbert Roscoe became Edward R.; he began to discover his voice in debating, playacting, and sportscasting on the radio; he became cadet colonel of the ROTC and president of the student body; as a senior he was voted president of the National Student Federation. At graduation in 1930, he received a Phi Beta Kappa key. That summer he got over to Europe, wearing a straw hat and carrying a cane. In the fall, the National Student Federation presidency took him to New York, with $25 a week for expenses and no salary. He got on CBS that September, with a talk of some dramatic interest in those dark days: "Looking Forward with Students," then got a job as assistant to the director of the Institute for International Education. Sometime before 1941, he did a bit of impression-management of his own, as a curriculum vitae he put together shows. He added three years to his age; his speech major at Washington State became political science and international relations at the University of Washington—with a master's degree from Stanford thrown in for good measure, a logging year with his father became "two years as compassman and topographer for timber cruisers in Northwest Washington, British Columbia and Alaska." Perhaps that enhanced history helped him start his radio career, as CBS's director of radio talks and education. Then in 1937 came what looked like a bad break: reassignment as CBS's European director, replacing an incumbent bored with recording children's choirs to fill unsellable network time. Thus it was that Edward R. Murrow was in Vienna for CBS the night before Hitler arrived.

Murrow was there, broadcasting all the way, when the German bombers came to London, and came back, again and again. He fell in love with British cool:

August 18, 1940

I spent five hours this afternoon on the outskirts of London. Bombs fell out there today. It is indeed surprising how little damage a bomb will do unless, of course, it scores a direct hit. But I found that one bombed house looks pretty much like another bombed house. It's about the people I'd like to talk, the little people who live in those little houses, who have no uniforms and get no decorations for bravery. Those men whose only uniform was a tin hat were digging unexploded bombs out of the ground this afternoon. There were two women who gossiped across the narrow strip of tired brown grass that separated their houses. They didn't have to open their kitchen windows in order to converse. The glass had been blown out. There was a little man with a pipe in his mouth who walked up and looked at a bombed house and said, "One fell there and that's all." Those people were calm and courageous. About an hour after the all clear had sounded, people were sitting in deck chairs on their lawns, reading the Sunday papers. The girls in light, cheap dresses were strolling along the streets. There was no bravado, no loud voices, only a quiet acceptance of the situation. To me those people were incredibly brave and calm. They are the unknown heroes of this war.*

That was his constant theme: "This is London at 3:30 in the morning. This has been what might be called a 'routine night'—air-raid alarm at about nine o'clock and intermittent bombing ever since." There were parallel themes— the muted British hope that sooner or later their friends across the sea would lend a hand, the persistence of old class distinctions in the midst of chaos, for example. But Murrow kept coming back to how these peculiar people shook off the shock of personal disaster and got on with the war. One night in London he put his microphone on the sidewalk, so America could hear the unhurried steps of people on their way to the bomb shelters.

One time during the war he wrote his parents, "I remember you once wanted me to be a preacher, but I had no faith, except in myself. But now I am preaching from a powerful pulpit. Often I am wrong but I am trying to talk as I would have talked were I a preacher. One need not wear a reversed collar to be honest." But like many another effective preacher, he learned to stand aside and let what he had to say shine forth. Murrow more than anyone else brought the power of the parable to broadcast journalism. His prose, knocked together in the midst of the fog of battle, needs no improvement. Story is what held it together. Murrow's performance set a standard for broadcast journalism for years to come. Two examples show what he could do with what he saw.

June 2, 1940—An airfield on the southeast coast of England.

. . . . When the squadron took off, one of [the pilots] remarked quite casually that he'd be back in time for tea. About that time a boy of twenty drove up in a station wagon. He weighed about 115 pounds. He asked the squadron leader if he could have someone fly him back to his own field. His voice was loud and flat; his uniform was torn, had obviously been wet. He wore a pair of brown tennis shoes three sizes too big. After he'd gone I asked one of the men what was the matter with him. "Oh," he replied, "he was shot down over at Dunkirk on the first patrol this morning, landed in the sea, swam to the beach, was bombed for a couple of hours, came home in a paddle steamer. His voice sounds like that because he can't hear himself. You get that way after you've been bombed for a few hours," he said.

April 15, 1945—Germany.

. . . . If you are at lunch, or if you have no appetite to hear what Germans have done, now is a good time to switch off the radio, for I propose to tell you about Buchenwald. It is on a small hill about four miles outside Weimar, and it is one of the largest concentration camps in Germany, and it was built to last. . . . We drove on, reached the main gate. The prisoners crowded up behind the wire. We entered.

* Edward Bliss, Jr., ed., *In Search of Light: The Broadcasts of Edward R. Murrow 1938–1961* (New York: Alfred A. Knopf, 1967), p. 39.

And now, let me tell this in the first person, for I was the least important person there, as you shall hear. There surged around me an evil-smelling horde. Men and boys reached out to touch me; they were in rags and the remnants of uniform. Death had already marked many of them, but they were smiling with their eyes. I looked out over that mass of men to the green fields beyond where well-fed Germans were ploughing. . . .

In another part of the camp they showed me the children, hundreds of them. Some were only six. One rolled up his sleeve, showed me his number. It was tattooed on his arm. D–6030, it was. The others showed me their numbers; they will carry them till they die.

An elderly man standing beside me said, "The children, enemies of the state." I could see their ribs through their thin shirts. . . . The children clung to my hands and stared. We crossed to the courtyard. Men kept coming up to speak to me and to touch me, professors from Poland, doctors from Vienna, men from all Europe. Men from the countries that made America. . . .

If I've offended you by this rather mild account of Buchenwald, I'm not in the least sorry. I was there on Thursday, and many men in many tongues blessed the name of Roosevelt. For long years his name had meant the full measure of their hope. These men who had kept close company with death for many years did not know that Mr. Roosevelt would, within hours, join their comrades who had laid their lives on the scale of freedom.

Back in 1941, Mr. Churchill said to me with tears in his eyes, "One day the world and history will recognize and acknowledge what it owes to your President." I saw and heard the first installment of that at Buchenwald on Thursday. It came from men from all over Europe. Their faces, with more flesh on them, might have been found anywhere at home. To them the name "Roosevelt" was a symbol, the code word for a lot of guys named "Joe" who are out in the blue with the armor heading east. At Buchenwald they spoke of the President just before he died. If there be a better epitaph, history does not record it.*

Murrow's clear, understated, spare, fact-anchored, narrative reporting brought to broadcast journalism a revolution in style comparable to that which *Time* had brought to the magazines. Fortunately for the future, Murrow brought along a whole generation of "Murrow's boys" in broadcasting, and on into television. Howard K. Smith, Eric Sevareid, Charles Collingwood, and others all would go off in their own directions for good or ill—but they have carried over to today the ideal of Murrow's literary precision, direct observation, and, from the war years at least, his independence from the nervous Nellies of the networks.

Indeed the three most strikingly effective broadcasting personalities of the Roosevelt era broke through to the mass audience by telling what was happening—out there—in crisis. Roosevelt himself, from his first Fireside Chat explaining the banking crisis, used the mode of objective description—not haranguement—to rally the nation against the deadly threat of collapsing confidence and, later, to prepare them for war. Kaltenborn came to the fore with his Munich broadcasts, the interest of which derived not from his rep-

---

*Ibid., pp. 26–27, 90–95.

resentation of himself but from his representation of a fast-moving, peace-threatening, historical avalanche. It was not "This is Murrow" but "This is London" that got across to millions of comfortable Americans what it must have been like to have war come home to one's own.

All three, in their different ways, stood as steady hands against the hysterics of their day. All three sensed the primacy of story over sermon, in the midst of that time's clashing ideologies. Those modes would stick. In later times, when the issues were not so clear and the eminences not so heroic, broadcasting's calmness and anecdotal manner would come to serve darker purposes.

Through the Roosevelt years, it helped keep the political show on the road.

Exit the Champ

In 1944, the nation for the second time in its history held a Presidential election in the middle of a war, a harmonizing election of conciliation. We voted to continue, to push on to peace. Roosevelt, sensing the mood, took it easy. His most widely noted speech was a little conversation with the Teamsters Union and radio listeners that September, beginning, "Mr. Tobin—I should say Dan, I always have—Ladies and Gentlemen." He blithely mocked his Republican critics, especially for attacking his "little dog Fala." His opponent, Thomas Dewey, out of phase with the national mood, tried to get a fight going, advertising his youth to make Roosevelt look geriatric. Such Republican hope as there was would depend on low turnout; near the end the Democrats worried that this would be *too* quiet an election. On October 20, FDR demonstrated his vigor by parading in an open car in a cold, pouring rain through the streets of New York on his way to a foreign-policy broadcast. He laughed and waved. Radio bulletins through the day reported his apparent pleasure and health. Then on election eve, Norman Corwin produced a most unusual turnout-stimulator for the Democrats.

Both NBC and CBS policy forbade "dramatization" in political messages. So Corwin got people—not actors—to speak briefly for themselves and for Roosevelt—a soldier and sailor back from the war, a depression apple-seller, a Republican, an old man getting ready to vote in his fifteenth Presidential election, a young girl about to vote for the first time, who introduced the President. Then the music came on, a pounding locomotive beat for the "Roosevelt Special," to which a succession of celebrities pledged their allegiance:

CHORUS: *All aboard for tomorrow!*
LUCILLE BALL: This is Lucille Ball. I'm on this train.
CHORUS: *Vote!*
JOAN BENNETT: Joan Bennett—for the champ.
CHORUS: *Vote!*

IRVING BERLIN: Irving Berlin—
MRS. BERLIN: And Mrs. Berlin.
CHORUS: *For Roosevelt!*
. . . .
JOHN DEWEY: Dewey—John, not Tom. Philosopher.*

The effect was electric. The Republicans had bought time for a program right after the "Roosevelt Special" rolled off the air, but by a stroke of Roosevelt luck, a star comedian pulled out of the Corwin program at the last moment, leaving a few minutes extra at the end. Radio listeners heard an interlude of lugubrious organ music, suggesting bedtime. One could hear the sets switching off all over the country.

In the returns, Roosevelt did about as well as he had in 1940. The following April he died, and, as ever when we lose a sitting President, the nation went into intense mourning. Among the projects he was working on was the draft for a Jefferson Day broadcast:

> Today we are faced with the pre-eminent fact that, if civilization is to survive, we must cultivate the science of human relationships—the ability of all peoples, of all kinds, to live together and work together, in the same world, at peace. Let me assure you that my hand is the steadier for the work that is to be done, that I move more firmly into the task, knowing that you—millions and millions of you—are joined with me in the resolve to make this work endure. . . .†

Whatever history makes of Roosevelt's policies, there is no doubt he was a superb political actor. He had an incredible sense of strategic timing, an incredible ability to see through the details to the larger tides of action and reaction that lent force to the political drama. And he was clearly the radio candidate *par excellence,* reaching past the politicians and the editors to the people at home. He caught on early to the living-room style. He grasped the enormous power of the parable to hold and convince an audience. He was a real pro, a natural. "I know what I'll do when I retire," he once said, "I'll be one of those high-powered commentators."

*Quoted in Barnouw, *Golden Web*, p. 209.
†Quoted in ibid., p. 211.

13

Dwight Eisenhower 1956

DESTINY COULD HARDLY have arranged a neater conjunction than that of Eisenhower, the popular mood of the 1950s, and the sudden rise of television broadcasting. The fighting election of 1948 set the backdrop for Eisenhower's emergence in 1952 as a man of conscience, indignant at the degeneration of the Presidency into a merely political office. But, by 1956, Eisenhower, running against Adlai Stevenson for the second time, shifted with the moodswing to become a hero of harmony, a conciliator *par excellence*. We needed that by then.

The rise of television broadcasting, with its emphasis on brevity and intimacy, was transforming the political dialogue from a discussion to a disjointed series of personalized symbolic assertions. The medium's traditional informality and good humor helped blur the distinctions reasoned political debate requires. Eisenhower, from a sense of duty, went along with what more experienced politicians told him was necessary. Stevenson at first resisted the demands the showmen shoved at him, tried instead to win over the electorate by offering a fresh diagnosis of their political condition, as a political professor in the Wilson tradition. But he eventually began to come around to the new mode. He is about as good an example as we are likely to see of a politician out of phase with the tides of his times.

These two good men, neither of whom really wanted to be President, played to an audience grappling with the challenges of radical life improvement. The way the drama worked out shows that the rhythm of electoral action and reaction swings on to its easing phase even when no Great Depression or Great War threatens the commonweal.

Ike

Eisenhower's first election in 1952 suited the Wilson-Hoover-Willkie pattern. "America"—helped along by a journalist, this time once again Henry Luce—sought and found yet another outsider, sprung from nativist soil, devoted to simple values, a nonpolitician whose successes far surpassed his humble beginnings. As the script required, he had to be coaxed.

David Dwight Eisenhower (as he was christened) was born in Texas but grew up in Abilene, Kansas, a dot on the vast, featureless plain of mid-America, in a little house where the family of eight had to learn to get along. "The Lord deals the cards," his mother told him, "you play them." His stern father came home and whipped the boys from time to time and laid down hard rules. Mother softened the blows: "Hatred was a futile sort of thing," her grown-up son remembered her saying after he got switched, "because hating anyone or anything meant that there was little to be gained." He took the lesson; their talk was, he said, "one of the most valuable moments of my life . . . to this day I make it a practice to avoid hating anyone."

After high school he almost made it into the naval academy, but it turned out he was overage, so he got into West Point instead, when another candidate failed his physical. Away from home and on his own, he became Dwight David, "Ike" to his friends, who soon were many. His ambition focused on sports. By vigorous eating he got his weight up from 152 to 174 and went out for football; he made the varsity and won his letter—but then tore up his leg in a game and reinjured it in a riding exercise, suddenly ending his sporting life. After a period of despondency, he found a role he could play: umpire.

Through the dull years of the peacetime army, sparked occasionally by such adventures as helping Douglas MacArthur disperse the Bonus Marchers, Ike rose through the ranks on the strength of his organizational abilities. His ideal was duty. His method was cooperation. Once again he was umpire. As Supreme Allied Commander in Europe, General Eisenhower led the greatest cooperative endeavor of his generation. *"The thing you must strive for,"* he wrote Lord Mountbatten, his counterpart in the Southeast Asian theater, *"is the utmost in mutual respect and confidence among the group of seniors making the overall command."* After the war he became president of Columbia University in 1948, a not altogether felicitous union. Two years later he had enough of that and returned to Europe as Supreme Commander of the Allied Forces. As for politics, he had no use for it. He saw himself as a soldier, his country's man, prepared to serve all the people, not to head up some faction thereof.

To the public he was a war hero, to the politicians he was a mystery. No one seemed to know which party he liked. As early as 1945, President Truman sounded him out as a potential Democratic candidate for President. In 1948, Republicans tried to enter his name in primaries and the Americans for Democratic Action led the way in the boom for Ike as a substitute for Truman. In the fall of 1950, Thomas Dewey withdrew from contention, endorsing Eisenhower. By the following summer the trail of Ike-wooers on pilgrimage to Paris grew crowded, as the General tried to run the allied military headquarters there. He backed and filled; too modest to say yes, he was too patriotic to say no. He did let it be known that he was a Republican. At last a "media event" tipped the balance. In February 1952, his supporters put together a giant rally in Madison Square Garden—following a prizefight—and filmed fifteen thousand enthusiasts roaring "We like Ike!" The film was flown to Paris. Ike said it affected him more "than had all the arguments presented by the individuals who had been plaguing me with political questions for many months." His name was entered in the New Hampshire primary and he won hands down. His response combined enthusiasm and obscurity: "Any American who would have that many Americans pay him that compliment would be proud or he would not be an American." Eight days later, in Minnesota where he was not even on the ballot, he got 108,692 write-in votes. *Time* announced that "an Eisenhower boom of tremendous proportions is sweeping across the land."

Henry Luce was out in front of the wave. Luce chose Eisenhower by deduction: "I felt that it was of paramount importance to the United States that a Republican should be put in the White House—almost any Republican," he said. After two decades of Democratic rule, "the American people should have the experience of living under a Republican Administration and discovering that they were not thereby reduced to selling apples on street corners." Surely Ike had the Republican spirit: "Ike was raised a Kansas Republican; he learned at his mother's knee faith in God and adherence to such basic Republican principles as sound money and balanced budgets."

Life began the Presidential year with an editorial making "The Case for Ike." In reply, Ike wrote "Dear Harry" that though the piece had "erred grossly on the side of generosity in your estimate of my capacity," it was "one of the factors that helped influence me to break my policy of complete silence." Luce went to see Ike in Paris, coming away "happily under the agreeable spell of a great personality." Eisenhower talked all around a *Time* reporter sent to interview him; Luce was disappointed—in the reporter. But if Eisenhower was doubtful, *Time* was not. When Ike visited Abilene, *Time* peered into the national psyche and found that people like Ike "in a way they could scarcely explain. . . . He made them proud of themselves and all the half-forgotten best that was in them and in the nation." The "Eisenhower boom of tremendous proportions" swept on into the convention in Chicago where the Eisenhower forces managed to turn a technical argument about which Texas delegation to seat into a moral issue of "fair play." That set up a direct confrontation between Ohio Senator Robert A. Taft—"Mr. Republican," a party regular down to his shoelaces—and Eisenhower, backed by the eastern establishment, convinced, as the *New York Times* put it for them, that "Mr. Taft Can't Win." The first nomination ballot gave Ike the prize, edging out Taft by 595 to 500 before the vote switching started and progressed to unanimity. *Time* and the *Times* and their Manhattan allies had their way. One ballot had transformed the face of the Republican party.

Ike's manager Henry Cabot Lodge welcomed Luce's fervent backing, writing to thank him for being such a "tower of strength." Lodge bought a pile of copies of *Time* and passed them out to every visitor. His letter to Luce said, "One of the lasting satisfactions of this adventure has been the fact that you and I have worked so closely for such a great cause." *Time* editors C. D. Jackson and Emmet Hughes took leave to write for Ike.

Adlai

Eisenhower's opponent was almost a polar opposite—in family, political experience, lifestyle, cast of mind. Born in 1900, Adlai Ewing Stevenson grew up in the good old days before the Great War, child of a leading family in Bloomington, Illinois, namesake of his grandfather, formerly Grover Cleveland's Vice-President, who lived nearby. "The household atmosphere," writes biographer Stuart Gerry Brown, "was one of gaiety mingled with idealism and the ethics of liberal Protestantism." Politics pervaded family conversation. At nine he sat on the speakers' platform when his grandfather and William Jennings Bryan spoke; the latter's sonorous and lengthy address put Adlai "peacefully to sleep," his sister noted. In August 1912, he sat quietly on a porch in New Jersey while his father, Lewis Stevenson, and Woodrow Wilson discussed the coming campaign. In 1916, his father, now a candidate for a full term as Illinois secretary of state, took Adlai to both the Bull Moose and the Republican conventions, though the boy had to go home before the Democrats met to celebrate Wilson's second ascension. He worked in Lewis Stevenson's campaign but came home to organize a college group for the Cox-Roosevelt ticket. In 1924, father and son were again on the convention scene—and working behind it—when the Democrats took 103 ballots to anoint John W. Davis. Adlai's father was the convention's "honorary secretary" that time; when, next time, in 1928, Lewis Stevenson was considered seriously for the Vice-Presidential nomination, Adlai was at his side. By 1933, when Roosevelt came in, young Stevenson, by then an accomplished and experienced Chicago lawyer and president of the Chicago Council on Foreign Relations, was ready to stop watching and start working in public office. "Louie Stevenson's boy" from the farm belt was a natural for the new Agricultural Adjustment Administration; he went to Washington as assistant counsel. In 1940, Navy Secretary Frank Knox tried to get him as his assistant, but Stevenson was by then a leading Midwest light in the Committee to Defend America by Aiding the Allies, battling with Colonel McCormick's *Chicago Tribune*, which blasted him as a "warmonger" and "a bloodthirsty Anglophile." Stevenson held up his end of that struggle until 1941, when he took Knox's offer. He was "assistant to the secretary of the navy"— almost what young Franklin Roosevelt had been in the Wilson administration. From there it was onward and upward, through a series of increasingly responsible wartime assignments that culminated in Stevenson's leading role in constructing the United Nations Organization and his 1948 gubernatorial victory in Illinois by the greatest margin ever. Illinois was one of the tougher states to be governor of, and he had achieved concrete results, as he noted in 1952:

We have eliminated the useless payrollers, put state purchasing on a business-like basis, enacted a great road construction program, raised the sights of the Illinois school system, put the state police on a professional non-political basis, taken the Commerce Commission out of politics, put Illinois out in front in the care and treatment of our mental patients, amended the Constitution, extended aid to tuberculosis hospitals, reorganized many aspects of government, knocked out commercial gambling, enforced the truck weight laws to protect our highways, instilled a new sense of public responsibility among the state's employees—and I could go on and on. And in contrast to most all other states, we have not raised taxes for the general purposes of the state.*

That was the experience and the record that sent Harry Truman—anxious to pass the torch to a winner—in hot pursuit of Stevenson. But Stevenson hung back. It took months of cajoling and persuading to get him back into the fight.

Stevenson had to be dragged into candidacy. The Democratic powers were in desperate search for an alternative to Tennessee Senator Estes Kefauver, who had surprised them with his popularity in the primaries. Truman tried to argue Stevenson into it; at last, a month before the convention in Chicago, Stevenson said he would accept a draft—but pleaded not to be drafted. Not until the fourth day of the convention proceedings did he agree to take the nomination. The bosses wheeled into action and barely got him over.

The Crusade of '52

The Eisenhower 1952 campaign was a "crusade" again, gathering "Citizens for Eisenhower" from every political faith, a process facilitated by the fact that no one had much of an idea what the candidate stood for. Basically, he came out for goodness: "In spite of the difficulties of the problems we have, I ask you this one question: If each of us in his own mind would dwell more upon those simple virtues—integrity, courage, self-confidence, an unshakable belief in the Bible—would not some of these problems tend to simplify themselves?" Stevenson, like Eisenhower, dragooned into candidacy by appeals to his conscience, also leaned on the Bible, accepting nomination despite his prayer to God "to let this cup pass from me," promising the delegates to try "to do justly and to love mercy and to walk humbly with my God." But instead of reiterating simple virtue, Stevenson, a sophisticated Unitarian, set out "to educate and elevate a people," to "talk sense" to them, which he proceeded to do in a campaign of eloquent and forceful addresses, often urging his audiences to an awareness of moral ambiguity. The Eisenhower Crusade was not a lecture series; whatever it was for, it was clearly against Harry Truman's administration, accusing Truman of failing to

* Quoted in Stuart Gerry Brown, *Adlai E. Stevenson* (Woodbury, N.Y.: Barron's Woodbury Press, 1965), p. 73.

stand up to the communists, irresolution in the negotiations to end the war in Korea, and corrupt practices alleged to reach near the Oval Office throne—in short, for "Communism, Korea, and Corruption."

Time's coverage of the campaign lacked ambiguity. Ike appeared as an "amazingly good campaigner," shining with "innate kindliness and modesty," and "great humility and clarity," his "force, sincerity and spontaneity" beaming over crowds of "glowing enthusiasts." Stevenson, with his "nervous laughter," "tried desperately," but his "standard Democratic formula" failed to "rouse his audience." Five months of such prose, accompanied by similarly slanted photographic selections, left readers with little doubt as to where the path of virtue led.

Ike left the hardball politics to Nixon, his running mate, whose taste in campaigning ran to accusations of Stevenson as "Adlai the appeaser," a "Ph.D. graduate of Dean Acheson's cowardly College of Communist Containment." The General held his nose and did what he had to, as he saw it, accepting Nixon's defense against a political bribery charge, welcoming Senator Joseph McCarthy to his campaign train, embracing another senator who had called his old friend General George Marshall "a front man for traitors," somehow all the while maintaining his reputation as a high-minded man of principle. He clinched his case with a promise: "I will go to Korea." In 1952, the Republican pitchmen applied the lessons of broadcasting to the merchandising of Ike and Dick. They saw that "set speeches, by their very nature, cannot impart the real warmth of personality with which both candidates are endowed." Oratory was dead and gone. Instead, "informal intimate television productions addressed directly to the individual American and his family, their problems and their hopes, are necessary to make the most of the ticket's human assets." They helped the star system ride over from the theater into politics. "Don't spend your money on anyone but the candidate," one of them urged back then. "Only the candidate can really get listeners—or the President of the United States—and we don't have him." Television spots, prepared to reach "the height of simplicity," would drive "an all-out saturation blitz" into forty-nine key counties. There would be set speeches, too, also carefully plotted as television mini-dramas:

The drama was conceived in shots: Ike coming through the door at the *back* of auditorium; Ike greeting crowd; people in gallery going wild, craning necks; Ike, escorted, making his way down the aisle; Mamie Eisenhower in box; Ike mounting platform; crowd going wild; Ike at rostrum, waving; Ike looking over toward Mamie; Mamie in box smiling; on cue, Ike holding up arms as if to stop applause; crowd going wild.*

The speech itself, and Ike's departure, were carefully planned for television effect. Privately, Eisenhower disliked the hoopla: "The candidate . . . steps

* Erik Barnouw, *A History Of Broadcasting in the United States*, vol. 2, *The Golden Web: 1933 to 1953* (New York: Oxford University Press, 1968), p. 299.

blithely out to face the crowd, doing his best to conceal with a big grin the ache in his bones, the exhaustion in his mind," he wrote. "I keep telling you fellows I don't like to do this sort of thing. I can think of nothing more boring, for the American public, than to have to sit in their living rooms for a whole half hour looking at my face on their television screens." The advertising men had no quarrel with that. Their strategy called for short, intimate shots of Eisenhower answering questions from ordinary American citizens. The "citizens," carefully selected, were filmed on location. Eisenhower's answers, fifty of them, were put on film in one day in a Manhattan studio, as the General, reading from cue cards, did what he was told. He shook his head: "That an old soldier should come to this . . . ," he said. But if that was what his duty required, he would go along with it for a day. The product was pure commercial guff:

> ANNOUNCER: Eisenhower answers the nation!
> CITIZEN: What about the cost of living, General?
> EISENHOWER: My wife, Mamie, worries about the same thing. I tell her it's our job to change that on November fourth!*

and

> ANNOUNCER: Eisenhower answers the nation!
> CITIZEN: Mr. Eisenhower, can you bring taxes down?
> EISENHOWER: Yes. We will work to cut billions in Washington spending and bring your taxes down.†

Ike himself, like a farmer's daughter suddenly thrust into a debutante ball, let those who knew tell him what to do.

Television played a moralizing role in that season's ethical feature: the drama of Nixon's Secret Fund. To answer charges that he had taken money from California businessmen to boost their fortunes in Washington, Nixon went on the air with a sentimental speech. He had accepted a little dog, "Checkers," for his little girls, but no naughty money, he said. Pressured by Dewey and others to drop Nixon from the ticket, Ike hesitated, but then, as the cameras whirred, met and embraced his wayward mate—"my boy," he called him.

Stevenson, on the other hand, brought to the fifties a public personality clashingly dissonant with the decade's dominant moods. To the strident moralism of 1952, he counterposed irony, even humor, moralism's most threatening enemy. He, too, was for virtue, but also for tolerance and reason. But what Stevenson saw—and undertook to convey—in 1952 was a world fraught with contradiction and ambiguity. The Yahoos were abroad with their simple-minded moral solutions for everything, as were the cold warriors and witch-hunters and race-baiters and the go-getters after their

---

* Ibid.
† Stanley Kelley, Jr., *Professional Public Relations and Political Power* (Baltimore: The Johns Hopkins University Press, 1956), p. 189.

share of the pie. The first problem of 1952, as Stevenson seemed to see it, was to break through the sophomoric shibboleths and certainties blinding a free people to their real possibilities. He set out with his rich vocabulary to preach complexity to a nation hungry for definite, principled reform. His very mode of address conveyed his message, as when he began paragraphs spoken to the American Legion convention with prefaces of uncertainty: "I am not sure that . . . ," "Yet all is not perfect . . . ," "Some of us are reluctant to admit that . . . ," "We have not yet really faced up to the problem . . . ," "And many only partly understand or are loath to acknowledge . . ." "The anatomy of patriotism is complex," he told the patriots. Eisenhower, in contrast, speaking to the same convention, came out loud and clear for his list of principles: "The course of peace is the establishment of conditions that will abolish fear and build confidence. There are three areas of immediate demand upon us. First, America must be militarily and productively strong. . . ." Listening to Stevenson's Chicago acceptance speech at a ranch in Colorado, an aide told Eisenhower, "He's too accomplished an orator; he'll be easy to beat."

The disdain was mutual. The way the Republicans were selling Ike in spot commercials was "the ultimate indignity to the democratic process," Stevenson said. Stevenson would not let himself be merchandised "like a breakfast food." Stevenson backer George Ball said the Republicans had "conceived not an election campaign in the usual sense, but a super colossal, multi-million dollar production designed to sell an inadequate ticket to the American people in precisely the way they sell soap, ammoniated toothpaste, hair tonic and bubble gum." The Democrats did put on a few ads of their own—about $77,000 worth, reminding people of the depression and the benefits of the New Deal. But the candidate himself was out to win with reason, not hucksterism. "For years I have listened to the nauseous nonsense, the pie-in-the-sky appeals to cupidity and greed, the cynical trifling with passion and prejudice and fear; the slander, the fraudulent promises, and the all-things-to-all-men demagoguery that are too much a part of our political campaigns," he said. Like Hoover, though with substantially superior literary results, Stevenson wrote and rewrote his own speeches. Typically he could be seen at the head table of the banquet, scribbling changes in his text as the chairman introduced him. The newspapermen, literary men themselves, liked his language, especially compared with Ike's "little moral lectures" and "dynamic platitudes," as James Reston called them. But they could not help but notice that Eisenhower got the better public reception. Newspaperman Cabell Phillips contrasted the two candidates: "One tries to persuade his hearers, the other to move them." Ike had the better of it, as "he conveys a sense of indignation, of sincere and honest anger over trusts that have been violated, over tragedy induced by stupidity or wickedness." Phillips saw that "the crowd is with him. Idolatry shows in their solemn, upturned faces."

Stevenson on television was a disaster in 1952. He did not use a teleprompter and his timing was terrible—as often as not he went off the air still turning pages as he read on and on. But television was small potatoes in 1952.

On the night before the 1952 election, the advertising crusade reached its climax in a televised "Report to the General on the Work of the Citizens for Eisenhower Committee." The question was "What inspired this spontaneous demonstration of sincere devotion?" The answer was "An old American habit! A matter of principle, a matter of issues!" From a close-up of the General, the camera switched to a living room where a "little group of friends and well wishers" had gathered to watch Ike and Mamie. There followed an incredible hour of flickering impressions—eighty-one switches from live to film and from city to city. Ike's little home in Abilene, Ike with Churchill, Ike with GIs and with his family and a new grandchild. A cash register ringing up higher prices, an influence peddler, Korean war scenes. A Korean vet, stoppped on the street, saying, "Well, all the guys I knew out in Korea figure there's only one man for the job, General, and that's you. We've been getting kind of tired of politicians." Groups from "Tykes for Ike" to "Nisei for Eisenhower-Nixon" were shown. The whole zippy business closed with the Eisenhowers cutting a victory cake. On election eve in 1952, when the Crusade for Eisenhower extravaganza dashed hither and yon, the Democrats presented four set speeches, by Truman, Alben Barkley, John Sparkman, and Stevenson himself, reviewing a campaign in which he had tried, "diligently, day and night, to talk sensibly, honestly and candidly." If he lost, he said, he would take it like a good sport. If he won, he would ask the Lord to help him. Impactwise, as they say, it was no contest. The landslide win the next day seemed to confirm what television could do for politics, given a smiling general, a great deal of money, and a nation in the mood to hear the message. More people had turned out to vote than ever before. Eisenhower's inaugural address in January 1953 began with a prayer that God might give us "the power to discern clearly right from wrong." The first float in the inaugural parade was "God's float."

Once again, the drama of politics as morals played to a nation tired of "politics," ready for a revival of values as personified in a hero of virtue. At long last, Henry Luce saw his man elected. Luce's predictable disillusionment was to cap the case. At Luce's request, Eisenhower appointed Mrs. Luce ambassador to Italy, but eventually Luce got fed up with the administration's "do-nothingism." Time, Inc. would go on to back Ike in 1956, despite such doubts.

The Age of Anxiety

Eisenhower followed up his moralizing victory of 1952 with action: an armistice was finally signed in Korea in July 1953, and a new Red scare began in earnest. Secretary of State John Foster Dulles glowered from the television screens as he applied his militant religious principles to the communist menace, threatening to "unleash" Chiang Kai-shek and his forces on Taiwan to invade the Chinese mainland, promising active support for resistance behind the Iron Curtain, threatening "massive retaliation" against the Soviets if communist aggression broke out anywhere. At home the anti-Red crusade fell into the hands of Senator Joseph McCarthy, slack-jawed, ranting propounder of the paranoid logic of "absolute security." McCarthy said he had discovered "a conspiracy so immense and an infamy so black as to dwarf any previous venture in the history of man." Before long, fearful folk all over America were caught up in the rage against the Reds. Dulles saw to the removal of such dangerous books as *The Selected Works of Tom Paine*—that revolutionary—from State Department libraries; McCarthy went after the Voice of America. J. Edgar Hoover, FBI director, sent memos to the FCC describing license applicants—inaccurately—as "members of the Communist Party or [who] have affiliated themselves sympathetically with the activities of the communist movement." Following a congressional investigation of communism in the film industry in 1947 (by a committee including young Representative Richard M. Nixon), featuring testimony that some films were guilty of "poking fun at our political system," ten Hollywood writers were sentenced to prison. Broadcasting was next: blacklists of supposed Red televisers, from Gypsy Rose Lee to Howard K. Smith, were circulated. Intimidated, the networks set up their own loyalty oaths and "security" investigations. The slippery smear language of McCarthyism—"pinks," "dupes," "stooges"—began to shape casting decisions and news commentaries. Ed Sullivan's variety show put on a dancer accused of being "procommunist in sympathy"; a furor resulted and Sullivan apologized. The whole preposterous business—which nevertheless seemed very serious at the time—led to the discovery that Lucille Ball, star of "I Love Lucy," television's most popular program, actually had been a member of the Communist party in 1936. That was too much; Lucy was quickly "cleared" when it was explained that she had only signed up to please her grandfather.

Even prosperity was, in some way, disconcerting and alarming because it led to spectacular changes in the American way of life. Millions bought homes, cars, college educations, as real income went up 29 percent between 1947 and 1960. Families brought up with iceboxes, brooms, and scrub tubs accumulated refrigerators (96 percent by 1956), vacuum cleaners (67 percent), and washing machines (89 percent). New life itself—babies—sprang forth at incredible rates and survived; the fifties saw a sudden, spectacular surge in population, adding 29 million more people. The newly proliferating psychological and social scientists kept discovering a new malady: "anxiety." Many people, it seemed, were not so much afraid—with that gut-twisting fear of 1932—as they were worried. There may have been some subtle reasons for that, something about guilt after war, something about surpassing your parents, something about a certain wariness that can come along when you get what you want, but there were also material concerns. Debt, for instance. People went on the cuff for big purchases, many for the first time in their lives. In early 1953, only about 6 percent of the GI housing loans were made without down payments; two years later, nearly 40 percent. By 1955 some 60 percent of car buys were on credit—often $100 down and three years to pay. Debt was rising a good deal faster than income. In human terms, that meant many a family was taking big chances. The drift to the suburbs drained taxable wealth from the cities, which began to fill up with poorer people, black and white, many of them strangers to urban life. The strain in the mushrooming suburbs fell on schools, to which the rising middle class naturally turned to ensure that their children would stay middle class. Nationwide, from 1946 to 1956, enrollments in grades one through eight went up 50 percent, which translated into crowded classrooms and a serious teacher shortage. Farther out in the unsuburbed countryside, the farm life Norman Rockwell had pictured as quintessentially American continued its inexorable erosion, leaving the folks who stayed behind feeling left behind.

Work life shifted on its axis. The 1950s saw "service industry" employment surpass work producing the goods to be moved and sold and delivered. Automation abstracted work; "human relations" became the relations of production to worry about. The depression and the war had given millions of women a crack at paying jobs and even promising careers. But expectations were often frustrated; now when father went off each morning to fight the traffic on the way to whatever it was he did downtown, mother stayed back with the children, who, like electrons in the nuclear family, had to be protected from deviating influences and spun off in the car to various enriching experiences. If father was to rise and shine in the ranks of management, mother had to help see to his appearance as an up-and-coming fellow with the right attitudes and a wife just as gung ho as he was for the Company.

Such relatively delicate anxieties were not yet the privilege of other millions left out of the progressive statistics. City blacks, Appalachian miners, mill workers in fading New England towns, and the rural poor of the South—perhaps one of five Americans—got along on less than what the government said it took to subsist. They would not be "discovered" until the sixties, by John Kennedy and Hubert Humphrey campaigning in West Virginia, by Michael Harrington's account of The Other America and Kenneth Clark's Dark Ghetto. If in the fifties they were scattered and invisible to prospering white people, who, after all, lacked occasion for social intercourse with them, the poor could now see how the other half lived—how "ordinary" Americans supposedly lived. A great many poor people scraped up enough to buy television sets; by the end of the decade more homes had television than had indoor plumbing or running water. There the poor saw a casual affluence that mocked their daily grind, a sense of assumed independence totally foreign to their feudal condition. They were used to fear;

knowledge of the gap between their life style and "America's" heightened their anxiety.

Blacks had special cause to worry. After economic gains in the late thirties and forties, the fifties brought a downturn in relative income compared to that of whites. Especially in the Confederate South, blacks got the short end of everything, and as late as 1957 only one in four even had a chance to vote. In the North, those few blacks who could afford to move to suburbia ran smack up against a wall of economic terror: white folks had moved out there to have a nice, safe place for themselves and they were not about to jeopardize their tenuous hold on progress by letting in such foreigners. Thus one white citizen of Levittown, Pennsylvania, the model suburb, said of a black father who wanted to be his neighbor, "[He is] probably a nice guy, but every time I look at him I see $2,000 drop off the value of my house."

On the civil-rights front Ike was not an aggressive soldier. He made a move here and there along the route to racial justice. He saw to the quiet desegregation of military installations and veterans' hospitals and the District of Columbia. Then in 1954 the Supreme Court dropped a bomb. Drawing on social science research, the Justices unanimously declared separate schools for black and white children, however equal they might be in facilities and the like—and usually they were not—"inherently unequal" *because* separate. They spoke for the Founders, for the Constitution. To most of the country, it was revolutionary doctrine—not because America had believed otherwise, but because actual social behavior might be affected. Blacks who thought the Court had ushered in the Year of Jubilee were quickly disillusioned. Eisenhower thought the decision was wrong: "I don't believe you can change the hearts of men with laws and decisions," he said. He seemed disinclined to carry out the mandate of the Court. He did nothing when, early in 1956, the University of Alabama expelled one young black girl as a threat to public safety. Or when race riots broke out that election-year fall in towns in Texas, Arkansas, and Tennessee. Or when that same year a young black Baptist minister, Martin Luther King, Jr., led a successful bus boycott against separate and unequal seats for blacks in Montgomery, Alabama. Racial tensions heightened the country's nervous unease.

What all this added up to as the 1956 election approached was a sense of fragility and vulnerability and uncertainty in the face of massive social change. Looming over the immediate threats to quiet luxury was the threat of instant death. Julius and Ethel Rosenberg were put to death in Sing Sing prison, a few months into Eisenhower's first term, for passing nuclear secrets to Soviet agents. In 1955, Soviet pilots succeeded in dropping the first hydrogen bomb. American pilots could not match that until May 1956. People, already worried about their jobs and kids and homes and how a person was supposed to act in this crazy new country, had the Bomb to worry about as well, and the possibility that the Reds might steal away the country's power. Pollster Samuel Lubell discovered, as the 1956 election approached, "Rarely

in American history has the craving for tranquility and moderation commanded more general public support."

Cooling the News

The coincidence that television grew up—suddenly, like Jack's bean-
stalk—in the fertilizer of the Eisenhower years shaped its meaning. It blossomed out of the postwar troubles and flowered most luxuriantly just as the
country found its need for another quiet time an urgent psychological
necessity. In 1952, radio still had the larger audience. There were only about
fifteen million television sets out, though broadcasters assumed the viewers
were "influentials." By the 1956–57 season, forty million homes had television—more than four out of five homes—with the average set turned on five
hours a day. Revenues for television stations more than tripled in those few
years, and political party advertising spending through broadcasting shot up
by 62 percent. A television license became, as the saying went, a license to
print your own money. The boom was swinging as it had for radio; television
as a commercial medium, addressing an enormous mass audience, took in
riches beyond the fondest dreams of avarice. Thus it was even more important than ever to offer people what it was thought they wanted and not to offend anybody. Through those burgeoning years, television's domination by
entertainment programming could hardly have been exceeded. For every
hour of the real world, there were at least a dozen hours of the imaginary
one. It was not until the 1960s that the now familiar half hour of evening
network news came along, not until the late 1970s that intensive local news
was appended. And again, as had happened with radio, commercials advertising every sort of relief and reward proliferated like mosquitoes in the summertime. And again, those who paid the piper increasingly insisted on calling the tune, so that before long identifying the "author" of anything on
television became well-nigh impossible. Teams made television. In the
1950s they made cowboy shows like "Gunsmoke" and "Bonanza," with a
little news at the edges of the day. The Red scare helped create an atmosphere of tension and fear in a highly intimidatable medium. On taking office, Eisenhower appointed one Joe McCarthy devotee to the Federal Communications Commission and another later in 1953. Edward R. Murrow
managed to get three excellent news documentaries shown: on an air force
lieutenant thrown out of the service because his father and sister had al-
legedly read "subversive newspapers" and engaged in other "questionable"
activities; one famous one on McCarthy; and another on the controversial
nuclear physicist J. Robert Oppenheimer. Each time Murrow and Fred
Friendly, his producer, had to buck enormous management pressures. The
network refused to advertise the programs; Murrow and Friendly bought
ads with their own money. Murrow was called on the carpet by the network
president. Before long his pioneering "See It Now" series was eased off the

air and Murrow became the host of "Person to Person"—charming little visits with celebrities in their very own homes. As television became immensely popular and lucrative, Murrow-type news got shorter and shorter shrift—a sideline to the quiz shows like "Twenty-Questions" (animal, vegetable, mineral) and the scandal-ridden "$64,000 Question," and more cowboy shows to boost the ratings.

But Murrow left an example later broadcasters would come back to. The medium need not confine itself to banalities and to fragments of real life scattered through the newscasts. Particularly when television focused on events beyond its studios, showing important developments in sustained, narrative sequences, it could preach with a vengeance. In years to come, from the Army-McCarthy hearings to the civil-rights marches to the Watergate drama, television would rise to the moral occasion, putting aside for the moment at least its traditional offering of corn and pap. Such moments would be few and far between, for the tradition was strong.

As Murrow faded out, broadcast news faded back into its old coloration, mixing reporting and entertainment. "The Today Show," invented by genial Dave Garroway, typified the shift. Garroway was first noticed beyond his circle of friends when, covering army maneuvers put on by Lieutenant Colonel Dwight D. Eisenhower in 1940, he scooped John Daly and Eric Sevareid by picking up on his microphone a platoon of plowboys singing "Onward Christian Soldiers," as they marched in the waning light of the setting sun. As a disc jockey in Pearl Harbor, and after the war in Chicago, Garroway developed an easy style—"as though I was talking to a friend over a highball," he said. In 1948, NBC put him on television for half an hour every Sunday night. He wondered if that was a promotion. "Television was kind of a nuisance," he said. "We thought of radio as hot stuff." On January 14, 1952, ten days after Henry Cabot Lodge the younger entered Eisenhower as a candidate in the New Hampshire primary, "The Today Show" flickered on at 7:00 A.M., with Garroway as host.

From the first, the designer of "Today" a visionary show-business impresario named Pat Weaver, sensed what might suit the television audience:

> We cannot and should not try to build a show that will make people sit down in front of their sets and divert their attention to the screen. We want America to shave, to eat, to dress, to get to work on time. But we also want America to be well informed, to be amused, to be lightened in spirit and in heart, and to be reinforced in inner resolution through knowledge.*

Weaver saw Garroway as "a calm relaxed guy" who would be "the news center of the world." Seated behind a big, horseshoe-shaped desk surrounded by clocks showing the time in various world capitals, Garroway announced "Today in two minutes." Headlines and photos flashed by from the morning newspapers—"Indochina Rebels Get Red-Built Radar Guns: Down

* Quoted in Robert Metz, *The Today Show* (Chicago: Playboy Press, 1977), p. 25.

Ten French Planes" a picture of Justice William O. Douglas saying he did not want to be President, a golf prize-winner being kissed by Bob Hope, and the like. "That's Today in capsule. Cut to two minutes," said Garroway. "That is the day you are going to live." The reviews were unencouraging. John Crosby wondered in the *Herald-Tribune*, "Who the hell wants to know what time it is in Tokyo?" But in its first two weeks "Today" received 65,000 letters. A woman wrote in to plead, "And please, Mr. Garroway, say something about the kiddies—they've got to get dressed and get out to school or they'll be late." A nurse wrote that Garroway was "someone wonderful to have into the house for breakfast." Garroway came on like the family's bachelor uncle, a mildly intellectual but egregiously easygoing fellow in a bow tie and spectacles, moving about the set with a kind of lumbering grace. Nothing rattled his aplomb. Right after a moving obituary, for instance, there he would be again, introducing a pretty girl as "Miss E. Z. Pop" or "Miss Concrete Life Preserver," or hokey visual attractions such as an underwater weather girl and a highly intelligent chimpanzee named J. Fred Muggs. Garroway built a following. In 1954, "Today," according to *Billboard*, had become "probably the largest-grossing venture in the history of show business within a period of one year"—beyond even *Gone With The Wind.*

Garroway the newsgiver also gave commercials, though he drew the line at eating the products after once sampling cake icing that turned out to be shaving cream. He stuck with "Today" year after year, until at last he fell apart. Like many another newsman, he began to think he understood the events he reported, began to believe he had answers to the big problems, began to deliver himself of sentient solutions on the air. When nothing changed, he felt the frustration of one only paid to be funny. Becoming more and more depressed and demanding, at last one day he lay down on the floor shortly before air time and said he would not get up until his demands were met. NBC let him go. He was replaced by three journalists—newsmen—John Chancellor, Edwin Newman, and Frank Blair—at celebrity salaries to compensate for the weird way of life the show forced on them: sleeping through the afternoon and early evening, rising in the black of night, isolated as a little band of midnight oilers cut off from ordinary social intercourse. Hugh Downs took over after a year, at half a million dollars, exuding a Jimmy Stewart charm, a nice, easygoing young fellow mothers could identify as just the type their daughters ought to marry. "Today" lasted, progressing from Frank McGee to Barbara Walters. Sincere young Tom Brokaw took over on August 30, 1976, with an interview: the camera panned across a plowed field in Georgia to Jimmy Carter, speaking softly from a rocking chair on a porch. The success of "Today" naturally led to imitation on the other two networks and the style spilled over into "happy talk" news on local stations, in which zippy young fellows and girls in blazers wisecrack their way through the horrors and hopes of the day. Television had inherited radio's easygoing, harmonizing mode.

Television offered one slight but appealing advantage over radio: a look at the faces and body language of the newsteller and, often, the newsmakers, themselves bringing across an Eisenhower in a richer, more human, intimate, almost touching way. What was lost was a kind of literature: Murrow describing the English on the radio, for example, could be better drama than the real English on television. What was gained was a certain realism: one could get a sense of the whole person as an embodied spirit, could catch him in the act of making up his mind, choosing his words, defining himself. Television pictured what before had to be depicted—the set, the surround, the actor in motion. With respect to news, that was a marginal plus. For particularly in the relatively pacific Eisenhower years, but also in most periods of "normal" life, most news of significance is not readily conveyed by pictures, as anyone knows who has had the sound go off during a news program. The exceptions leap to mind: a coronation, a Presidential funeral, a battle, a space shot, a riot, a fire, a storm. They remain exceptions. Day to day, the news that may make a difference is to be found in the turning of minds, not the motions of bodies. Yet television abhorred "talking heads" as though thought were a vacuum.

Selling Eisenhower

Republican National Chairman Leonard Hall advised an audience in 1955, "We must choose able and personable candidates who can 'sell themselves' because TV has changed the course of campaigns." Ike had proved out on television, as had Richard Nixon. But Eisenhower was no more anxious to continue as President than he had been to begin. Near the end of his first year in office, Ike wrote his brother Milton, "If ever a second time I should show any signs of yielding to persuasion, please call in the psychiatrist—or even better the sheriff." Then on September 23, 1955, he suffered a severe heart attack. The urgent question was whether he would live, the idea that he would run again the following year seemed out of the question. As he slowly recovered, Americans tuned in to Eisenhower performances on television much as they would to a session with Marcus Welby, M.D.—not so much to hear what he said as to see how he looked. By November he felt better. But not until February 29, 1956, did his sense of duty overcome his personal reluctance; on television from the Oval Office, he told the people he would run. That drama over, he made a second fateful decision, to keep Nixon on the ticket as his running mate. On June 8, Ike went into serious surgery for ileitis, and again the medical bulletins dominated the news. Again the public waited for a look at him; when he reappeared he looked fine, with the old smile and vigorous posture.

The Republicans gathered in San Francisco on August 22 to celebrate their allegiance to Ike. Nothing else happened. Bored newsmen got one good little story: a delegate from Nebraska, just for the hell of it, nominated a nonexistent "Joe Smith" to take Nixon's place on the ticket. Scurrying news-men invaded the floor, but no Joe Smith was found. It was a minor episode in a congratulatory festival.

Eisenhower and his managers readied a new-style campaign. Television, a relatively minor factor in 1952, *was* the Eisenhower campaign of 1956. As in 1952, the Republicans hired a big-time advertising agency, Batten, Barton, Durstine & Osborn, fabulously successful touters of the wares of United States Steel, Du Pont, General Electric, and American Tobacco, to see to it that the Ike product moved off the shelves and into the shopping bags. Noting that in 1952 Ike's opponent had caught hell from viewers for preempting their favorite shows ("I Love Lucy, I like Ike, drop dead"), the admen persuaded wealthy and sympathetic sponsors to run their programs five minutes short so a bit of Eisenhower appeal could be shown with minimal disruption of the entertainment fare. The Democrats, in contrast, could hardly find an ad agency to take their account.

By 1956, with nearly five times the hundred television stations of 1952, the Eisenhower campaign for peace, prosperity, and unity at home focused on the new mass audience. The planning was sophisticated, the product was simple—purposefully so. The emerging national sample surveys, some of them run by academic social scientists determined to discern in a fundamental way who "the People" were on whom democracy was based, turned up shocking findings. The long and the short of it was that an enormous number of Americans were ignorant of their government, indifferent to political affairs, and illiterate in the very language of political discourse. Millions of eligible voters did not know even the rough shape of the Constitution, how elections worked, who their representatives or senators were, what the parties stood for—even when such questions were posed in the simplest possible way. When a pollster appeared on the citizen's doorstep offering alternative opinions to be checked, the citizen would cooperate by choosing one, thus conveying the impression that about 70 percent of the public had an "opinion" on nearly anything. But when the questions did not offer answers—questions such as, "Is there anything in particular about Eisenhower that might make you want to vote for him?"—typically nearly half the respondents stood mute, answerless, unopinionated, don't knows. The standard vocabularies so readily bandied about by the editorialists, such as their calculations of degrees of "liberalism" and "conservatism" along the "left" to "right" continuum, passed right over the heads of huge segments of the democracy; they did not think in those terms. A surface allegiance to "freedom of speech" and other generalities, shared by nearly everyone, crumbled when the questioning moved from vague abstractions to simple, concrete cases.

As science progressed, scholars began to inquire how people were using the media. Network executives and their advertising clients kept close track of "ratings," which they took to show millions of families "watching" television for long hours every day, their sense glued to their sets. But, in fact, the ratings merely showed how many sets were tuned to which channels, not whether or not anyone was watching or, if watching, taking in what was conveyed. It seems likely that in the early days of television, people in large numbers did sit still and stare at the screen. It was small and a little blurry and jumpy and it was a new presence in the house. One could remember the early days of radio at home, when the family sat around in the living room, listening to sounds emerging from the old cathedral-style receivers. But radio had become household Muzak. Television was on the way to the same destination. Studies—competent studies—showed that a great many people who had just "watched" the evening news could not remember what they had seen or heard shortly after the program was over. It was a chilling thought.

Such revelations called forth the predictable indignations. The schools were lying down on the job. The politicans talked gibberish. The media obfuscated everything. Television took much of this heat, because the social scientists found out that it was (by and large, on the average) the medium of choice of the ill-informed, the political ignoramuses, while the better-informed relied on print.

The Eisenhower admen brushed aside the indignations and got on with the business of meeting that audience where it was. The message had to be simple, emotional, dramatic, and personal. Eisenhower cooperated, willingly this time; unable to go on the road in an active campaign, he took to television with a new enthusiasm. Building on the lessons of 1952, his managers got him up front in a friendly format. In a typical television performance, carefully selected "citizens" tossed great puffy softball questions for their President to pole out of the ball park. A "discerning Democrat": "Will you tell the nation who is in charge, sir?" A UAW member: "Some fellers feel that the Democratic party is on their side. I happen to know that you are on their side even more so. . . . And I wish, Mr President, that you would explain and enlighten my buddies back home as to your stand on labor unions and the things that they are inclined to do?" A New York State dairy farmer: "What does the soil bank offer a farmer from the Northeast?" A black Chicago pastor: "Will you be an ambassador of good will to all the homes in America, so that we can be one nation indivisible?"

Ike himself came up with the perfect final touch. Told the program was running out of time, he said, "I'm going to stay here as long as anyone wants to. If we go off the air, why all right. But I'll stay here because I'm thoroughly enjoying this." Garroway could not have done it better.

Talking Sense Again

After the 1952 Democratic debacle Stevenson had continued to speak out; he rose to the top of the Democratic preference polls and announced his candidacy for 1956 early—in November 1955. He set out to beat his principal opponent, Kefauver again, campaigning in a coonskin cap. Stevenson let New Hampshire pass, but when Kefauver beat him in Minnesota, he had had enough: "I am tired of losing elections—I don't intend to lose any more!" Asked if that meant he would go handshaking in the Kefauver style, he allowed, "Well, a certain identity *is* established between the shaker and the shakee!" By the California primary, Professor Stevenson had gone all out to meet the American middle class. In Los Banos, he rode into town on a strawberry roan, decked out in blue jeans and denim jacket with tasseled shoulders, a red string tie and a ten-gallon hat, preceded by Miss Merced County. In grand stylistic irony, he there encountered Kefauver—in a tailored, Swiss silk suit, calmly puffing an expensive cigar. The parade over, Stevenson told his handlers to "get me out of this ridiculous costume" the image-makers had talked him into. A Stevenson-Kefauver debate followed, Adlai as usual penning notes till the last minute. He gave them a lecture on farm prices, sprinkled with witticisms over the farmers' heads and with dogged tries at the common touch—Ike "a-stumblin' and a-fallin' " and the like. On he went, well past the limit, quoting a paradoxical Scripture passage and an ironical reference to farmers as "parasites." Kefauver, in his turn, noting that the day was Mother's Day, and Sunday to boot, said he would make no partisan remarks, and observed "I never saw more beautiful children in my life" than were there. Going on he said the day was "one of compassion, and if we could get that message across to the world, why, ah think everythin' would be all right." He drew to a close: "I would like to end right there, and then step among you and shake your hands. I would like to pay a humble tribute to those of you *who have lost fine mothers!*" Nevertheless, Stevenson won in California, two to one over Kefauver. In Florida he posed on courthouse steps, awkwardly holding a broom to symbolize sweeping Washington clean. The televisers persuaded him that the indignity of five-minute commercials fell short of the ultimate; he acted in a series of them, as "The Man from Libertyville."

Before the convention, Kefauver capitulated and after Stevenson's name was placed in nomination by young Senator John F. Kennedy, he won on the first ballot. In a surprise move, he threw the Vice-Presidential nomination open to the convention's choice. Kennedy tried and lost, to coonskin Kefauver. Stevenson's acceptance speech signaled a fighting campaign. Gone were the apologies of 1952: "I accept your nomination and your program. And I pledge to you every resource of mind and strength I possess to make your deed today a good one for our country and for our party. Four years ago I stood in this same place and uttered those same words to you. But four years ago we lost. This time we will win!"

Stevenson was out of sync. Radically misreading the climate of the country, he said, "Tonight, after an interval of marking time and aimless drifting, we are on the threshold of another great, decisive era." He called for a "New America." He would "get America moving again." Against the advice of his close advisers, he lambasted Eisenhower on—of all things—military issues: he championed an end to hydrogen-bomb testing and the draft. Ike called it "a national theatrical gesture." Stevenson was, in effect, a prophet, but prophets are seldom elected President. Once more Stevenson was running against the grain, this time against the overwhelming national sentiment for "peace, prosperity and unity at home"—and for Ike, who symbolized all three. Right on to the end he bucked the tide: "I ask your support not because I offer promises of peace and prosperity but because I do not. . . . I ask your support not because I say that all is well, but because I say that we must work hard, with tireless dedication, to make the small gains out of which, we may hope, large gains will ultimately be fashioned." And in the ultimate misunderstanding of what the fifties were meaning to American millions, Stevenson said, "I ask your support not in the name of complacency but in the name of anxiety."

The contrast between the candidates was not a matter of ideology. Stevenson was no more a radical than Eisenhower. Indeed they both came out four-square for moderation. Ike said:

> The middle of the road is derided by all of the right and the left. They deliberately misrepresent the central position as a neutral, wishy-washy one. Yet here is the truly creative area within which we may obtain agreement for constructive social action compatible with basic American principles, and with the just aspirations of every sincere American.*

Stevenson said to an old friend, "Mrs. Roosevelt, I understand that an opponent of mine—and I give you one guess as to who he is—has referred to me as a moderate. I had not realized that this word was an epithet or an accusation." Mrs. Roosevelt cooperatively responded, "As a matter of fact, moderation is a wise word. . . ." Thus these two moderates, both reluctant candidates, had much in common. But as the challenger, it was up to Stevenson to demonstrate his differences. His televised addresses, helped by such brilliant writers as John Hersey, Arthur Schlesinger, Jr., and John Kenneth Galbraith, glittered with occasional literary gems—but every time he seemed to get hold of an issue it crumbled in his hands. Complexity turned on him: he wanted hydrogen-bomb testing stopped without requiring inspection, because a test could be detected anyway from afar. As for lesser atomic weapons, he did not say. Eisenhower had but to sweep over the complications and stand on his superior military prowess and judgment. The health issue—Eisenhower as an ill, "part-time President"—revived, but there on the television set was Ike, beaming salubriously. Fire was directed at Nixon, that "man of many masks"—"the only human being I have ever actually hated," Stevenson once said in private. In public he scathed the Old

* Quoted in John M. Blum et al., *The National Experience: A History of The United States*, 2d ed. (New York: Harcourt, Brace & World, 1968), p. 790.

Nixon, "a man whose greatest political talent is a mastery of personal innuendo, who cries 'treason' and spreads fear and doubt, a man who uses language to conceal issues rather than explore them, a man whose trademark is slander." But how could that be? Here on the television screen was Nixon the Statesman, the man who had filled in for Ike when he got sick, a calm and earnest gentleman, gently advising "The kind of people we are counts much more than what we say."

But none of these blunted charges cut much ice with the people in 1956. Stevenson went out railing against the country's political climate, sneering at "this mealymouthed Republican campaign talk, this squeaky chorus—peace, prosperity and progress." Eisenhower had a different vision: traveling America, "We see a glow of happiness on people's faces. They are believing something. They are holding a faith."

Stevenson tried to get a partisan fight over issues underway at a time when the nation wanted ease and harmony. Worst of all, he was eloquent. Both Truman and Eisenhower came right out of the middle of the middle class—and sounded that way, but in the age of Lawrence Welk, Stevenson sounded like the Budapest String Quartet. He managed to get himself typecast as a namby-pamby "egghead" with delusions of literary grandeur. Harry Truman called him "a country-club, tweedy snob." Eisenhower recalled friends who saw Stevenson as "a real lemon." Ike thought the 1956 Stevenson-Kefauver ticket "the weakest they could have named." Stevenson had a way with words, but if that were to be the criterion, "we ought to elect Ernest Hemingway," Ike said.

The real Adlai Stevenson had a record that belied the effete image thrust upon him by political opponents. Nor was he, as it had become fashionable to conclude, a Hamlet-like neurotic perpetually testing the world's tolerance for his indecision. Years later it was this supposedly weak and wordy snob who, as United States ambassador to the United Nations during the Cuban missile crisis, let the Soviet ambassador have it between the eyes: "You are in the courtroom of world opinion. You have denied [the missiles] exist, and I want to know if I understand you correctly. I am prepared to wait for my answer until hell freezes over."

"All Men of Good Will"

As if the gods of history wanted to take no chances, world events nailed down the Eisenhower victory with exquisite timing. On October 21, Soviet Premier Bulganin, no doubt trying to be helpful, praised Stevenson's test ban idea—which had approximately the effect of the Mafia endorsing a candidate for police chief. On October 23, Hungarian rebels, who had taken seriously Dulles's talk of liberation, stormed through the streets of Budapest demanding an end to Soviet tyranny. Soviet tanks and troops roared in. Days of street fighting followed before the last resistance was crushed on November 4, as forlorn patriots on rooftops scanned the skies for American help. On

October 29, Israel invaded Egypt's Sinai Peninsula; Egypt in July had seized the Suez Canal. Ceasefire pleas from France and Britain were rejected—so France and Britain bombed Egypt on October 31 and landed troops on November 5 and 6. The United States denounced that; the United Nations called for a cease-fire. But the whole thing was up in the air on election day, November 6. This was no time for amateurs in the Presidency. Rather a time for steady Ike, a man of peace.

Eisenhower won in a walk. His plurality numbered more than nine million votes, better by a third than he had done in 1952. Significantly, he ran ahead of the Republican congressional ticket by more than 6,500,000 votes. Walter Johnson, a vigorous and early Stevenson backer, gave Ike due credit:

Without Eisenhower as the head of the Republic party, the venom that disgraced democratic politics in the closing years of Truman's presidency would have been rife in the nation. He purged national life of rancor. And by presenting himself continuously as standing at the moderate and reasonable center of American life, he was able to tune in on the deepest instincts of the people, who, at this stage in their history, desired pause, comfort and repose; a mood which reflected the spectacular expansion of the middle class base of American life.*

Walter Lippmann was not so sure:

The campaign has been clean and decent, but not enlightening or interesting. It takes two to bring on a debate, and the President refused to be provoked into debating anything. Since there was a great contented majority behind him, he did not have to admit there was any issue to debate. . . .†

But it was Dwight Eisenhower, in an inaugural address markedly contrasting to his last one, who put into words the hope for harmony and national union that anxious America wanted to hear:

Before all else, we seek, upon our common labor as a nation, the blessings of Almighty God. And the hopes in our hearts fashion the deepest prayers of our whole people.

May we pursue the right without self-righteousness.

May we know unity without conformity.

May we grow in strength without pride in self.

May we, in our dealings with all peoples of the earth, ever speak and serve justice.

And so shall America—in the sight of all men of good will—prove true to the honorable purposes that bind and rule us as a people in all this time of trial through which we pass.‡

---

* Walter Johnson, *1600 Pennsylvania Avenue: Presidents and the People, 1929–1959* (Boston: Little, Brown, 1960), pp. 317–18.

† Quoted in Charles A. H. Thomson and Frances M. Shattuck, *The 1956 Presidential Campaign* (Washington: The Brookings Institution, 1960), p. 321.

‡ *Inaugural Addresses of the Presidents of the United States* (USGPO, 1961), p. 263.

Eisenhower yanked a substantial part of the Grand Old Party out of its troglodyte negativism into the modern age. Eisenhower was a pragmatist, and not having been excessively educated in the reactionary version of Republicanism, he was open enough to see that a return to the days before the New Deal was not a live option. Under Ike, Republicanism slid toward the center, where it had a chance to win. Eisenhower demonstrated that a President could attain and sustain popularity of Rooseveltian proportions, not as a vigorous, activist experimenter in the Roosevelt fashion, but as a presiding presence letting the national nature take its course. The legacy of his calm would be the chaos of the next decade, chaos that, ironically, would make many long for another period of peace and prosperity. President-watchers, reared in the Roosevelt era, only slowly grasped the virtues of Presidential restraint. Not many paid enough attention, for example, to Eisenhower's warning, as he stepped down from the Presidency, against "the recurring temptation to feel that some spectacular and costly action could become the miraculous solution to current difficulties" in a revolutionary world, against "a huge increase in newer elements in our defense," against "the acquisition of unwarranted influence, whether sought or unsought, by the military-industrial complex." His successor, Fighting Jack Kennedy, gave the military 27 percent more money in his first budget than Eisenhower had granted them in his last. Ike's lesson was slow to sink in: from time to time, less vigor in the White House might be a virtue.

Yet a profounder lesson from Eisenhower's political life instructed ambitious candidates and their managers who, in future years, would leaf back through history for hints on how to get and keep the White House. The Eisenhower phenomenon showed as never before how personal stardom could substitute for party unity. Roosevelt had been a personal star, but he came out of his party and he brought his party along with him. Willkie had been a personal star, but Willkie lost. Eisenhower the popular President soared way on out past his party, leaving droves of Republican candidates behind among the defeated as he won an unprecedented victory. He sustained his popularity better than any other postwar President. He took that affection with him when he left the White House. Long after he was President, Eisenhower's opinion of Presidential contenders would count heavily in the calculations of those who chose the nominees. Had he used the authority to good effect, the nation might have been spared the distortions of Barry Goldwater and the disaster of Richard Nixon.

14

Richard Nixon 1968

ISENHOWER, the conciliator of 1956, gave us Nixon, the conciliator of 1968. In between, Presidential politics changed at least as radically as they had between Harding and Roosevelt. The anxiety of the mid-fifties deepened to the desperation of the mid-sixties. By the time Nixon reappeared—apparently having undergone a personality transplant—responsible observers saw the American union ripping itself to shreds. From sea to shining sea, every Presidential candidate, of whatever ideological stripe or personal predilection, cried out for order and peace. In the end, the "peacemaker" we chose in 1968 delivered massive destruction and eventual rout in Vietnam, the most divisive administration of the twentieth century, and our first historical example of a President resigning in the face of certain impeachment and conviction. The Nixon win of 1968 turned out to be a truce, a temporary tactical pause between the gut-fighting Nixon of the past and future. The way he brought that off—by the most adroit and systematic manipulation of the mass media yet seen—is an object lesson in the perils of modern democracy.

On the night of August 7, 1968, as Chairman Gerald Ford, representative from Michigan, introduced Spiro Agnew, governor of Maryland, to nominate Richard Nixon for President at the Republican convention, mayhem exploded across town in Miami's black ghetto, Liberty City. Seventy policemen armed with shotguns moved against the rioters, part of a coordinated security force more numerous than the entire collection of the Republican delegates. The next night it happened again, and the next. By then three blacks had been shot dead and six hundred soldiers had marched in to quell the looting and sniper fire. None of that came anywhere near Nixon's 200-room headquarters in a beach hotel, except on television. But it suited Agnew's rhetoric as he recommended "a man who had the courage to rise up from the depths of defeat six years ago and make the greatest political comeback in history. When a nation is in crisis and history speaks firmly to that nation," Agnew said, "it needs a man to match the time." The balloting went forward. Nixon—tan, serene—sat in an easy chair in the middle of his room, chatting with Eisenhower's son as they watched the voting on television while a television crew filmed their reactions. Wisconsin did it: 667 votes. Mrs. Nixon walked over and patted him on the shoulder and walked off camera. Nelson Rockefeller phoned. "Nice of him to call," said Nixon.

The next night Nixon began his acceptance speech with a confident smile: "Sixteen years ago I stood before this convention to accept your nomination as the running mate of one of the greatest Americans of our time or any time—Dwight D. Eisenhower." Then the applause. Then the prediction of victory. Then:

> General Eisenhower, as you know, lies critically ill in Walter Reed Hospital tonight. I have talked, however, with Mrs. Eisenhower on the telephone. She tells me that his heart is with us. She says that there is nothing that he lives for, and there is nothing that would lift him more than for us to win in November. And I say let's win this one for Ike.

Then to the message, the theme for the campaign:

> As we look at America, we see cities enveloped in smoke and flame. We hear sirens in the night. We see Americans dying on distant battlefields abroad. We see Americans hating each other; fighting each other; killing each other at home. And as we see and hear these things, millions of Americans cry out in anguish: Did we come all this way for this? Did American boys die in Normandy and Korea and in Valley Forge for this?
>
> Listen to the answers to these questions. It is another voice, it is a quiet voice in the tumult of the shouting. It is the voice of the great majority of Americans, the forgotten Americans, the non-shouters, the non-demonstrators. They're not racists or sick; they're not guilty of the crime that plagues the land; they are black, they are white; they're native born and foreign born; they're young and they're old. They work in American factories, they run American businesses. They serve in government; they provide most of the soldiers who die to keep it free. They give drive to the spirit of America. They give lift to the American dream. They give steel to the backbone of America. They're good people. They're decent people; they work and they save and they pay their taxes and they care.

Thus the diagnosis: chaos. Thus the prescription: quiet. Thus the invocation of the good citizens as the bearers of the needed values. Nixon went on, choosing peace and order at every stop. Amid his rhetorical echoes of Kennedy and Martin Luther King sounded an echo of Franklin Roosevelt: "We shall re-establish freedom from fear in America, so that America can take the lead in re-establishing freedom from fear in the world." And then the peroration: the love of children.

> And tonight, therefore, as we make this commitment, let us look into our hearts, and let us look down into the faces of our children. Is there anything in the world that should stand in their way? None of the old hatreds mean anything when you look down into the faces of our children. In their faces is our hope, our love and our courage.

And at the last, the singling out of a special child, who grew up to meet his destiny: to guide his people to peace. Once upon a time that child . . .

hears a train go by. At night he dreams of far away places where he'd like to go. It seems like an impossible dream. But he is helped on his journey through life. A father who had to go to work before he finished the sixth grade sacrificed everything he had so that his sons could go to college. A gentle Quaker mother with a passionate concern for peace, quietly wept when he went to war but she understood why he had to go. A great teacher, a remarkable football coach, an inspirational minister encouraged him on his way. A courageous wife and loyal children stood by him in victory and also in defeat. And in his chosen profession of politics, first there were scores, then hundreds, then thousands, and finally millions who worked for his success. And tonight he stands before you, nominated for President of the United States of America. You can see why I believe so deeply in the American dream.

It was hard to quarrel with Nixon's diagnosis. Back in January, Johnson's case had seemed so plausible—if not morally, at least militarily. Who could doubt that half a million fighting Americans, equipped with the world's most sophisticated engines of human destruction, would bring to heel a scattered mélange of ragged peasants running around in the jungle with their rusty rifles? Over the years since Johnson had begun to turn a minor mission into an all-out massacre, the doubters had been preaching against him, their case buttressed from time to time by television scenes of American soldiers casually setting fire to a peaceful village, chasing old men and women and children, laughing about their inability to distinguish enemy soldiers from terrified civilians. But until the Tet offensive of 1968, few could really doubt the eventual outcome. Television, the "consensus medium" as CBS's William Paley called it, and Lyndon Johnson, the consensus President, got along; with very rare exceptions, the scenes that came into American living rooms showed our planes taking off from our carriers, our boys on the march up the highways, our headquarters in the easy bustle of Saigon. At NBC and ABC, producers instructed editors to cut out pictures of bleeding bodies because they would disturb viewers at dinner time. In any case, the Viet Cong was given to attacking at night, when filming was impossible. Thus the image of the war before Tet encouraged Americans to see Vietnam as victory in progress. Nearly two-thirds, in a 1967 poll, agreed that the television coverage made them more supportive of the American effort.

Tet knocked the bottom out of that consensus. Enemy forces attacked simultaneously seven major cities in South Vietnam; American planes burned on the ground at the Danang airfield; the old city of Hue fell to the enemy. Saigon itself was set afire and the television audience saw a gun battle on the very grounds of the American Embassy. The most important member of that audience was Walter Cronkite, CBS anchorman. Cronkite took off to see for himself what was happening in Vietnam. When he got there, the military refused to let him go to Khe Sanh, where the fighting was hot, and sent him instead to Hue, then thought safe. He arrived in time to witness American marines in a desperate battle to retake the city. He talked with reporters who had covered the war. He came home mad—and he said so, in four special reports in February and March, each capped by his own personal commentary. "We have been too often disappointed by the optimism of the American leaders, both in Vietnam and Washington, to have faith any longer in the silver linings they find in the darkest clouds," he said, "for it seems now more certain than ever that the bloody experience of Vietnam is to end in a stalemate." Cronkite's most important audience was Lyndon Johnson, who saw, and told friends, that if he had lost Cronkite he had lost America. On March 31, Johnson announced he would not run for reelection.

The Appeal of Peace

One strong motive for Johnson's renunciation was the threat that he would be defeated by, of all things, a movement among Democrats led by, of all people, Senator Eugene McCarthy, who had very nearly bested the President in the March 12 New Hampshire primary and, polls showed, would probably best him resoundingly in Wisconsin on April 2. McCarthy, hitherto an obscure senator from Minnesota whose style seemed to alternate between disdain and bemusement, had gathered to him the political phalanx of the "student revolution," yet another dramatic disrupter of American life in 1968. By that year, the college student population had grown to 6,900,000— roughly six times as many as before World War II, three times as many collegians as there were farmers in America. An enormous flood of them arrived as freshmen just as Johnson's escalation brought on the military draft. Thousands exercised their idealism in the civil-rights movement of the sixties, vivified by television where they began a long course in the practice of social change. By 1968, the cause was the War, and by then students had learned something about how to get noticed in an indifferent world. Thousands bought the strategy of political action; they poured into New Hampshire and Wisconsin—the men shaved and necktied, the women in skirts to canvass for McCarthy. Other thousands, especially at the impersonal multiversities like Berkeley and Chicago and Columbia, went in for local provocation, an old protest art form given new dimension by television. In October 1967, some thousands put on a dramatically videogenic demonstration at the Pentagon. In January 1968, the Student Mobilization Committee met at the University of Chicago where speakers, flailing around for ideological bearings, extolled armed revolutionaries, produced posters calling for "Victory to the Vietcong," and ripped rhetorically into "the Enemy"—namely, the government of the United States. That spring at Columbia University, rioting students broke into offices, "occupied" buildings on campus, dumped files and destroyed research, captured a dean, and brought to a halt any semblance of teaching and learning. The police waded in, with television recording every move. Bloody mayhem—on April 19, 148 injuries, 711 arrests; on May 22, 68 injuries, 177 arrests—found its way onto the screens and into the living rooms. Parents who had scrimped and saved to give their kids a chance at higher education were appalled. The rioting students, relatively few in number, were excessively visible; to many watchers it seemed a whole generation had turned against a system constructed, at considerable sacrifice, to lift them up and send them on.

But that was peanuts compared to the black rebellion. In retrospect, the uprising of city blacks in 1967 and 1968 looks predictable. Take millions of poor, rural, undereducated, visually identifiable, distinct people and isolate them in ghettos in the great metropolises. Remove therefrom millions of middle-class whites and put them in suburban circles around the cities. "Give" middle-class blacks a taste of progress in response to their demands: somewhat better jobs and schools and housing, as you let the slums deteriorate, the streets wandered by jobless black youth. Lay on the principle that all of them have a right to full participation, as integrated equals, in the society at large—but add the qualification that that will take time, that many will have to wait, perhaps for a generation, for what they have a right to. Sell them television sets to show them, hour after hour, a vision of luxury as the American norm. Stir in episodes of police overreaction and a few articulate revolutionaries—and watch the resultant explosion.

In the summer of 1967, city after city—scores of them by summer's end—blew up in a violent contagion of fires and mobs and battles with the police. Television spread the anger to blacks and the terror to whites, 164 riots, 83 dead in that one summer, the pictures of smoke spiraling up from downtown Detroit and Newark and Cincinnati, the faces and voices of young American orators raging to excited crowds to "burn, baby, burn," to "smash everything Western civilization has created," to "wage guerrilla war on the honky white man." That May, armed Black Panthers came into the galleries of the California legislature. By the next March in 1968, big department stores in Chicago and New York were burning. On the evening of April 4, 1968, four days after Johnson's renunciation, the country's leading advocate of nonviolent progress, Martin Luther King, Jr., was murdered in Memphis. Riot and arson broke out in more than one hundred cities in a paroxysm of grief and anger; the flames shot up within two blocks of the White House. Two months later, on the night of June 6, 1968, the country's leading white politician capable of being heard in the black ghettos, Robert F. Kennedy, the late President's brother, was murdered in Los Angeles—on television—just as he was about to win the California primary.

Random crime and violence were also up. In America's safest big city, New York, 904 persons, black and white, were murdered in 1968, nearly tripling the annual murder rate of fifteen years before. Individual crime, mob crime, national crime in Vietnam, the butchering of leaders—instantly pictured on television—ripped at America's self-respect. James Reston saw a "plague of lawlessness and violence . . . sweeping the globe." A Nixon staff man thought the country was on the verge of a nervous breakdown. Nixon's call for a restoration of the peaceable kingdom echoed through all the candidates' camps that year. Withdrawing from the race, President Johnson asked "all Americans, whatever their personal interest or concern, to guard against divisiveness and all its ugly consequences." All his political life, he said, he had "put the unity of the people first," striving as President at "binding up our wounds, healing our history." Johnson's reason for pulling out of office was that he could "not permit the Presidency to become involved in the partisan divisions that are developing in this political year." Robert Kennedy, hoping to "heal the race question," had said "You must appeal to the generous spirit of Americans. This is what a campaign is about." Hubert Humphrey declared his candidacy as "the way politics ought to be in America, the politics of happiness, the politics of purpose, the politics of joy. And that's the way it's going to be, all the way, from here on in!"—a campaign based on "the concept of human brotherhood." Eugene McCarthy puckishly promised that if elected he would go to the Pentagon; his whole campaign focused on an end to the carnage in Vietnam, a return to reason as the cure for insanity.

The Humphrey Alternative

Nixon was the puzzling one. He had come into politics as a fighter, a modern-day political Jack the Ripper, from his first contest in 1946 through his hatchet work for Eisenhower down to his failing fight for the governorship of California in 1962. In 1966 he campaigned hard and assisted a remarkable Republican comeback in Congress; at that time the old Nixon seemed alive and well: "We'll kick their toes off in 1968," he said. Now, apparently transformed, he was coming on as the personification of peace. But in the campaign of 1968, for all its apparent contrast to the ways of the old Nixon, a strong continuity would prevail, the continuity with Nixon the self-manager, Nixon the perpetual molder and shaper of Nixon, Nixon overridingly concerned with the theatrical production of his character. He read the signs and acted accordingly. He could see why Nelson Rockefeller's insistence that "law and order" had to be based on "justice and opportunity" fell flat; he would offer themes, not programs. He could see that Robert Kennedy's passion came across on television to many viewers as frenzy—even "ruthlessness"; he would stay cool. He could see that Hubert Humphrey's verbosity could seem silly; he would act—would be, for the time being—dignified and sparing of talk. Thus much of the Nixon of 1968 would take hold as courses he would not follow, distractions he would carefully avoid. "The entire Nixon campaign, through the primaries and down to the election itself," wrote Theodore White, "hung on this thought—that the nation had had its fill of turbulence, bloodshed, killing, violence and adventure." The ruling strategy was "a strategy of blandness," reflected nowhere as clearly as in the superbland Republican convention, which left reporters groggy with ennui. Nixon the gut-fighter was replaced at Miami by Nixon the serene, yet another switch in the continuing sage of "New Nixons" parading adroitly through the 1960s, as he manufactured whatever persona his dramatic perceptiveness required. He had not really had to worry about the nomination; he won the New Hampshire primary and then the Wisconsin primary by nearly 80 percent of the vote in each case, stayed far ahead in the polls, and took the nomination on the first convention ballot.

The national convention itself, variously titled "a coronation," a "mirage," "an illusion of unity" by book-writing journalists, was staged primarily to beguile the television teams that descended on Miami with their enormously expensive technologies. No stone was left unturned. Down South, Roy Acuff could be heard, on carefully selected country and western radio shows, twanging "Bring Our Country Back": "How far down the road has our country gone, In this time of trouble and strife? How can we bring our country back, To the good and decent life? . . . Dick Nixon is a decent man, Who can bring our country back." And there came his voice over the radio, minus that reminding face, intoning, "The next President must unite America. He must calm its angers, ease its terrible frictions and bring its people together once again in peace and mutual respect."

Democratic party politics in early 1968 was electric with tension. Eugene McCarthy, enigmatic poet of the northland, was having charisma forced on him by his youthful admirers. Down South George Wallace growled, his talent for mobilizing discontent attracting new support far beyond the wilds of Alabama. Robert Kennedy, the "ruthless" Kennedy, was emerging as a compassionate friend of the poor and the blacks. Lyndon Johnson, though withdrawn from the race, was not about to let control of it fall out of his hands if he could help it.

That spring Robert Kennedy was shot to death. The ups and downs of the primaries left standing to take the nomination only Hubert Horatio Humphrey, Johnson's own Vice-President. His job was to get everyone together, an endeavor that suited his habits just fine.

Like Nixon, Humphrey was a small-town boy—and there the resemblance stopped. Born in 1911, Humphrey grew up in Doland, South Dakota. "My father was a man in love his whole life," Humphrey wrote. "He had a sense of wonder about the United States that rubbed off on all of us, the kind of love and obligation that was true of a lot of immigrants." Father Humphrey was converted to the Democratic faith by that great political lover William Jennings Bryan; his mother broke ranks to vote for another conciliator, Warren Harding, in 1920. The family talked politics nonstop, long after bedtime. "Never go to bed," Dad told Hubert, "stay out of bed as long as you can; ninety percent of all people die in bed." The son grew up with a remarkable spirit of indomitable optimism and loquacious energy, rooted in his memory of those formative years: "My childhood was happy—much of the summertime on the farm, many hours of winter out-of-doors, skating and sliding on the snow, and all of the time being part of a family filled with love and warmth, concerned with people and ideas."

He got all the way through graduate school and became a professor of political science. Color blindness and a hernia barred him from service in World War II, so he tried to serve in politics, running for mayor of Minneapolis in 1943 and losing, running again in 1945 and winning. In 1947 he helped found the Americans for Democratic Action, and in 1948 got into the Democratic action directly. At the national convention, he gave a stirring speech: "I ask this Convention to say in unmistakable terms that we proudly hail and we courageously support our President and leader, Harry Truman, in his great fight for civil rights in America." That fall he was elected to the Senate, where he made his mark; over the years he modified much of his early prairie radicalism, but not on civil rights. It was Hubert Humphrey, the Democratic Whip, who, in eighty-three days of cajolery and compromise got through Lyndon Johnson's landmark Civil Rights Act of 1964. But the word got around that year that "Hubert has mellowed." Johnson tapped him for the Vice-Presidential nomination and they went in together.

Johnson had barely pulled out of the race for 1968 when Humphrey got attention with a speech about "the politics of joy"—announcing his candidacy for President. But joy in that year of turmoil and tragedy was in short supply. Wallace was making strong headway early in the season, not only cutting away Democratic votes, but agitating "the atmosphere of heightened hostility and anger in the country; the irritability and the grating antagonisms," as Humphrey saw it. The antagonism that raked and sawed at his own spirit was Vietnam; Humphrey went over there once and talked to the generals, coming back an enthusiastic hawk, then went again and talked to the reporters, coming back a wavering but private dove. At the convention in July in Chicago, just as he thought he had a compromise platform plank on Vietnam worked out, Lyndon Johnson blistered him on the telephone: "Well, this plank just undercuts our whole policy and, by God, the Democratic party ought not to be doing that to me and you ought not to be doing it; you've been a part of this policy." Humphrey yielded. The last thing he would need was an enraged Lyndon Johnson zapping him from the White House.

A Nixon media adviser, Frank Shakespeare, had thought he saw "a tide of history which will guarantee Nixon's election this year." "Without television," Shakespeare said, "Richard Nixon would not have a chance . . . but because he is so good on television he will get through despite the press." Events would demonstrate powerfully how right Shakespeare was. The tide of conflict swept into the Democratic convention in Chicago, first with the news that the Soviet Union had suddenly invaded and occupied Czechoslovakia, then with pictures of bloody mayhem on the streets of Chicago itself.

Several thousand unarmed but provocative peace demonstrators, male and female, were attacked by berserk police squads, flailing the longhairs with their clubs, spraying Mace, dragging bleeding prisoners across the pavements—as the television cameras ground away and the crowd chanted "The whole world is watching!" Camera crews and reporters were attacked and arrested. Just as Mayor Joseph Alioto of San Francisco finished nominating Hubert Humphrey, television cut away to the street scene—and that's the way it was: alternating visions of the Democratic convention and the police riot on Michigan Avenue. The images ran together. Out on the street, Theodore White wrote in his notebook, "The Democrats are finished." Humphrey raged at "that instrument," his hotel television set, for "playing up the kooks and rioters," as the tear gas began to filter into his air conditioning.

Actually the networks put on only about half an hour of demonstration coverage in more than seventy times that much coverage of the convention. But it looked like powerful stuff. For a moment in the cool politics of 1968, television had gone hot, had shown blood. The pictures plainly showed a police riot, as any attentive viewer could see, and later official reports confirmed that fact. But that is not what the public perceived. Instead they "saw" what a year of seemingly endless strife had prepared them for; the reaction was overwhelmingly antidemonstrator and propolice, in poll after poll and in a great outpouring of wires and letters. The image of violence rubbed off on the Democrats. Walter Cronkite, the country's most respected anchorman, contributed to that result with what he later called "a very bad interview." Only a few months earlier, Cronkite had stepped out of his neutral role to express his view of what he had seen in Vietnam. Lyndon Johnson had let him know how *he* felt about *that.* Then one night at the Democratic convention, his CBS colleague Dan Rather was slugged by one of Mayor Daley's goons. Cronkite's voice shook as he said—on camera—"It looks like we've got a bunch of thugs in here," and, "If this sort of thing continues, it makes us, in our anger, want to just turn off our cameras and pack up our microphones and our typewriters and get the devil out of this town and leave the Democrats to their agony." The next day he interviewed Mayor Daley for twenty-three minutes. "I was deeply involved emotionally," he explained later, "and I was seeking desperately to maintain my objectivity." He bent over backwards, saying, "Maybe this is a kiss-and-make-up session but it's not intended that way. . . . I think we've always been friends." Daley was allowed to convey his wholly false version: that a revolution had been halted by police courage. Cronkite was reduced to carping: the evidence was not yet in as to whether or not the demonstration leaders were Communists, he insisted. (In fact, they were not.) The Walker Report later termed it, boldly, a "police riot."

Humphrey accepted his party's nomination in the persona of Saint Francis of Assisi, in a sort of political prayer:

Listen to this immortal saint: "Where there is hatred, let me know love. Where there is injury, pardon. Where there is doubt, faith. Where there is despair, hope. Where there is darkness, light. . . ."

We do not want a police state, but we need a state of law and order, and neither mob violence nor police brutality have any place in America. . . .

I take my stand—we are and must be one nation under God, with liberty and justice for all. This is our America. . . .

I say to America: Put aside recrimination and dissension. Turn away from violence and hatred. . . .*

Nixon at the Controls

Nixon's campaign centered on television technique. Reading another 1968 sign, the suspicion of manipulation, Nixon said, "I'm not going to have any damn image experts telling me how to part my hair" and "I am not going to barricade myself into a television studio and make this an antiseptic campaign." But from the start those were just his intentions. "We're going to build this whole campaign around television," he told his advisers. "You fellows just tell me what you want me to do and I'll do it." In fact, Nixon would manage much of his own television imagery, demonstrating sophisticated expertise in timing and technique, instructing the cameramen at a commercial-making session, "Now when you give me the fifteen-second cue, give it to me right under the camera. So I don't shift my eyes." Along the way he got the advice and consent of some of the sharpest brains in advertising. The new Nixon was no accident. As early as November 1967, his adviser Ray Price called it "the growth idea" and italicized: *The great advantage of the growth idea is that it doesn't require a former Nixon-hater to admit that he was wrong in order to become a Nixon supporter now.*

The candidate himself had had long and intense schooling in television. Two experiences especially added to the store of "lessons" Nixon was forever deriving from his experience, one a dazzling success, the other a dismal failure.

The first was the famous Checkers Speech of 1952, when Nixon, as Eisenhower's running mate, was discovered to have accepted some $18,000 from California businessmen. Eisenhower himself stood aside from the issue, but nearly all of his close advisers recommended that Nixon remove himself from the ticket—and they let Nixon know that. In a counterstrategy Nixon went on television, nationwide, following Milton Berle's show, with a maudlin, soap-opera defense, pleading the plainness of his life style, invoking the loyalty of his cloth-coated wife and his children's love for their little dog, Checkers. It was a smash hit. Nearly 200,000 telegrams poured in to the Republican National Committee, overwhelmingly favoring Nixon. Ei-

* Quoted in Theodore White, *The Making of the President 1968* (New York: Atheneum, 1969), pp. 306–7.

senhower relented: "You're my boy," he said when they met, and put his paternal arm around the weeping prodigal. Television had rescued Nixon. He would remember how.

But in 1960, late in his campaign against the upstart Kennedy, television had helped strike Nixon down. From the first shot of the first of that year's "Great Debates," replacing Andy Griffith in prime time, viewers saw Ike's experienced Vice-President reduced to equality with Kennedy. Kennedy seemed to know what he was talking about, spouting statistics, confidently speaking past his opponent to the audience of seventy million Americans. Nixon, approaching the debate as if it were a debate, concentrated on answering Kennedy—scoring points to impress the judges as he had in high school. Kennedy looked tan and vigorous. Nixon looked as he was, haggard, exhausted, convalescing from a bout of fever, distracted by sharp pain from a sore knee he had reinjured on the way to the studio. When it was over Nixon's mother called from California to ask if he was "feeling all right." The Gallup poll showed that nearly two out of three viewers thought Kennedy had won. Gloom descended on the Nixon campaign as Kennedy's crowds picked up. Kennedy went on to win the election by a hair. "It was TV more than anything else that turned the tide," he said afterward.

Nixon came out of 1960 believing that "television has increasingly become the medium through which the great majority of the voters get their news and develop their impressions of the candidates." Thus "one bad camera angle on television can have more effect on the election outcome than a major mistake in writing a speech which is then picked up and criticized by columnists and editorial writers." Nixon concluded that "where votes are concerned," a proverb of Khrushchev's "could not be more controlling: 'one TV picture is worth ten thousand words.' "

In contrast, the press—the print press—had become, at least by 1962, Nixon's private enemy. It liked a fighter but not Nixon's style: banal, secretive, clumsy. That grim November morning when the returns showed he had lost his race for governor of California, Nixon responded to his aides' insistence that he had to go down and meet the press with "Screw them," and again, "Screw them." But he went and delivered his famous "last press conference," a rambling plaint inviting them to "think how much you're going to be missing. You won't have Nixon to kick around anymore." He smashed at the *Los Angeles Times*—his ardent sponsor in his early career—for reporting his gaffe (that he was running for "governor of the United States") while ignoring his opponent Pat Brown's gaffe (that people should vote for a Republican senator). Television actually had both. "I can only say thank God for television and radio for keeping the newspapers a little more honest," Nixon said.

Try as he did, Nixon could never learn to win over the print reporters, who grimaced at his jokes and mocked his seriousness in comic songs. From his perspective, Lyndon Johnson had that medium right when he said, "Cast your bread on the waters, and the sharks will get it." But the seas of television could be channeled, the message floated past the sharks.

It had dawned on Nixon by 1968 that television could be *controlled*—molded to his purpose—in ways the print press never could be. The Checkers Speech showed how incredibly successfully Nixon could come across when he produced his own performance. The debates disaster showed how dangerous it was for Nixon to step before the cameras when control was beyond his grasp.

Campaigning had been revolutionized. A century before, Andrew Johnson had invented the modern go-to-the-people strategy in his famous "Swing Around the Circle." Now, as Nixon's new adviser, advertising man H. R. Haldeman, put it, "The reach of the individual campaigner doesn't add up to diddly-squat in votes." What counted was the one story a day the candidate could get out through the media, especially television, to the millions who would never encounter him in the flesh. Thus: save his energy, target his messages, and above all, control the presentation of his image on television. Nixon's campaign would spend at least half of its $24,000,000 expense—by far the largest campaign fund in history—on television.

That kind of money could buy a lot of professional advice. From the beginning, the Nixon campaign sought and found experts in the arcane arts of modern imagemaking. John Mitchell, Nixon's senior law partner, rode herd. His job, he said, was to "program the candidate." Politicians simply got in the way; Mitchell said, "We don't have any of them around here. That's why it seems so professional. Politicians are always after self-status. I don't want people who spend most of their time worrying over their own position or image. We're interested in the candidate." The program was designed down to the last detail. For instance, "participation politics"—the then popular desire to open the system to citizen "input"—was carefully engineered. At Nixon headquarters around the country, citizens spoke their questions into tape recorders. The messages were communicated to a central office where a computer, preprogrammed with sixty-seven Nixon answers, typed out a four-paragraph letter personally addressed to the questioner, each and every letter with its individualized variation, each machine-signed as if by the hand of the candidate. Thus "participation," handled with extraordinary dispatch by the appropriate equipment, left the candidate's hands free for other tasks.

With the print media, newspapers and magazines, the method was more subtle but no less deliberate. Nixon's basic task was to avoid controversy—the stuff of the newspaper story—while building up his "new Nixon" image.

The strategy was, therefore, essentially negative: how to keep them distracted and satisfied, and above all how to protect the candidate from reportable error. Nixon saw how George Romney was suddenly eliminated from contention by a casual remark to the effect that he had been "brainwashed" in Vietnam. Nixon avoided scenes of conflict or challenge or spontaneity: no debates, no "Meet the Press" or "Face the Nation," no forays to ghettoes or campuses where sharp questions or heckling might arise—and very few question-and-answer sessions with the horde of reporters trailing after him. When he did let them in, it was as smiling host—he even played "Let Me Call You Sweetheart" on the piano for them at one of his lavish hotel parties—or, on rare occasions, as a candidate suddenly available for an unprepared private interview. Otherwise they had to be content with making something of his public speeches, press releases, and position papers, all designed to dampen debate. He saw to it that they were well fed and amply refreshed, their comings and goings smoothly arranged as if by a personal tour guide; they called the Nixon campaign "The Country Club." At first they complained at being shut out, but before long the print reporters sank into what a British journalist called "astounded torpor." The fact that Nixon was unavailable for comment could be reported once, maybe twice, but then his nonresponsiveness lost its newsworthiness and reporters turned to reconstruing what they could get. They could take notes on the celebrities lending their presence to one of the "Dick Nixon community receptions," where roped-off lines of citizens waited patiently to shake the hands of Dick, Pat, Tricia, Julie, and David Eisenhower, as the cameras ground. They could write up theatrical reviews of the great Nixon indoor rallies, composed by show business experts, where a carefully culled crowd—"Anyone who doesn't look right is pulled from the line" at the gate—experienced the big brass band, the huge choir singing "The Battle Hymn of the Republic," the mammoth shower of balloons. What they could rarely do was ask the candidate, to his face, how he differed from anybody else who wanted to be President.

Other citizens were more fortunate. All over the country, local audiences saw Nixon on television being questioned by panels of ordinary community folks—a scene that seemed to give the lie to the accusation that he was hiding from inquiry. The casual audience could hardly realize that these hometown panel shows were put together with approximately the same degree of spontaneity permitted in the construction of a space satelite. The panelists were meticulously selected by interview—no psychiatrists, no reporters, no unreliable characters. The studio audience was also there by invitation. Print reporters could watch on monitors in an adjoining room, but not until after the warm-up: "Now, when Mr. Nixon comes in," the host would say to the gathering, "I want you to tear the place apart. Sound like ten thousand people. I'm sure, of course, that you'll also want to stand up at that point. So what do you say we try it now. Come on, stand up. And let me hear it." Mr. Nixon came in and they did it again. Then came the questions, floating through the studio air like milkweed seeds in a warm spring breeze: "Mr Nixon, at this point in the campaign, what do you find as the greatest concerns of the people? . . . Have you encountered any surprises at all? I suppose not? . . . Is there any hazard at all to being a leader? . . . What is there about your leadership that America needs?" The Nixon who in the 1960 debates had reminded media philosopher Marshall McLuhan of "the railway lawyer who signs leases that are not in the best interests of the folks of the town" now stood there cool and comfortable, chatting with the townspeople and, it seemed, with their neighbors at home. The best exchanges were snipped from the tape for reuse in commercials.

The Nixon commercials were designed with the aid of unpublicized "semantic differential" polls—asking people to check where they would put Nixon on scales running from "shifty" to "direct," from "insincere" to "sincere," from "politician" to "statesman." In their private deliberations, Nixon's hardheaded media men wasted little time on sentimentality. One technique, the use of rapidly exposed series of still photographs accompanied by narration, was explicitly designed to keep the candidate off the screen. "He says such incredible pap," one of his advisers said in private. "Nixon has not only developed the use of the platitude, he's raised it to an art form. It's mashed potatoes." That was a plus, mediawise: "It appeals to the lowest common denominator of American taste"—the triter the better. But Nixon himself, in the flesh, on camera, roused up a lot of old negative impressions. Adviser Roger Ailes explained:

Let's face it, a lot of people think Nixon is dull. Think he's a bore, a pain in the ass. They look at him as the kind of kid who always carried a bookbag. Who was forty-two years old the day he was born. They figure other kids got footballs for Christmas, Nixon got a briefcase and he loved it. He'd always have his homework done and he'd never let you copy.

Now you put him on television, you've got a problem right away. He's a funny-looking guy. He looks like somebody hung him in a closet overnight and he jumps out in the morning with his suit all bunched up and starts running around saying, "I want to be President."[*]

The panel shows, with Nixon carefully made up and lighted, helped "make them forget all that." The still-photo commercials did it better: up to forty images a minute flashing past—faces anxious and smiling, vigorous and despairing, scenes of sunset and riot, in an indeterminate blur—with Nixon's voice imposing Nixon's meaning on the visual impression. Thus the video script for a commercial titled "Order," available in sixty and forty-second versions, ripped along:

Fadeup on rapidly moving sequence of rioting, urban mob motivating to crowds taunting police authorities. Flaming apartment house dissolving to police patrolling deserted streets in aftermath of violence. Perplexed faces of Americans. Sequence of shots of people moving through battered streets bordered by destroyed shops and homes. Eloquent faces of Americans who have lived through such experiences. . . .[†]

* Joe McGinniss, *The Selling of the President 1968* (New York: Pocket Books, 1970), p. 103–4.
† Ibid., pp. 260–61.

The audio script had Nixon's message framed in music, steady and serene in contrast to the pictures. "It is time for some honest talk about the problem of order in the United States," he said. "Dissent is a necessary ingredient of change. But in a system of government that provides for peaceful change— there is no cause that justifies violence. There is no cause that justifies rule by mob instead of by reason." That was it. Nixon the narrator, whose guidance had to be accepted if the viewer wanted to enter into the little drama, need never appear on the screen.

From first to last, the Nixon forces controlled the Nixon image. Nixon kept his angers under tight control, quickly checking his ire at arrogant reporters. In his speeches, typically delivered without a single note and with precise timing, Nixon was given to constructing his own little dialogues— "As the President of Chile told me just last week, 'Mr. Nixon. . . .' " At his rare press conferences, he gained control by anticipating questions, thus enabling him to pose them in his own form—"You're going to say to that, 'Well, just a minute there now, Mr. Nixon, if what you say is so, then how about . . . ?' And I say. . . ." He went off to Key Biscayne every three weeks to relax and refresh his tan. He saw to it that his running mate, Spiro Agnew, who had begun to make disturbingly aggressive statements, was reined in and smoothed out. The basic half-hour Nixon documentary was titled "Nixon Now"—the new Nixon, the winning Nixon.

But behind the individual techniques for presenting Nixon as a calm, warm, human pacifier of the season's rages was a profounder set of guiding principles, derived from his media managers' vision of the new electronic mode of perception. In their private memos put together in the fall of 1967, they propounded nothing less than a new political epistemology. In the age of television, the very nature of political persuasion had to change. Nixon adviser William Gavin, whose typewriter, it appears, lacked capital letters, recommended for New Hampshire "saturation with a film" showing "only the best moments" of Nixon, "a quick parading" of him "not saying anything, just being seen." He offered this view of the requirements of the political dialogue:

reason pushes the viewer back, it assaults him it demands that he agree or disagree; impression can envelop him invite him in, without making an intellectual demand, or a demand on his intellectual energies. he can receive the impression without having to think about it in a linear, structured way. when we argue with him we demand that he make the effort of replying. we seek to engage his intellect, and for most people this is the most difficult work of all. the emotions are more easily roused, closer to the surface, more malleable.*

Gavin saw "the tv-oriented" voter as "emotional, unstructured, uncompartmented, direct." One must "lead 'em to the brink of the idea, but don't push them across the brink."

* Ibid., pp. 198–99.

Thus Nixon adviser Ray Price struggled with the problem that Nixon had been "viewed as a partisan figure first, a national figure second; as devious and unfair in his debating tactics—a master of unsupported innuendo, etc." Price wrote in a memo:

Let's leave realities aside—because what we have to deal with now is not the facts of history, but an image of history. The history we have to be concerned with is not what happened, but what's remembered, which may be quite different. Or, to put it another way, the historical untruth may be a political reality.

We can't do anything about what *did* happen, and there's not much we can *directly* do about people's *impressions* of what happened; for better or for worse, these are part of the political folklore. Thus what we have to do to persuade people that they're irrelevant to 1968. How? This has three prongs:

1. The passage of time; this has clearly worked in our favor. The sharp edge of memory has dulled, the image has mellowed; people don't maintain their passions forever. . . .

2. A dawning recognition on the part of some voters that they (or the chroniclers) might have been wrong, and that maybe the horror stories weren't all true after all; and

3. The natural phenomenon of growth. This is where I think there's the most gold to be mined. People understand growth, readily and instinctively; they expect people to mellow as they mature, and to learn from experience. . . .

. . . . *We have to be very clear on this point: that the response is to the image, not to the man.* . . . It's not what's *there* that counts, it's what's projected—and, carrying it one step further, it's not what *he* projects but rather what the voter receives.*

Thus what was to be controlled in the Nixon campaign was not the course of an argument or the revision of a history, but an emotional impression. Most of the public could be counted on not to pay close attention to what he said. The people would be invited to "leave realities aside," to relax and let the Nixon imagery "envelop" them—precisely what the theater audience is supposed to do as the lights go down and the curtain goes up: the suspension of disbelief. Along with troublesome reason, memory would be set aside; the Nixon campaign would signal a grand act of popular amnesia, declaring Nixon's checkered past "irrelevant to 1968," as if he had dropped from the sky, tan and warm and smiling, to symbolize the fun of forgetting.

Many observers that season shared Theodore White's view that "the Nixon of 1968 was so different from the Nixon of 1960 that the whole personality required re-exploration." White "came to believe that one must respect this man: there was about all he said a conviction and a sincerity" . . . "a total absence of bitterness, of the rancor and venom that had once colored his remarks." He thought, "There had indeed come to be a new Nixon"—"a firmer, wiser, thoroughly mature man," a "mellowed" man, "genuine and authentic." Walter Lippmann agreed: "I believe that there really is a 'new Nixon,' a maturer and mellower man who is no longer clawing his way to the top." Richard Nixon agreed: "I do want to say this: there certainly is a new

* Ibid., pp. 203–4.

Nixon." Calm and relaxed, Nixon reiterated his plea for reconciliation and unity and peace; commentators (lacking other news) began to suspect him of conversion—not marginally, but at the center of his being.

The reality of Nixon, before, during and after 1968, is now better known than any politician's reality. Long before his Presidential demise in the summer of 1974, Nixon the producer of "Nixon" was to be found, as he dodged and distorted, narrating his performance as "being perfectly candid," "speaking quite frankly," "putting it bluntly." In 1968, as never before, the link between reality and rhetoric in political discourse was broken—consciously, even proudly. As author Jonathan Schell later described the Nixon administration then yet to come, "What the Nixon men thought was unconnected to what they said. What they said was unconnected to what they did. What they did or said they were doing at one moment was unconnected to what they did or said they were doing the next moment." But none of that was perfectly clear as Nixon performed his waltz past the electorate in 1968.

Decision

As for Hubert Humphrey, he was in a nearly impossible position. His campaign, springing from that frighteningly riotous convention, was an organizational disaster—without money, without even an advertising agency. As Lyndon Johnson's Vice-President and Lyndon Johnson's pick for the Presidential nomination, Humphrey felt he could not back all the way away from support for the Vietnam war, so he backed part way, in a series of ambiguous retreats, while Nixon teasingly intimated that he had a secret plan to end the war soon. Plagued by chanting antiwar demonstrators wherever he went, a sad aftermath for the battered liberal hero, Humphrey tried desperately to recapture the old New Deal allegiances, an appeal that now sounded old and irrelevant. Not until September 30, 1968, could the Democrats even raise enough money for a nationwide telecast. By then it was nearly all over, despite a last-gasp try at rescue by Johnson.

On the Thursday night before the Tuesday voting in November, President Johnson appeared, announcing: "I have now ordered that all air, naval, and artillery bombardment of North Vietnam cease as of eight A.M. Washington time, Friday morning. I have reached this decision . . . in the belief that this action can lead to progress toward a peaceful settlement of the Vietnamese war. . . . What we now expect . . . are prompt, productive, serious and intensive negotiations in an atmosphere that is conducive to progress." Humphrey's chances picked up. Over the next few days, complex peace rumors floated confusingly about but, at the same time, Democratic voters once again began to ask themselves whether they were really ready to vote for Richard Nixon, Republican. The last-minute, quick surveys indicated that the women's vote might be crucial—they were slipping toward Humphrey.

On election eve, the rival candidates did "telethons." Humphrey's was a characteristically confused meander of various Democratic celebrities among the camera cables splayed across the studio floor. Nixon's was a characteristically slick operation: questions phoned in to a photogenic bank of Nixon enthusiasts were translated into precomposed questions on related topics and referred to the candidate for his precomposed answers. The final Humphrey documentary featured the candidate in a heart-rending relationship with his mentally retarded granddaughter. The final Nixon documentary—lavished over soap-opera time in every American region—played up, in Checkers' style, peacemaking Richard the pacific son of a quiet Quaker mother.

By an eyelash, 517,000 votes of the 73,359,762 votes cast, Richard Nixon became President of the United States. Humphrey issued a statement: "I have done my best. I have lost. Mr. Nixon has won. The democratic process has worked its will, so now let's get on with the urgent task of uniting our country." At Nixon's inauguration, the new President seemed to have heard Humphrey. "The greatest honor history can bestow is the title of peacemaker. This honor now beckons America—the chance to help lead the world at last out of the valley of turmoil and on to that high ground of peace that man has dreamed of since the dawn of civilization." And he continued:

We are caught in war, wanting peace. We are torn by division, wanting unity. We see around us empty lives, wanting fulfillment. We see tasks that need doing, waiting for hands to do them. To a crisis of the spirit, we need an answer of the spirit.

To find the answer, we need only look within ourselves. When we listen to "the better angels of our nature," we find that they celebrate the simple things, and the basic things—such as goodness, decency, love, kindness.

Greatness comes in simple trappings. The simple things are the ones most needed today if we are to surmount what divides us, and cement what unites us.

To lower our voices would be a simple thing.

In these difficult years, America has suffered from a fever of words: from inflated rhetoric that promises more than it can possibly deliver; from angry rhetoric that fans discontent into hatreds; from bombastic rhetoric that postures instead of persuading.

We cannot learn from one another until we stop shouting at one another—until we speak quietly enough so that our words can be heard as well as our voices.*

Chalmers Roberts of the *Washington Post* summed up a popular impression: "In short, the new President's speech was intended to be in tune with the times as with the mood of the voters who put him in the White House. He had heard their voices, at least their majority voice and he was reflecting it."

That was January. In March, the President ordered the bombing of another country, Cambodia, in a secret move kept secret even from the secretary of the air force. In May, that leaked. Wiretaps were ordered for five newsmen and for high officials in the State Department, the Defense Department, the White House itself. . . .

* Quoted in Jules Witcover, *The Resurrection of Richard Nixon* (New York: G. P. Putnam's Sons, 1979), pp. 477–78.

The Television Reality

Again and again in its modern history, television journalism was there to display, in live coverage, the denouement of a crisis it had helped to build in its ordinary news reports. Thus in the 1950s, Senator Joseph McCarthy had learned how to put on his little playlets of accusation for the evening newscast, counting on brevity and immediacy to preclude close checking of what he had to say. At last Murrow and his partner Fred Friendly—fighting their network managers all the way—let the camera dwell on McCarthy at length, revealing his offensive and unfair behavior, and, later, McCarthy's rapid destruction at the hands of a Yankee lawyer, Joseph Welch, in the televised Army-McCarthy hearings. Television news had dutifully reported Nixon's daily denunciation of supposed Democratic corruption in 1952, leading up to the drama of the Checkers Speech—live. The campaign of 1960, day by day, was a contest between experienced Nixon and brash John Kennedy, until the Great Debates—live and unedited—redressed the balance. Then came the romance of Kennedy's Camelot, the first real television Presidency, ending in bloody horror in Dallas and then in the long, live weary mourning of his death. The sixties saw the riot of the day and the zealot of the hour, and demonstration after demonstration designed to get television coverage, reach their dramatic fruition in Martin Luther King's grand March on Washington, the funeral following his murder, Robert Kennedy's televised death, and the Chicago convention police war. The real war in Vietnam zipped along on television news as a brave adventure until at long last the live reality of it was brought home to a shocked America. For better or for worse, the television news productions that stand out in memory are almost all direct depictions of history happening—out there in the world, not in a studio or the little framed performance of a commentator on the White House lawn.

Nixon's television campaign of 1968 had been designed to ensure that nothing happened, that is, nothing that would lend itself to intense, focused television coverage. The productions he could control were essentially nonevents meant to convey an impression: Nixon as Walter Cronkite, calm, rational, warm and avuncular, and above all, reconciling. Much of that played off the medium's primary mission of entertainment—the celebrity aura, the soap-opera biography, the folksy panel shows and telethons aping Johnny Carson, the blurred pointillism of the commercials. But Nixon also managed to slip by the evening news into the White House. He could not control the network news, but he could take advantage of the way network news had learned, over a long history, to control itself. Nixon's baseline problem in 1968 was his own history. To evaluate his soft-spoken appeal for peace, his pledge of "absolute candor," his promise of an "open administration," and, more broadly, his character as a potential President, the public had only two lines of evidence to go on: Nixon past and Nixon present—his background and his performance in the campaign. Nixon's baseline strategy was to concentrate attention on the latter and to suggest that the former was irrelevant.

Journalism in all the media, with its emphasis on the immediate and the novel, cooperated; the old Nixon was old news. But television news in particular had a hard time piercing the soft veil of Nixon's new image, especially on the dinnertime news shows.

The newsmen in television—those who devoted all their effort to journalism, as distinguished from the morning show entertainers who did a little news along the way—were an endangered species. In the decades after the war, they struggled to tell their truth against powerful forces intent on instructing them what to say—and especially what not to say: their own network managements, the government, the commercial sponsors. Over the same period, they elaborated a form and a manner of news presentation in broadcasting that hung around their necks like an iron collar, making it ever more difficult for them to convey to the public a reliable image of the real world.

Television news was affected by the government as no other medium had been from broadcasting's birth. The fear that the FCC might lift a license now and then, even though the threat was rarely carried out, inhibited departures from "balance." The Red scare left its scars, not just in the imagination but in memories of the blasting of actual careers. Wildly exaggerated estimates of television's hypnotic influence seemed to justify demands for caution. Perhaps most powerfully, television's extraordinary reach to the mass market, which brought it immense wealth, made doing again what had worked before seem the only prudent course.

Thus when Nixon reemerged on the national stage, television news already had behind it an extraordinarily nervous history. President Johnson had been given to raging telephone calls to network presidents, always with the implied threat of government interference. Once in office, Nixon would assault the newscasters with all the instruments at his command, from irate threats to FBI surveillance of reporters. But even in 1968, he could count on the inherited tradition of caution to dampen any controversial news initiatives challenging his new reputation. While the print reporters were lapsing into "astounded torpor," Nixon saw to it that television had plenty of pictures of his travels and celebrity scenes—but not much else.

Its history gave television news its style, as every weekday evening it flickered forth as a kind of prelude for the entertainments to follow. The typical newscast opened with a welcoming "good evening" by the familiar anchorman, seated quietly at a desk. He began with the day's most important story, but only that positioning signaled its importance—the anchorman moved rapidly on to other items. Each had its minute or so of time, and then was gone. Brevity meant that only the sketchiest account of what happened could be related, in bulletin style, largely without explanation, until the end of the story, when the anchorman or another reporter gave a brief interpretation, balancing the most plausible meanings, typically concluding in ambivalence. A short film might illustrate the story, with a calm voice telling the viewer what he was seeing and what he could not see. For a moment a story might seem shocking—even horrifying—but then came a commercial showing the relief of some ill, and then the return of the anchorman, calm and steady, apparently unaffected by the terrors he had just recounted. As the sequence loped along, facts were interlarded with opinions—not of the newsmen but of personalities in the news, nearly always two of them so that "both sides" were represented. Nearly always one such personality was the President and, in the election season, the major Presidential candidates. Near the end of the half hour might come a short sermon by a commentator, taking his text from one of the day's events, typically propounding some mild moral we would all do well to remember in these troubled times. Then the "light piece," a humorous or sympathetic human interest item to cap off with happiness the ill fortunes previously portrayed. And at the end, the anchorman again, giving his benediction, as if to absolve everyone involved, sending the audience, having done its duty, on in peace to the pleasures of the night.

Thus to television's traditional caution was added a mode of presentation markedly contrasting to the glaring headlines of the newspapers, the leisurely pace of the magazine piece, or the old-style staccato excitement of radio newscasts by the Kaltenborns and Murrows. The news was fragmented and rhythmed, the viewer guided gently along by the confident, reappearing anchorman, like the chorus in a Shakespeare play. All in all, it was a gentling experience most nights, its style and manner working to soften the harsh edges of the news.

If television lacked the time and inclination to dig hard for the Nixon story, it also lacked the capacity. The top newsmen, especially the anchormen, made star-type salaries, but the networks, for all their burgeoning wealth and their massive investments in equipment, went light on research. The news was written almost entirely from wire service reports—themselves composed in neutral style so as to be useful to newspapers of any persuasion. Background materials were virtually unexploited; the networks did not even keep tapes of their own news broadcasts in those days, much less historical data on Presidential candidates. As long as Nixon left his past alone, television news would also. And because his message of union and restraint and peace so suited the propensity of television—everybody's medium—he had little doubt they would report it.

Thus way back in 1968 we got a President who would have to be pardoned. He rose to power like a dove, sensing the drift of the wind.

Downfall

Five years later, Nixon resigned, because, he said, he no longer had "a strong enough political base in the Congress to justify continuing." There was a truth to that: Nixon's assault on the law and the Constitution had created an overwhelming majority in the House of Representatives for his impeachment, an overwhelming majority in the Senate for conviction—both majorities including many of his most ardent, last-ditch supporters. Television—his favored medium—had helped to bring him down, mainly by simply turning the cameras on the congressmen as they uncovered his massive malfeasance in office. By then virtually the whole of journalism had discovered the Old Nixon alive and kicking, the real Nixon, his 1968 mask of conciliation destroyed. In the fall of 1972, as he pretended indifference to the charges of corruption George McGovern kept raising, Nixon in private took a different view of his situation: "This is a war." A year later, as the Watergate cover-up was falling apart, he let "the electronic media" have it between the eyes; at a press conference on October 26, 1973, he said, "I have never heard or seen such outrageous, distorted reporting in 27 years of public life," damning "frantic, hysterical reporting." The following month, his performance in office led *Time*, the *New York Times*, and even the *National Review*, among many other periodicals, to call for his resignation. Nearly a year would go by before that wish came true. The press, and in particular the "electronic media," had become Nixon's Enemy Number One. The success of his perpetual image-propping operations depended on the cooperation of those who conveyed the images. In the conciliating election that brought him to Presidential power, television had served him well, lifting him out of his reputation as a political alley-fighter. Now television brought him down, as day after day, in living color, Americans saw their President's crimes unfold.

But even at the end, commenting on his resignation speech, television newsmen found words to temper the pain. The newsman Nixon felt had given him the hardest of times, Dan Rather, said that this might well be "his finest hour." Turning to Walter Cronkite, Rather said, "He did give—and I would agree with, Walter, what you said—he gave to this moment a touch of class—more than that—a touch of majesty—touching that nerve in most people that says to their brain: Revere the presidency and respect the President; the Republic and the country comes first. . . ." Nixon the majestic, to balance Nixon the malfeasant.

PROPOSAL

15

A Vision Beyond the Myth

LIKE HUMANS IN OTHER AGES, we tend to go along with the stories current in our culture. Even the exception proves the rule: a legend strong in our mythology is the story of the maverick, the lone individual bucking the tide of society, finding his own way, attracting our interest as a prophet or a symbol or a warning. Our own history is a story we tell again and again in periodic celebrations and in pilgrimages to the shrines that mark heroic deeds. We search for present meaning in a version of the past, in our roots as we want to remember them. Even more powerfully in America, this New World, we hold to the sense that the national story continues into the adventures of the future. From the start, we have been a people about to be, a nation of becomers. Whether in shock or satisfaction, Americans tune in to the new—and thus the news—to catch the sound and shape of the next episode, lest we be left behind as the country moves forward. And with an optimism absurd to the Old World sophisticates and determinists, we democrats—those who demand a return to a better past and those who insist on an advance to a better future—cling to the faith that we ourselves are the makers of our destiny. That faith falters from time to time, but then springs up again. "In God We Trust," yes, but we The People are the authors of liberty.

Yet in fact we depend, far more profoundly than we have realized, on storytellers to pluck from the chaos of experience the plot of the next adventure. From the beginning, even geography had to give way to the force of myth: Columbus, flying in the face of the science of his day, believing instead in Marco Polo's tales of the Indies, the Puritans, aiming for Virginia and hitting Cape Cod, sustained by the vision of a New Zion, on down to the wildly improbable but mythically compelling idea of putting a man on the moon. The pictures in our heads conquered the ground beneath our feet. The painters of those pictures, when they can get them believed, exercise a power that is nothing less than the power to set a course of civilization. In modern politics, lacking grander visions, we make do with glimpses of possibility and shades of meaning—a kaleidoscope of fact and metaphor and judgment. Journalism, our composite Homer, delivers those partial sightings, which substitute for heroic myth. If it is the default of the political parties that burdens journalism with sorting out candidates, it is the default of the contemporary intellectuals that leaves to journalists the task of composing our ruling ideas.

Being American, my purpose is improvement. But just as it seems to me quite unlikely that the pulse of politics will suddenly beat to a halt or that the basic political system now in place will change radically in the near future, so certain basics of the craft of political journalism probably have to be taken as given. Two such basics stand out: haste and drama. Journalism will continue to be history in a hurry. That is the major stumbling block in the path of improvement. Haste fights reflection, and an unreflective journalism drifts into dependence on standard and fashionable story forms. That risk can be cut to some extent by a variety of palliatives, such as alternating long and short deadlines, study leaves for reporters and editors, closer links between the more leisurely academic world and the journalistic rush to judgment, and the development of a steadier and more responsible corps of press critics. New information-retrieval technologies should make possible far quicker access to background and context data. And some journalists have already grasped the fact that it is the relevance of information, not simply its recency, that grips the reader as he tries to understand today's situation. But such changes at the edges will leave intact the main focus of journalism: current events hurrying into tomorrow.

Critics who preach against journalistic drama per se are also likely to be disappointed. The audience cannot be forced to attend; they must be attracted. Critics who urge the publication of stories no one wants to write, and they themselves would not read, deserve particular neglect. The drama can be better done. It can steer clear of fiction. It does not require brevity—as witness sustained public attention to the Army-McCarthy hearings, the Watergate saga, Theodore White's campaign books, and the like. The drama inheres in the strong, engaging narrative development that stretches the attention span. Even the quickest medium, television, has discovered that in the popular appeal of "Sixty Minutes." But drama itself is an inherent—essential—element of journalism. In a Presidential election year, the nation is not a classroom; it is a street theater.

The main line of improvement is obvious. We need all three stories every time, to test the candidates from different angles, lest we wind up with an expert mood-reader who sails in on the tide of the dominant story of the year and then founders when it turns out he cannot handle the other challenges of the Presidency. Journalism's modern talent and enterprise and taste for variety can meet that responsibility. But the stories themselves can also stand improvement. Their promise as guides to the choice of a President has yet to be fulfilled.

The story of politics as conflict has distorted and diverted Presidential politics repeatedly. Candidates who had experienced the terrors and thrills of combat, directly or vicariously, carried over into politics an entirely inappropriate rhetoric of battle. For in a real battle, the rights and wrongs are already decided. The appeal to arms cancels the appeal for deliberation. The question of arousal overwhelms the question of understanding. In each of the battle campaigns illustrated here, and as could easily be illustrated from those left out, the national debate degenerated into mere castigation, often over picayune "issues" and the thrust and parry of personal accusation. Candidates who tried to stir a debate about the major actualities of their time quickly learned that what counted with the press was not substance but difference. In Theodore Roosevelt's time, and in Truman's old-fashioned shout, the drama of attack and defense at least had the virtue of a certain visceral definiteness, the sparkle and lurch of combative action and event. But by the time Adlai Stevenson and then George McGovern entered the fray, controversy had lapsed into shadowboxing. No candidate could advance a position seriously, as a Presidential intention, without its being reduced immediately to a tactical ploy in the contest for popularity. When John Kennedy offered a different vision of what the Americans might hold themselves to, a vision of achievement considered in the light of resources, he quickly discovered how irrelevant that seemed to a press prepared to light up over Quemoy and Matsu.

The transformation of the election from an event to a saga set the stage for the appearance of new militant vocabularies, as campaign organizations maneuvered over the expanded primary terrain, month after month, exercising their logistics and strategies to build momentum and avoid erosion. Campaign maneuver itself became the featured story; the Presidential implications of what the candidates were saying faded into the distance. Horserace imagery gave way to Parcheesi politics—war against the scoreboard—a new game of expectations and scenarios and surprises played as vigorously by the candidates as by the press reporting them. By the end of the 1970s, journalism, increasingly conscious of its own interpretative influence, took to reporting how the candidates were going over with the press itself. Campaign reporting became a speciality distinct from government reporting; the battle story drifted away from Washington, lost its connection with the reality the victor would encounter there. Public opinion polling, grown reliable after the 1948 fiasco, set up another dynamic: the front-runner, identified long before the first voting, emerging from the pack and fighting off the challengers. Front-runners far enough in front avoided debate like the plague: Dewey dodged debate in 1948 and nearly won; Eisenhower floated above the contest; Nixon, learning his lesson from 1960, played above it all in 1968 and 1972; Ford, to his sorrow, let himself be persuaded to debate on television in 1976. Candidates coming from behind sought to co-opt rather than confront the positions of the more popular contender.

Thus over the years inventive candidates and journalists translated the battle story into a tale of calculation and maneuver set off from the story of governing the country. We have come a long way from the Lincoln-Douglas debates. The televised debate series in 1960 and 1976 verged on deliberation—but their substance was immediately swallowed up by reporting on "who won" in the instant polls. As arousers of an apathetic citizenry, the story dragged; voting turnout drifted downward, the public turned away from the fight.

Critics of the fighting story call for "issues not personalities," for a rational debate on the candidates' programs and party platforms. But as President after President has discovered, particularly in recent years, the gap between what he wants to do in January of an election year and what he can do the following January is enormous. Pressed for specifics during the campaign, the candidate and his aides and advisers expend their intellectual energies composing tedious position papers. They are not frequently cited after inauguration day. The fundamental reason is not that the candidates lie, though some do, but that such detailed blueprints for government action are drawn up abstractly, disconnected from an as yet unknown context of forces and chances in Washington, and of necessity shaped for an immediate purpose: to win the election. It is like asking a doctor to prescribe for a patient he has yet to meet. The party platforms try to beat those uncertainties by including a little of everything. At best they become registries of access—who could marshal enough clout to nail in a plank—and at worst mere laundry lists of more or less plausible hopes. To center campaign debate on specific candidate plans is to shift the conversation away from evidence and toward opinions that cannot readily be tested, however sincerely they are advanced. The story of conflict reduces itself to a competition among assertions. Reporters closeted with the candidates on the campaign trail badger them for statements of intention, hoping for some bit of quotable idiocy, usually making do with some hypothetical clash between what A says and what B says. Their reports from the field become grist for the editorial mill; the columnists and commentators take over, producing analysis after analysis in which their own confident opinions on issues are contrasted with the uncertain and ineloquent proposals candidates make. In practice, the battle between candidate and journalist supersedes the battle among the candidates themselves. Because an issue's focus must by definition highlight the hypothetical and abstract, a story told in the subjunctive language of what one would do *if* certain conditions prevailed, the way is opened for endless speculation, and theory rules the roost.

Journalism's strength is not theory but fact. And to reason toward a choice, the public's first need is to get a grip on the contemporary reality. As for candidates, each offers a picture of the facts as he sees them, a picture very likely to shape whatever he would try to do as President. A battle among *those* visions—visions of what is actually happening—could prove much more enlightening and enlivening than war stories out of New Hampshire or Wisconsin. In 1932, for example, Hoover claimed the economy was picking up, Roosevelt the opposite. Their visions of reality clashed. The facts of life were there to report—and bore directly on the task of assessing the candidates. Hoover favored local, voluntary relief. Whatever the philosophical validity of his viewpoint, it rested on a fact question: what local and private resources were available to relieve how many of the unemployed? In the 1950s, Joe McCarthy's charges and threats rattled through the press, randomly ruining lives, until the facts of "Communists in government" finally smashed him. In 1960, John Kennedy charged the Eisenhower administration with allowing a dangerous "missile gap" to widen between the United States and the Soviet Union. Not until after the election did the facts blow that vision out of the water. Through the sixties, candidates posturing about the state of welfare too rarely had the facts thrown at them: how many American families lacked the money to feed their children properly? What were the actual effects of the programs in place? How typical among those aided was the able but lazy "welfare cheater"? In 1964 and beyond, Vietnam was importantly a moral issue, but what eventually turned it around was not the logic of antiwar opinion, but the revelation of what was actually happening out there in the field. Similarly Watergate—more broadly, the corruption in government charge—barely rippled the surface of national debate until after the election of 1972. McGovern's eloquent damnations failed to convince. Two young reporters fought their way through to the facts and set in motion the fall of a President. And late in the 1970s, amid much speculation about Jimmy Carter's state of mind, the facts of an energy crisis limped late into the public consciousness.

Modern journalism clearly has the capacity to handle the battle over facts. Journalism has attracted some of the best brains in the country. In the colleges, very bright students insist on struggling their way into that overcrowded line of work. Mammoth news organizations have the requisite money and manpower. Compared to just a few years ago, today's government "secrets" are there for the reporter's asking as are the piles of scholarly studies issued by the universities. The central problem is not access but selectivity—but there journalism has just begun to exploit the incredible speed of the new information-retrieval technologies that will enable a reporter to survey a month's worth of data in an afternoon, posing question after question. A war over the facts, every four years, could help journalism break out of its losing preoccupation with the nuances of hypothetical opinion, symbolic epistemology, electoral bookie work, and the tired search for someone to quote, and do what it does best: get relevant information, quickly and accurately. Citizens, now woefully mis- and un- and underinformed on the way things work in a fast-changing world, might begin to see through the fog of rhetoric to the shape of reality. The drama of revelation might grip the public imagination a good deal more firmly than do the campaign gossip and ideological chitchat that now drone through so many eminently forgettable paragraphs.

But the main virtue of a quadrennial war about the facts would be its contribution to the central electoral task: the choice of a President. Testing potential Presidents on the facts of the national condition would test their capacity for realistic perception and judgment, their grasp of the actual shape of the situation at home and abroad. That would be an important test of a genuine Presidential ability. For time and again, in recent decades, we have seen a President cut himself off from the real world, isolate himself in the White House with his cozy crew of flattering advisers, and drift into illusion and tragedy. It happened to as cool a rationalist as John F. Kennedy, when he fell for the Bay of Pigs invasion mirage, though he quickly recovered his bearings. We need a President highly curious about what in the world is happening—and ready to respond to the evidence of change. The time to assess a President's worldview is before, not after, he raises his hand on inauguration day and swears to preserve, protect and defend the Constitution. During the campaign, his fantasies should be held to the fire of fact. Whatever he may hope to do, can he bear to see the truth? Does he know what he is talking about? Presidents-to-be should never again be allowed to pass through the gate of an election without paying the admission of realism, talking sense to the American people about the realities he and they must face together.

At the heart of the story of politics as conscience is the question of character. A candidate may be in full possession of the facts of his time, but that does not determine what he makes of them, his orientation toward action. He can be counted on to present a character in the campaign, calling attention to himself as he wants to be seen. But that may be a temporary guise donned for the immediate task and shucked aside when it has served his purpose. Wilson's campaign "conservatism" is an example; Johnson's restrained reasonableness in 1964 makes the point. The problem is to get behind the mask to the man, to the permanent basics of the personality that bear on Presidential performance. That quest does not deny the possibility of fundamental change after age forty or the possibility that the candidate may be a better person than he makes himself out to be. Possible—but not likely enough to justify the risk. The "New Nixon" seduction argues caution.

Nor does the quest for character deny the relevance of ideology. The confusion that arises from the contemporary "liberal's" defense of the big government status quo and the "conservative's" demand for a radical dismantling of government does not dismiss the ideological question. For in a crude and simple sense, there is an important distinction: historically Democratic Presidents have pressed for government action to relieve popular distress, while Republicans prefer free-market mechanisms. The distinction is politically important but not ultimate; it is a distinction of means, not ends.

Republicans as well as Democrats aim to make people better off; they disagree about how. And in the reality of American politics, "better off" means a grab bag of common values—security and opportunity, money and liberty, fairness and variety—not some tightly derived logical product of metaphysical demonstration.

That is where the Wilsons and Luces go wrong, wrenching the story of morals away from its American plot. Claiming that their political preferences are derived from eternal principles, they wind up investing debatable policies with the force of holy writ. Goldwaterism follows: sweeping away the conditional uncertainties of the historical present as simply irrelevant, demanding not calculation but application of received truth. That stance stops argument dead in its tracks. If it is God who prescribes the League of Nations or militant anticommunism or free enterprise, the Devil must be running the opposition—and you turn your back on the Devil, you do not argue with him. History is seen as fundamentally beside the point. Therefore such superficially startling leaps as Wilson's shift from peace to war and such low-level contradictions as Goldwater's desire to cut federal spending while financing much stronger military forces are not so surprising. The political fundamentalist looks up the answer in his book of natural laws or divine revelations and pronounces—Q.E.D., like Euclid with his triangles. Nor is it so surprising that moralizing candidates so often wind up practicing the wily arts of public relations and psychological manipulation. Since the derivation from principle to policy is perfectly clear, the obstacles to implementation must be emotional—problems of the will, not the mind. People need selling, not convincing. That leads a Dwight Eisenhower to the commercial-making studio where, however reluctantly, he mouths little inspirational platitudes for his admen.

What is missing in this line of political philosophy is the common sense that political values are contingent. Values are not irrelevant; a politics without values reduces the democratic adventure to a dismal pull and tug among interests. But politics is not theology; there is no salvation in it. At its best, it sets the conditions for a virtuous life. Its arena is a messy middle ground between the best and the probable, as philosophers from Thomas Aquinas to Reinhold Niebuhr have clearly understood. The genius of American politics operates in that territory, not above it all (Eisenhower's malady) or lost in mere manipulation (Nixon's penchant). If modern political history shows anything, it is that the right to speak for God in politics may be claimed by any sort of character—and probably will be.

The moralizing story comes up as a reaction to the battle story, which, like a war gone on too long, seems to degenerate from adventure to butchery. The moralists in journalism seek to recapture innocence in the person of an outsider who will clean up the Capitol. Each of the moralizing candidates discussed above, including Willkie and Eisenhower, was a politician in the broad sense of the word—a man of affairs already tainted with the rot of compromise. But romantic idealization sets in, beginning with the mythology of the man's upbringing in some island of innocence far from Washington and progressing to his uncanny talent for cutting through the tangles of intrigue with the sword of principle. Once that process of perfectionism takes hold it is hard to stop, short of a kind of secular deification. Criticism seems somehow blasphemous, as if one crack in the dike of personal virtue would destroy the whole. Intimations of ambition are especially dangerous; the ideal candidate should be dragged into office despite his protestations of reluctance.

This earthly elevation reflects and contributes to the popular fantasy of the President as Superman. The moralizing tales find their way into the textbooks and movies, teaching the young to expect miracles from the White House. The regularity of disillusionment follows as the night follows the day. Instead of miracles come halting progress and/or crashed hopes, as the President discovers how short a distance his independent powers can take him. His moralizing sponsors find him disappointing, partly because they mistook his personal virtue for agreement with their particular deductions from natural law. As the country runs through that cycle of uplift and downfall again and again, the force of the story wanes and skepticism sets in. In reaction to the romantic version of the discovery of the best natural American for President, journalists turn to the equally romantic notion that every candidate is a secret crook.

The modern skeptical story of conscience fumbles after character in the Campaign Street Test—the totally unrealistic supposition that he who is good at running for President will be good at running the Presidency. Especially since the race became a marathon, campaigning, with its endless exhaustions, brief encounters, and pleadings for money and attention, tests qualities of physical endurance and superficial plausibility, but not much else. The story's prize is the gaffe. Carter's "ethnic purity" mistake and Ford's "Polish blunder" were the great gaffes of 1976, neither of which bore the slightest relationship to their public policies, much less their characters. But the story takes off and lives, sometimes for weeks of front-page attention and editorial fulmination, before it finds its rightful place in oblivion. The gaffe is our era's prime example of symbolic politics run wild. Its early retirement would make space for the story we eventually turn to for enlightenment on the question of Presidential character.

That is the life story, the biography. As the early magazine moralists discovered, that was their most appealing product. It sold far better than all the shrill denunciations and atmospheric pontifications put together. People could connect with it. Everyone lives a life history. Everyone is interested in how to do that and, through the human connection, how lives very different from their own take shape and plunge on. The poetic saga of Odysseus, the history of Moses, the parable of the life of Christ, Caesar's story, the tragedies of King Oedipus and Prince Hamlet, on down to the lives of Napoleon and Lincoln and Victoria and Churchill, to our age's fascination with the biographies of every sort of hero and villain from Gandhi to Hitler—the story of a person grips the imagination as nothing else can. The stories of "ordinary" people (each, in fact, extraordinary), told by the likes of Robert Coles or Studs Terkel, light up the contemporary scene with a clarity unmatched by any public-opinion poll. For people sense that all our theoretical constructs and elaborate fantasies take their human meaning from their incarnation in the flesh and blood of persons. The theory no one lives by remains a theory only. Biography brings theory down to earth, history to focus, fantasy to reality. It is the narrative of existence, of being-in-becoming. No wonder people indifferent to mere speculation take to biography as if the life they read might be their own.

In the journalism of Presidential campaigns, biography occupies an increasingly important place. The news magazines in particular, but also long newspaper stories and television documentaries, have moved past the romantic "son of the soil" versions to review candidate histories from a Presidential perspective. In 1976 those stories came late in the game, but they were unusual in their thoroughness and incisiveness. Some made use of the scheme I developed in *The Presidential Character* to try to sort out the major biographical themes relevant to performance in the White House, but each developed its own focus, often explicitly stated, on the main biographical questions. Special attention went to the roots, in family, school, local culture, and early political experience, of the candidates' habits of mind and approaches to action. After Nixon and Johnson, writers were specially tuned in to evidence bearing on the character as compulsive or open to learning, self-doubting or confident, moved primarily by narrow ambition or larger values. The strength of those analyses was not only their narrative appeal but also their reach beyond the manipulatable and invariably manipulated images of the campaign to a record of performance already in place. Unsatisfied with little gaffey glimpses into character, the authors checked out candidate experiences over the years. The result was the best writing yet from the interpreters of the political meanings and values and probabilities embodied in the real men then making their way toward the Presidency. An example was set; whether it would carry forward to the next campaign and the one after that was yet to be seen.

Political observers of the "realist" school are forever underrating the problem of conciliation in American democracy. The appeal that celebrates the common hope for harmony is dismissed as mere rhetoric, masking darker purposes. Every candidate is assumed to be consumed with personal ambition and to possess an infinite capacity for meaningless blather. Conflict is real; concord is an illusion. Thus the tough-minded wordsmith, who need never bear the responsibility of action, sets out to unmask the fakers and correct the naïve. In fact, of course, it is not possible for the government to move forward except by developing alliances among politicians—the politics of conciliation.

The story of that search periodically dominates the national narrative. Too often, the hunger for the relief of tension and anxiety has led us to accept the terms of a peace too fragile to last, a truce in place of a social contract. Three features of that story raise that risk.

The first is the drift toward fiction. Politics as theater, politics as a "great game," campaign politics as a story cut loose from the story of government—those themes reinforce that drift. Somehow as the Presidential election season approaches the signal goes out that a brand new "epic struggle" is beginning in which the ordinary rules of judgment are to be set aside—the theatrical suspension of disbelief. History stops; amnesia sets in, encouraged by candidates who, unable to resolve the conflicts they inherit, invite us to forget them. People turn to the story, particularly as presented in the entertaining broadcast media, as if they were attending a spectacle, as essentially passive spectators. The question of judgment is transformed into a question of appreciation—did we like the show, or not? How did the candidate do? Did he give a good performance? Were we impressed? The typical television interviewer asks the candidate how he feels about this and that, making a connection between his feelings and the audience's feelings, defining the exchange as an emotional occasion. Harding's rhetoric, reduced to print, says nothing. Harding's performance, in person, conveyed, when the audience was ready for him, powerful feelings. Today the fragmented brevity of television news sends the message by too fast to call the mind into play. Emotion is quicker but shallower. A parade of impressions jogs gently along the edge of attention, barely disturbing the rational faculties, leaving behind a blur of affective responses. Candidates like Nixon pick up the lesson: the impression is everything. The appearance of the candidate in the watcher's emotional imagination is what counts. Politics is cut adrift from its real-world moorings and floats out into the seas of fiction.

The second risk, in a time of high anxiety, is the raising of expectations impossible to fulfill. Candidates normally overpromise and voters learn to apply a discount rate. But judging from the cases reviewed, from Bryan's silver panacea to Nixon's secret plan to end the war, there is a deeper danger: the seductiveness of a magic answer to cut through all the complexities and bring back the good old days. Even more powerfully appealing than specific magic tricks of policy may be the message that all will be well if people will just be nice to one another. That reaches the frustrated and confused citizen with an answer he can understand: Big Bill Taft's "Smile, Smile, Smile," Franklin Roosevelt's "nice jolly understanding of their problems," Eisenhower's infectious grin, Nixon's "bring us together." The hometown booster spirit is transposed to the national community; positive thinking prevails, in the hope that thinking will make it so, that acting as if one were confident will create confidence. Differences are papered over with a veneer of happy talk. The needed unity is not composed, it is assumed and celebrated. Political discussion collapses into cheerleading.

The third risk in the conciliation story springs from the direct and seemingly intimate relationship between candidate and audience, facilitated as never before by television. Harmony among the followers comes to depend almost entirely on shared allegiance to the leader. He is the celebrity. They are the fans. In between is nothing but the vibrating airwaves. When the camera moves away from him, interest evaporates. Recognizing that, the candidate and his managers seize control of his appearances and choreograph them for maximum effect. They play to a mass, undifferentiated audience, strangers to one another, focusing their friendship on the lone star on the stage. Some citizens may be brought in to pose vague and easy questions of a general nature. But throughout his varied appearances the candidate conveys the impression that he as President, backed by The People at large, will comprise the political system soon to be.

That of course is nonsense, but it points the way to a more productive path for the story of politics as conciliation to take. That story could tell of the gathering of forces and persons who might well wind up leading the nation, not just to victory at the polls but in the years thereafter. Journalists would press Presidential candidates to articulate the areas of agreement they share with actual and potential congressmen and senators, governors and cabinet members, advisers and interest-group leaders—with the range of politicians preparing to join in running the country. Stories on the interesting characters running for "lesser" offices, highlighting their connections with the Presidential candidates, would enrich the drama. Even during the primary season, now so preoccupied with conflict, emerging candidates would be asked not just what they would do with power, but with whom they might do it and what the basis for their concord could be. At and after the national convention, now a television extravaganza of doubtful instructional benefit, reporters could press the candidate for President not to name his cabinet, but to elaborate where he and leaders of cabinet stature come together. That challenge would test a genuine Presidential skill, because in fact the government works by an endless round of negotiation.

To attract that support committed to the long haul, the candidate would have to offer more than his person. Nor is it likely that the crew would sign on merely because they liked one another or were like one another or shared some sense of organizational neatness. They would want to work out with him a sense of purpose and direction of policy, not in unrealistic detail but in a broad outline of priorities. Together they would strain their intelligence to discover and articulate formulae of alliance, expressing those "ideas whose time has come" capable of attracting wide support before and after the election. Effort would be expended to bring in the broadest possible representation of the policy's main interests, an effort further testing the candidate's power of negotiation and formulation. Out of such experiments in purposeful unity might eventually emerge an organization lasting on into the following election. One might call it a political party.

The long-run need for such networks of cooperators between leader and followers is evident. Leader-mass politics is inherently unstable; given our Constitutional arrangements it is governmentally unworkable. There are grave risks in proceeding as at present. John Kennedy brought his young campaign hotshots into the White House to run the show—and so did Nixon and so did Carter—a kitchen cabinet of dependent devotees. Officers in the other cabinet are too occupied with their departments to function as general advisers. Modern congressmen run continuous district-oriented campaigns; senators preen themselves for their turn at the Presidency. Governors relate to Washington as the enemy and interest groups concentrate on their narrowly defined aims. When an incumbent President discovers, too late, that his "open administration" has gone anarchical and he seeks to force unity upon it, he winds up splintering and suppressing his official family in the name of "loyalty."

But however obvious these general malfunctions may be, pointing them out will not correct them. Reformers who urge the revival of parties as abstract good things in themselves or look to the reinvigoration of the jumbo coalitions of years gone by are marching up a blind alley. Purpose comes first, then party. In the rush of campaigning, the urgent work is to discover themes of unity so compelling that they will attract allies whose allegiance might survive the selection. In the larger and longer-range picture, discerning the basic shape of the emerging future and the broad strategies that might bend it in beneficient directions is the challenging task of the intellectuals. Unless and until people who are paid to think put their minds to work on that task and learn to articulate their ideas in a language politicians and journalists can understand, the search for harmony will falter.

"Where there is no vision," Proverbs warns, "the people perish." The vision of the intellectual in America has too often in recent years been narrowly focused on technical specialities or diffused in romantic or cynical generalities. Some have done positive harm, placing their brains in the service of sinister causes. Few have ventured to look beyond the imperfections of the present to develop progressive, realistic, and humane alternatives to our current course. It is that work, if we are lucky, that might yet produce harmonies that will hold a basis for union worth its price.

The American faith is that no law of necessity bars us from molding our destiny. The story of our peculiar democracy shows how, from time to time, we have overcome old prejudices and replaced them with new visions. Sooner or later we will shuck off the myths that, in our own experience, prove to serve us ill. Those who tell the story, those who act in it, and those who think through what it yet might mean have the chance to breathe new life into our old adventure.

A Note of Appreciation

M Y FIRST DEBT is to the scholars who provided the material and insights on which *The Presidential Character* was based. That book led into this one. I am indebted to all those students of Presidential politics who kept asking how one might acquire the information needed to assess a potential President. Those inquiries set the question; the researchers who provided the data for *The Pulse of Politics*—the historians, the biographers, the political philosophers whose understandings I have so freely borrowed in the pages above—I thank for their contributions to whatever is true in the answers I have offered. I am particularly thankful for the guidance and correction of Jeffrey Pressman, Donald Matthews, Christopher Arterton, and William Bicker, political science colleagues who educated me about the contexts and meanings of the most recent Presidential season. Professors at Duke who took time for clarifying conversations on this book's topic include Irving Alexander, Keith Brodie, Taylor Cole, Walter Dellinger, Walter Devries, Joel Fleishman, Ernestine Friedl, Lawrence Goodwyn, William Green, Hugh Hall, Ole Holsti, Jerry Hough, David Lange, Arthur Larson, Thomas McCollough, John McConahay, David Paletz, David Price, Reynolds Price, Ronald Rogowski, and Terry Sanford. Professors elsewhere whose counsel has been particularly helpful include Ben Bagdikian, James MacGregor Burns, Thomas Cronin, Lewis Anthony Dexter, Edwin Diamond, Clifford Geertz, Fred Greenstein, Elihu Katz, Herbert Kaufman, Stanley Kelley, Robert Lane, Harold Lasswell, Michael Maccoby, Michael Novak, Thomas Patterson, Ithiel de Sola Pool, George Reedy, David Riesman, Michael Robinson, Robert Louis Stevenson, and Aaron Wildavsky. All the participants in the Duke Fellows in Communication Program, *Washington Post*-Duke Fellows Program, and the *Time*-Duke Fellows Program have contributed to my education, as have the many other journalists who have paused to reflect with me about their craft. Particularly patient informants were Bonnie Angelo, R. W. Apple, Michael Arlen, Benjamin Bradlee, David Broder, Lou Cannon, John Chancellor, Stanley Cloud, Hedley Donovan, Saul Friedman, Philip Geyelin, Peter Goldman, William Greider, Henry Grunwald, James Hogue, Robert Kaiser, Haynes Johnson, Ward Just, Anthony Lewis, Suzannah Lessard, Marshal Loeb, Jason McManus, Robert MacNeil, Bill Moyers, Martin Nolan, Charles Peters, Dan Rather, Harry Rosenthal, Vermont Royster, Daniel Schorr, Robert Sherrill, Hugh Sidey, John Siegenthaler, Howard Simons, Claude Sitton, William Small, Helen Thomas, Frank Trippett, Sander Vanocur, Wallace Westfeldt, Tom Wicker, George Will, Jules Witcover, and Ed Yoder. I am thankful for the chance to have talked about the Presidential selection process with some of those who have competed in it: Jimmy Carter, Barry Goldwater, Fred Harris, George McGovern, Edmund Muskie, Ronald Reagan, Adlai Stevenson, and Harry Truman.

Research contributing to this volume has been generously supported by the Ford Foundation, whose Robert Goldmann gave sage judgment from the start, and by the John and Mary Markle Foundation, whose Jean Firstenberg contributed her steady vision. Along the way, Douglass Cater of the Aspen Institute, Clifford Nelson of the American Assembly, and Arthur Singer of the Sloan Foundation provided opportunities for trial runs.

My first debt for essential guidance in the shaping of the manuscript is to Jeannette Hopkins, that brilliant editor who thinks as she imagines, and to Donald Lamm, Norton's president, whose faith sustained this project from its earliest days. Salena Rapp Kern did a first-rate job of copy editing. At Duke, the production depended on the heroic reproductions of Patricia McFarland, ably assisted by Nancy Kiefer and Doris Ralston, while Louise Walker presided to ensure that my interests were advanced. David Garrow, my research assistant, offered his independent criticisms. I thank W. D. Davies, William Willis, and especially Harry Levy for their advice on classical languages. And without the patient, loving care of Jean Lassiter for the serenity of my household, this project could never have been.

By the authority vested in authors, I hereby absolve each and every one of these collaborators from blame for the result. They have given, but what I have taken is my own.

James David Barber

Cullowhee Spring
Durham, North Carolina

Bibliography

THE FOLLOWING SOURCES are essential to an understanding of the twentieth-century Presidential elections and the connection of journalism therewith.

Barnouw, Erik. *A History of Broadcasting in the United States*. 3 vols. New York: Oxford University Press, 1970.
Mott, Frank Luther. *American Journalism: A History 1690–1960*. 3d ed. New York: Macmillan, 1962.
Schlesinger, Arthur M., Jr.; Israel, Fred L.; and Hansen, William P., eds. *History of American Presidential Elections: 1789–1968*. Vols. 3 and 4. New York: Chelsea House Publishers, 1971.
Tebbel, John. *The Media in America*. New York: Thomas Y. Crowell Company, 1974.
White, Theodore H. *The Making of the President 1960—and 1964, 1968, 1972*, and *Breach of Faith: The Fall of Richard Nixon*. New York: Atheneum, 1961 et seq.

1. The Presidential Beat

Price, Reynolds. *A Palpable God*. New York: Atheneum, 1978.
Ransome, Arthur. *A History of Story-Telling: Studies in the Development of Narrative*. New York: Frederick A. Stokes Company, undated (ca. 1910).
Roseboom, Eugene H. *A History of Presidential Elections: From George Washington to Richard M. Nixon*. New York: Macmillan, 1970.

3. Theodore Roosevelt 1900

Argyris, Chris. *Behind the Front Page*. San Francisco: Jossey-Bass, 1974.
Bishop, Joseph Bucklin, ed. *Theodore Roosevelt's Letters to His Children*. New York: Charles Scribner's Sons, 1928.
Blum, John M. et al. *The National Experience*. 2d ed. New York: Harcourt, Brace & World, 1968.
Cornwell, Elmer E., Jr. *Presidential Leadership of Public Opinion*. Bloomington: Indiana University Press: 1965.
Davis, Charles Belmont, ed. *Adventures and Letters of Richard Harding Davis*. New York: Charles Scribner's Sons, 1917.
Douglas, George William. *The Many-Sided Roosevelt*. New York: Dodd, Mead, 1907.
Downey, Fairfax. *Richard Harding Davis: His Day*. New York: Charles Scribner's Sons, 1933.
Harbaugh, William H. "Election of 1904." In *History of American Presidential Elections 1789–1968*, edited by Schlesinger et al., vol. 3.
———. *The Life and Times of Theodore Roosevelt*. New York: Collier Books, 1963.
Hoover, Irwin Hood *Forty-Two Years in the White House*. New York: Houghton Mifflin Co., 1934.

Huxley, Aldous. *After Many a Summer Dies the Swan*. New York and London: Harper and
     Brothers, 1939.
Josephson, Matthew. *The Politicos*. Vol. 3. New York: Harcourt, Brace & World, 1938.
Kent, Frank R. *The Great Game of Politics: An Effort to Present the Elementary Human Facts
     about Politics, Politicians, and Political Machines*. New York: Arno Press, 1974.
Knightley, Phillip. *The First Casualty*. New York: Harcourt Brace Jovanovich, 1975.
Koenig, Louis W. *Bryan*. New York: G. P. Putnam's Sons, 1971.
LaFeber, Walter. "Election of 1900." In *History of American Presidential Elections 1789–1968*,
     edited by Schlesinger et al., vol. 3.
Leach, Margaret. *In the Days of McKinley*. New York: Harper, 1959.
Mott, Frank Luther. *American Journalism*. Rev. ed. New York: Macmillan, 1950.
Pringle, Henry F. *Theodore Roosevelt: A Biography*. New York: Harcourt, Brace & Company,
     1931.
Rammelkamp, Julian S. *Pulitzer's Post-Dispatch 1878–1883*. Princeton, N.J.: Princeton Univer-
     sity Press, 1967.
Riis, Jacob A. *Theodore Roosevelt the Citizen*. New York: Grosset & Dunlap, 1904.
Roosevelt, Theodore. *The Works of Theodore Roosevelt*. Edited by Hermann Hagedorn. New
     York: Charles Scribner's Sons, 1926.
Roshco, Bernard. *Newsmaking*. Chicago: University of Chicago Press, 1975.
Swanberg, W. A. *Citizen Hearst*. New York: Charles Scribner's Sons, 1961.
———. *Pulitzer*. New York: Charles Scribner's Sons, 1967.
Talese, Gay. *The Kingdom and the Power*. New York: Bantam Books, 1970.
Tebbel, John. *The Media in America*. New York: Thomas Y. Crowell Company, 1974.
Tugwell, Rexford G. *How They Became President*. New York: Simon & Schuster, 1965.
Zweig, Paul. *The Adventurer*. New York: Basic Books, 1974.

Newspapers and Periodicals

New York World. 17 May 1895, 8 June 1895, 14 November 1896, 22 October 1900, and 5
     November 1900.
New York Evening Journal. 6 April 1898 and 6 May 1898.

4. Harry Truman 1948

Johnson, Walter. *1600 Pennsylvania Avenue: Presidents and the People 1929–1959*. Boston:
     Little, Brown & Company, 1960.
Kirkendall, Richard S. "Election of 1948." In *History of American Presidential Elections—1789–
     1968*, edited by Schlesinger et al., vol. 4.
Phillips, Cabell. *The Truman Presidency: The History of a Triumphant Succession*. New York:
     Macmillan, 1966.
Pollard, James E. *The Presidents and the Press: Truman to Johnson*. Washington, D.C.: Public
     Affairs Press, 1964.
Ross, Irwin. *The Loneliest Campaign: The Truman Victory of 1948*. New York: New American
     Library, 1968.
Steinberg, Alfred. *The Man from Missouri: The Life and Times of Harry S. Truman*. New York:
     G. P. Putnam's Sons, 1962.
Stone, Irving. *They Also Ran: The Story of the Men Who Were Defeated for the Presidency*.
     Garden City, N.Y.: Doubleday & Co., 1966.
Weisbord, Marvin R. *Campaigning for President*. Washington, D.C.: Public Affairs Press,
     1964.

5. John Kennedy 1960

Blair, Clay, Jr., and Blair, Joan. *The Search for JFK*. New York: G. P. Putnam's Sons, 1976.
Crouse, Timothy. *The Boys on the Bus*. New York: Ballantine Books, 1973.
Crown, James Tracy. *The Kennedy Literature: A Biographical Essay on John F. Kennedy*. New
     York: New York University Press, 1968.
Kennedy, John. *Why England Slept*. New York: Wilfred Funk, Inc., 1940.
———. "The Speeches, Remarks, Press Conferences, and Statements of Senator John F. Ken-
     nedy, August 1 through November 7, 1960." *Freedom of Communications*. Part 1
     87th Cong., 1st sess., Sen. Rept. 994.

Salinger, Pierre. *With Kennedy.* Garden City, N.Y.: Doubleday & Co., 1966.
Schlesinger, Arthur M., Jr. *A Thousand Days: John F. Kennedy in the White House.* Boston: Houghton Mifflin Co., 1965.
Sorensen, Theodore C. *Kennedy.* New York: Harper & Row, 1965.
———. *The Making of the President 1960.* New York: Atheneum, 1961.
Williams, Delos F. "The American Newspaper: A Study in Social Psychology." *Annals of the American Academy of Political and Social Science,* July 1900.
Williamson, Henry. *The Wet Flanders Plain.* New York: E. P. Dutton & Co., 1929.

Periodicals

Rosten, Leo. *Journalism Quarterly,* vol. 14, no. 3 (September 1937), pp. 221–25.

6. George McGovern 1972

Anson, Sam. *McGovern: A Biography.* New York: Holt, Rinehart & Winston, 1972.
Arterton, Christopher. *Media Politics: The News Strategies of Presidential Campaigns.* Forthcoming.
Barber, James David, ed. *Choosing the President.* Englewood Cliffs, N.J.: Prentice-Hall, 1974.
Bernstein, Carl, and Woodward, Bob. *All the President's Men.* New York: Simon & Schuster, 1974.
Crouse, Timothy. *The Boys on the Bus.* New York: Ballantine Books, 1973.
Dougherty, Richard. *Goodbye Mr. Christian: A Personal Account of McGovern's Rise and Fall.* Garden City, N.Y.: Doubleday & Co., 1973.
Hadley, Arthur. *The Invisible Primary.* Englewood Cliffs, N.J.: Prentice-Hall, 1976.
Lukas, Anthony. *Nightmare: The Underside of the Nixon Years.* New York: The Viking Press, 1976.
McGovern, Eleanor. *Uphill: A Personal Story.* Boston: Houghton Mifflin Co., 1974.
McGovern, George. *An American Journey: The Presidential Campaign Speeches of George McGovern.* New York: Random House, 1974.
Matthews, Donald R. "Presidential Nominations: Process and Outcomes." In *Choosing the President,* edited by James David Barber. Englewood Cliffs, N.J.: Prentice-Hall, 1974.
Perry, James M. *Us and Them: How the Press Covered the 1972 Election.* New York: Clarkson N. Potter, 1973.
Ranney, Austin. "Changing the Rules of the Nominating Game." In *Choosing the President,* edited by James David Barber. Englewood Cliffs, N.J.: Prentice-Hall, 1974.
Schell, Jonathon. *The Time of Illusion.* New York: Alfred A. Knopf, 1976.
Schram, Martin. *Running for President: A Journal of the Carter Campaign.* New York: Pocket Books, 1976.
Weil, Gordon L. *The Long Shot: George McGovern Runs for President.* New York: W. W. Norton & Co., 1973.
White, Theodore H. *Breach of Faith: The Fall of Richard Nixon.* New York: Atheneum, 1975.
———. *The Making of the President 1972.* New York: Atheneum, 1973.
Witker, Kristi. *How to Lose Everything in Politics Except Massachusetts.* New York: Mason & Lipscomb Publishers, 1974.

7. Woodrow Wilson 1916

Bragdon, Henry Wilkinson. *Woodrow Wilson: The Academic Years.* Cambridge, Mass.: Harvard University Press, 1967.
Busch, Noel F. *Briton Hadden.* New York: Farrar, Straus & Co., 1949.
Elson, Robert T. *Time Inc.: The Intimate History of a Publishing Enterprise 1923–1941.* New York: Atheneum, 1968.
Fuchs, Lawrence H. "Election of 1928." In *History of American Presidential Elections—1789–1968,* edited by Schlesinger et al., vol. 3.
George, Alexander L., and George, Juliette L. *Woodrow Wilson and Colonel House: A Personality Study.* New York: The John Day Company, 1956.
Johnson, Willis Fletcher. *George Harvey: A Passionate Patriot.* Boston: Houghton Mifflin Co., 1929.
Kramer, Dale. *Ross and the New Yorker.* Garden City, N.Y.: Doubleday & Co., 1951.

Link, Arthur S. "Portrait of the President." In *Philosophy and Policies of Woodrow Wilson*, edited by Earl Latham. Chicago: University of Chicago Press, 1958.
——. *Wilson: The Road to the White House*. Princeton, N.J.: Princeton University Press, 1947.
——, and Leary, William M., Jr. "Election of 1916." In *History of American Presidential Elections—1789–1968*, edited by Schlesinger et al., vol. 3.
O'Brien, Francis William, ed. *The Hoover-Wilson Correspondence: September 24, 1914 to November 11, 1918*. Ames, Iowa: The Iowa State University Press, 1974.
Russell, Francis. *The President Makers: From Mark Hanna To Joseph P. Kennedy*. Boston: Little, Brown & Co., 1976.
Tebbel, John. *George Horace Lorimer and the Saturday Evening Post*. Garden City, N.Y.: Doubleday & Co., 1948.
Wilson, Carol Green. *Herbert Hoover: A Challenge for Today*. New York: Evans Publishing Company, 1968.
Wood, James Playsted. *Of Lasting Interest: The Story of the Reader's Digest*. Garden City, N.Y.: Doubleday & Co., 1967.

Periodicals

Collier's. 14 October 1916.
Inglis, William. "Helping to Make a President." *Collier's*, 7 October 1916.
Tarbell, Ida. "A Talk with the President." *Collier's*, 28 October 1916.

8. Wendell Willkie 1940

Berger, Meyer. *The Story of the New York Times 1851–1951*. New York: Simon & Schuster, 1951.
Bernstein, Barton, J. "Election of 1952." In *History of American Presidential Elections—1789–1968*, edited by Schlesinger et al., vol. 4.
Boorstin, Daniel, J., ed. *An American Primer*. Chicago: University of Chicago Press, 1966.
Brayman, Harold. *The President Speaks off the Record*. Princeton, N.J.: Dow Jones Books, 1976.
Burke, Robert. "Election of 1940." In *History of American Presidential Elections—1789–1968*, edited by Schlesinger et al., vol. 4.
Busch, Noel. *Briton Hadden*. New York: Farrar, Straus & Co., 1949.
Childs, Marquis. *Eisenhower: Captive Hero*. New York: Harcourt Brace & World, 1958.
Dillon, Mary Earhart. *Wendell Willkie, 1892–1944*. Philadelphia: J.P. Lippincott Co., 1952.
Elson, Robert T. *Time Inc.: The Intimate History of a Publishing Enterprise 1923–1941*. New York: Atheneum, 1968.
Entrikin, Isabelle Webb. *Sarah Josepha Hale and Godey's Lady's Book*. Lancaster, Penn.: Lancaster Press, 1946.
Finley, Ruth E. *The Lady of Godey's: Sarah Josepha Hale*. Philadelphia: J. P. Lippincott Co., 1931.
Fisher, Charles. *The Columnists*. New York: Howell, Soskin, 1944.
Goldman, Eric F. *Rendezvous with Destiny*. New York: Vintage Books, 1956.
Harbaugh, William H., ed. *The Writings of Theodore Roosevelt*. Indianapolis and New York: The Bobbs-Merrill Co., 1967.
James, Edward T. et al, eds. *Notable American Women 1607–1950: A Biographical Dictionary*. Cambridge: Harvard University Press, 1971.
Johnson, Walter. *1600 Pennsylvania Avenue*. Boston: Little Brown & Co. 1960.
Kobler, John. *Luce: His Time, Life, and Fortune*. Garden City: N.Y.: Doubleday & Co., 1968.
Larson, Arthur. *Eisenhower: The President Nobody Knew*. New York: Charles Scribner's Sons, 1968.
Lubell, Samuel. *Revolt of the Moderates*. New York: Harper and Brothers, 1956.
McClure, S. S. *My Autobiography*. New York: Frederick Ungar Publishing Co., 1963.
Mott, Frank Luther. *American Journalism*. 3d ed. New York: Macmillan, 1962.
Novak, Michael. *Choosing Our King*. New York: Macmillan, 1974.
Rukeyser, Muriel. *One Life*. New York: Simon & Schuster, 1957.
Severn, Bill. *Toward One World: The Life of Wendell Willkie*. New York: Ives Washburn, Inc., 1967.

Swanberg, W. A. *Luce and His Empire*. New York: Charles Scribner's Sons: 1972.

Tarbell, Ida M. *All In the Day's Work*. New York: Macmillan, 1939.

———. *The History of the Standard Oil Company*. New York: McClure Phillips and Co., 1904.

Tebbel, John. *The American Magazine: A Compact History*. New York: Hawthorne Books, 1969.

Tomkins, Mary E. *Ida M. Tarbell*. New York: Twayne Publishers, 1974.

Willkie, Wendell. *This Is Wendell Willkie*. New York: Dodd Mead & Co., 1940.

Wilson, Harold S. *McClure's Magazine and the Muckrakers*. Princeton, N.J.: Princeton University Press, 1970.

Periodicals

Brooks, N. C. "The Parting Hour; or, The Three Separations." *The Lady's Book*, August 1835.

Hamilton, Virginia Van der Veer. "The Gentlewoman and the Robber Baron." *American Heritage*, April 1970.

9. Barry Goldwater 1964

Berger, Meyer. *The Story of the New York Times 1851–1951*. New York: Simon & Schuster, 1951.

Elson, Robert T. *Time Inc*. New York: Atheneum, 1968.

Faber, Harold, ed. *The Road to the White House: The Story of the 1964 Election by the Staff of the New York Times*. New York: McGraw-Hill, 1965.

Fisher, Charles. *The Columnists*. New York: Howell, Soskin, 1944.

Goldwater, Barry. *The Conscience of a Conservative*. New York: Hillmann Books, 1960.

McDowell, Charles, Jr. *Campaign Fever: The National Folk Festival from New Hampshire to November, 1964*. New York: William Morrow & Co., 1965.

Mott, Frank Luther. *American Journalism*. 3d ed. New York: Macmillan, 1962.

Roseboom, Eugene H. *A History of Presidential Elections*. New York: Macmillan, 1970.

Rovere, Richard H. *The Goldwater Caper*. New York: Harcourt, Brace & World, Inc., 1965.

Steinberg, Alfred. *Sam Johnson's Boy: A Close Up of the President from Texas*. New York: Macmillan, 1968.

Stone, Irving. *They Also Ran: The Story of the Men Who Were Defeated for the Presidency*. Garden City, N.Y.: Doubleday & Co., 1966.

Talese, Gay. *The Kingdom and the Power*. New York: Bantam Books, 1970.

White, Theodore. *The Making of the President 1964*. New York: Atheneum, 1965.

Williams, T. Harry, ed. *Abraham Lincoln: Selected Speeches, Messages, and Letters*. New York: Rinehart and Co., 1957.

10. Jimmy Carter 1976

Arterton, F. Christopher. "The Media Politics of Presidential Campaigns: A Study of the Carter Nomination Drive." In *Race for the Presidency*, edited by James David Barber. Englewood Cliffs, N.J.: Prentice-Hall, 1978.

Hadley, Arthur T. *The Invisible Primary*. Englewood Cliffs, N.J.: Prentice-Hall, 1976.

MacDougall, Malcolm D. *We Almost Made It*. New York: Crown Publishers, 1977.

Miller, William Lee. *Yankee from Georgia: The Emergence of Jimmy Carter*. New York: New York Times Books, 1978.

Novak, Michael. *Choosing Our King*. New York: Macmillan, 1974.

Pomper, Gerald et al. *The Election of 1976*. New York: David Mackay Co., 1977.

Schram, Martin. *Running for President: A Journal of the Carter Campaign*. New York: Pocket Books, 1976.

Stroud, Kandy. *How Jimmy Won*. New York: William Morrow & Co., 1977.

Witcover, Jules. *Marathon: The Pursuit of the Presidency 1972–1976*. New York: Viking Press, 1977.

Wooten, James. *Dasher: The Roots and Rising of Jimmy Carter*. New York: Summit Books, 1978.

Periodicals

Brill, Steven. *"Jimmy Carter's Pathetic Lies."* Harper's, March 1976.

Chicago Tribune. 31 August 1975.

Chicago Tribune. 29 September 1975.

Diamond, Edwin. "The Mid-Life Crisis of the Newsweeklies." *New York,* 7 June 1976.

Germond, Jack W. "Attack on Carter By Liberals Fierce." *Washington Star,* 4 February 1976.

Greider, William. "A Carter Album." *Washington Post,* 24 October 1976.

Halberstam, David. "Time, Inc.'s Internal War over Vietnam." *Esquire,* January 1978.

Helm, Charles. "Jimmy Carter and the Press." *Illinois Quarterly,* spring 1977.

Just, Ward, and Kaiser, Robert. "To Time, Inc., As to All Institutions, Come Winds of Change." *Washington Post,* 3 December 1968.

Lapham, Lewis, H. "The Wizard of Oz." *Harper's,* August 1976.

Lydon, Christopher. "Jimmy Carter Revealed: He's a Rockefeller Republican." *Atlantic Monthly,* July 1977.

Pollak, Richard. "Time: After Luce." *Harper's,* July 1969.

Sheahan, Denis. "Editor's Note." *Women's Wear Daily,* 5 June 1972.

Stanford, Phil. " 'The Most Remarkable Piece of Fiction' Jimmy Carter Ever Read." *Columbia Journalism Review,* July–August 1976.

Time. 23 December 1974.

Time. 13 October 1975.

Wilkes, Paul. "Time vs. Newsweek." *New York,* 16 June 1969.

Wright, Robert A. "New Editor of Time 'Bending Old Formula' to Give Magazine a Different Approach." *New York Times,* 30 November 1968.

11. Warren Harding 1920

Adams, Samuel Hopkins. *Incredible Era: The Life and Times of Warren Gamaliel Harding.* New York: Capricorn Books, 1964.

Barber, James David. *The Presidential Character: Predicting Performance in The White House.* Rev. ed. Englewood Cliffs, N.J.: Prentice-Hall, 1977.

Harrison, Harry P. *Culture under Canvas: The Story of Tent Chautauqua.* New York: Hastings House, 1958.

McCoy, Donald R. "Election of 1920." In *History of American Presidential Elections—1789–1968,* edited by Schlesinger et al., vol. 3.

Russell, Francis. *The Shadow of Blooming Grove: Warren G. Harding in His Times.* New York: McGraw-Hill, 1968.

Tugwell, Rexford G. *How They Became President: Thirty-Five Ways to the White House.* New York: Simon & Schuster, 1964.

12. Franklin Roosevelt 1932

Allen, Steve. *The Funny Men.* New York: Simon & Schuster, 1956.

Asbell, Bernard. *The F.D.R. Memoirs.* New York: Doubleday & Co., 1973.

Barnouw, Erik. *A History of Broadcasting in the United States,* vol. 1, *A Tower in Babel: To 1933.* New York: Oxford University Press, 1966.

———. *A History of Broadcasting in the United States,* vol. 2, *The Golden Web: 1933 to 1953.* New York: Oxford University Press, 1968.

Bliss, Edward, Jr., ed. *In Search of Light: The Broadcasts of Edward R. Murrow 1938–1961.* New York: Alfred A. Knopf, 1967.

Crosby, Bing. (As told to Pete Martin.) *Call Me Lucky.* New York: Simon & Schuster, 1953.

Culbert, David Holbrook. *News for Everyman: Radio and Foreign Affairs in Thirties America.* Westport, Connecticut: Greenwood Press, 1976.

Edmondson, Madeleine, and Rounds, David. *The Soaps: Daytime Serials of Radio and TV.* New York: Stein & Day, 1973.

Farley, James A. *Behind the Ballots.* New York: Harcourt, Brace & Company, 1938.

Freidel, Frank. "Election of 1932." In *History of American Presidential Elections—1789–1968,* edited by Schlesinger et al., vol. 3.

———. *Franklin D. Roosevelt: The Triumph.* Boston: Little, Brown & Co., 1956.

Friedman, Leon. "Election of 1964." In *History of American Presidential Elections—1789–1968,* edited by Schlesinger et al., vol. 4.

Gates, Gary Paul. *Air Time: The Inside Story of CBS News.* New York: Harper & Row, 1978.

Goldman, Eric F. *Rendezvous with Destiny.* New York: Vintage Books, 1956.

Gunther, John. *Roosevelt in Retrospect*. New York: Pyramid Books, 1962.
Harrity, Richard, and Martin, Ralph G. *The Human Side of FDR*. New York: Duell, Sloan and Pearce, 1960.
Hofstadter, Richard. *The American Political Tradition*. New York: Vintage Books, 1954.
Johnson, Walter. *1600 Pennsylvania Avenue*. Boston: Little, Brown & Co., 1960.
Kaltenborn, H. V. *I Broadcast the Crisis*. New York: Random House, 1938.
Lash, Joseph P. *Eleanor and Franklin*. New York: W. W. Norton & Co., 1971.
Leuchtenburg, William E. "Election of 1936." In *History of American Presidential Elections—1789–1968*, edited by Schlesinger et al., vol. 3.
Mencken, H. L. *Making a President*. New York: Alfred A. Knopf, 1932.
Perkins, Francis. *The Roosevelt I Knew*. New York: Harper & Row, 1946.
Schlesinger, Arthur M., Jr. *The Crisis of the Old Order*. Boston: Houghton Mifflin Company, 1957.
Seldes, Gilbert. *The Years of the Locust*. Boston: Little, Brown & Co., 1933.
Tugwell, Rexford G. *The Democratic Roosevelt*. Baltimore: Penguin Books, 1969.
Weisbord, Marvin R. *Campaigning for President*. Washington: Public Affairs Press, 1964.

Periodicals

Nevins, Allan. "The Place of Franklin D. Roosevelt in History." The Sir George Watson Lecture delivered at the University of Leicester, 17 May 1965, published by the Humanities Press in New York in 1965.

13. Dwight Eisenhower 1956

Barnouw, Erik. *A History of Broadcasting in the United States*, vol. 2, *The Golden Web: 1933 to 1953*. New York: Oxford University Press, 1968.
Blum, John M. et al. *The National Experience: A History of the United States*. 2d ed. New York: Harcourt, Brace & World, 1968.
Brown, Stuart Gerry. *Adlai E. Stevenson*. Woodbury, N.Y.: Barron's Woodbury Press, 1965.
Inaugural Addresses of the Presidents of the United States. USGPO, 1961.
Johnson, Walter. *1600 Pennsylvania Avenue: Presidents and the People, 1929–1959*. Boston: Little, Brown & Company, 1960.
Kelley, Stanley, Jr. *Professional Public Relations and Political Power*. Baltimore: The Johns Hopkins University Press, 1956.
Metz, Robert. *The Today Show*. Chicago: Playboy Press, 1977.
Sterling, Christopher H., and Haight, Timothy R. *The Mass Media: Aspen Institute Guide to Communication Industry Trends*. New York: Praeger, 1978.
Thomson, Charles A. H., and Shattuck, Frances M. *The 1956 Presidential Campaign*. Washington: The Brookings Institution, 1960.

14. Richard Nixon 1968

Abrahamsen, David, M.D. *Nixon vs. Nixon: An Emotional Tragedy*. New York: Farrar, Straus & Giroux, 1977.
Barber, James David. *The Presidential Character: Predicting Performance in the White House*. Englewood Cliffs, N.J.: Prentice-Hall, 1977.
Barnouw, Erik. *Tube of Plenty*. New York: Oxford University Press, 1975
Broder, David S. "Election of 1968." In *History of American Presidential Elections—1789–1968*, edited by Schlesinger et al., vol. 4.
Chesen, Eli S., M.D. *President Nixon's Psychiatric Profile*. New York: Basic Books, 1972.
Chester, Lewis, Hodgson, Godfrey, and Page, Bruce. *An American Melodrama*. New York: Viking Press, 1969.
Gates, Gary Paul. *Air Time: The Inside Story of CBS News*. New York: Harper & Row, 1978.
Humphrey, Hubert H. *The Education of a Public Man*. Garden City, N.Y.: Doubleday & Co., 1976.
Keogh, James. *President Nixon and the Press*. New York: Funk & Wagnalls, 1972.
McGinniss, Joe. *The Selling of the President 1968*. New York: Pocket Books, 1970.
Mankiewicz, Frank. *Perfectly Clear: Nixon from Whittier to Watergate*. New York: Popular Library, 1973.

Mazlish, Bruce. *In Search of Nixon: A Psychohistorical Inquiry*. New York: Basic Books, 1972.
Schell, Jonathon. *The Time of Illusion*. New York: Alfred A. Knopf, 1976.
Small, William. *To Kill a Messenger: Televison News and the Real World*. New York: Hastings
    House, 1970.
White, Theodore. *The Making of the President 1968*. New York: Atheneum, 1969.
Wills, Garry. *Nixon Agonistes: The Crisis of the Self-Made Man*. Boston: Houghton Mifflin
    Company, 1970.
Witcover, Jules. *The Resurrection of Richard Nixon*. New York: G. P. Putnam's Sons, 1979.

Index